INSTITUTES OF THE CHRISTIAN RELIGION

BOOK II

INSTITUTES OF THE CHRISTIAN RELIGION

BOOK II: OF THE KNOWLEDGE OF
GOD THE REDEEMER, IN CHRIST,
AS FIRST MANIFESTED TO THE
FATHERS, UNDER THE LAW, AND
THEREAFTER TO US UNDER THE
GOSPEL

JOHN CALVIN

Translated by Henry Beveridge
with an Introduction by Ben Merkle
& Discussion Questions and Answers by Douglas Wilson

The Christian Heritage Series
Published by Canon Press
P.O. Box 8729, Moscow, Idaho 83843
800.488.2034 | www.canonpress.com

John Calvin, *Institutes of the Christian Religion*
Christian Heritage Series edition copyright ©2020.
Introduction, copyright ©2020 by Ben Merkle
This modernized Christian Heritage Series edition based on the CCEL edition, copyright ©20xx by
Christian Classics Ethereal Library. Used by permission.
First published in 1845.
Discussion questions taken from Douglas Wilson, *A Study Guide to Calvin's Institutes*, copyright
©2011.

Cover design by James Engerbretson
Cover illustration by Forrest Dickison
Interior design by Valerie Anne Bost and James Engerbretson

Printed in the United States of America.

20 21 22 23 24 25   10 9 8 7 6 5 4 3 2 1

CONTENTS

INTRODUCTION

Book II is a systematic walk through who Jesus Christ was. Calvin's goal is to leave the reader with a clear understanding of Jesus' nature and the work that he performed as our Savior. But in order to do that, he is going to take a few unexpected turns to give you the background that will give you a much deeper understanding of who Jesus was.

The full title of book II reads "Of the knowledge of God the Redeemer, in Christ, as first manifested to the fathers, under the law, and thereafter to us under the gospel." If you recall Calvin's opening observation from book I, then you will remember that knowledge of God and knowledge of self are necessarily intertwined. So this knowledge of God the Redeemer is all tied up with man's knowledge of himself, and his rightful understanding of his own desperate need for redemption. Men must know themselves and their sinful condition if they are to understand who Christ their Savior is. All men are fallen as a result of original sin—"... a hereditary corruption and depravity of our nature, extending to all the parts of the soul, which first makes us obnoxious to the wrath of God, and then produces in us works which in Scripture are termed works of the flesh" (14).[1] The

---

1. All quotes are taken from this edition unless otherwise noted.

effect of this sin on Adam and on all of his descendants was total, leaving him in need of not just a savior, but a sovereign Savior.

In this book Calvin sketches out the soteriology, or doctrine of salvation, that has become synonymous with his name—what we now know as "Calvinism." Calvin explains that man's fallen condition is so severe that it amounts to a prison of the will, such that man can't even decide on his own to turn to God. He moves from his description of fallen man (ch. 1) to a careful explanation of how an enslaved will is still capable of a free choice since it is free from external compulsion (ch. 2-5). This section is really worth a very close read and a good bit of reflection. Calvin's detractors, who think his doctrine of salvation turns men into robots, tend to miss his distinction between compulsion and necessity—two terms that must be carefully defined to understand Calvin's argument. As you read this section, note how much Calvin is actually appealing to the earlier work of Augustine. You can see why, from Calvin's perspective, he was arguing nothing new, but simply recovering the ancient faith. Calvin's soteriology differed very little from that of Martin Luther at this point, though later Lutheranism would diverge significantly from Reformed soteriology.

With this understanding of man's dire situation understood, Calvin turns to the revelation of Jesus Christ, our Savior who came to rescue man from this doomed condition. Jesus came as our "Redeemer," that is a person who came to "redeem" or to pay a penalty owed by man. Considering Christ from this angle takes Calvin first of all to the law of God (ch. 7-8), as summarized by the Ten Commandments. This is another strange turn. Why would you put a summary of the Ten Commandments in a book that is supposed to be about describing Jesus?

Well, consider that these laws describe the moral perfection of God which Adam violated and which Jesus Christ, the second Adam, came to fulfill. So, if Jesus was the fulfillment of the law that mankind has continually fallen short of, then it follows that to understand who Jesus was, we must understand God's law. It is actually a description of Jesus.

You should notice two things in Calvin's teaching on the law. First, Calvin describes two different functions that the law can serve. This is a pretty typical way to approach the law, saying that the law reveals man's fallenness and need for a Savior, while it also provides a standard for the civil magistrate to use to restrain ungodly men. But Calvin adds a third use of the law, one which Calvin describes as the law's "principle use." For the regenerate man, one who has been redeemed and empowered by the Holy Spirit, the law provides the ongoing standard for godly obedience.

Second, be sure to catch Calvin's explanation of the role of "synecdoches" in understanding the Ten Commandments. "Obviously, in almost all the commandments there are such manifest synecdoches that he who would confine his understanding of the law within the narrowness of the words deserves to be laughed at."[2] A synecdoche is a figure of speech where a part is used to represent the whole. For instance, when the captain calls for "all hands on deck" he is employing a synecdoche, since he definitely expects the sailors' entire personages on the deck, not just their hands. Therefore, when Calvin unpacks each of the Ten Commandments, you will see that he employs a kind maximalism, meaning he doesn't simply ask "what is the commandment specifically about?" Rather, he asks, "What all does this commandment imply?" So the command to not murder is also a positive command to seek the safety and well-being of others, etc. By interpreting the Ten Commandments this way, Calvin seeks to paint a larger picture of the righteousness of God, which Christ came to fulfill. He is describing Jesus.

And so, throughout the Old Testament, the Gospel of Christ was foretold both through the teaching of the law, which described the perfection of Christ, and through the prophets who foretold, in types

---

2. *Calvin: Institutes of the Christian Religion*, translated by Ford Lewis Battles and edited by John T. McNeill (Louisville, KY: Westminster John Knox Press, 1960), 1:374.

and shadows, the coming of the Savior. Calvin insists that there was a continuity in the story of salvation from the Old Testament to the New, all united by Christ (ch. 9-11). However, the New Testament was different because now, Christ having come and fulfilled those Old Testament types and shadows, we can see clearly what was previously dim and vague. Calvin writes, "By the Gospel, I understand the clear manifestation of the mystery of Christ" (252). Thus, the New Testament launches the age of the Gospel—not a new salvation story, but the clear proclamation of a long-awaited story.

From here, Calvin turns to the subject of Christology, which is the precise theological definition of the person, nature, and work of Jesus Christ (ch. 12-14). Much of the important work on this subject was accomplished in the early councils and creeds of the Christian church and Calvin shows little interest in deviating significantly from this tradition. But he still has to walk very carefully through this topic. The definitions of Christology had been crafted and honed by the greatest theologians in the church over a millennium and had been passed down through church tradition. But, as a protestant reformer, Calvin believed that all theology ultimately received its authority from the clear testimony of Scripture, an authority that trumped human tradition. In fact, as a protestant reformer, Calvin was a leader in overthrowing a number of unbiblical church traditions like the Roman mass. So how can he teach a Christology which had been handed down by tradition, while at the same time rejecting other teachings that had been passed down by tradition?

The answer was that Calvin was not opposed to tradition in and of itself, but simply insisted that tradition understand its place underneath the authority of Scripture. Scripture is the ultimate and infallible standard for all theology—Scripture and Scripture alone. Tradition serves as a secondary authority to assist us in unpacking the riches of Scripture our primary authority. So in this section on Christology you will see Calvin, with a deft hand, give a simple account of the nature, person, and work of Jesus Christ, rooted in and illuminated by the biblical text, but consistent with and informed by the larger Christian Christological tradition. In this section, you see Calvin distance himself from contemporary adversaries like Osiander and Servetus, while establishing his like-mindedness with the orthodox Christian fathers like Athanasius, Augustine, and Anselm.[3] Calvin's position is fairly straightforward (well, as much as it is possible for the mystery of Christology to be straightforward). Christ was fully man and fully God (ch. 12-13), yet these two natures were perfectly united, but not mingled, in one person (ch. 14).

You should note this quote at the very end of chapter 13—"The Son of God descended miraculously from heaven, yet without abandoning heaven, was pleased to be conceived miraculously in the Virgin's womb, to live on the earth, and hang upon the cross, and yet always filled the world as from the beginning" (331). Here Calvin is setting up a Christological premise which will play a key role in his doctrine of the Lord's Supper. Although this will be fleshed out later on in Book IV, just make a mental note to yourself that Calvin stresses the fact that in the incarnation, Christ's divine nature remained omnipresent throughout the universe, while his human nature was fixed within the limitations of space and time. This bit of Christology, though by no means invented by Calvin, later became known as the *Calvinistic Extra* and came to be one of the main indicators for identifying Calvin's theological successors.

---

3. Andreas Osiander was an early Lutheran theologian who argued that our justification was not a result of a legal imputation of Christ's sacrifice but rather an infusion of God's divine nature. Michael Servetus argued that the Reformers did not go far enough in their reformation of Catholic teaching and that if they were consistent in their application of the "sola scriptura" policy, then they would see that the doctrine of the Trinity was a later Catholic teaching imposed upon the biblical text. He was especially antagonistic towards Calvin and ended up burned at the stake in Geneva for his heretical rejection of the doctrine of the Trinity in one of the most controversial episodes of Calvin's career.

After having described the nature and person of Jesus Christ, Calvin goes on to describe Christ's work, which Calvin sets forth through a profoundly insightful summary of the three offices that Christ held—prophet, king, and priest (ch. 15). Calvin was not entirely unique in describing Christ's work according to these three offices, but the device is still largely credited to him because of how effectively he used those three offices to draw together all of Scripture to explain the work of Christ. All the Old Testament looks forward to the Messiah because those three offices, prominent throughout the Hebrew scriptures, were always pointing towards the one true Prophet, Priest, and King, and the New Testament, that final, clear proclamation of the Gospel, sets Christ before us in terms of those same three offices.

Calvin then turns to Christ's saving work in his meritorious death, burial, resurrection, and ascension. He uses the Apostles' Creed to structure the key events in Christ's work (ch. 16). Again, you should notice that Calvin is structuring his argument according to a received tradition, the Apostles' Creed, while arguing for his position through the testimony of Scripture. But his concluding focus is on the profound totality of the work of Christ, which he illustrates through a discussion of "merit." Where is all the merit in our salvation? At what point was our salvation earned? Was it when God mercifully decided to forgive our sins? Or was it when Christ suffered on the cross to atone for our sins? Are those two things in conflict with one another in their claim for meriting our salvation? Calvin answers that those two things are harmoniously synthesized in the fact that God graciously predestined the death of Christ as the means for forgiving our sins. Therefore, all the merit in our salvation was a gracious gift from God (by grace alone), given to us by means of the salvific work of Christ (by Christ alone).

Please remember that Calvin's goal in writing the *Institutes* was not to distill out of Scripture the "theology things" that we all ought to be thinking. To do so would be to attempt to replace Scripture. Rather, his goal was to give us a map so that we could run back into Scripture and better understand what we find there. And as we read book II of the *Institutes*, what we find is that throughout Scripture what we should always see is Christ set before us. When we see man's sinful fallenness, we see our need for Christ. When we see the law, we see the perfection of Christ's fulfillment. When we see Old Testament types and shadows, like the prophets, kings, and priests, we see a looking forward to Christ. And when we read the New Testament, we see the Gospel and Christ and his perfect work set before us clearly.

~Ben Merkle

SUMMARY

To his most Christian Majesty, the most mighty and illustrious
monarch, Francis, King of the French, his sovereign; John Calvin prays
peace and salvation in Christ

The First Part of the Apostles' Creed—viz. the knowledge of God the Creator, being disposed of, we now come to the Second Part, which relates to the knowledge of God as a Redeemer in Christ. The subjects treated of accordingly are, first, the Occasion of Redemption—viz. Adam's fall; and, secondly, Redemption itself. The first five chapters are devoted to the former subject, and the remainder to the latter.

Under the Occasion of Redemption, the Fall is considered not only in a general way, but also specially in its effects. Hence the first four chapters treat of original sin, free will, the corruption of human nature, and the operation of God in the heart. The fifth chapter contains a refutation of the arguments usually urged in support of free will.

The subject of redemption may be reduced to five particular heads:

I. The character of him in whom salvation for lost man must be sought, Chap. 6.

II. How he was manifested to the world, namely, in a twofold manner. First, under the Law. Here the Decalogue is expounded, and some other points relating to the law discussed, Chap. 7 and 8. Secondly, under the Gospel. Here the resemblance and difference of the two dispensations are considered, Chap. 9, 10, 11.

III. What kind of person Christ was, and behaved to be, in order to perform the office of Mediator—viz. God and man in one person, Chap. 12, 13, 14.

IV. For what end he was sent into the world by the Father. Here Christ's prophetical, kingly, and priestly offices are considered, Chap. 15.

V. In what way, or by what successive steps, Christ fulfilled the office of our Redeemer, Chap. 16. Here are considered his crucifixion, death, burial, descent to hell, resurrection, ascension to heaven, and seat at the right hand of the Father, together with the practical use of the whole doctrine. Chapter 17 contains an answer to the question, Whether Christ is properly said to have merited the grace of God for us.

CHAPTER 1

Through the fall and revolt of Adam, the whole human race made
accursed and degenerate of original sin.

Outline:

How necessary the knowledge of ourselves is, its nature, the danger of mistake, its leading parts, sections 1, 2, 3. II. The causes of Adam's fearful fall, section 4. III. The effects of the fall extending to Adam's posterity, and all the creatures, section 5, to the end of the Chapter, where the nature, propagation, and effect of original sin are considered.

1. The knowledge of ourselves most necessary. To use it properly we must be divested of pride, and clothed with true humility, which will dispose us to consider our fall, and embrace the mercy of God in Christ.

2. Though there is plausibility in the sentiment which stimulates us to self-admiration, the only sound sentiment is that which inclines us to true humbleness of mind. Pretexts for pride. The miserable vanity of sinful man.

3. Different views taken by carnal wisdom and by conscience, which appeals to divine justice as its standard. The knowledge of ourselves, consisting of two parts, the former of which having already been discussed, the latter is here considered.

4. In considering this latter part, two points to be considered; 1. How it happened that Adam involved himself and the whole human race in this dreadful calamity. This, the result not of sensual intemperance but of infidelity (the source of other heinous sins), which led to revolt from God, from whom all true happiness must be derived. An enumeration of the other sins produced by the infidelity of the first man.

5. The second point to be considered is the extent to which the contagious influence of the fall extends. It extends, 1. To all the creatures, though unoffending; and, 2. To the whole posterity of Adam. Hence hereditary corruption, or original sin, and the deprivation of a nature which was previously pure and good. This deprivation communicated to the whole posterity of Adam, but not in the way supposed by the Pelagians and Celestians.

6. Deprivation communicated not merely by imitation, but by propagation. This proved, 1. From the contrast drawn between Adam and Christ. Confirmation from passages of Scripture; 2 From the general declaration that we are the children of wrath.

7. Objection, that if Adam's sin is propagated to his posterity, the soul must be derived by transmission. Answer. Another objection—viz. that children cannot derive corruption from pious parents. Answer.

8. Definition of original sin. Two parts in the definition. Exposition of the latter part. Original sin exposes us to the wrath of God. It also produces in us the works of the flesh. Other definitions considered.

9. Exposition of the former part of the definition—viz. that hereditary depravity extends to all the faculties of the soul.

10. From the exposition of both parts of the definition it follows that God is not the author of sin, the whole human race being corrupted by an inherent viciousness.

11. This, however, is not from nature, but is an adventitious quality. Accordingly, the dream of the Manichees as to two principles vanishes.

It was not without reason that the ancient proverb so strongly recommended to man the knowledge of himself. For if it is deemed disgraceful to be ignorant of things pertaining to the business of life, much more disgraceful is self-ignorance, in consequence of which we miserably deceive ourselves in matters of the highest moment, and so walk blindfold. But the more useful the precept is, the more careful we must be not to use it preposterously, as we see certain philosophers have done. For they, when exhorting man to know himself, state the motive to be that he may not be ignorant of his own excellence and dignity. They wish him to see nothing in himself but what will fill him with vain confidence, and inflate him with pride. But self-knowledge consists in this, first: when reflecting on what God gave us at our creation, and still continues graciously to give, we perceive how great the excellence of our nature would have been had its integrity remained, and, at the same time, remember that we have nothing of our own, but depend entirely on God, from whom we hold at pleasure whatever he has seen it meet to bestow; secondly, when viewing our miserable condition since Adam's fall, all confidence and boasting are overthrown, we blush for shame, and feel truly humble. For as God at first formed us in his own image, that he might elevate our minds to the pursuit of virtue, and the contemplation of eternal life, so to prevent us from heartlessly burying those noble qualities which distinguish us from the lower animals, it is of importance to know that we were endued with reason and intelligence, in order that we might cultivate a holy and honorable life, and regard a blessed immortality as our destined aim. At the same time, it is impossible to think of our primeval dignity without being immediately reminded of the sad spectacle of our ignominy and corruption, ever since we fell from our original in the person of our first parent. In this way, we feel dissatisfied with ourselves, and become truly humble, while we are inflamed with new desires to seek after God, in whom each may regain those good qualities of which all are found to be utterly destitute.

2. In examining ourselves, the search which divine truth enjoins, and the knowledge which it demands, are such as may indispose us to every thing like confidence in our own powers, leave us devoid of all means of boasting, and so incline us to submission. This is the course which we must follow, if we would attain to the true goal, both in speculation and practice. I am not unaware how much more plausible the view is, which invites us rather to ponder on our good qualities, than to contemplate what must overwhelm us with shame—our miserable destitution and ignominy. There is nothing more acceptable to the human mind than flattery, and, accordingly, when told that its endowments are of a high order, it is apt to be excessively credulous. Hence it is not strange that the greater part of mankind have erred so egregiously in this matter. Owing to the innate self-love by which all are blinded, we most willingly persuade ourselves that we do not possess a single quality which is deserving of hatred; and hence, independent of any countenance from without, general credit is given to the very foolish idea that man is perfectly sufficient of himself for all the purposes of a good and happy life. If any are disposed to think more modestly, and concede somewhat to God, that they may not seem to arrogate every thing as their own, still, in making the division, they apportion matters so, that the chief ground of confidence and boasting always remains with themselves. Then, if a discourse is pronounced which flatters the pride spontaneously springing up in man's inmost heart, nothing seems more delightful. Accordingly, in every age, he who is most forward in extolling the excellence of human nature is received with the loudest applause. But be this heralding of human excellence what it may, by teaching man to rest in himself, it does nothing more than fascinate by its sweetness, and, at the same time, so delude as to drown in perdition all who assent to it. For what avails it to proceed in vain confidence, to deliberate, resolve, plan, and attempt what we deem pertinent to the purpose, and, at the very outset, prove deficient and destitute both of sound intelligence

and true virtue, though we still confidently persist till we rush headlong on destruction? But this is the best that can happen to those
who put confidence in their own powers. Whosoever, therefore, gives
heed to those teachers, who merely employ us in contemplating our
good qualities, so far from making progress in self-knowledge, will be
plunged into the most pernicious ignorance.

3. While revealed truth concurs with the general consent of
mankind in teaching that the second part of wisdom consists in
self-knowledge, they differ greatly as to the method by which this
knowledge is to be acquired. In the judgment of the flesh man deems
his self-knowledge complete, when, with overweening confidence in
his own intelligence and integrity, he takes courage, and spurs himself
on to virtuous deeds, and when, declaring war upon vice, he uses his
utmost endeavor to attain to the honorable and the fair. But he who
tries himself by the standard of divine justice, finds nothing to inspire
him with confidence; and hence, the more thorough his self-exam-
ination, the greater his despondency. Abandoning all dependence on
himself, he feels that he is utterly incapable of duly regulating his
conduct. It is not the will of God, however, that we should forget the
primeval dignity which he bestowed on our first parents—a dignity
which may well stimulate us to the pursuit of goodness and justice. It
is impossible for us to think of our first original, or the end for which
we were created, without being urged to meditate on immortality, and
to seek the kingdom of God. But such meditation, so far from raising
our spirits, rather casts them down, and makes us humble. For what
is our original? One from which we have fallen. What the end of our
creation? One from which we have altogether strayed, so that, weary
of our miserable lot, we groan, and groaning sigh for a dignity now
lost. When we say that man should see nothing in himself which can
raise his spirits, our meaning is that he possesses nothing on which
he can proudly plume himself. Hence, in considering the knowledge
which man ought to have of himself, it seems proper to divide it thus,

first, to consider the end for which he was created, and the qualities—by no means contemptible qualities—with which he was endued, thus urging him to meditate on divine worship and the future life; and, secondly, to consider his faculties, or rather want of faculties—a want which, when perceived, will annihilate all his confidence, and cover him with confusion. The tendency of the former view is to teach him what his duty is, of the latter, to make him aware how far he is able to perform it. We shall treat of both in their proper order.

4. As the act which God punished so severely must have been not a trivial fault, but a heinous crime, it will be necessary to attend to the peculiar nature of the sin which produced Adam's fall, and provoked God to inflict such fearful vengeance on the whole human race. The common idea of sensual intemperance is childish. The sum and substance of all virtues could not consist in abstinence from a single fruit amid a general abundance of every delicacy that could be desired, the earth, with happy fertility, yielding not only abundance, but also endless variety. We must, therefore, look deeper than sensual intemperance. The prohibition to touch the tree of the knowledge of good and evil was a trial of obedience, that Adam, by observing it, might prove his willing submission to the command of God. For the very term shows the end of the precept to have been to keep him contented with his lot, and not allow him arrogantly to aspire beyond it. The promise, which gave him hope of eternal life as long as he should eat of the tree of life, and, on the other hand, the fearful denunciation of death the moment he should taste of the tree of the knowledge of good and evil, were meant to prove and exercise his faith. Hence it is not difficult to infer in what way Adam provoked the wrath of God. Augustine, indeed, is not far from the mark, when he says (in Psal. 19), that pride was the beginning of all evil, because, had not man's ambition carried him higher than he was permitted, he might have continued in his first estate. A further definition, however, must be derived from the kind of temptation which Moses describes. When,

by the subtlety of the devil, the woman faithlessly abandoned the command of God, her fall obviously had its origin in disobedience. This Paul confirms when he says that by the disobedience of one man, all were destroyed. At the same time, it is to be observed that the first man revolted against the authority of God, not only in allowing himself to be ensnared by the wiles of the devil, but also by despising the truth, and turning aside to lies. Assuredly, when the word of God is despised, all reverence for Him is gone. His majesty cannot be duly honored among us, nor his worship maintained in its integrity, unless we hang as it were upon his lips. Hence infidelity was at the root of the revolt. From infidelity, again, sprang ambition and pride, together with ingratitude; because Adam, by longing for more than was allotted him, manifested contempt for the great liberality with which God had enriched him. It was surely monstrous impiety that a son of earth should deem it little to have been made in the likeness, unless he were also made the equal of God. If the apostasy by which man withdraws from the authority of his Maker, nay, petulantly shakes off his allegiance to him, is a foul and execrable crime, it is in vain to extenuate the sin of Adam. Nor was it simple apostasy. It was accompanied with foul insult to God, the guilty pair assenting to Satan's calumnies when he charged God with malice, envy, and falsehood. In fine, infidelity opened the door to ambition, and ambition was the parent of rebellion, man casting off the fear of God, and giving free vent to his lust. Hence, Bernard truly says that in the present day a door of salvation is opened to us when we receive the gospel with our ears, just as by the same entrance, when thrown open to Satan, death was admitted. Never would Adam have dared to show any repugnance to the command of God if he had not been incredulous as to his word. The strongest curb to keep all his affections under due restraint would have been the belief that nothing was better than to cultivate righteousness by obeying the commands of God, and that the highest possible felicity was to be loved by him. Man, therefore, when carried

away by the blasphemies of Satan, did his very utmost to annihilate
the whole glory of God.

5. As Adam's spiritual life would have consisted in remaining united
and bound to his Maker, so estrangement from him was the death of his
soul. Nor is it strange that he who perverted the whole order of nature
in heaven and earth deteriorated his race by his revolt. "The whole creation groaneth," saith St Paul, "being made subject to vanity, not willingly" (Rom. 8:20, 22). If the reason is asked, there cannot be a doubt that
creation bears part of the punishment deserved by man, for whose use all
other creatures were made. Therefore, since through man's fault a curse
has extended above and below, over all the regions of the world, there
is nothing unreasonable in its extending to all his offspring. After the
heavenly image in man was effaced, he not only was himself punished
by a withdrawal of the ornaments in which he had been arrayed—viz.
wisdom, virtue, justice, truth, and holiness, and by the substitution in
their place of those dire pests, blindness, impotence, vanity, impurity, and
unrighteousness, but he involved his posterity also, and plunged them in
the same wretchedness. This is the hereditary corruption to which early
Christian writers gave the name of Original Sin, meaning by the term
the deprivation of a nature formerly good and pure. The subject gave
rise to much discussion, there being nothing more remote from common apprehension, than that the fault of one should render all guilty,
and so become a common sin. This seems to be the reason why the oldest
doctors of the church only glance obscurely at the point, or, at least, do
not explain it so clearly as it required. This timidity, however, could not
prevent the rise of a Pelagius with his profane fiction—that Adam sinned
only to his own hurt, but did no hurt to his posterity. Satan, by thus craft-
ily hiding the disease, tried to render it incurable. But when it was clearly
proved from Scripture that the sin of the first man passed to all his posterity, recourse was had to the cavil, that it passed by imitation, and not
by propagation. The orthodox, therefore, and more especially Augustine,
labored to show, that we are not corrupted by acquired wickedness, but

bring an innate corruption from the very womb. It was the greatest impudence to deny this. But no man will wonder at the presumption of the Pelagians and Celestians, who has learned from the writings of that holy man how extreme the effrontery of these heretics was. Surely there is no ambiguity in David's confession, "I was shapen in iniquity; and in sin did my mother conceive me" (Ps. 51:5). His object in the passage is not to throw blame on his parents; but the better to commend the goodness of God towards him, he properly reiterates the confession of impurity from his very birth. As it is clear, that there was no peculiarity in David's case, it follows that it is only an instance of the common lot of the whole human race. All of us, therefore, descending from an impure seed, come into the world tainted with the contagion of sin. Nay, before we behold the light of the sun we are in God's sight defiled and polluted. "Who can bring a clean thing out of an unclean? Not one," says the Book of Job (Job 14:4).

6. We thus see that the impurity of parents is transmitted to their children, so that all, without exception, are originally depraved. The commencement of this depravity will not be found until we ascend to the first parent of all as the fountain head. We must, therefore, hold it for certain that in regard to human nature, Adam was not merely a progenitor, but, as it were, a root, and that, accordingly, by his corruption, the whole human race was deservedly vitiated. This is plain from the contrast which the Apostle draws between Adam and Christ, "Wherefore, as by one man sin entered into the world, and death by sin; and so death passed upon all men, for that all have sinned; even so might grace reign through righteousness unto eternal life by Jesus Christ our Lord" (Rom. 5:19-21). To what quibble will the Pelagians here recur? That the sin of Adam was propagated by imitation! Is the righteousness of Christ then available to us only in so far as it is an example held forth for our imitation? Can any man tolerate such blasphemy? But if, out of all controversy, the righteousness of Christ, and thereby life, is ours by communication, it follows that both of these were lost in Adam that they might be recovered

in Christ, whereas sin and death were brought in by Adam, that they might be abolished in Christ. There is no obscurity in the words, "As by one man's disobedience many were made sinners, so by the obedience of one shall many be made righteous." Accordingly, the relation subsisting between the two is this: as Adam, by his ruin, involved and ruined us, so Christ, by his grace, restored us to salvation. In this clear light of truth I cannot see any need of a longer or more laborious proof. Thus, too, in the First Epistle to the Corinthians, when Paul would confirm believers in the confident hope of the resurrection, he shows that the life is recovered in Christ which was lost in Adam (1 Cor. 15:22). Having already declared that all died in Adam, he now also openly testifies that all are imbued with the taint of sin. Condemnation, indeed, could not reach those who are altogether free from blame. But his meaning cannot be made clearer than from the other member of the sentence, in which he shows that the hope of life is restored in Christ. Everyone knows that the only mode in which this is done is when by a wondrous communication Christ transfuses into us the power of his own righteousness, as it is elsewhere said, "The Spirit is life because of righteousness" (1 Cor. 15:22). Therefore, the only explanation which can be given of the expression, "in Adam all died," is that he by sinning not only brought disaster and ruin upon himself, but also plunged our nature into like destruction; and that not only in one fault, in a matter not pertaining to us, but by the corruption into which he himself fell, he infected his whole seed. Paul never could have said that all are "by nature the children of wrath" (Eph. 2:3), if they had not been cursed from the womb. And it is obvious that the nature there referred to is not nature such as God created, but as vitiated in Adam; for it would have been most incongruous to make God the author of death. Adam, therefore, when he corrupted himself, transmitted the contagion to all his posterity. For a heavenly Judge, even our Savior himself, declares that all are by birth vicious and depraved, when he says that "that which is born of the flesh is fleshly" (John 3:6), and that therefore the gate of life is closed against all until they have been regenerated.

7. To the understanding of this subject, there is no necessity for an anxious discussion (which in no small degree perplexed the ancient doctors) as to whether the soul of the child comes by transmission from the soul of the parent. It should be enough for us to know that Adam was made the depository of the endowments which God was pleased to bestow on human nature, and that therefore, when he lost what he had received, he lost not only for himself but for us all. Why feel any anxiety about the transmission of the soul, when we know that the qualities which Adam lost he received for us not less than for himself, that they were not gifts to a single man, but attributes of the whole human race? There is nothing absurd, therefore, in the view, that when he was divested, his nature was left naked and destitute that he having been defiled by sin, the pollution extends to all his seed. Thus, from a corrupt root corrupt branches proceeding, transmit their corruption to the saplings which spring from them. The children being vitiated in their parent, conveyed the taint to the grandchildren; in other words, corruption commencing in Adam, is, by perpetual descent, conveyed from those preceding to those coming after them. The cause of the contagion is neither in the substance of the flesh nor the soul, but God was pleased to ordain that those gifts which he had bestowed on the first man, that man should lose as well for his descendants as for himself. The Pelagian cavil, as to the improbability of children deriving corruption from pious parents, whereas, they ought rather to be sanctified by their purity, is easily refuted. Children come not by spiritual regeneration but carnal descent. Accordingly, as Augustine says, "Both the condemned unbeliever and the acquitted believer beget offspring not acquitted but condemned, because the nature which begets is corrupt." Moreover, though godly parents do in some measure contribute to the holiness of their offspring, this is by the blessing of God; a blessing, however, which does

not prevent the primary and universal curse of the whole race from previously taking effect. Guilt is from nature, whereas sanctification is from supernatural grace.

8. But lest the thing itself of which we speak be unknown or doubtful, it will be proper to define original sin. (Calvin, in *Conc. Trident.* 1, Dec. Sess. 5). I have no intention, however, to discuss all the definitions which different writers have adopted, but only to adduce the one which seems to me most accordant with truth. Original sin, then, may be defined a hereditary corruption and depravity of our nature, extending to all the parts of the soul, which first makes us obnoxious to the wrath of God, and then produces in us works which in Scripture are termed works of the flesh. This corruption is repeatedly designated by Paul by the term sin (Gal. 5:19); while the works which proceed from it, such as adultery, fornication, theft, hatred, murder, revelings, he terms, in the same way, the fruits of sin, though in various passages of Scripture, and even by Paul himself, they are also termed sins. The two things, therefore, are to be distinctly observed— viz. that being thus perverted and corrupted in all the parts of our nature, we are, merely on account of such corruption, deservedly condemned by God, to whom nothing is acceptable but righteousness, innocence, and purity. This is not liability for another's fault. For when it is said that the sin of Adam has made us obnoxious to the justice of God, the meaning is not that we, who are in ourselves innocent and blameless, are bearing his guilt, but that since by his transgression we are all placed under the curse, he is said to have brought us under obligation. Through him, however, not only has punishment been derived, but pollution instilled, for which punishment is justly due. Hence Augustine, though he often terms it another's sin (that he may more clearly show how it comes to us by descent), at the same time asserts that it is each individual's own sin. And the Apostle most distinctly testifies, that "death passed upon all men, for that all have sinned" (Rom. 5:12); that is, are involved in original sin, and polluted

by its stain. Hence, even infants bringing their condemnation with them from their mother's womb, suffer not for another's, but for their own defect. For although they have not yet produced the fruits of their own unrighteousness, they have the seed implanted in them. Nay, their whole nature is, as it were, a seed-bed of sin, and therefore cannot but be odious and abominable to God. Hence it follows, that it is properly deemed sinful in the sight of God; for there could be no condemnation without guilt. Next comes the other point—viz. that this perversity in us never ceases, but constantly produces new fruits, in other words, those works of the flesh which we formerly described; just as a lighted furnace sends forth sparks and flames, or a fountain without ceasing pours out water. Hence, those who have defined original sin as the want of the original righteousness which we ought to have had, though they substantially comprehend the whole case, do not significantly enough express its power and energy. For our nature is not only utterly devoid of goodness, but so prolific in all kinds of evil, that it can never be idle. Those who term it concupiscence use a word not very inappropriate, provided it were added (this, however, many will by no means concede) that everything which is in man, from the intellect to the will, from the soul even to the flesh, is defiled and pervaded with this concupiscence; or, to express it more briefly, that the whole man is in himself nothing else than concupiscence.

9. I have said, therefore, that all the parts of the soul were possessed by sin, ever since Adam revolted from the fountain of righteousness. For not only did the inferior appetites entice him, but abominable impiety seized upon the very citadel of the mind, and pride penetrated to his inmost heart (Rom. 7:12; Book 4, chap. 15, sec. 10-12), so that it is foolish and unmeaning to confine the corruption thence proceeding to what are called sensual motions, or to call it an excitement, which allures, excites, and drags the single part which they call sensuality into sin. Here Peter Lombard has displayed gross ignorance (Lomb., lib. 2 Dist. 31). When investigating the seat of

corruption, he says it is in the flesh (as Paul declares), not properly, indeed, but as being more apparent in the flesh. As if Paul had meant that only a part of the soul, and not the whole nature, was opposed to supernatural grace. Paul himself leaves no room for doubt, when he says, that corruption does not dwell in one part only, but that no part is free from its deadly taint. For, speaking of corrupt nature, he not only condemns the inordinate nature of the appetites, but, in particular, declares that the understanding is subjected to blindness, and the heart to depravity (Eph. 4:17-18). The third chapter of the Epistle to the Romans is nothing but a description of original sin; The same thing appears more clearly from the mode of renovation. For the spirit, which is contrasted with the old man, and the flesh, denotes not only the grace by which the sensual or inferior part of the soul is corrected, but includes a complete reformation of all its parts (Eph. 4:23). And, accordingly, Paul enjoins not only that gross appetites be suppressed, but that we be renewed in the spirit of our mind (Eph. 4:23), as he elsewhere tells us to be transformed by the renewing of our mind (Rom. 12:2). Hence it follows, that that part in which the dignity and excellence of the soul are most conspicuous, has not only been wounded, but so corrupted, that mere cure is not sufficient. There must be a new nature. How far sin has seized both on the mind and heart, we shall shortly see. Here I only wished briefly to observe, that the whole man, from the crown of the head to the sole of the foot, is so deluged, as it were, that no part remains exempt from sin, and, therefore, everything which proceeds from him is imputed as sin. Thus Paul says that all carnal thoughts and affections are enmity against God, and consequently death (Rom. 8:7).

10. Let us have done, then, with those who dare to inscribe the name of God on their vices, because we say that men are born vicious. The divine workmanship, which they ought to look for in the nature of Adam, when still entire and uncorrupted, they absurdly expect to find in their depravity. The blame of our ruin rests with our own carnality,

not with God, its only cause being our degeneracy from our original condition. And let no one here glamour that God might have provided better for our safety by preventing Adam's fall. This objection, which, from the daring presumption implied in it, is odious to every pious mind, relates to the mystery of predestination, which will afterwards be considered in its own place (Tertull. *de Praescript.*, Calvin, Lib. *de Predest.*). Meanwhile let us remember that our ruin is attributable to our own depravity, that we may not insinuate a charge against God himself, the Author of nature. It is true that nature has received a mortal wound, but there is a great difference between a wound inflicted from without, and one inherent in our first condition. It is plain that this wound was inflicted by sin; and, therefore, we have no ground of complaint except against ourselves. This is carefully taught in Scripture. For the Preacher says, "Lo, this only have I found, that God made man upright; but they have sought out many inventions" (Eccl. 7:29). Since man, by the kindness of God, was made upright, but by his own infatuation fell away unto vanity, his destruction is obviously attributable only to himself (Athanas. *in Orat. Cont. Idola.*).

11. We say, then, that man is corrupted by a natural viciousness, but not by one which proceeded from nature. In saying that it proceeded not from nature, we mean that it was rather an adventitious event which befell man, than a substantial property assigned to him from the beginning. We, however call it natural to prevent any one from supposing that each individual contracts it by depraved habit, whereas all receive it by a hereditary law. And we have authority for so calling it. For, on the same grounds the apostle says, that we are "by nature the children of wrath" (Eph. 2:3). How could God, who takes pleasure in the meanest of his works be offended with the noblest of them all? The offense is not with the work itself, but the corruption of the work. Wherefore, if it is not improper to say, that, in consequence of the corruption of human nature, man is naturally hateful to God, it is not improper to say, that he is naturally vicious and depraved.

Hence, in the view of our corrupt nature, Augustine hesitates not to call those sins natural which necessarily reign in the flesh wherever the grace of God is wanting. This disposes of the absurd notion of the Manichees, who, imagining that man was essentially wicked, went the length of assigning him a different Creator, that they might thus avoid the appearance of attributing the cause and origin of evil to a righteous God.

Study Guide Questions

Section 1

1. What ancient proverb does Calvin commend?
2. What echo of an earlier point in Calvin does this make?
3. What are the two essential parts of self-knowledge?

Section 2

1. Instead of true self-knowledge, what do we tend to seek out instead?
2. What does this flattery appeal to?

Section 3

1. Does reflection on our original nobility create pride in us?
2. How are we then to divide our knowledge of ourselves?
3. What will this do?

Section 4

1. Does Calvin believe that Adam was allowed to eat from the tree of life?
2. Was Adam's sin simply gluttony?
3. What was the root of Adam's sin?
4. What was the progress of Adam's rebellion?

Section 5

1. How does Calvin define the "death of [Adam's] soul"?

2. How does Calvin define "original sin"?

3. What was Pelagius' "profane fiction"?

Section 6

1. When are children defiled by original sin?

2. What is Adam's position with regard to the human race?

3. What is, for Calvin, "out of all controversy"?

4. How does Calvin define that communication of righteousness from Christ?

Section 7

1. What should we be content to know with regard to all this?

2. Does the contagion spread through the substance of flesh or soul?

Section 8

1. How does Calvin define original sin?

2. Do infants bear the curse of original sin?

3. Is this original sin nothing more than the absence of righteousness?

Section 9

1. How far does original sin extend in a man?

2. Is it true that the flesh is fallen, but the soul is not?

Section 10

1. What is Calvin's response to those who would write God's name upon their faults?

2. What is wrong with asking the question "Why did God not prevent the Fall?"

Section 11

1. In what way is sin unnatural?

2. In what way is sin natural?

CHAPTER 2

Man now deprived of freedom of will, and miserably enslaved.

Having in the first chapter treated of the fall of man, and the corruption of the human race, it becomes necessary to inquire, Whether the sons of Adam are deprived of all liberty; and if any particle of liberty remains, how far its power extends? The four next chapters are devoted to this question. This second chapter may be reduced to three general heads: I. The foundation of the whole discussion. II. The opinions of others on the subject of human freedom, sections 2-9. III. The true doctrine on the subject, sections 10-27.

Outline:

1. Connection of the previous with the four following chapters. In order to lay a proper foundation for the discussion of free will, two obstacles in the way to be removed—viz. sloth and pride. The basis and sum of the whole discussion. The solid structure of this basis, and a clear demonstration of it by the argument a *majori ad minus*. Also from the inconveniences and absurdities arising from the obstacle of pride.

2. The second part of the chapter containing the opinions of others. The opinions of philosophers.

3. The labyrinths of philosophers. A summary of the opinion common to all the philosophers.

4. The opinions of others continued—viz. The opinions of the ancient theologians on the subject of free will. These composed partly of Philosophy and partly of Theology. Hence their falsehood, extravagance, perplexity, variety, and contradiction. Too great fondness for philosophy in the Church has obscured the knowledge of God and of ourselves. The better to explain the opinions of philosophers, a definition of Free Will given. Wide difference between this definition and these opinions.

5. Certain things annexed to Free Will by the ancient theologians, especially the Schoolmen. Many kinds of Free Will according to them.

6. Puzzles of scholastic divines in the explanation of this question.

7. The conclusion that so trivial a matter ought not to be so much magnified. Objection of those who have a fondness for new terms in the Church. Objection answered.

8. Another answer. The Fathers, and especially Augustine, while retaining the term Free Will, yet condemned the doctrine of the heretics on the subject, as destroying the grace of God.

9. The language of the ancient writers on the subject of Free Will is, with the exception of that of Augustine, almost unintelligible. Still they set little or no value on human virtue, and ascribe the praise of all goodness to the Holy Spirit.

10. The last part of the chapter, containing a simple statement of the true doctrine. The fundamental principle is, that man first begins to profit in the knowledge of himself when he becomes sensible of his ruined condition. This confirmed, 1. by passages of Scripture.

11. Confirmed, 2. by the testimony of ancient theologians.

12. The foundation being laid, to show how far the power both of the intellect and will now extends, it is maintained in general, and in conformity with the views of Augustine and the Schoolmen, that the natural endowments of man are corrupted, and the supernatural almost

entirely lost. A separate consideration of the powers of the Intellect and the Will. Some general considerations, 1. The intellect possesses some powers of perception. Still it labors under a twofold defect.

13. Man's intelligence extends both to things terrestrial and celestial. The power of the intellect in regard to the knowledge of things terrestrial. First, with regard to matters of civil polity.

14. The power of the intellect, secondly, with regard to the arts. Particular gifts in this respect conferred on individuals, and attesting the grace of God.

15. The rise of this knowledge of things terrestrial, first, that we may see how human nature, notwithstanding of its fall, is still adorned by God with excellent endowments.

16. Use of this knowledge continued. Secondly, that we may see that these endowments bestowed on individuals are intended for the common benefit of mankind. They are sometimes conferred even on the wicked.

17. Some portion of human nature still left. This, whatever be the amount of it, should be ascribed entirely to the divine indulgence. Reason of this. Examples.

18. Second part of the discussion, namely, that which relates to the power of the human intellect in regard to things celestial. These reducible to three heads, namely, divine knowledge, adoption, and will. The blindness of man in regard to these proved and thus tested by a simile.

19. Proved, moreover, by passages of Scripture, showing, 1. That the sons of Adam are endued with some light, but not enough to enable them to comprehend God. Reasons.

20. Adoption not from nature, but from our heavenly Father, being sealed in the elect by the Spirit of regeneration. Obvious from many passages of Scripture, that, previous to regeneration, the human intellect is altogether unable to comprehend the things relating to regeneration. This fully proved. First argument. Second argument. Third argument.

21. Fourth argument. Scripture ascribes the glory of our adoption and salvation to God only. The human intellect blind as to heavenly things until it is illuminated. Disposal of a heretical objection.

22. Human intellect ignorant of the true knowledge of the divine law. This proved by the testimony of an Apostle, by an inference from the same testimony, and from a consideration of the end and definition of the Law of Nature. Plato obviously mistaken in attributing all sins to ignorance.

23. Themistius nearer the truth in maintaining, that the delusion of the intellect is manifested not so much in generals as in particulars. Exception to this rule.

24. Themistius, however, mistaken in thinking that the intellect is so very seldom deceived as to generals. Blindness of the human intellect when tested by the standard of the Divine Law, in regard both to the first and second tables. Examples.

25. A middle view to be taken—viz. that all sins are not imputable to ignorance, and, at the same time, that all sins do not imply intentional malice. All the human mind conceives and plans in this matter is evil in the sight of God. Need of divine direction every moment.

26. The will examined. The natural desire of good, which is universally felt, no proof of the freedom of the human will. Two fallacies as to the use of terms, appetite and good.

27. The doctrine of the Schoolmen on this subject opposed to and refuted by Scripture. The whole man being subject to the power of sin, it follows that the will, which is the chief seat of sin, requires to be most strictly curbed. Nothing ours but sin.

Having seen that the dominion of sin, ever since the first man was brought under it, not only extends to the whole race, but has complete possession of every soul, it now remains to consider more closely, whether from the period of being thus enslaved, we have been deprived of all liberty; and if any portion still remains, how far its power extends. In order to facilitate the answer to this question it may be proper in passing to point out the course which our inquiry ought to take. The best method of avoiding error is to consider the dangers which beset us on either side. Man being devoid of all uprightness, immediately takes occasion from the fact to indulge in sloth, and having no ability in himself for the study of righteousness, treats the whole subject as if he had no concern in it. On the other hand, man cannot arrogate any thing, however minute, to himself, without robbing God of his honor, and through rash confidence subjecting himself to a fall. To keep free of both these rocks, our proper course will be, first, to show that man has no remaining good in himself, and is beset on every side by the most miserable destitution; and then teach him to aspire to the goodness of which he is devoid, and the liberty of which he has been deprived: thus giving him a stronger stimulus to exertion than he could have if he imagined himself possessed of the highest virtue. How necessary the latter point is, everybody sees. As to the former, several seem to entertain more doubt than they ought. For it being admitted as incontrovertible that man is not to be denied any thing that is truly his own, it ought also to be admitted, that he is to be deprived of every thing like false boasting. If man had no title to glory in himself, when, by the kindness of his Maker, he was distinguished by the noblest ornaments, how much ought he to be humbled now, when his ingratitude has thrust him down from the highest glory to extreme ignominy? At the time when he was raised to the highest pinnacle of honor, all which Scripture attributes to him is that he was created in the image of God, thereby intimating that the blessings in which his happiness consisted were not his own, but derived by divine communication. What remains, therefore, now that man is stripped of all his glory, than to acknowledge the God for whose kindness he failed to be grateful, when he was loaded with the riches of his grace? Not having glorified him by the acknowledgment of his blessings, now, at least, he ought to glorify him by the confession of his poverty. In truth, it is no less useful for us to renounce all the praise of wisdom and virtue than to aim at the glory of God. Those who invest us with more than we possess only add sacrilege to our ruin. For when we are taught to contend in our own strength, what more is done than to lift us up, and then leave us to lean on a reed which immediately gives way? Indeed, our strength is exaggerated when it is compared to a reed. All that foolish men invent and prattle on this subject is mere smoke. Wherefore, it is not without reason that Augustine so often repeats the well-known saying that free will is more destroyed than established by its defenders (August. *in Evang. Joann.* Tract. 81). It was necessary to premise this much for the sake of some who, when they hear that human virtue is totally overthrown, in order that the power of God in man may be exalted, conceive an utter dislike to the whole subject, as if it were perilous, not to say superfluous, whereas it is manifestly both most necessary and most useful.

2. Having lately observed that the faculties of the soul are seated in the mind and the heart, let us now consider how far the power of each extends. Philosophers generally maintain that reason dwells in the mind like a lamp, throwing light on all its counsels, and like a queen, governing the will—that it is so pervaded with divine light as to be able to consult for the best, and so endued with vigor as to be able perfectly to command; that, on the contrary, sense is dull and short-sighted, always creeping on the ground, groveling among inferior objects, and never rising to true vision; that the appetite, when it obeys reason, and does not allow itself to be subjugated by sense, is borne to the study of virtue, holds a straight course, and becomes transformed into will; but that when enslaved by sense, it is corrupted and depraved so as to degenerate into lust. In a word, since, according to their opinion, the faculties which I have mentioned above, namely, intellect, sense, and appetite, or will (the latter being the term in ordinary use), are seated in the soul, they maintain that the intellect

is endued with reason, the best guide to a virtuous and happy life, provided it duly avails itself of its excellence, and exerts the power with which it is naturally endued; that, at the same time, the inferior movement, which is termed sense, and by which the mind is led away to error and delusion, is of such a nature that it can be tamed and gradually subdued by the power of reason. To the will, moreover, they give an intermediate place between reason and sense, regarding it as possessed of full power and freedom, whether to obey the former, or yield itself up to be hurried away by the latter.

3. Sometimes, indeed, convinced by their own experience, they do not deny how difficult it is for man to establish the supremacy of reason in himself, inasmuch as he is at one time enticed by the allurements of pleasure; at another, deluded by a false semblance of good; and, at another, impelled by unruly passions, and pulled away (to use Plato's expression) as by ropes or sinews (Plato, *De Legibus*, lib. 1). For this reason, Cicero says, that the sparks given forth by nature are immediately extinguished by false opinions and depraved manners (Cicero, *Tusc. Quaest.* lib. 3). They confess that when once diseases of this description have seized upon the mind, their course is too impetuous to be easily checked, and they hesitate not to compare them to fiery steeds, which, having thrown off the charioteer, scamper away without restraint. At the same time, they set it down as beyond dispute, that virtue and vice are in our own power. For (say they), If it is in our choice to do this thing or that, it must also be in our choice not to do it: again, if it is in our choice not to act, it must also be in our choice to act, but both in doing and abstaining we seem to act from free choice; and, therefore, if we do good when we please, we can also refrain from doing it; if we commit evil, we can also shun the commission of it (Aristot. *Ethic.* lib. 3 c. 5). Nay, some have gone the length of boasting (Seneca, passim), that it is the gift of the gods that we live, but our own that we live well and purely. Hence Cicero says, in the person of Cotta, that as every one acquires virtue for himself,

no wise man ever thanked the gods for it. "We are praised," says he, "for virtue, and glory in virtue, but this could not be, if virtue were the gift of God, and not from ourselves" (Cicero, *De Nat. Deorum*). A little after, he adds, "The opinion of all mankind is, that fortune must be sought from God, wisdom from ourselves." Thus, in short, all philosophers maintain that human reason is sufficient for right government; that the will, which is inferior to it, may indeed be solicited to evil by sense, but having a free choice, there is nothing to prevent it from following reason as its guide in all things.

4. Among ecclesiastical writers, although there is none who did not acknowledge that sound reason in man was seriously injured by sin, and the will greatly entangled by vicious desires, yet many of them made too near an approach to the philosophers. Some of the most ancient writers appear to me to have exalted human strengths from a fear that a distinct acknowledgment of its impotence might expose them to the jeers of the philosophers with whom they were disputing, and also furnish the flesh, already too much disinclined to good, with a new pretext for sloth. Therefore, to avoid teaching anything which the majority of mankind might deem absurd, they made it their study, in some measure, to reconcile the doctrine of Scripture with the dogmas of philosophy, at the same time making it their special care not to furnish any occasion to sloth. This is obvious from their words. Chrysostom says, "God having placed good and evil in our power, has given us full freedom of choice; he does not keep back the unwilling, but embraces the willing" (Homil. *de Prodit. Judae*). Again, "He who is wicked is often, when he so chooses, changed into good, and he who is good falls through sluggishness, and becomes wicked. For the Lord has made our nature free. He does not lay us under necessity, but furnishing apposite remedies, allows the whole to depend on the views of the patient" (Homily. 18, *in Genesis*). Again, "As we can do nothing rightly until aided by the grace of God, so, until we bring forward what is our own, we cannot obtain favor from above" (Homily.

52). He had previously said, "As the whole is not done by divine assistance, we ourselves must of necessity bring somewhat." Accordingly, one of his common expressions is, "Let us bring what is our own, God will supply the rest." In unison with this, Jerome says, "It is ours to begin, God's to finish: it is ours to offer what we can, his to supply what we cannot" (Dialog. 3 *Cont. Pelag.*).

From these sentences, you see that they have bestowed on man more than he possesses for the study of virtue, because they thought that they could not shake off our innate sluggishness unless they argued that we sin by ourselves alone. With what skill they have thus argued we shall afterwards see. Assuredly we shall soon be able to show that the sentiments just quoted are most inaccurate. Moreover although the Greek Fathers, above others, and especially Chrysostom, have exceeded due bounds in extolling the powers of the human will, yet all ancient theologians, with the exception of Augustine, are so confused, vacillating, and contradictory on this subject that no certainty can be obtained from their writings. It is needless, therefore, to be more particular in enumerating every separate opinion. It will be sufficient to extract from each as much as the exposition of the subject seems to require. Succeeding writers (every one courting applause for his acuteness in the defense of human nature) have uniformly, one after the other, gone more widely astray, until the common dogma came to be that man was corrupted only in the sensual part of his nature, that reason remained entire, and will was scarcely impaired. Still the expression was often on their lips, that man's natural gifts were corrupted, and his supernatural taken away. Of the thing implied by these words, however, scarcely one in a hundred had any distinct idea. Certainly, were I desirous clearly to express what the corruption of nature is, I would not seek for any other expression. But it is of great importance attentively to consider what the power of man now is when vitiated in all the parts of his nature, and deprived of supernatural gifts. Persons professing to be the disciples of Christ have spoken too much like the philosophers on this subject. As if human nature were still in its integrity, the term free will has always been in use among the Latins, while the Greeks were not ashamed to use a still more presumptuous term—viz. *autexousion*, as if man had still full power in himself.

But since the principle entertained by all, even the vulgar, is that man is endued with free will, while some, who would be thought more skillful, know not how far its power extends; it will be necessary, first to consider the meaning of the term, and afterwards ascertain, by a simple appeal to Scripture, what man's natural power for good or evil is. The thing meant by free will, though constantly occurring in all writers, few have defined. Origen, however, seems to have stated the common opinion when he said it is a power of reason to discern between good and evil; of will, to choose the one or other. Nor does Augustine differ from him when he says it is a power of reason and will to choose the good, grace assisting—to choose the bad, grace desisting. Bernard, while aiming at greater acuteness, speaks more obscurely, when he describes it as consent, in regard to the indestructible liberty of the wills and the inalienable judgment of reason. Anselm's definition is not very intelligible to ordinary understandings. He calls it a power of preserving rectitude on its own account. Peter Lombard and the Schoolmen preferred the definition of Augustine, both because it was clearer, and did not exclude divine grace, without which they saw that the will was not sufficient of itself. They however add something of their own, because they deemed it either better or necessary for clearer explanation. First, they agree that the term will (*arbitrium*) has reference to reason, whose office it is to distinguish between good and evil, and that the epithet free properly belongs to the will, which may incline either way. Wherefore, since liberty properly belongs to the will, Thomas Aquinas says (Part 1 Quast. 83, Art. 3), that the most congruous definition is to call free will an elective power, combining intelligence and appetite, but inclining more to appetite. We now perceive in what it is they suppose the faculty of free will to consist—viz. in reason and will. It remains to see how much they attribute to each.

5. In general, they are wont to place under the free will of man only intermediate things—viz. those which pertain not to the kingdom of God, while they refer true righteousness to the special grace of God and spiritual regeneration. The author of the work, *De Vocatione Gentium* (On the Calling of the Gentiles), wishing to show this, describes the will as threefold—viz. sensitive, animal, and spiritual. The two former, he says, are free to man, but the last is the work of the Holy Spirit. What truth there is in this will be considered in its own place. Our intention at present is only to mention the opinions of others, not to refute them. When writers treat of free will, their inquiry is chiefly directed not to what its power is in relation to civil or external actions, but to the obedience required by the divine law. The latter I admit to be the great question, but I cannot think the former should be altogether neglected; and I hope to be able to give the best reason for so thinking (sec. 12 to 18). The schools, however, have adopted a distinction which enumerates three kinds of freedom (see Lombard, lib. 2 Dist. 25); the first, a freedom from necessity; the second, a freedom from sin; and the third, a freedom from misery: the first naturally so inherent in man that he cannot possibly be deprived of it; while through sin the other two have been lost. I willingly admit this distinction, except in so far as it confounds necessity with compulsion. How widely the things differ, and how important it is to attend to the difference, will appear elsewhere.

6. All this being admitted, it will be beyond dispute that free will does not enable any man to perform good works, unless he is assisted by grace; indeed, the special grace which the elect alone receive through regeneration. For I stay not to consider the extravagance of those who say that grace is offered equally and promiscuously to all (Lomb. lib. 2 Dist. 26). But it has not yet been shown whether man is

entirely deprived of the power of well-doing, or whether he still possesses it in some, though in a very feeble and limited degree—a degree
so feeble and limited that it can do nothing of itself, but when assisted
by grace, is able also to perform its part. The Master of the Sentences
(Lombard, ibid.) wishing to explain this, teaches that a twofold grace
is necessary to fit for any good work. The one he calls Operating. To
it, it is owing that we effectually will what is good. The other, which
succeeds this good will, and aids it, he calls Co-operating. My objection to this division (see infra, chap. 3 sec. 10, and chap. 7 sec. 9) is,
that while it attributes the effectual desire of good to divine grace, it
insinuates that man, by his own nature, desires good in some degree,
though ineffectually. Thus Bernard, while maintaining that a good
will is the work of God, concedes this much to man—viz. that of his
own nature he longs for such a good will. This differs widely from the
view of Augustine, though Lombard pretends to have taken the division from him. Besides, there is an ambiguity in the second division,
which has led to an erroneous interpretation. For it has been thought
that we co-operate with subsequent grace, inasmuch as it pertains
to us either to nullify the first grace, by rejecting its or to confirm
it, by obediently yielding to it. The author of the work *De Vocatione
Gentium* expresses it thus: It is free to those who enjoy the faculty of
reason to depart from grace, so that the not departing is a reward, and
that which cannot be done without the co-operation of the Spirit is
imputed as merit to those whose will might have made it otherwise
(lib. 2 cap. 4). It seemed proper to make these two observations in
passing, that the reader may see how far I differ from the sounder of
the Schoolmen. Still further do I differ from more modern sophists,
who have departed even more widely than the Schoolmen from the
ancient doctrine. The division, however, shows in what respect free
will is attributed to man. For Lombard ultimately declares (lib. 2,
Dist. 25) that our freedom is not to the extent of leaving us equally
inclined to good and evil in act or in thought, but only to the extent of

freeing us from compulsion. This liberty is compatible with our being depraved, the servants of sin, able to do nothing but sin.

7. In this way, then, man is said to have free will, not because he has a free choice of good and evil, but because he acts voluntarily, and not by compulsion. This is perfectly true: but why should so small a matter have been dignified with so proud a title? An admirable freedom! that man is not forced to be the servant of sin, while he is, however, εθελοδουλω (a voluntary slave); his will being bound by the fetters of sin. I abominate mere verbal disputes, by which the Church is harassed to no purpose; but I think we ought religiously to eschew terms which imply some absurdity, especially in subjects where error is of pernicious consequence. How few are there who, when they hear free will attributed to man, do not immediately imagine that he is the master of his mind and will in such a sense, that he can of himself incline himself either to good or evil? It may be said that such dangers are removed by carefully expounding the meaning to the people. But such is the proneness of the human mind to go astray that it will more quickly draw error from one little word, than truth from a lengthened discourse. Of this, the very term in question furnishes too strong a proof. For the explanation given by ancient Christian writers having been lost sight of, almost all who have come after them, by attending only to the etymology of the term, have been led to indulge a fatal confidence.

8. As to the Fathers (if their authority weighs with us), they have the term constantly in their mouths; but they, at the same time, declare what extent of meaning they attach to it. In particular, Augustine hesitates not to call the will a slave. In another passages he is offended with those who deny free will; but his chief reason for this is explained when he says, "Only lest any one should presume so to deny freedom of will, from a desire to excuse sin." It is certain, he elsewhere admits, that without the Spirit the will of man is not free, inasmuch as it is subject to lusts which chain and master it. And again, that nature began to want liberty the moment the will was vanquished by

the revolt into which it fell. Again, that man, by making a bad use of free will, lost both himself and his will. Again, that free will having been made a captive, can do nothing in the way of righteousness. Again, that no will is free which has not been made so by divine grace. Again, that the righteousness of God is not fulfilled when the law orders, and man acts, as it were, by his own strength, but when the Spirit assists, and the will (not the free will of man, but the will freed by God) obeys. He briefly states the ground of all these observations, when he says that man at his creation received a great degree of free will, but lost it by sinning. In another place, after showing that free will is established by grace, he strongly inveighs against those who arrogate any thing to themselves without grace. His words are, "How much soever miserable men presume to plume themselves on free will before they are made free, or on their strength after they are made free, they do not consider that, in the very expression free will, liberty is implied. 'Where the Spirit of the Lord is, there is liberty,'" (2 Cor. 3:17). If, therefore, they are the servants of sin, why do they boast of free will? He who has been vanquished is the servant of him who vanquished him. But if men have been made free, why do they boast of it as of their own work? Are they so free that they are unwilling to be the servants of Him who has said, "Without me ye can do nothing?" (John 15:5). In another passage he even seems to ridicule the word, when he says, "That the will is indeed free, but not freed—free of righteousness, but enslaved to sin." The same idea he elsewhere repeats and explains, when he says, "That man is not free from righteousness save by the choice of his will, and is not made free from sin save by the grace of the Savior." Declaring that the freedom of man is nothing else than emancipation or manumission from righteousness, he seems to jest at the emptiness of the name. If anyone, then, chooses to make use of this term, without attaching any bad meaning to it, he shall not be troubled by me on that account; but as it cannot be retained without very great danger, I think the abolition of it would be of great advantage to the Church. I am unwilling to use it myself; and others if they will take my advice, will do well to abstain from it.

9. It may, perhaps, seem that I have greatly prejudiced my own view by confessing that all the ecclesiastical writers, with the exception of Augustine, have spoken so ambiguously or inconsistently on this subject that no certainty is attainable from their writings. Some will interpret this to mean that I wish to deprive them of their right of suffrage because they are opposed to me. Truly, however, I have had no other end in view than to consult, simply and in good faith, for the advantage of pious minds, which, if they trust to those writers for their opinion, will always fluctuate in uncertainty. At one time they teach that man having been deprived of the power of free will must flee to grace alone; at another, they equip or seem to equip him in armor of his own. It is not difficult, however, to show that notwithstanding of the ambiguous manner in which those writers express themselves, they hold human virtue in little or no account, and ascribe the whole merit of all that is good to the Holy Spirit. To make this more manifest, I may here quote some passages from them. What, then, is meant by Cyprian in the passage so often lauded by Augustine, "Let us glory in nothing, because nothing is ours," unless it be, that man being utterly destitute, considered in himself, should entirely depend on God? What is meant by Augustine and Eucherius, when they expound that Christ is the tree of life, and that whoso puts forth his hand to it shall live; that the choice of the will is the tree of the knowledge of good and evil, and that he who, forsaking the grace of God, tastes of it shall die? What is meant by Chrysostom, when he says, "That every man is not only naturally a sinner, but is wholly sin?" If there is nothing good in us; if man, from the crown of the head to the sole of the foot, is wholly sin; if it is not even lawful to try how far the power of the will extends—how can it be lawful to share the merit of a good work between God and man? I might quote many passages to the same effect from other writers; but lest

any caviler should say that I select those only which serve my purpose, and cunningly pass by those which are against me, I desist. This much, however, I dare affirm, that though they sometimes go too far in extolling free will, the main object which they had in view was to teach man entirely to renounce all self-confidence, and place his strength in God alone. I now proceed to a simple exposition of the truth in regard to the nature of man.

10. Here however, I must again repeat what I premised at the outset of this chapter, that he who is most deeply abased and alarmed, by the consciousness of his disgrace, nakedness, want, and misery, has made the greatest progress in the knowledge of himself. Man is in no danger of taking too much from himself, provided he learns that whatever he wants is to be recovered in God. But he cannot arrogate to himself one particle beyond his due without losing himself in vain confidence and, by transferring divine honor to himself, becoming guilty of the greatest impiety. And, assuredly, whenever our minds are seized with a longing to possess a somewhat of our own, which may reside in us rather than in God, we may rest assured that the thought is suggested by no other counselor than he who enticed our first parents to aspire to be like gods, knowing good and evil. It is sweet, indeed, to have so much virtue of our own as to be able to rest in ourselves; but let the many solemn passages by which our pride is sternly humbled, deter us from indulging this vain confidence: "Cursed be the man that trusteth in man, and maketh flesh his arm" (Jer. 17:5). "He delighteth not in the strength of the horse; he taketh not pleasure in the legs of a man. The Lord taketh pleasure in those that fear him, in those that hope in his mercy" (Ps. 147:10-11). "He giveth power to the faint; and to them that have no might he increaseth strength. Even the youths shall faint and be weary, and the young men shall utterly fall: But they that wait upon the Lord shall renew their strength" (Is. 40:29-31). The scope of all these passages is that we must not entertain any opinion whatever of our own strength,

if we would enjoy the favor of God, who "resisteth the proud, but giveth grace unto the humble" (James 4:6). Then let us call to mind such promises as these, "I will pour water upon him that is thirsty, and floods upon the dry ground" (Is. 44:3); "Ho, every one that thirsteth, come ye to the waters" (Is. 55:1). These passages declare, that none are admitted to enjoy the blessings of God save those who are pining under a sense of their own poverty. Nor ought such passages as the following to be omitted: "The sun shall no more be thy light by day; neither for brightness shall the moon give light unto thee: but the Lord shall be unto thee an everlasting light, and thy God thy glory" (Is. 60:19). The Lord certainly does not deprive his servants of the light of the sun or moon, but as he would alone appear glorious in them, he dissuades them from confidence even in those objects which they deem most excellent.

11. I have always been exceedingly delighted with the words of Chrysostom, "The foundation of our philosophy is humility;" and still more with those of Augustine, "As the orator, when asked, What is the first precept in eloquence? answered, Delivery: What is the second? Delivery: What the third? Delivery: so, if you ask me in regard to the precepts of the Christian Religion, I will answer, first, second, and third, Humility." By humility he means not when a man, with a consciousness of some virtue, refrains from pride, but when he truly feels that he has no refuge but in humility. This is clear from another passage, "Let no man," says he, "flatter himself: of himself he is a devil: his happiness he owes entirely to God. What have you of your own but sin? Take your sin which is your own; for righteousness is of God." Again, "Why presume so much on the capability of nature? It is wounded, maimed, vexed, lost. The thing wanted is genuine confession, not false defense." "When anyone knows that he is nothing in himself, and has no help from himself, the weapons within himself are broken, and the war is ended." All the weapons of impiety must be bruised, and broken, and burnt in the fire; you must remain unarmed,

having no help in yourself. The more infirm you are, the more the Lord will sustain you. So, in expounding the seventieth Psalm, he forbids us to remember our own righteousness, in order that we may recognize the righteousness of God, and shows that God bestows his grace upon us that we may know that we are nothing; that we stand only by the mercy of God, seeing that in ourselves eve are altogether wicked. Let us not contend with God for our right, as if anything attributed to him were lost to our salvation. As our insignificance is his exaltation, so the confession of our insignificance has its remedy provided in his mercy. I do not ask, however, that man should voluntarily yield without being convinced, or that, if he has any powers, he should shut his eyes to them, that he may thus be subdued to true humility; but that getting quit of the disease of self-love and ambition, φιλαυτια και φιλονεικια, under the blinding of which he thinks of himself more highly than he ought to think, he may see himself as he really is, by looking into the faithful mirror of Scripture.

12. I feel pleased with the well-known saying which has been borrowed from the writings of Augustine that man's natural gifts were corrupted by sin, and his supernatural gifts withdrawn; meaning by supernatural gifts the light of faith and righteousness, which would have been sufficient for the attainment of heavenly life and everlasting felicity. Man, when he withdrew his allegiance to God, was deprived of the spiritual gifts by which he had been raised to the hope of eternal salvation. Hence it follows, that he is now an exile from the kingdom of God, so that all things which pertain to the blessed life of the soul are extinguished in him until he recover them by the grace of regeneration. Among these are faith, love to God, charity towards our neighbor, the study of righteousness and holiness. All these, when restored to us by Christ, are to be regarded as adventitious and above nature. If so, we infer that they were previously abolished. On the other hand, soundness of mind and integrity of heart were, at the same time, withdrawn, and it is this which constitutes the corruption

of natural gifts. For although there is still some residue of intelligence and judgment as well as will, we cannot call a mind sound and entire which is both weak and immersed in darkness. As to the will, its depravity is but too well known. Therefore, since reason, by which man discerns between good and evil, and by which he understands and judges, is a natural gift, it could not be entirely destroyed; but being partly weakened and partly corrupted, a shapeless ruin is all that remains. In this sense it is said that "the light shineth in darkness, and the darkness comprehended it not" (John 1:5); these words clearly expressing both points—viz. that in the perverted and degenerate nature of man there are still some sparks which show that he is a rational animal, and differs from the brutes, inasmuch as he is endued with intelligence, and yet that this light is so smothered by clouds of darkness that it cannot shine forth to any good effect. In like manner, the will, because inseparable from the nature of man, did not perish, but was so enslaved by depraved lusts as to be incapable of one righteous desire. The definition now given is complete, but there are several points which require to be explained. Therefore, proceeding agreeably to that primary distinction (Book 1 c. 15 sec. 7 and 8) by which we divided the soul into intellect and will, we will now inquire into the power of the intellect.

To charge the intellect with perpetual blindness, so as to leave it no intelligence of any description whatever, is repugnant not only to the Word of God, but to common experience. We see that there has been implanted in the human mind a certain desire of investigating truth, to which it never would aspire unless some relish for truth antecedently existed. There is, therefore, now, in the human mind, discernment to this extent, that it is naturally influenced by the love of truth, the neglect of which in the lower animals is a proof of their gross and irrational nature. Still it is true that this love of truth fails before it reaches the goal, forthwith falling away into vanity. As the human mind is unable, from dullness, to pursue the right path of investigation, and, after various wanderings, stumbling every now and then like one groping in darkness, at length gets completely bewildered, so its whole procedure proves how unfit it is to search the truth and find it. Then it labors under another grievous defect, in that it frequently fails to discern what the knowledge is which it should study to acquire. Hence, under the influence of a vain curiosity, it torments itself with superfluous and useless discussions, either not adverting at all to the things necessary to be known, or casting only a cursory and contemptuous glance at them. At all events, it scarcely ever studies them in sober earnest. Profane writers are constantly complaining of this perverse procedure, and yet almost all of them are found pursuing it. Hence Solomon, throughout the Book of Ecclesiastes, after enumerating all the studies in which men think they attain the highest wisdom, pronounces them vain and frivolous.

13. Still, however, man's efforts are not always so utterly fruitless as not to lead to some result, especially when his attention is directed to inferior objects. Nay, even with regard to superior objects, though he is more careless in investigating them, he makes some little progress. Here, however, his ability is more limited, and he is never made more sensible of his weakness than when he attempts to soar above the sphere of the present life. It may therefore be proper, in order to make it more manifest how far our ability extends in regard to these two classes of objects, to draw a distinction between them. The distinction is that we have one kind of intelligence of earthly things, and another of heavenly things. By earthly things, I mean those which relate not to God and his kingdom, to true righteousness and future blessedness, but have some connection with the present life, and are in a manner confined within its boundaries. By heavenly things, I mean the pure knowledge of God, the method of true righteousness, and the mysteries of the heavenly kingdom. To the former belong matters of policy and economy, all mechanical arts and liberal studies. To the latter (as to which, see the eighteenth and following sections) belong

the knowledge of God and of his will, and the means of framing the life in accordance with them. As to the former, the view to be taken is this: since man is by nature a social animal, he is disposed from natural instinct to cherish and preserve society; and accordingly we see that the minds of all men have impressions of civil order and honesty. Hence it is that every individual understands how human societies must he regulated by laws, and also is able to comprehend the principles of those laws. Hence the universal agreement in regard to such subjects, both among nations and individuals, the seeds of them being implanted in the breasts of all without a teacher or lawgiver. The truth of this fact is not affected by the wars and dissensions which immediately arise, while some, such as thieves and robbers, would invert the rules of justice, loosen the bonds of law, and give free scope to their lust; and while others (a vice of most frequent occurrence) deem that to be unjust which is elsewhere regarded as just, and, on the contrary, hold that to be praiseworthy which is elsewhere forbidden. For such persons do not hate the laws from not knowing that they are good and sacred, but, inflamed with headlong passion, quarrel with what is clearly reasonable, and licentiously hate what their mind and understanding approve. Quarrels of this latter kind do not destroy the primary idea of justice. For while men dispute with each other as to particular enactments, their ideas of equity agree in substance. This, no doubt, proves the weakness of the human mind, which, even when it seems on the right path, halts and hesitates. Still, however, it is true that some principle of civil order is impressed on all. And this is ample proof that, in regard to the constitution of the present life, no man is devoid of the light of reason.

14. Next come manual and liberal arts, in learning which, as all have some degree of aptitude, the full force of human acuteness is displayed. But though all are not equally able to learn all the arts, we have sufficient evidence of a common capacity in the fact, that there is scarcely an individual who does not display intelligence in some particular art.

And this capacity extends not merely to the learning of the art, but to the devising of something new, or the improving of what had been previously learned. This led Plato to adopt the erroneous idea that such knowledge was nothing but recollection. So cogently does it oblige us to acknowledge that its principle is naturally implanted in the human mind. But while these proofs openly attest the fact of a universal reason and intelligence naturally implanted, this universality is of a kind which should lead every individual for himself to recognize it as a special gift of God. To this gratitude we have a sufficient call from the Creator himself, when, in the case of idiots, he shows what the endowments of the soul would be were it not pervaded with his light. Though natural to all, it is so in such a sense that it ought to be regarded as a gratuitous gift of his beneficence to each. Moreover, the invention, the methodical arrangement, and the more thorough and superior knowledge of the arts, being confined to a few individuals cannot be regarded as a solid proof of common shrewdness. Still, however, as they are bestowed indiscriminately on the good and the bad, they are justly classed among natural endowments.

15. Therefore, in reading profane authors, the admirable light of truth displayed in them should remind us, that the human mind, however much fallen and perverted from its original integrity, is still adorned and invested with admirable gifts from its Creator. If we reflect that the Spirit of God is the only fountain of truth, we will be careful, as we would avoid offering insult to him, not to reject or condemn truth wherever it appears. In despising the gifts, we insult the Giver. How, then, can we deny that truth must have beamed on those ancient lawgivers who arranged civil order and discipline with so much equity? Shall we say that the philosophers, in their exquisite researches and skillful description of nature, were blind? Shall we deny the possession of intellect to those who drew up rules for discourse, and taught us to speak in accordance with reason? Shall we say that those who, by the cultivation of the medical art, expended their industry in our behalf

were only raving? What shall we say of the mathematical sciences? Shall we deem them to be the dreams of madmen? Nay, we cannot read the writings of the ancients on these subjects without the highest admiration; an admiration which their excellence will not allow us to withhold. But shall we deem anything to be noble and praiseworthy, without tracing it to the hand of God? Far from us be such ingratitude; an ingratitude not chargeable even on heathen poets, who acknowledged that philosophy and laws, and all useful arts were the inventions of the gods. Therefore, since it is manifest that men whom the Scriptures term carnal, are so acute and clear-sighted in the investigation of inferior things, their example should teach us how many gifts the Lord has left in possession of human nature, notwithstanding of its having been despoiled of the true good.

16. Moreover, let us not forget that there are most excellent blessings which the Divine Spirit dispenses to whom he will for the common benefit of mankind. For if the skill and knowledge required for the construction of the Tabernacle behaved to be imparted to Bezaleel and Aholiab, by the Spirit of God (Exod. 31:2; 35:30), it is not strange that the knowledge of those things which are of the highest excellence in human life is said to be communicated to us by the Spirit. Nor is there any ground for asking what concourse the Spirit can have with the ungodly, who are altogether alienated from God? For what is said as to the Spirit dwelling in believers only is to be understood of the Spirit of holiness by which we are consecrated to God as temples. Notwithstanding of this, He fills, moves, and invigorates all things by the virtue of the Spirit, and that according to the peculiar nature which each class of beings has received by the Law of Creation. But if the Lord has been pleased to assist us by the work and ministry of the ungodly in physics, dialectics, mathematics, and other similar sciences, let us avail ourselves of it, lest, by neglecting the gifts of God spontaneously offered to us, we be justly punished for our sloth. Lest anyone, however, should imagine a man to be very

happy merely because, with reference to the elements of this world, he has been endued with great talents for the investigation of truth, we ought to add, that the whole power of intellect thus bestowed is, in the sight of God, fleeting and vain whenever it is not based on a solid foundation of truth. Augustine (supra, sec. 4 and 12), to whom, as we have observed, the Master of Sentences (lib. 2 Dist. 25), and the Schoolmen, are forced to subscribe, says most correctly that as the gratuitous gifts bestowed on man were withdrawn, so the natural gifts which remained were corrupted after the fall. Not that they can be polluted in themselves in so far as they proceed from God, but that they have ceased to be pure to polluted man, lest he should by their means obtain any praise.

17. The sum of the whole is this: from a general survey of the human race, it appears that one of the essential properties of our nature is reason, which distinguishes us from the lower animals, just as these by means of sense are distinguished from inanimate objects. For although some individuals are born without reason, that defect does not impair the general kindness of God, but rather serves to remind us that whatever we retain ought justly to be ascribed to the Divine indulgence. Had God not so spared us, our revolt would have carried along with it the entire destruction of nature. In that some excel in acuteness, and some in judgment, while others have greater readiness in learning some peculiar art, God, by this variety commends his favor toward us, lest any one should presume to arrogate to himself that which flows from His mere liberality. For whence is it that one is more excellent than another, but that in a common nature the grace of God is specially displayed in passing by many and thus proclaiming that it is under obligation to none. We may add that each individual is brought under particular influences according to his calling. Many examples of this occur in the Book of Judges, in which the Spirit of the Lord is said to have come upon those whom he called to govern his people (Judges 6:34). In short, in every distinguished act there is

a special inspiration. Thus it is said of Saul that "there went with him a band of men whose hearts the Lord had touched" (1 Sam. 10:26). And when his inauguration to the kingdom is foretold, Samuel thus addresses him, "The Spirit of the Lord will come upon thee, and thou shalt prophesy with them, and shalt be turned into another man" (1 Sam. 10:6). This extends to the whole course of government, as it is afterwards said of David, "The Spirit of the Lord came upon David from that day forward" (1 Sam. 16:13). The same thing is elsewhere said with reference to particular movements. Nay, even in Homer, men are said to excel in genius, not only according as Jupiter has distributed to each, but according as he leads them day by day, οιον επ ημαρ αγησι. And certainly experience shows when those who were most skillful and ingenious stand stupefied, that the minds of men are entirely under the control of God, who rules them every moment. Hence it is said, that "He poureth contempt upon princes, and causeth them to wander in the wilderness where there is no way" (Ps. 107:40). Still, in this diversity we can trace some remains of the divine image distinguishing the whole human race from other creatures.

18. We must now explain what the power of human reason is, in regard to the kingdom of God, and spiritual discernments which consists chiefly of three things—the knowledge of God, the knowledge of his paternal favor towards us, which constitutes our salvation, and the method of regulating of our conduct in accordance with the Divine Law. With regard to the former two, but more properly the second, men otherwise the most ingenious are blinder than moles. I deny not, indeed, that in the writings of philosophers we meet occasionally with shrewd and apposite remarks on the nature of God, though they invariably savor somewhat of giddy imagination. As observed above, the Lord has bestowed on them some slight perception of his Godhead that they might not plead ignorance as an excuse for their impiety, and has, at times, instigated them to deliver some truths, the confession of which should be their own condemnation. Still, though

seeing, they saw not. Their discernment was not such as to direct them to the truth, far less to enable them to attain it, but resembled that of the bewildered traveler, who sees the flash of lightning glance far and wide for a moment, and then vanish into the darkness of the night, before he can advance a single step. So far is such assistance from enabling him to find the right path. Besides, how many monstrous falsehoods intermingle with those minute particles of truth scattered up and down in their writings as if by chance. In short, not one of them even made the least approach to that assurance of the divine favor, without which the mind of man must ever remain a mere chaos of confusion. To the great truths, what God is in himself, and what he is in relation to us, human reason makes not the least approach. (See Book 3 c. 2 sec. 14, 15, 16).

19. But since we are intoxicated with a false opinion of our own discernment, and can scarcely be persuaded that in divine things it is altogether stupid and blind, I believe the best course will be to establish the fact, not by argument, but by Scripture. Most admirable to this effect is the passage which I lately quoted from John, when he says, "In him was life; and the life was the light of men. And the light shineth in darkness; and the darkness comprehended it not" (John 1:4-5). He intimates that the human soul is indeed irradiated with a beam of divine light, so that it is never left utterly devoid of some small flame, or rather spark, though not such as to enable it to comprehend God. And why so? Because its acuteness is, in reference to the knowledge of God, mere blindness. When the Spirit describes men under the term darkness, he declares them void of all power of spiritual intelligence. For this reason, it is said that believers, in embracing Christ, are "born, not of blood, nor of the will of the flesh, nor of the will of man, but of God" (John 1:13); in other words, that the flesh has no capacity for such sublime wisdom as to apprehend God, and the things of God, unless illumined by His Spirit. In like manner

our Savior, when he was acknowledged by Peter, declared that it was by special revelation from the Father (Matt. 16:17).

20. If we were persuaded of a truth which ought to be beyond dispute—viz. that human nature possesses none of the gifts which the elect receive from their heavenly Father through the Spirit of regeneration, there would be no room here for hesitation. For thus speaks the congregation of the faithful, by the mouth of the prophet: "With thee is the fountain of life: in thy light shall we see light" (Ps. 36:9). To the same effect is the testimony of the Apostle Paul, when he declares, that "no man can say that Jesus is the Lord, but by the Holy Ghost" (1 Cor. 12:3). And John the Baptist, on seeing the dullness of his disciples, exclaims, "A man can receive nothing, unless it be given him from heaven" (John 3:27). That the gift to which he here refers must be understood not of ordinary natural gifts, but of special illumination, appears from this—that he was complaining how little his disciples had profited by all that he had said to them in commendation of Christ. "I see," says he, "that my words are of no effect in imbuing the minds of men with divine things, unless the Lord enlighten their understandings by His Spirit." Nay, Moses also, while upbraiding the people for their forgetfulness, at the same time observes, that they could not become wise in the mysteries of God without his assistance. "Ye have seen all that the Lord did before your eyes in the land of Egypt, unto Pharaoh, and unto all his servants, and unto all his land; the great temptations which thine eyes have seen, the signs, and these great miracles: yet the Lord has not given you an heart to perceive, and eyes to see, and ears to hear, unto this, day" (Deut. 29:2-4). Would the expression have been stronger had he called us mere blocks in regard to the contemplation of divine things? Hence the Lord, by the mouth of the Prophet, promises to the Israelites as a singular favor, "I will give them an heart to know me" (Jer. 24:7); intimating that in spiritual things the human mind is wise only in so far as he enlightens it. This was also clearly confirmed

by our Savior when he said, "No man can come to me, except the Father which has sent me draw him" (John 6:44). Nay, is not he himself the living image of his Father, in which the full brightness of his glory is manifested to us? Therefore, how far our faculty of knowing God extends could not be better shown than when it is declared, that though his image is so plainly exhibited, we have not eyes to perceive it. What? Did not Christ descend into the world that he might make the will of his Father manifest to men, and did he not faithfully perform the office? True! He did; but nothing is accomplished by his preaching unless the inner teacher, the Spirit, open the way into our minds. Only those, therefore, come to him who have heard and learned of the Father. And in what is the method of this hearing and learning? It is when the Spirit, with a wondrous and special energy, forms the ear to hear and the mind to understand. Lest this should seem new, our Savior refers to the prophecy of Isaiah, which contains a promise of the renovation of the Church. "For a small moment have I forsaken thee; but with great mercies will I gather thee" (Is. 54:7). If the Lord here predicts some special blessing to his elect, it is plain that the teaching to which he refers is not that which is common to them with the ungodly and profane.

It thus appears that none can enter the kingdom of God save those whose minds have been renewed by the enlightening of the Holy Spirit. On this subject the clearest exposition is given by Paul, who, when expressly handling it, after condemning the whole wisdom of the world as foolishness and vanity, and thereby declaring man's utter destitution, thus concludes, "The natural man receiveth not the things of the Spirit of God: for they are foolishness unto him: neither can he know them, for they are spiritually discerned" (1 Cor. 2:14). Whom does he mean by the "natural man"? The man who trusts to the light of nature. Such a man has no understanding in the spiritual mysteries of God. Why so? Is it because through sloth he neglects them? Nay, though he exert himself, it is of no avail; they are "spiritually discerned." And what does this mean? That altogether hidden from human discernment, they are made known only by the revelation of the Spirit; so that they are accounted foolishness wherever the Spirit does not give light. The Apostle had previously declared, that "Eye has not seen, nor ear heard, neither have entered into the heart of man, the things which God has prepared for them that love him;" nay, that the wisdom of the world is a kind of veil by which the mind is prevented from beholding God (1 Cor. 2:9). What would we more? The Apostle declares that God has "made foolish the wisdom of this world" (1 Cor. 1:20); and shall we attribute to it an acuteness capable of penetrating to God, and the hidden mysteries of his kingdom? Far from us be such presumption!

21. What the Apostle here denies to man, he, in another place, ascribes to God alone, when he prays, "that the God of our Lord Jesus Christ, the Father of glory, may give unto you the spirit of wisdom and revelation" (Eph. 1:17). You now hear that all wisdom and revelation is the gift of God. What follows? "The eyes of your understanding being enlightened." Surely, if they require a new enlightening, they must in themselves be blind. The next words are, "that ye may know what is the hope of his calling" (Eph. 1:18). In other words, the minds of men have not capacity enough to know their calling. Let no prating Pelagian here allege that God obviates this rudeness or stupidity when, by the doctrine of his word, he directs us to a path which we could not have found without a guide. David had the law, comprehending in it all the wisdom that could be desired, and yet not contented with this, he prays, "Open thou mine eyes, that I may behold wondrous things out of thy law" (Ps. 119:18). By this expression, he certainly intimates, that it is like sunrise to the earth when the word of God shines forth; but that men do not derive much benefit from it until he himself, who is for this reason called the Father of lights (James 1:17), either gives eyes or opens them; because whatever is not illuminated by his Spirit is wholly darkness. The Apostles

had been duly and amply instructed by the best of teachers. Still, as they wanted the Spirit of truth to complete their education in the very doctrine which they had previously heard, they were ordered to wait for him (John 14:26). If we confess that what we ask of God is lacking to us, and He by the very thing promised intimates our want, no man can hesitate to acknowledge that he is able to understand the mysteries of God, only in so far as illuminated by his grace. He who ascribes to himself more understanding than this is the blinder for not acknowledging his blindness.

22. It remains to consider the third branch of the knowledge of spiritual things—viz. the method of properly regulating the conduct. This is correctly termed the knowledge of the works of righteousness, a branch in which the human mind seems to have somewhat more discernment than in the former two, since an Apostle declares, "When the Gentiles, which have not the law, do by nature the things contained in the law, these, having not the law, are a law unto themselves: which show the work of the law written in their hearts, their conscience also bearing witness, and their thoughts the meantime accusing or else excusing one another" (Rom. 2:14-15). If the Gentiles have the righteousness of the law naturally engraven on their minds, we certainly cannot say that they are altogether blind as to the rule of life. Nothing, indeed is more common, than for man to be sufficiently instructed in a right course of conduct by natural law, of which the Apostle here speaks. Let us consider, however, for what end this knowledge of the law was given to men. For from this it will forthwith appear how far it can conduct them in the way of reason and truth. This is even plain from the words of Paul, if we attend to their arrangement. He had said a little before, that those who had sinned in the law will be judged by the law; and those who have sinned without the law will perish without the law. As it might seem unaccountable that the Gentiles should perish without any previous judgment, he immediately subjoins that conscience served them instead of the law

and was therefore sufficient for their righteous condemnation. The end of the natural law, therefore, is to render man inexcusable, and may be not improperly defined—the judgment of conscience distinguishing sufficiently between just and unjust, and by convicting men on their own testimony depriving them of all pretext for ignorance. So indulgent is man towards himself that, while doing evil, he always endeavors as much as he can to suppress the idea of sin. It was this, apparently, which induced Plato (in his *Protagoras*) to suppose that sins were committed only through ignorance. There might be some ground for this, if hypocrisy were so successful in hiding vice as to keep the conscience clear in the sight of God. But since the sinner, when trying to evade the judgment of good and evil implanted in him, is ever and anon dragged forward, and not permitted to wink so effectually as not to be compelled at times, whether he will or not, to open his eyes, it is false to say that he sins only through ignorance.

23. Themistius is more accurate in teaching (Paraphr. in Lib. 3 *de Anima*, cap. 46) that the intellect is very seldom mistaken in the general definition or essence of the matter; but that deception begins as it advances farther, namely, when it descends to particulars. That homicide, putting the case in the abstract, is an evil, no man will deny; and yet one who is conspiring the death of his enemy deliberates on it as if the thing was good. The adulterer will condemn adultery in the abstract, and yet flatter himself while privately committing it. The ignorance lies here: that man, when he comes to the particular, forgets the rule which he had laid down in the general case. Augustine treats most admirably on this subject in his exposition of the first verse of the fifty-seventh Psalm. The doctrine of Themistius, however, does not always hold true: for the turpitude of the crime sometimes presses so on the conscience, that the sinner does not impose upon himself by a false semblance of good, but rushes into sin knowingly and willingly. Hence the expression—I see the better course, and approve it: I follow the worse (Medea of Ovid). For this reason, Aristotle seems

to me to have made a very shrewd distinction between incontinence and intemperance (*Ethic.* lib. 7 cap. 3) Where incontinence (ακρασια) reigns, he says, that through the passion (παθη) particular knowledge is suppressed: so that the individual sees not in his own misdeed the evil which he sees generally in similar cases; but when the passion is over, repentance immediately succeeds. Intemperance (ακολασια), again, is not extinguished or diminished by a sense of sin, but, on the contrary, persists in the evil choice which it has once made.

24. Moreover, when you hear of a universal judgment in man distinguishing between good and evil, you must not suppose that this judgment is, in every respect, sound and entire. For if the hearts of men are imbued with a sense of justice and injustice, in order that they may have no pretext to allege ignorance, it is by no means necessary for this purpose that they should discern the truth in particular cases. It is even more than sufficient if they understand so far as to be unable to practice evasion without being convicted by their own conscience, and beginning even now to tremble at the judgment-seat of God. Indeed, if we would test our reason by the Divine Law, which is a perfect standard of righteousness, we should find how blind it is in many respects. It certainly attains not to the principal heads in the First Table, such as, trust in God, the ascription to him of all praise in virtue and righteousness, the invocation of his name, and the true observance of his day of rest. Did ever any soul, under the guidance of natural sense, imagine that these and the like constitute the legitimate worship of God? When profane men would worship God, how often soever they may be drawn off from their vain trifling, they constantly relapse into it. They admit, indeed, that sacrifices are not pleasing to God, unless accompanied with sincerity of mind; and by this they testify that they have some conception of spiritual worship, though they immediately pervert it by false devices: for it is impossible to persuade them that every thing which the law enjoins on the subject is true. Shall I then extol the discernment of a mind which can neither acquire wisdom by itself, nor listen to

advice? As to the precepts of the Second Table, there is considerably more knowledge of them, inasmuch as they are more closely connected with the preservation of civil society. Even here, however, there is something defective. Every man of understanding deems it most absurd to submit to unjust and tyrannical domination, provided it can by any means be thrown off, and there is but one opinion among men, that it is the part of an abject and servile mind to bear it patiently, the part of an honorable and high-spirited mind to rise up against it. Indeed, the revenge of injuries is not regarded by philosophers as a vice. But the Lord condemning this too lofty spirit, prescribes to his people that patience which mankind deem infamous. In regard to the general observance of the law, concupiscence altogether escapes our animadversion. For the natural man cannot bear to recognize diseases in his lusts. The light of nature is stifled sooner than take the first step into this profound abyss. For, when philosophers class immoderate movements of the mind among vices, they mean those which break forth and manifest themselves in grosser forms. Depraved desires, in which the mind can quietly indulge, they regard as nothing (see infra, chap. 8 sect. 49).

25. As we have above animadverted on Plato's error in ascribing all sins to ignorance, so we must repudiate the opinion of those who hold that all sins proceed from preconceived gravity and malice. We know too well from experience how often we fall, even when our intention is good. Our reason is exposed to so many forms of delusion, is liable to so many errors, stumbles on so many obstacles, is entangled by so many snares, that it is ever wandering from the right direction. Of how little value it is in the sight of God, in regard to all the parts of life, Paul shows, when he says, that we are not "sufficient of ourselves to think any thing as of ourselves" (2 Cor. 3:5). He is not speaking of the will or affection; he denies us the power of thinking aright how any thing can be duly performed. Is it indeed true that all thought, intelligence, discernment, and industry, are so defective that in the sight of the Lord we cannot think or aim at any thing that is right?

To us, who can scarcely bear to part with acuteness of intellect (in our estimation a most precious endowment), it seems hard to admit this, whereas it is regarded as most just by the Holy Spirit, who "knoweth the thoughts of man, that they are vanity" (Ps. 94:11), and distinctly declares that "every imagination of the thoughts of his heart was only evil continually" (Gen. 6:5; 8:21). If everything which our mind conceives, meditates, plans, and resolves is always evil, how can it ever think of doing what is pleasing to God, to whom righteousness and holiness alone are acceptable? It is thus plain, that our mind, in what direction soever it turns, is miserably exposed to vanity. David was conscious of its weakness when he prayed, "Give me understanding, and I shall keep thy law" (Ps. 119:34). By desiring to obtain a new understanding, he intimates that his own was by no means sufficient. This he does not once only, but in one psalm repeats the same prayer almost ten times, the repetition intimating how strong the necessity which urged him to pray. What he thus asked for himself alone, Paul prays for the churches in general. "For this cause," says he, "we also, since the day we heard it, do not cease to pray for you, and to desire that ye might be filled with the knowledge of his will, in all wisdom and spiritual understanding; that you might walk worthy of the Lord," &c. (Col. 1:9-10). Whenever he represents this as a blessing from God, we should remember that he at the same time testifies that it is not in the power of man. Accordingly, Augustine, in speaking of this inability of human reason to understand the things of God, says, that he deems the grace of illumination not less necessary to the mind than the light of the sun to the eye (August. *de Peccat. Merit. et Remiss.* lib. 2 cap. 5). And, not content with this, he modifies his expression, adding that we open our eyes to behold the light, whereas the mental eye remains shut, until it is opened by the Lord. Nor does Scripture say that our minds are illuminated in a single day, so as afterwards to see of themselves. The passage, which I lately quoted from the Apostle Paul, refers to continual progress and increase. David, too, expresses this distinctly in these words: "With my whole heart have I sought thee: O let me not wander from thy commandments" (Ps. 119:10). Though he had been regenerated, and so had made no ordinary progress in true piety, he confesses that he stood in need of direction every moment, in order that he might not decline from the knowledge with which he had been endued. Hence, he elsewhere prays for a renewal of a right spirit, which he had lost by his sin, (Ps. 51:12). For that which God gave at first, while temporarily withdrawn, it is equally his province to restore.

26. We must now examine the will, on which the question of freedom principally turns, the power of choice belonging to it rather than the intellect, as we have already seen (supra, sect. 4). And at the outset, to guard against its being thought that the doctrine taught by philosophers, and generally received—viz. that all things by natural instinct have a desire of good, is any proof of the rectitude of the human will—let us observe that the power of free will is not to be considered in any of those desires which proceed more from instinct than mental deliberation. Even the schoolmen admit (Thomas, Part 1, Quaest. 83, art. 3) that there is no act of free will, unless when reason looks at opposites. By this they mean that the things desired must be such as may be made the object of choice, and that to pave the way for choice, deliberation must precede. And, undoubtedly, if you attend to what this natural desire of good in man is, you will find that it is common to him with the brutes. They, too, desire what is good; and when any semblance of good capable of moving the sense appears, they follow after it. Here, however, man does not, in accordance with the excellence of his immortal nature, rationally choose, and studiously pursue, what is truly for his good. He does not admit reason to his counsel, nor exert his intellect; but without reason, without counsel, follows the bent of his nature like the lower animals. The question of freedom, therefore, has nothing to do with the fact of man's being led by natural instinct to desire good. The question is, does man,

after determining by right reason what is good, choose what he thus knows, and pursue what he thus chooses? Lest any doubt should be entertained as to this, we must attend to the double misnomer. For this appetite is not properly a movement of the will, but natural inclination; and this good is not one of virtue or righteousness, but of condition—viz. that the individual may feel comfortable. In fine, how much soever man may desire to obtain what is good, he does not follow it. There is no man who would not be pleased with eternal blessedness; and yet, without the impulse of the Spirit, no man aspires to it. Since, then, the natural desire of happiness in man no more proves the freedom of the will, than the tendency in metals and stones to attain the perfection of their nature, let us consider, in other respects, whether the will is so utterly vitiated and corrupted in every part as to produce nothing but evil, or whether it retains some portion uninjured, and productive of good desires.

27. Those who ascribe our willing effectually to the primary grace of God (supra, sect. 6), seem conversely to insinuate that the soul has in itself a power of aspiring to good, though a power too feeble to rise to solid affection or active endeavor. There is no doubt that this opinion, adopted from Origin and certain of the ancient Fathers, has been generally embraced by the schoolmen, who are wont to apply to man in his natural state (*in puris naturalibus*, as they express it) the following description of the apostle: "For that which I do I allow not: for what I would, that do I not; but what I hate, that do I." "To will is present with me; but how to perform that which is good I find not" (Rom. 7:15, 18). But, in this way, the whole scope of Paul's discourse is inverted. He is speaking of the Christian struggle (touched on more briefly in the Epistle to the Galatians), which believers constantly experience from the conflict between the flesh and the Spirit. But the Spirit is not from nature, but from regeneration. That the apostle is speaking of the regenerate is apparent from this, that after saying, "in me dwells no good thing," he immediately adds

the explanation, "in my flesh." Accordingly, he declares, "It is no more I that do it, but sin that dwelleth in me." What is the meaning of the correction, "in me (that is, in my flesh?)" It is just as if he had spoken in this way: No good thing dwells in me, of myself, for in my flesh nothing good can be found. Hence follows the species of excuse: It is not I myself that do evil, but sin that dwelleth in me. This applies to none but the regenerate, who, with the leading powers of the soul, tend towards what is good. The whole is made plain by the conclusion, "I delight in the law of God after the inward man: but I see another law in my members, warring against the law of my mind" (Rom. 7:22-23). Who has this struggle in himself, save those who, regenerated by the Spirit of God, bear about with them the remains of the flesh? Accordingly, Augustine, who had at one time thought that the discourse related to the natural man (August. *ad Bonifac.* lib. 1 c. 10), afterwards retracted his exposition as unsound and inconsistent. And, indeed if we admit that men, without grace, have any motions to good, however feeble, what answer shall we give to the apostles who declares that "we are incapable of thinking a good thought?" (2 Cor. 3:6). What answer shall we give to the Lord, who declares by Moses that "every imagination of man's heart is only evil continually?" (Gen. 8:21). Since the blunder has thus arisen from an erroneous view of a single passage, it seems unnecessary to dwell upon it. Let us rather give due weight to our Savior's words, "Whosoever committeth sin is the servant of sin" (John 8:34). We are all sinners by nature, therefore we are held under the yoke of sin. But if the whole man is subject to the dominion of sin, surely the will, which is its principal seat, must be bound with the closest chains. And, indeed, if divine grace were preceded by any will of ours, Paul could not have said that "it is God which worketh in us both to will and to do" (Phil. 2:13). Away, then, with all the absurd trifling which many have indulged in with regard to preparation. Although believers sometimes ask to have their heart trained to the obedience of the divine law, as David does in several passages (Ps. 51:12), it is to be observed that even this longing in prayer is from God. This is apparent from the language used. When he prays, "Create in me a clean heart," he certainly does not attribute the beginning of the creation to himself. Let us therefore rather adopt the sentiment of Augustine, "God will prevent you in all things, but do you sometimes prevent his anger. How? Confess that you have all these things from God, that all the good you have is from him, all the evil from yourself" (August. *De Verbis Apost.* Serm. 10). Shortly after he says "Of our own we have nothing but sin."

Study Guide Questions

Section 1

1. What are the twin perils that threaten man, given his bondage to sin?
2. What does Augustine say that the defenders of free will do?

Section 2

1. What do the philosophers believe about reason?
2. Where do they believe our corruptions reside?
3. Where do they locate the will?

Section 3

1. Do the philosophers believe that things can go wrong?
2. At the same time, do they believe that virtue is a real possibility?
3. According to Cicero, should we thank the gods for our own virtue?

Section 4

1. Does Calvin believe that the church fathers handled the idea of free will scripturally?
2. What was the reason for this?
3. What two things were they concerned to avoid?
4. Which of the fathers was an exception to this?

Section 5

1. What were the three kinds of freedom that were distinguished in the schools?
2. Does Calvin accept this distinction?

Section 6

1. What is necessary before men can do good works truly?
2. What ambiguity does Calvin object to in the teaching of Lombard?

Section 7

1. What does Calvin think about "mere verbal disputes"?
2. So why then does he reject the words "free will" so strongly?

Section 8

1. What does Augustine teach about the will?
2. Does Augustine use the phrase "free will"?
3. What is Calvin's approach to the phrase?

Section 9

1. What is the problem with the other fathers?
2. What does Calvin say in their favor?

Section 10

1. When a man is utterly cast down in himself, what has he gained?
2. What is the problem with a man retaining to himself some of the honor found in "free will"?
3. Who may receive God's blessings?

Section 11

1. What did Augustine say were the three chief rules for eloquence?
2. In a similar vein, what does Calvin say are the three chief precepts of the Christian religion?

3. Instead of relying on human nature, which is "bruised, and broken, and burnt" and "having no help," what do we need?

4. In order for our war with God to be over, what must happen?

Section 12

1. In the Fall, what happened to our supernatural gifts like faith and righteousness?

2. What happened to our natural gifts, like soundness of mind and uprightness of heart?

3. Have we fallen to the level of the brute beasts?

Section 13

1. What are the two kinds of understanding according to Calvin?

2. What is included in the former?

3. The latter?

Section 14

1. What does virtually every human being possess?

2. What do we learn from imbeciles?

3. What is a natural gift?

Section 15

1. If we regard the Spirit of God as the sole fountain of truth, what follows?

2. What should our response be to the great accomplishments of unbelievers?

Section 16

1. What do we learn from Bezalel and Oholiab?

2. Is the Spirit's work limited to believers?

Section 17

1. What is proper to our nature?

2. What must we avoid claiming as our own?

Section 18
1. What are the three characteristics of spiritual insight?
2. What illustration does Calvin use to describe unbelievers when they have a true insight concerning God?

Section 19
1. Do unbelievers have some illumination concerning God?
2. How do we know men do not have spiritual understanding?

Section 20
1. How do men regain what nature lacks?
2. How far may a man become spiritually wise?

Section 21
1. Where the Spirit of God does not shine, what do we have?
2. What is the worst form of blindness?

Section 22
1. Does Calvin take the Gentiles in Romans 2:14–15 to be Christians or not?
2. Does Calvin believe in natural law?
3. How does he define it?
4. What is natural law for?

Section 23
1. Can unregenerate men affirm the right ethical choice generally?
2. Where then do they fail, according to Calvin?

Section 24
1. Where does human ethical knowledge fail utterly?

2. Where does it fail in a critical sense?

3. What do the philosophers recognize and what do they ignore?

Section 25

1. Does Calvin hold that men are evil in every respect?

2. But what is absolutely necessary in order for us to understand spiritual things?

Section 26

1. Choice belongs to what sphere in our makeup?

2. What is necessary before we can say that a true moral choice has been made?

Section 27

1. Does Calvin believe that the description in Romans 7 is of a Christian or not?

2. What does he make of the excuse "It is no more I that do it, but sin that dwelleth in me"?

CHAPTER 3

Everything proceeding from the corrupt nature of man damnable.

The principal matters in this chapter are—

I. A recapitulation of the former chapter, proving, from passages of Scriptures that the intellect and will of man are so corrupted, that no integrity, no knowledge or fear of God, can now be found in him, sect. 1 and 2.

II. Objections to this doctrine, from the virtues which shone in some of the heathen, refuted, sect. 3 and 4.

III. What kind of will remains in man, the slave of sin, sect. 5. The remedy and cure, sect. 6.

IV. The opinion of Neo-Pelagian sophists concerning the preparation and efficacy of the will, and also concerning perseverance and co-operating grace, refuted, both by reason and Scripture, sect. 7-12.

V. Some passages from Augustine confirming the truth of this doctrine, sect. 13 and 14. Sections.

Outline:

1. The intellect and will of the whole man corrupt. The term flesh applies not only to the sensual, but also to the higher part of the soul. This demonstrated from Scripture.

2. The heart also involved in corruption, and hence in no part of man can integrity, or knowledge or the fear of God, be found.

3. Objection, that some of the heathen were possessed of admirable endowments, and, therefore, that the nature of man is not entirely corrupt. Answer: corruption is not entirely removed, but only inwardly restrained. Explanation of this answer.

4. Objection still urged, that the virtuous and vicious among the heathen must be put upon the same level, or the virtuous prove that human nature, properly cultivated, is not devoid of virtue. Answer: that these are not ordinary properties of human nature, but special gifts of God. These gifts defiled by ambition, and hence the actions proceeding from them, however esteemed by man, have no merit with God.

5. Though man has still the faculty of willing there is no soundness in it. He falls under the bondage of sin necessarily, and yet voluntarily. Necessity must be distinguished from compulsion. The ancient Theologians acquainted with this necessity. Some passages condemning the vacillation of Lombard.

6. Conversion to God constitutes the remedy or soundness of the human will. This not only begun, but continued and completed; the beginning, continuance, and completion, being ascribed entirely to God. This proved by Ezekiel's description of the stony heart, and from other passages of Scripture.

7. Various Objections.—1. The will is converted by God, but, when once prepared, does its part in the work of conversion. Answer from Augustine. 2. Grace can do nothing without will, nor the will without grace. Answer. Grace itself produces will. God prevents the unwilling, making him willing, and follows up this preventing grace

that he may not will in vain. Another answer gathered from various passages of Augustine.

8. Answer to the second objection continued. No will inclining to good except in the elect. The cause of election out of man. Hence right will, as well as election, are from the good pleasure of God. The beginning of willing and doing well is of faith; faith again is the gift of God; and hence mere grace is the cause of our beginning to will well. This proved by Scripture.

9. Answer to second objection continued. That good will is merely of grace proved by the prayers of saints. Three axioms 1. God does not prepare man's heart, so that he can afterwards do some good of himself, but every desire of rectitude, every inclination to study, and every effort to pursue it, is from Him. 2. This desire, study, and effort, do not stop short, but continue to effect. 3. This progress is constant. The believer perseveres to the end. A third objection, and three answers to it.

10. A fourth objection. Answer. Fifth objection. Answer. Answer confirmed by many passages of Scripture, and supported by a passage from Augustine.

11. Perseverance not of ourselves, but of God. Objection. Two errors in the objection. Refutation of both.

12. An objection founded on the distinction of co-operating grace. Answer. Answer confirmed by the testimony of Augustine and Bernard.

13. Last part of the chapter, in which it is proved by many passages of Augustine, that he held the doctrine here taught.

14. An objection, representing Augustine at variance with himself and other theologians, removed. A summary of Augustine's doctrine on free will.

The nature of man, in both parts of his soul—viz. intellect and will—cannot be better ascertained than by attending to the epithets applied to him in Scripture. If he is fully depicted (and it may easily be proved that he is) by the words of our Savior, "that which

is born of the flesh is flesh" (John 3:6), he must be a very miserable
creature. For, as an apostle declares, "to be carnally minded is death"
(Rom. 8:8), "It is enmity against God, and is not subject to the law
of God, neither indeed can be." Is it true that the flesh is so perverse,
that it is perpetually striving with all its might against God? that it
cannot accord with the righteousness of the divine law? that, in short,
it can beget nothing but the materials of death? Grant that there is
nothing in human nature but flesh, and then extract something good
out of it if you can. But it will be said that the word flesh applies only
to the sensual, and not to the higher part of the soul. This, however,
is completely refuted by the words both of Christ and his apostle.
The statement of our Lord is that a man must be born again, because
he is flesh. He requires not to be born again with reference to the
body. But a mind is not born again merely by having some portion
of it reformed. It must be totally renewed. This is confirmed by the
antithesis used in both passages. In the contrast between the Spirit
and the flesh, there is nothing left of an intermediate nature. In this
way, everything in man which is not spiritual, falls under the denom-
ination of carnal. But we have nothing of the Spirit except through
regeneration. Everything, therefore, which we have from nature is
flesh. Any possible doubt which might exist on the subject is removed
by the words of Paul (Eph. 4:23), where, after a description of the
old man who, he says, "is corrupt according to the deceitful lusts," he
bids us "be renewed in the spirit" of our mind. You see that he places
unlawful and depraved desires not in the sensual part merely, but in
the mind itself, and therefore requires that it should be renewed. Indeed, he had a little before drawn a picture of human nature, which
shows that there is no part in which it is not perverted and corrupted.
For when he says that the "Gentiles walk in the vanity of their mind,
having the understanding darkened being alienated from the life of
God through the ignorance that is in them, because of the blindness
of their heart" (Eph. 4:17-18), there can be no doubt that his words

apply to all whom the Lord has not yet formed anew both to wisdom and righteousness. This is rendered more clear by the comparison which immediately follows, and by which he reminds believers that they "have not so learned Christ" these words implying that the grace of Christ is the only remedy for that blindness and its evil consequences. Thus, too, had Isaiah prophesied of the kingdom of Christ, when the Lord promised to the Church, that though darkness should "cover the earth, and gross darkness the people," yet that he should "arise" upon it, and "his glory" should be seen upon it (Isaiah 40:2). When it is thus declared that divine light is to arise on the Church alone, all without the Church is left in blindness and darkness. I will not enumerate all that occurs throughout Scripture, and particularly in the Psalms and Prophetical writings, as to the vanity of man. There is much in what David says, "Surely men of low degree are vanity, and men of high degree are a lie: to be laid in the balance, they are altogether lighter than vanity" (Ps. 62:10). The human mind receives a humbling blow when all the thoughts which proceed from it are derided as foolish, frivolous, perverse, and insane.

2. In no degree more lenient is the condemnation of the heart, when it is described as "deceitful above all things, and desperately wicked" (Jer. 17:9). But as I study brevity, I will be satisfied with a single passage: one, however, in which as in a bright mirror, we may behold a complete image of our nature. The Apostle, when he would humble man's pride, uses these words: "There is none righteous no, not one: there is none that understandeth, there is none that seeketh after God. They are all gone out of the way, they are together become unprofitable; there is none that does good, no, not one. Their throat is an open sepulcher; with their tongues they have used deceit; the poison of asps is under their lips; whose mouth is full of cursing and bitterness; their feet are swift to shed blood; destruction and misery are in their ways; and the way of peace have they not known; there is no fear of God before their eyes" (Rom. 3:10-18). Thus he thunders

not against certain individuals, but against the whole posterity of Adam—not against the depraved manners of any single age, but the perpetual corruption of nature. His object in the passage is not merely to upbraid men in order that they may repent, but to teach that all are overwhelmed with inevitable calamity, and can be delivered from it only by the mercy of God. As this could not be proved without previously proving the overthrow and destruction of nature, he produced those passages to show that its ruin is complete.

Let it be a fixed point, then, that men are such as is here described, not by vicious custom, but by depravity of nature. The reasoning of the Apostle, that there is no salvation for man, save in the mercy of God, because in himself he is desperate and undone, could not otherwise stand. I will not here labor to prove that the passages apply, with the view of removing the doubts of any who might think them quoted out of place. I will take them as if they had been used by Paul for the first time, and not taken from the Prophets. First, then, he strips man of righteousness, that is, integrity and purity; and, secondly, he strips him of sound intelligence. He argues that defect of intelligence is proved by apostasy from God. To seek Him is the beginning of wisdom, and, therefore, such defect must exist in all who have revolted from Him. He subjoins that all have gone astray, and become as it were mere corruption; that there is none that does good. He then enumerates the crimes by which those who have once given loose to their wickedness pollute every member of their bodies. Lastly, he declares that they have no fear of God, according to whose rule all our steps should be directed. If these are the hereditary properties of the human race, it is vain to look for anything good in our nature. I confess indeed that all these iniquities do not break out in every individual. Still it cannot be denied that the hydra lurks in every breast. For as a body, while it contains and fosters the cause and matter of disease, cannot be called healthy, although pain is not actually felt; so a soul, while teeming with such seeds of vice, cannot be called sound. This similitude, however, does not apply throughout. In a body however morbid the functions of life are performed; but the soul, when plunged into that deadly abyss, not only labors under vice, but is altogether devoid of good.

3. Here again we are met with a question very much the same as that which was previously solved. In every age there have been some who, under the guidance of nature, were all their lives devoted to virtue. It is of no consequence that many blots may be detected in their conduct; by the mere study of virtue, they evinced that there was somewhat of purity in their nature. The value which virtues of this kind have in the sight of God will be considered more fully when we treat of the merit of works. Meanwhile however, it will be proper to consider it in this place also, in so far as necessary for the exposition of the subject in hand. Such examples, then, seem to warn us against supposing that the nature of man is utterly vicious, since, under its guidance, some have not only excelled in illustrious deeds, but conducted themselves most honorably through the whole course of their lives. But we ought to consider that, notwithstanding of the corruption of our nature, there is some room for divine grace, such grace as, without purifying it, may lay it under internal restraint. For, did the Lord let every mind loose to wanton in its lusts, doubtless there is not a man who would not show that his nature is capable of all the crimes with which Paul charges it (Rom. 3 compared with Ps. 14:3ff). What? Can you exempt yourself from the number of those whose feet are swift to shed blood; whose hands are foul with rapine and murder; whose throats are like open sepulchers; whose tongues are deceitful; whose lips are venomous; whose actions are useless, unjust, rotten, deadly; whose soul is without God; whose inward parts are full of wickedness; whose eyes are on the watch for deception; whose minds are prepared for insult; whose every part, in short, is framed for endless deeds of wickedness? If every soul is capable of such abominations (and the Apostle declares this boldly), it is surely

easy to see what the result would be if the Lord were to permit human passion to follow its bent. No ravenous beast would rush so furiously; no stream, however rapid and violent, so impetuously burst its banks. In the elect, God cures these diseases in the mode which will shortly be explained; in others, he only lays them under such restraint as may prevent them from breaking forth to a degree incompatible with the preservation of the established order of things. Hence, how much soever men may disguise their impurity, some are restrained only by shame, others by a fear of the laws, from breaking out into many kinds of wickedness. Some aspire to an honest life, as deeming it most conducive to their interest, while others are raised above the vulgar lot that, by the dignity of their station, they may keep inferiors to their duty. Thus God, by his providence, curbs the perverseness of nature, preventing it from breaking forth into action, yet without rendering it inwardly pure.

4. The objection, however, is not yet solved. For we must either put Catiline on the same footing with Camillus, or hold Camillus to be an example that nature, when carefully cultivated, is not wholly void of goodness. I admit that the specious qualities which Camillus possessed were divine gifts, and appear entitled to commendation when viewed in themselves. But in what way will they be proofs of a virtuous nature? Must we not go back to the mind, and from it begin to reason thus? If a natural man possesses such integrity of manners, nature is not without the faculty of studying virtue. But what if his mind was depraved and perverted, and followed anything rather than rectitude? Such it undoubtedly was, if you grant that he was only a natural man. How then will you laud the power of human nature for good, if, even where there is the highest semblance of integrity, a corrupt bias is always detected? Therefore, as you would not commend a man for virtue whose vices impose upon you by a show of virtue, so you will not attribute a power of choosing rectitude to the human will while rooted in depravity (see August. lib. 4, *Cont. Julian*). Still, the

surest and easiest answer to the objection is that those are not common endowments of nature, but special gifts of God, which he distributes in divers forms, and, in a definite measure, to men otherwise profane. For which reason, we hesitate not, in common language, to say that one is of a good, another of a vicious nature; though we cease not to hold that both are placed under the universal condition of human depravity. All we mean is that God has conferred on the one a special grace which he has not seen it meet to confer on the other. When he was pleased to set Saul over the kingdom, he made him as it were a new man. This is the thing meant by Plato when, alluding to a passage in the Iliad, he says that the children of kings are distinguished at their birth by some special qualities—God, in kindness to the human race, often giving a spirit of heroism to those whom he destines for empire. In this way, the great leaders celebrated in history were formed. The same judgment must be given in the case of private individuals. But as those endued with the greatest talents were always impelled by the greatest ambitions (a stain which defiles all virtues and makes them lose all favor in the sight of God), so we cannot set any value on anything that seems praiseworthy in ungodly men. We may add, that the principal part of rectitude is wanting, when there is no zeal for the glory of God, and there is no such zeal in those whom he has not regenerated by his Spirit. Nor is it without good cause said in Isaiah that on Christ should rest "the spirit of knowledge, and of the fear of the Lord" (Isa. 11:2); for by this we are taught that all who are strangers to Christ are destitute of that fear of God which is the beginning of wisdom (Ps. 111:10). The virtues which deceive us by an empty show may have their praise in civil society and the common intercourse of life, but before the judgment-seat of God they will be of no value to establish a claim of righteousness.

5. When the will is enchained as the slave of sin, it cannot make a movement towards goodness, far less steadily pursue it. Every such movement is the first step in that conversion to God, which in

Scripture is entirely ascribed to divine grace. Thus Jeremiah prays, "Turn thou me, and I shall be turned" (Jer. 31:18). Hence, too, in the same chapter, describing the spiritual redemption of believers, the Prophet says, "The Lord has redeemed Jacob, and ransomed him from the hand of him that was stronger than he" (Jer. 31:11); intimating how close the fetters are with which the sinner is bound, so long as he is abandoned by the Lord, and acts under the yoke of the devil. Nevertheless, there remains a will which both inclines and hastens on with the strongest affection towards sin; man, when placed under this bondage, being deprived not of will, but of soundness of will. Bernard says not improperly that all of us have a will; but to will well is proficiency, to will ill is defect. Thus simply to will is the part of man, to will ill the part of corrupt nature, to will well the part of grace. Moreover, when I say that the will, deprived of liberty, is led or dragged by necessity to evil, it is strange that any should deem the expression harsh, seeing there is no absurdity in it, and it is not at variance with pious use. It does, however, offend those who know not how to distinguish between necessity and compulsion. Were any one to ask them, Is not God necessarily good, is not the devil necessarily wicked, what answer would they give? The goodness of God is so connected with his Godhead, that it is not more necessary to be God than to be good; whereas the devil, by his fall, was so estranged from goodness, that he can do nothing but evil. Should any one give utterance to the profane jeer (see Calvin *Adv. Pighium*) that little praise is due to God for a goodness to which he is forced, is it not obvious to every man to reply it is owing not to violent impulse, but to his boundless goodness, that he cannot do evil? Therefore, if the free will of God in doing good is not impeded, because he necessarily must do good; if the devil, who can do nothing but evil, nevertheless sins voluntarily; can it be said that man sins less voluntarily because he is under a necessity of sinning? This necessity is uniformly proclaimed by Augustine, who even when pressed by the invidious cavil of Celestius hesitated not to assert it in the following terms: "Man through liberty became a sinner, but corruption, ensuing as the penalty, has converted liberty into necessity" (August. *lib. de Perf. Justin*). Whenever mention is made of the subject, he hesitates not to speak in this way of the necessary bondage of sin (August. *de Nature et Gratia*, et alibi). Let this, then, be regarded as the sum of the distinction. Man, since he was corrupted by the fall, sins not forced or unwilling, but voluntarily, by a most forward bias of the mind; not by violent compulsion, or external force, but by the movement of his own passion; and yet such is the depravity of his nature, that he cannot move and act except in the direction of evil. If this is true, the thing not obscurely expressed is that he is under a necessity of sinning. Bernard, assenting to Augustine, thus writes: "Among animals, man alone is free, and yet sin intervening, he suffers a kind of violence, but a violence proceeding from his will, not from nature, so that it does not even deprive him of innate liberty" (Bernard, *Sermo. super Cantica*, 81). For that which is voluntary is also free. A little after he adds, "Thus, by some means strange and wicked, the will itself, being deteriorated by sin, makes a necessity; but so that the necessity, in as much as it is voluntary, cannot excuse the will, and the will, in as much as it is enticed, cannot exclude the necessity." For this necessity is in a manner voluntary. He afterwards says that "we are under a yoke, but no other yoke than that of voluntary servitude; therefore, in respect of servitude, we are miserable, and in respect of will, inexcusable; because the will, when it was free, made itself the slave of sin." At length he concludes, "Thus the soul, in some strange and evil way, is held under this kind of voluntary, yet sadly free necessity, both bond and free; bond in respect of necessity, free in respect of will: and what is still more strange, and still more miserable, it is guilty because free, and enslaved because guilty, and therefore enslaved because free." My readers hence perceive that the doctrine which I deliver is not new, but the doctrine which of old Augustine delivered with the consent of all the godly, and which was afterwards shut up in the cloisters of monks for almost a thousand years. Lombard, by not knowing how to distinguish between necessity and compulsion, gave occasion to a pernicious error.

6. On the other hand, it may be proper to consider what the remedy is which divine grace provides for the correction and cure of natural corruption. Since the Lord, in bringing assistance, supplies us with what is lacking, the nature of that assistance will immediately make manifest its converse—viz. our penury. When the Apostle says to the Philippians, "Being confident of this very thing, that he which has begun a good work in you, will perform it until the day of Jesus Christ" (Phil. 1:6), there cannot be a doubt that by the good work thus begun, he means the very commencement of conversion in the will. God, therefore, begins the good work in us by exciting in our hearts a desire, a love, and a study of righteousness, or (to speak more correctly) by turning, training, and guiding our hearts unto righteousness; and he completes this good work by confirming us unto perseverance. But lest any one should cavil that the good work thus begun by the Lord consists in aiding the will, which is in itself weak, the Spirit elsewhere declares what the will, when left to itself, is able to do. His words are, "A new heart also will I give you, and a new spirit will I put within you: and I will take away the stony heart out of your flesh, and I will give you an heart of flesh. And I will put my Spirit within you, and cause you to walk in my statutes, and ye shall keep my judgments, and do them" (Ezek. 36:26-27). How can it be said that the weakness of the human will is aided so as to enable it to aspire effectually to the choice of good, when the fact is, that it must be wholly transformed and renovated? If there is any softness in a stone; if you can make it tender, and flexible into any shape, then it may be said, that the human heart may be shaped for rectitude, provided that which is imperfect in it is supplemented by divine grace. But if the Spirit, by the above similitude, meant to show that no good can ever be extracted from our heart until it is made altogether new, let us not attempt to

share with Him what He claims for himself alone. If it is like turning a stone into flesh when God turns us to the study of rectitude, everything proper to our own will is abolished, and that which succeeds in its place is wholly of God. I say the will is abolished, but not in so far as it is will, for in conversion everything essential to our original nature remains; I also say that it is created anew, not because the will then begins to exist, but because it is turned from evil to good. This I maintain is wholly the work of God, because, as the Apostle testifies, we are not "sufficient of ourselves to think any thing as of ourselves" (2 Cor. 3:5). Accordingly, he elsewhere says, not merely that God assists the weak or corrects the depraved will, but that he worketh in us to will (Phil. 2:13). From this it is easily inferred, as I have said, that everything good in the will is entirely the result of grace. In the same sense, the Apostle elsewhere says, "It is the same God which worketh all in all" (1 Cor. 12:6). For he is not there treating of universal government, but declaring that all the good qualities which believers possess are due to God. In using the term "all," he certainly makes God the author of spiritual life from its beginning to its end. This he had previously taught in different terms, when he said that there is "one Lord Jesus Christ, by whom are all things, and we by him" (1 Cor. 8:6); thus plainly extolling the new creation, by which everything of our common nature is destroyed. There is here a tacit antithesis between Adam and Christ, which he elsewhere explains more clearly when he says, "We are his workmanship, created in Christ Jesus unto good works, which God has before ordained that we should walk in them" (Eph. 2:10). His meaning is to show in this way that our salvation is gratuitous because the beginning of goodness is from the second creation which is obtained in Christ. If any, even the minutest, ability were in ourselves, there would also be some merit. But to show our utter destitution, he argues that we merit nothing, because we are created in Christ Jesus unto good works, which God has prepared; again intimating by these words that all the fruits of good works are originally and immediately from God. Hence the Psalmist, after saying that the Lord "has made us," to deprive us of all share in the work, immediately adds, "not we ourselves." That he is speaking of regeneration, which is the commencement of the spiritual life, is obvious from the context, in which the next words are, "we are his people, and the sheep of his pasture" (Psalm 100:3). Not contented with simply giving God the praise of our salvation, he distinctly excludes us from all share in it, just as if he had said that not one particle remains to man as a ground of boasting. The whole is of God.

7. But perhaps there will be some who, while they admit that the will is in its own nature averse to righteousness, and is converted solely by the power of God, will yet hold that, when once it is prepared, it performs a part in acting. This they found upon the words of Augustine, that grace precedes every good work; the will accompanying, not leading; a handmaid, and not a guide (August. *ad Bonifac.* Ep. 106). The words thus not improperly used by this holy writer, Lombard preposterously wrests to the above effect (Lombard, lib. 2, Dist. 25). But I maintain that as well in the words of the Psalmist which I have quoted, as in other passages of Scripture, two things are clearly taught—viz. that the Lord both corrects, or rather destroys, our depraved will, and also substitutes a good will from himself. In as much as it is prevented by grace, I have no objection to your calling it a handmaid; but in as much as when formed again, it is the work of the Lord, it is erroneous to say, that it accompanies preventing grace as a voluntary attendant. Therefore, Chrysostom is inaccurate in saying that grace cannot do any thing without will, nor will any thing without grace (Serm. *de Invent. Sanct. Crucis*); as if grace did not, in terms of the passage lately quoted from Paul, produce the very will itself. The intention of Augustine, in calling the human will the handmaid of grace, was not to assign it a kind of second place to grace in the performance of good works. His object merely was to refute the pestilential dogma of Pelagius, who made human merit the first cause of salvation.

As was sufficient for his purpose at the time, he contends that grace is prior to all merit, while, in the meantime, he says nothing of the other question as to the perpetual effect of grace, which, however, he handles admirably in other places. For in saying, as he often does, that the Lord prevents the unwilling in order to make him willing, and follows after the willing that he may not will in vain, he makes Him the sole author of good works. Indeed, his sentiments on this subject are too clear to need any lengthened illustration. "Men," says he, "labor to find in our will something that is our own, and not God's; how they can find it, I wot not" (August. *de Remiss. Peccat.*, lib. 2 c. 18). In his First Book against Pelagius and Celestius, expounding the saying of Christ, "Every man therefore that has heard, and has learned of the Father, cometh unto me" (John 6:45), he says, "The will is aided not only so as to know what is to be done, but also to do what it knows." And thus, when God teaches not by the letter of the Law, but by the grace of the Spirit, he so teaches, that every one who has learned, not only knowing, sees, but also willing, desires, and acting, performs.

8. Since we are now occupied with the chief point on which the controversy turns, let us give the reader the sum of the matter in a few, and those most unambiguous, passages of Scripture; thereafter, lest any one should charge us with distorting Scripture, let us show that the truth, which we maintain to be derived from Scripture, is not unsupported by the testimony of this holy man (I mean Augustine). I deem it unnecessary to bring forward every separate passage of Scripture in confirmation of my doctrine. A selection of the most choice passages will pave the way for the understanding of all those which lie scattered up and down in the sacred volume. On the other hand, I thought it not out of place to show my accordance with a man whose authority is justly of so much weight in the Christian world. It is certainly easy to prove that the commencement of good is only with God, and that none but the elect have a will inclined to good. But the cause of election must be sought out of man; and hence it

follows that a right will is derived not from man himself, but from the same good pleasure by which we were chosen before the creation of the world. Another argument much akin to this may be added. The beginning of right will and action being of faith, we must see whence faith itself is. But since Scripture proclaims throughout that it is the free gift of God, it follows that when men, who are with their whole soul naturally prone to evil, begin to have a good will, it is owing to mere grace. Therefore, when the Lord, in the conversion of his people, sets down these two things as requisite to be done—viz. to take away the heart of stone and give a heart of flesh, he openly declares that in order to our conversion to righteousness, what is ours must be taken away, and that what is substituted in its place is of himself. Nor does he declare this in one passage only. For he says in Jeremiah "I will give them one heart, and one way, that they may fear me for ever;" and a little after he says, "I will put my fear in their hearts, that they shall not depart from me" (Jer. 32:39-40). Again, in Ezekiel, "I will give them one heart, and I will put a new spirit within you; and I will take the stony heart out of their flesh, and will give them an heart of flesh" (Ezek. 11:19). He could not more clearly claim to himself, and deny to us, everything good and right in our will, than by declaring that in our conversion there is the creation of a new spirit and a new heart. It always follows, both that nothing good can proceed from our will until it be formed again, and that after it is formed again in so far as it is good, it is of God, and not of us.

9. With this view, likewise the prayers of the saints correspond. Thus Solomon prays that the Lord may "incline our hearts unto him, to walk in his ways, and keep his commandments" (1 Kings 8:58); intimating that our heart is perverse, and naturally indulges in rebellion against the Divine law, until it be turned. Again, it is said in the Psalms, "Incline my heart unto thy testimonies" (Ps. 119:36). For we should always note the antithesis between the rebellious movement of the heart, and the correction by which it is subdued to obedience.

David feeling for the time that he was deprived of directing grace, prays, "Create in me a clean heart, O God; and renew a right spirit within me" (Ps. 51:10). Is not this an acknowledgment that all the parts of the heart are full of impurity, and that the soul has received a twist, which has turned it from straight to crooked? And then, in describing the cleansing, which he earnestly demands as a thing to be created by God, does he not ascribe the work entirely to Him? If it is objected that the prayer itself is a symptom of a pious and holy affection, it is easy to reply that although David had already in some measure repented, he was here contrasting the sad fall which he had experienced with his former state. Therefore, speaking in the person of a man alienated from God, he properly prays for the blessings which God bestows upon his elect in regeneration. Accordingly, like one dead, he desires to be created anew, so as to become, instead of a slave of Satan, an instrument of the Holy Spirit. Strange and monstrous are the longings of our pride. There is nothing which the Lord enjoins more strictly than the religious observance of his Sabbath, in other words resting from our works; but in nothing do we show greater reluctance than to renounce our own works, and give due place to the works of God. Did not arrogance stand in the way, we could not overlook the clear testimony which Christ has borne to the efficacy of his grace. "I," said he, "am the true vine, and my Father is the husbandman." "As the branch cannot bear fruit of itself, except it abide in the vine; no more can ye, except ye abide in me" (John 15:1, 4). If we can no more bear fruit of ourselves than a vine can bud when rooted up and deprived of moisture, there is no longer any room to ask what the aptitude of our nature is for good. There is no ambiguity in the conclusion, "For without me ye can do nothing." He says not that we are too weak to suffice for ourselves; but, by reducing us to nothing, he excludes the idea of our possessing any, even the least ability. If, when engrafted into Christ, we bear fruit like the vine, which draws its vegetative power from the moisture of the ground, and the dew of heaven, and the fostering warmth of the sun, I see nothing in a good work, which we can call our own, without trenching upon what is due to God. It is vain to have recourse to the frivolous cavil that the sap and the power of producing are already contained in the vine, and that, therefore, instead of deriving everything from the earth or the original root, it contributes something of its own. Our Savior's words simply mean that when separated from him, we are nothing but dry, useless wood, because, when so separated, we have no power to do good, as he elsewhere says, "Every plant which my heavenly Father has not planted, shall be rooted up" (Matt. 15:13). Accordingly, in the passage already quoted from the Apostle Paul, he attributes the whole operation to God, "It is God which worketh in you both to will and to do of his good pleasure" (Phil. 2:13). The first part of a good work is the will, the second is vigorous effort in the doing of it. God is the author of both. It is, therefore, robbery from God to arrogate anything to ourselves, either in the will or the act. Were it said that God gives assistance to a weak will, something might be left us; but when it is said that he makes the will, everything good in it is placed without us. Moreover, since even a good will is still weighed down by the burden of the flesh, and prevented from rising, it is added that to meet the difficulties of the contest, God supplies the persevering effort until the effect is obtained. Indeed, the Apostle could not otherwise have said, as he elsewhere does, that "it is the same God which worketh all in all" (1 Cor. 12:6); words comprehending, as we have already observed (sec. 6), the whole course of the spiritual life. For which reason, David, after praying, "Teach me thy way, O Lord, I will walk in thy truths" adds, "unite my heart to fear thy name" (Ps. 86:11); by these words intimating that even those who are well-affected are liable to so many distractions that they easily become vain, and fall away, if not strengthened to persevere. And hence, in another passage, after praying, "Order my steps in thy word," he requests that strength also may be given him to carry on the war, "Let not any iniquity have dominion over me" (Ps. 119:133). In this way, the Lord both begins and perfects the good work in us, so that it is due to Him: first, that the will conceives a love of rectitude, is inclined to desire, is moved and stimulated to pursue it; secondly, that this choice, desire, and endeavor fail not, but are carried forward to effect; and, lastly, that we go on without interruption, and persevere even to the end.

10. This movement of the will is not of that description which was for many ages taught and believed—viz. a movement which thereafter leaves us the choice to obey or resist it, but one which affects us efficaciously. We must, therefore, repudiate the oft-repeated sentiment of Chrysostom, "Whom he draws, he draws willingly;" insinuating that the Lord only stretches out his hand, and waits to see whether we will be pleased to take his aid. We grant that, as man was originally constituted, he could incline to either side, but since he has taught us by his example how miserable a thing free will is if God works not in us to will and to do, of what use to us were grace imparted in such scanty measure? Nay, by our own ingratitude, we obscure and impair divine grace. The Apostle's doctrine is not, that the grace of a good will is offered to us if we will accept of it, but that God himself is pleased so to work in us as to guide, turn, and govern our heart by his Spirit, and reign in it as his own possession. Ezekiel promises that a new spirit will be given to the elect, not merely that they may be able to walk in his precepts, but that they may really walk in them (Ezek. 11:19; 36:27). And the only meaning which can be given to our Savior's words, "Every man, therefore, that has heard and learned of the Father, cometh unto me" (John 6:45), is, that the grace of God is effectual in itself. This Augustine maintains in his book *De Praedestinatione Sancta.* This grace is not bestowed on all promiscuously, according to the common brocard (of Occam, if I mistake not), that it is not denied to any one who does what in him lies. Men are indeed to be taught that the favor of God is offered, without exception, to all who ask it; but since those only begin to ask whom heaven by

grace inspires, even this minute portion of praise must not be withheld from him. It is the privilege of the elect to be regenerated by the
Spirit of God, and then placed under his guidance and government.
Wherefore Augustine justly derides some who arrogate to themselves
a certain power of willing, as well as censures others who imagine
that that which is a special evidence of gratuitous election is given to
all (August. *de Verbis Apost.* Serm. 21). He says, "Nature is common
to all, but not grace;" and he calls it a showy acuteness "which shines
by mere vanity, when that which God bestows, on whom he will is
attributed generally to all." Elsewhere he says, "How came you? By
believing. Fear, lest by arrogating to yourself the merit of finding the
right way, you perish from the right way. I came, you say, by free
choice, came by my own will. Why do you boast? Would you know
that even this was given you? Hear Christ exclaiming, No man com-
ets unto me, except the Father which has sent me draw him.' "And
from the words of John (6:44), he infers it to be an incontrovertible fact, that the hearts of believers are so effectually governed from
above, that they follow with undeviating affection. "Whosoever is
born of God does not commit sin; for his seed remaineth in him" (1
John 3:9). That intermediate movement which the sophists imagine,
a movement which every one is free to obey or to reject, is obviously
excluded by the doctrine of effectual perseverance.

11. As to perseverance, it would undoubtedly have been regarded as
the gratuitous gift of God, had not the very pernicious error prevailed
that it is bestowed in proportion to human merit, according to the re-
ception which each individual gives to the first grace. This having given
rise to the idea that it was entirely in our own power to receive or reject
the offered grace of God, that idea is no sooner exploded than the error
founded on it must fall. The error, indeed, is twofold. For, besides teaching that our gratitude for the first grace and our legitimate use of it is
rewarded by subsequent supplies of grace, its abettors add that, after
this, grace does not operate alone, but only co-operates with ourselves.

As to the former, we must hold that the Lord, while he daily enriches his servants, and loads them with new gifts of his grace, because he approves of and takes pleasure in the work which he has begun, finds that in them which he may follow up with larger measures of grace. To this effect are the sentences, "To him that has shall be given." "Well done, good and faithful servant: thou hast been faithful over a few things, I will make thee ruler over many things" (Matt. 25:21, 23, 29; Luke 19:17, 26). But here two precautions are necessary. It must not be said that the legitimate use of the first grace is rewarded by subsequent measures of grace, as if man rendered the grace of God effectual by his own industry, nor must it be thought that there is any such remuneration as to make it cease to be the gratuitous grace of God. I admit, then, that believers may expect as a blessing from God, that the better the use they make of previous, the larger the supplies they will receive of future grace; but I say that even this use is of the Lord, and that this remuneration is bestowed freely of mere good will. The trite distinction of operating and co-operating grace is employed no less sinistrously than unhappily. Augustine, indeed, used it, but softened it by a suitable definition—viz. that God, by co-operating, perfects what he begins by operating—that both graces are the same, but obtain different names from the different manner in which they produce their effects. Whence it follows that he does not make an apportionment between God and man, as if a proper movement on the part of each produced a mutual concurrence. All he does is to mark a multiplication of grace. To this effect, accordingly, he elsewhere says, that in man good will precedes many gifts from God; but among these gifts is this good will itself. (August. *Enchiridion ad Laurent.* cap. 32). Whence it follows, that nothing is left for the will to arrogate as its own. This Paul has expressly stated. For, after saying, "It is God which worketh in you both to will and to do," he immediately adds, "of his good pleasure" (Phil. 2:13); indicating by this expression, that the blessing is gratuitous. As to the common saying, that after we have given admission to the first grace,

our efforts co-operate with subsequent grace, this is my answer: If it is
meant that after we are once subdued by the power of the Lord to the
obedience of righteousness, we proceed voluntarily, and are inclined to
follow the movement of grace, I have nothing to object. For it is most
certain that where the grace of God reigns, there is also this readiness to
obey. And whence this readiness, but just that the Spirit of God being
everywhere consistent with himself, after first begetting a principle of
obedience, cherishes and strengthens it for perseverance? If, again, it is
meant that man is able of himself to be a fellow-laborer with the grace
of God, I hold it to be a most pestilential delusion.

12. In support of this view, some make an ignorant and false application of the Apostle's words: "I labored more abundantly than they
all: yet not I, but the grace of God which was with me" (1 Cor. 15:10).
The meaning they give them is that as Paul might have seemed to
speak somewhat presumptuously in preferring himself to all the other
apostles, he corrects the expression so far by referring the praise to
the grace of God, but he, at the same time, calls himself a co-oper-
ator with grace. It is strange that this should have proved a stum-
bling-block to so many writers, otherwise respectable. The Apostle
says not that the grace of God labored with him so as to make him
a co-partner in the labor. He rather transfers the whole merit of the
labor to grace alone, by thus modifying his first expression, "It was not
I," says he, "that labored, but the grace of God that was present with
me." Those who have adopted the erroneous interpretation have been
misled by an ambiguity in the expression, or rather by a preposterous
translation, in which the force of the Greek article is overlooked. For
to take the words literally, the Apostle does not say that grace was a
fellow-worker with him, but that the grace which was with him was
sole worker. And this is taught not obscurely, though briefly, by Augustine when he says, "Good will in man precedes many gifts from
God, but not all gifts, seeing that the will which precedes is itself
among the number." He adds the reason, "for it is written, 'the God

of my mercy shall prevent me,' (Ps. 59:10), and 'Surely goodness and mercy shall follow me,'" (Ps. 23:6); it prevents him that is unwilling, and makes him willing; it follows him that is willing, that he may not will in vain." To this Bernard assents, introducing the Church as praying thus, "Draw me, who am in some measure unwilling, and make me willing; draw me, who am sluggishly lagging, and make me run" (Serm. 2 in *Cantic.*).

13. Let us now hear Augustine in his own words, lest the Pelagians of our age, I mean the sophists of the Sorbonne, charge us after their wont with being opposed to all antiquity. In this indeed they imitate their father Pelagius, by whom of old a similar charge was brought against Augustine. In the second chapter of his *Treatise De Correptione et Gratis*, addressed to Valentinus, Augustine explains at length what I will state briefly, but in his own words, that to Adam was given the grace of persevering in goodness if he had the will; to us it is given to will, and by will overcome concupiscence; that Adam, therefore, had the power if he had the will, but did not will to have the power, whereas to us is given both the will and the power; that the original freedom of man was to be able not to sin, but that we have a much greater freedom—viz. not to be able to sin. And lest it should be supposed, as Lombard erroneously does (lib. 2 Dist. 25), that he is speaking of the perfection of the future state, he shortly after removes all doubt when he says, "For so much is the will of the saints inflamed by the Holy Spirit, that they are able, because they are willing; and willing, because God worketh in them so to will." For if, in such weakness (in which, however, to suppress pride, "strength" must be made "perfect,") their own will is left to them, in such sense that, by the help of God, they are able, if they will, while at the same time God does not work in them so as to make them will; among so many temptations and infirmities the will itself would give way, and, consequently, they would not be able to persevere. Therefore, to meet the infirmity of the human will, and prevent it from failing, how weak

soever it might be, divine grace was made to act on it inseparably and uninterruptedly. Augustine (ibid. cap. 14) next entering fully into the question, how our hearts follow the movement when God affects them, necessarily says, indeed, that the Lord draws men by their own wills; wills, however, which he himself has produced. We have now an attestation by Augustine to the truth which we are specially desirous to maintain—viz. that the grace offered by the Lord is not merely one which every individual has full liberty of choosing to receive or reject, but a grace which produces in the heart both choice and will: so that all the good works which follow after are its fruit and effect; the only will which yields obedience being the will which grace itself has made. In another place, Augustine uses these words, "Every good work in us is performed only by grace" (August. Ep. 105).

14. In saying elsewhere that the will is not taken away by grace, but out of bad is changed into good, and after it is good is assisted—he only means that man is not drawn as if by an extraneous impulse without the movement of the heart, but is inwardly affected so as to obey from the heart. Declaring that grace is given specially and gratuitously to the elect, he writes in this way to Boniface: "We know that Divine grace is not given to all men, and that to those to whom it is given, it is not given either according to the merit of works, or according to the merit of the will, but by free grace: in regard to those to whom it is not given, we know that the not giving of it is a just judgment from God" (August. *ad Bonifac.* Ep. 106). In the same epistle, he argues strongly against the opinion of those who hold that subsequent grace is given to human merit as a reward for not rejecting the first grace. For he presses Pelagius to confess that gratuitous grace is necessary to us for every action, and that merely from the fact of its being truly grace, it cannot be the recompense of works. But the matter cannot be more briefly summed up than in the eighth chapter of his Treatise *De Correptione et Gratia*, where he shows, first, that human will does not by liberty obtain grace, but by grace obtains liberty.

Secondly, that by means of the same grace, the heart being impressed with a feeling of delight, is trained to persevere, and strengthened with invincible fortitude. Thirdly, that while grace governs the will, it never falls; but when grace abandons it, it falls forthwith. Fourthly, that by the free mercy of God, the will is turned to good, and when turned, perseveres. Fifthly, that the direction of the will to good, and its constancy after being so directed, depend entirely on the will of God, and not on any human merit. Thus the will (free will, if you choose to call it so), which is left to man, is, as he in another place (Ep. 46) describes it, a will which can neither be turned to God, nor continue in God, unless by grace; a will which, whatever its ability may be, derives all that ability from grace.

Study Guide Questions

Section 1

1. Is all of man's nature fleshly?

2. What is the only way to obtain anything of spiritual value from the Spirit?

3. Whatever we have from nature is what?

Section 2

1. What passage does Paul turn to in order to throw down the arrogance of mankind?

2. Is this passage limited to some men?

3. What are the two reasons men are this way?

Section 3

1. Does Calvin agree that some unbelievers have some nobility in their nature?

2. How does Calvin account for this?

Section 4

1. Does Calvin agree that we must "put Catiline on the same footing with Camillus"?
2. Which way does Calvin take it?
3. How?
4. Do these virtues put these men in a right standing with God?

Section 5

1. We must attribute conversion entirely to what?
2. What drives evil will, and what drives good will?
3. Those who are offended by this do not know how to do what?
4. If necessity is the same as compulsion, what must be said about God?
5. Calvin agrees with whom in these matters?

Section 6

1. What must we not divide?

Section 7

1. What does Calvin think of Lombard's idea of "preventing grace"?
2. What is prior to all merit?

Section 8

1. Why does Calvin cite Augustine?
2. What is the basis for Calvin's assertions on this topic?
3. How do we know that faith is a free gift of God?

Section 9

1. What antithesis must we always remember?
2. How does Calvin describe the license of our pride?

Section 10

1. Does God's grace give us a chance to be good or not?

2. What must we not claim?

Section 11
1. What is perseverance *not?*
2. Is grace a co-worker with us?

Sections 12–13
1. Can man take credit for even one good work apart from grace?
2. What, according to Augustine, brings about every good work in us?

Section 14
1. Does grace eliminate the will?
2. What is the right relationship of grace and freedom?

CHAPTER 4

How God works in the hearts of men.

The leading points discussed in this chapter are,
I. Whether in bad actions anything is to be attributed to
God; if anything, how much. Also, what is to be attributed to the
devil and to man, sec. 1-5.

II. In indifferent matters, how much is to be attributed to God, and
how much is left to man, sec. 6.

III. Two objections refuted, sec. 7-8.

Outline:

1. Connection of this chapter with the preceding. Augustine's similitude of a good and bad rider. Question answered in respect to the devil.

2. Question answered in respect to God and man. Example from
the history of Job. The works of God distinguished from the works of
Satan and wicked men. 1. By the design or end of acting. How Satan
acts in the reprobate. 2. How God acts in them.

3. Old objection, that the agency of God in such cases is referable
to prescience or permission, not actual operation. Answer, showing

that God blinds and hardens the reprobate, and this in two ways; 1. By deserting them; 2. By delivering them over to Satan.

4. Striking passages of Scripture, proving that God acts in both ways, and disposing of the objection with regard to prescience. Confirmation from Augustine.

5. A modification of the former answer, proving that God employs Satan to instigate the reprobate, but, at the same time, is free from all taint.

6. How God works in the hearts of men in indifferent matters. Our will in such matters not so free as to be exempt from the overruling providence of God. This confirmed by various examples.

7. Objection, that these examples do not form the rule. An answer, fortified by the testimony of universal experience, by Scripture, and a passage of Augustine.

8. Some, in arguing against the error of free will, draw an argument from the event. How this is to be understood.

That man is so enslaved by the yoke of sin, that he cannot of his own nature aim at good either in wish or actual pursuit, has, I think, been sufficiently proved. Moreover, a distinction has been drawn between compulsion and necessity, making it clear that man, though he sins necessarily, nevertheless sins voluntarily. But since, from his being brought into bondage to the devil, it would seem that he is actuated more by the devil's will than his own, it is necessary, first, to explain what the agency of each is, and then solve the question, Whether in bad actions anything is to be attributed to God, Scripture intimating that there is some way in which he interferes? Augustine (in Psalm 31 and 33) compares the human will to a horse preparing to start, and God and the devil to riders. "If God mounts, he, like a temperate and skillful rider, guides it calmly, urges it when too slow, reins it in when too fast, curbs its forwardness and over-action, checks its bad temper, and keeps it on the proper course; but if the devil has seized the saddle, like an ignorant and rash rider, he hurries it over broken ground, drives it into ditches, dashes it over precipices, spurs it into obstinacy or fury." With this simile, since a better does not occur, we shall for the present be contented. When it is said, then, that the will of the natural man is subject to the power of the devil, and is actuated by him, the meaning is not that the will, while reluctant and resisting, is forced to submit (as masters oblige unwilling slaves to execute their orders), but that, fascinated by the impostures of Satan, it necessarily yields to his guidance, and does him homage. Those whom the Lord favors not with the direction of his Spirit, he, by a righteous judgment, consigns to the agency of Satan. Wherefore, the Apostle says, that "the god of this world has blinded the minds of them which believe not, lest the light of the glorious gospel of Christ, who is the image of God, should shine into them." And, in another passage, he describes the devil as "the spirit that now worketh in the children of disobedience" (Eph. 2:2). The blinding of the wicked, and all the iniquities consequent upon it, are called the works of Satan; works the cause of which is not to be Sought in anything external to the will of man, in which the root of the evil lies, and in which the foundation of Satan's kingdom, in other words, sin, is fixed.

2. The nature of the divine agency in such cases is very different. For the purpose of illustration, let us refer to the calamities brought upon holy Job by the Chaldeans. They having slain his shepherds, carry off his flocks. The wickedness of their deed is manifest, as is also the hand of Satan, who, as the history informs us, was the instigator of the whole. Job, however, recognizes it as the work of God, saying, that what the Chaldeans had plundered, "the Lord" had "taken away." How can we attribute the same work to God, to Satan, and to man, without either excusing Satan by the interference of God, or making God the author of the crime? This is easily done, if we look first to the end, and then to the mode of acting. The Lord designs to exercise the patience of his servant by adversity; Satan's plan is to drive him

to despair, while the Chaldeans are bent on making unlawful gain by plunder. Such diversity of purpose makes a wide distinction in the act. In the mode there is not less difference. The Lord permits Satan to afflict his servant; and the Chaldeans, who had been chosen as the ministers to execute the deed, he hands over to the impulses of Satan, who, pricking on the already depraved Chaldeans with his poisoned darts, instigates them to commit the crime. They rush furiously on to the unrighteous deed, and become its guilty perpetrators. Here Satan is properly said to act in the reprobate, over whom he exercises his sway, which is that of wickedness. God also is said to act in his own way; because even Satan when he is the instrument of divine wrath, is completely under the command of God, who turns him as he will in the execution of his just judgments. I say nothing here of the universal agency of God, which, as it sustains all the creatures, also gives them all their power of acting. I am now speaking only of that special agency which is apparent in every act. We thus see that there is no inconsistency in attributing the same act to God, to Satan, and to man, while, from the difference in the end and mode of action, the spotless righteousness of God shines forth at the same time that the iniquity of Satan and of man is manifested in all its deformity.

3. Ancient writers sometimes manifest a superstitious dread of making a simple confession of the truth in this matter, from a fear of furnishing impiety with a handle for speaking irreverently of the works of God. While I embrace such soberness with all my heart, I cannot see the least danger in simply holding what Scripture delivers. When Augustine was not always free from this superstition, as when he says, that blinding and hardening have respect not to the operation of God, but to prescience (*Lib. de Predestina. et Gratia*). But this subtlety is repudiated by many passages of Scriptures which clearly show that the divine interference amounts to something more than prescience. And Augustine himself, in his book against Julian, contends at length that sins are manifestations not merely of divine

permission or patience, but also of divine power, that thus former sins may be punished. In like manner, what is said of permission is too weak to stand. God is very often said to blind and harden the reprobate, to turn their hearts, to incline and impel them, as I have elsewhere fully explained (Book 1 c. 18). The extent of this agency can never be explained by having recourse to prescience or permission. We, therefore, hold that there are two methods in which God may so act. When his light is taken away, nothing remains but blindness and darkness; when his Spirit is taken away, our hearts become hard as stones; when his guidance is withdrawn, we immediately turn from the right path; and hence he is properly said to incline, harden, and blind those whom he deprives of the faculty of seeing, obeying, and rightly executing. The second method, which comes much nearer to the exact meaning of the words, is when executing his judgments by Satan as the minister of his anger, God both directs men's counsels, and excites their wills, and regulates their efforts as he pleases. Thus when Moses relates that Simon, king of the Amorites, did not give the Israelites a passage, because the Lord "had hardened his spirit, and made his heart obstinate," he immediately adds the purpose which God had in view—viz. that he might deliver him into their hand (Deut. 2:30). As God had resolved to destroy him, the hardening of his heart was the divine preparation for his ruin.

4. In accordance with the former methods it seems to be said, "The law shall perish from the priests and counsel from the ancients." "He poureth contempt upon princes, and causeth them to wander in the wilderness, where there is no way." Again "O Lord, why hast thou made us to err from thy ways, and hardened our heart from thy fear?" These passages rather indicate what men become when God deserts them, than what the nature of his agency is when he works in them. But there are other passages which go farther, such as those concerning the hardening of Pharaoh: "I will harden his heart, that he shall not let the people go." The same thing is afterwards repeated

in stronger terms. Did he harden his heart by not softening it? This is, indeed, true; but he did something more: he gave it in charge to Satan to confirm him in his obstinacy. Hence he had previously said, "I am sure he will not let you go." The people come out of Egypt, and the inhabitants of a hostile region come forth against them. How were they instigated? Moses certainly declares of Sihon, that it was the Lord who "had hardened his spirit, and made his heart obstinate" (Deut. 2:30). The Psalmists relating the same history says, "He turned their hearts to hate his people" (Psalm 105:25). You cannot now say that they stumbled merely because they were deprived of divine counsel. For if they are hardened and turned, they are purposely bent to the very end in view. Moreover, whenever God saw it meet to punish the people for their transgression, in what way did he accomplish his purpose by the reprobate? In such a way as shows that the efficacy of the action was in him, and that they were only ministers. At one time he declares, "that he will lift an ensign to the nations from far, and will hiss unto them from the end of the earth;" at another, that he will take a net to ensnare them; and at another, that he will be like a hammer to strike them. But he specially declared that he was not inactive among them when he called Sennacherib an axe, which was formed and destined to be wielded by his own hand. Augustine is not far from the mark when he states the matter thus, that men sin, is attributable to themselves: that in sinning they produce this or that result, is owing to the mighty power of God, who divides the darkness as he pleases (August. *de Praedest. Sanct*).

5. Moreover, that the ministry of Satan is employed to instigate the reprobate, whenever the Lord, in the course of his providence, has any purpose to accomplish in them, will sufficiently appear from a single passage. It is repeatedly said in the First Book of Samuel, that an evil spirit from the Lord came upon Saul, and troubled him (1 Sam. 16:14; 18:10; 19:9). It were impious to apply this to the Holy Spirit. An impure spirit must therefore be called a spirit from the

Lord, because completely subservient to his purpose, being more an instrument in acting than a proper agent. We should also add what Paul says, "God shall send them strong delusion, that they should believe a lie: that they all might be damned who believed not the truth" (2 Thess. 2:11-12). But in the same transaction there is always a wide difference between what the Lord does, and what Satan and the ungodly design to do. The wicked instruments which he has under his hand and can turn as he pleases, he makes subservient to his own justice. They, as they are wicked, give effect to the iniquity conceived in their wicked minds. Every thing necessary to vindicate the majesty of God from calumny, and cut off any subterfuge on the part of the ungodly, has already been expounded in the Chapters on Providence (Book 1 Chapter 16-18). Here I only meant to show, in a few words, how Satan reigns in the reprobate, and how God works in both.

6. In those actions, which in themselves are neither good nor bad, and concern the corporeal rather than the spiritual life, the liberty which man possesses, although we have above touched upon it (supra, Chap. 2 sect. 13-17), has not yet been explained. Some have conceded a free choice to man in such actions; more, I suppose, because they were unwilling to debate a matter of no great moment, than because they wished positively to assert what they were prepared to concede. While I admit that those who hold that man has no ability in himself to do righteousness, hold what is most necessary to be known for salvation, I think it ought not to be overlooked that we owe it to the special grace of God, whenever, on the one hand, we choose what is for our advantage, and whenever our will inclines in that direction; and on the other, whenever with heart and soul we shun what would otherwise do us harm. And the interference of Divine Providence goes to the extent not only of making events turn out as was foreseen to be expedient, but of giving the wills of men the same direction. If we look at the administration of human affairs with the eye of sense, we will have no doubt that, so far, they are placed at man's disposal;

but if we lend an ear to the many passages of Scripture which proclaim that even in these matters the minds of men are ruled by God,
they will compel us to place human choice in subordination to his
special influence. Who gave the Israelites such favor in the eyes of the
Egyptians that they lent them all their most valuable commodities?
(Exod. 11:3). They never would have been so inclined of their own accord. Their inclinations, therefore, were more overruled by God than
regulated by themselves. And surely, had not Jacob been persuaded
that God inspires men with divers affections as seems to him good, he
would not have said of his son Joseph (whom he thought to be some
heathen Egyptian), "God Almighty give you mercy before the man"
(Gen. 43:14). In like manner, the whole Church confesses that when
the Lord was pleased to pity his people, he made them also to be pitied of all them that carried them captives (Ps. 106:46). In like manner,
when his anger was kindled against Saul, so that he prepared himself
for battle, the cause is stated to have been, that a spirit from God fell
upon him (1 Sam. 11:6). who dissuaded Absalom from adopting the
counsel of Ahithophel, which was wont to be regarded as an oracle?
(2 Sam. 17:14). Who disposed Rehoboam to adopt the counsel of the
young men? (1 Kings 12:10). Who caused the approach of the Israelites to strike terror into nations formerly distinguished for valor?
Even the harlot Rahab recognized the hand of the Lord. Who, on the
other hand, filled the hearts of the Israelites with fear and dread (Lev.
26:36), but He who threatened in the Law that he would give them a
an "trembling heart"? (Deut. 28:65).

7. It may be objected, that these are special examples which cannot
be regarded as a general rule. They are sufficient, at all events, to prove
the point for which I contend—viz. that whenever God is pleased to
make way for his providence, he even in external matters so turns and
bends the wills of men, that whatever the freedom of their choice may
be, it is still subject to the disposal of God. That your mind depends
more on the agency of God than the freedom of your own choice,

daily experience teaches. Your judgment often fails, and in matters of no great difficulty, your courage flags; at other times, in matters of the greatest obscurity, the mode of explicating them at once suggests itself, while in matters of moment and danger, your mind rises superior to every difficulty. In this way, I interpret the words of Solomon, "The hearing ear, and the seeing eye, the Lord hath made even both of them" (Prov. 20:12). For they seem to me to refer not to their creation, but to peculiar grace in the use of them, when he says, "The king's heart is in the hand of the Lord as the rivers of water; he turneth it whithersoever he will" (Prov. 21:1), he comprehends the whole race under one particular class. If any will is free from subjection, it must be that of one possessed of regal power, and in a manner exercising dominion over other wills. But if it is under the hand of God, ours surely cannot be exempt from it. On this subject there is an admirable sentiment of Augustine, "Scripture, if it be carefully examined, will show not only that the good wills of men are made good by God out of evil, and when so made, are directed to good acts, even to eternal life, but those which retain the elements of the world are in the power of God, to turn them whither he pleases, and when he pleases, either to perform acts of kindness, or by a hidden, indeed, but, at the same time, most just judgment to inflict punishment" (August. *De Gratia et Lib. Arb. ad Valent.* cap. 20).

8. Let the reader here remember that the power of the human will is not to be estimated by the event, as some unskillful persons are absurdly wont to do. They think it an elegant and ingenious proof of the bondage of the human will that even the greatest monarchs are sometimes thwarted in their wishes. But the ability of which we speak must be considered as within the man, not measured by outward success. In discussing the subject of free will, the question is not whether external obstacles will permit a man to execute what he has internally resolved, but whether, in any matter whatever, he has a free power of judging and of willing. If men possess both of these, Attilius

Regulus, shut up in a barrel studded with sharp nails, will have a will no less free than Augustus Caesar ruling with imperial sway over a large portion of the globe.

Study Guide Questions

Section 1

1. Does man sin willingly, even though of necessity?
2. What comparison of Augustine's does Calvin approve?

Section 2

1. Who was involved in Job's loss?
2. What distinguishes these various agents?
3. What aspect of God's sovereignty is Calvin not addressing here?

Section 3

1. Why do the early fathers not want to attribute "hardening" to God?
2. What does Calvin think of this?
3. What does Calvin call the idea that hardening is nothing but permission or a matter of foreknowledge?
4. Considering the editor's footnote, how does Calvin chide Augustine unnecessarily?

Section 4

1. Are there passages that describe God as acting on the godless by simply "deserting" them?
2. Does this explanation cover all the scriptural data?

Section 5

1. What error must be avoided when discussing the "evil spirit from the Lord"?
2. Can God and Satan work in the same man at the same time?

Section 6

1. When actions are neither good nor evil, is God still involved?

Section 7

1. How is God's control of kingly actions (Prov. 21:1) a "how much more" argument?

Section 8

1. For Calvin, is free will to be determined by whether or not a man chooses what he wants?

CHAPTER 5

The arguments usually alleged in support of free will refuted.

Objections reduced to three principal heads:
I. Four absurdities advanced by the opponents of the orthodox doctrine concerning the slavery of the will, stated and refuted, sec. 1-5.

II. The passages of Scripture which they pervert in favor of their error, reduced to five heads, and explained, sec. 6-15.

III. Five other passages quoted in defense of free will expounded, sec. 16-19.

Outline:

1. Absurd fictions of opponents first refuted, and then certain passages of Scripture explained. Answer by a negative. Confirmation of the answer.

2. Another absurdity of Aristotle and Pelagius. Answer by a distinction. Answer fortified by passages from Augustine, and supported by the authority of an Apostle.

3. Third absurdity borrowed from the words of Chrysostom. Answer by a negative.

4. Fourth absurdity urged of old by the Pelagians. Answer from the works of Augustine. Illustrated by the testimony of our Savior. Another answer, which explains the use of exhortations.

5. A third answer, which contains a fuller explanation of the second. Objection to the previous answers. Objection refuted. Summary of the previous answers.

6. First class of arguments which the Neo-Pelagians draw from Scripture in defense of free will. 1. The Law demands perfect obedience and therefore God either mocks us, or requires things which are not in our power. Answer by distinguishing precepts into three sorts. The first of these considered in this and the following section.

7. This general argument from the Law of no avail to the patrons of free will. Promises conjoined with precepts, prove that our salvation is to be found in the grace of God. Objection, that the Law was given to the persons living at the time. Answer, confirmed by passages from Augustine.

8. A special consideration of the three classes of precepts of no avail to the defenders of free will. 1. Precepts enjoining us to turn to God. 2. Precepts which simply speak of the observance of the Law. 3. Precepts which enjoin us to persevere in the grace of God.

9. Objection. Answer. Confirmation of the answer from Jeremiah. Another objection refuted.

10. A second class of arguments in defense of free will drawn from the promises of God—viz. that the promises which God makes to those who seek him are vain if it is not in our power to do, or not do, the thing required. Answer, which explains the use of promises, and removes the supposed inconsistency.

11. Third class of arguments drawn from the divine upbraidings—that it is in vain to upbraid us for evils which it is not in our power to avoid. Answer. Sinners are condemned by their own consciences, and, therefore, the divine upbraidings are just. Moreover, there is a twofold

use in these upbraidings. Various passages of Scripture explained by means of the foregoing answers.

12. Objection founded on the words of Moses. Refutation by the words of an Apostle. Confirmation by argument.

13. Fourth class of arguments by the defenders of free will. God waits to see whether or not sinners will repent; therefore they can repent. Answer by a dilemma. Passage in Hosea explained.

14. Fifth class of arguments in defense of free will. Good and bad works described as our own, and therefore we are capable of both. Answer by an exposition, which shows that this argument is unavailing. Objection drawn from analogy. Answer. The nature and mode of divine agency in the elect.

15. Conclusion of the answer to the last class of arguments.

16. Third and last division of the chapter discussing certain passages of Scripture. 1. A passage from Genesis. Its true meaning explained.

17. 2. Passage from the Epistle to the Romans. Explanation. Refutation of an objection. Another refutation. A third refutation from Augustine. 3. A passage from First Corinthians. Answer to it.

18. 4. A passage from Ecclesiastes. Explanation. Another explanation.

19. 5. A passage from Luke. Explanation. Allegorical arguments weak. Another explanation. A third explanation. A fourth from Augustine. Conclusion and summary of the whole discussion concerning free will.

Enough would seem to have been said on the subject of man's will, were there not some who endeavor to urge him to his ruin by a false opinion of liberty and at the same time, in order to support their own opinion, assail ours. First, they gather together some absurd inferences, by which they endeavor to bring odium upon our doctrine, as if it were abhorrent to common sense, and then they oppose it with certain passages of Scripture (infra, sec. 6). Both devices we shall dispose of in their order. If sin, say they, is necessary, it ceases to be sin; if it is voluntary, it may be avoided. Such, too, were the weapons with which Pelagius assailed Augustine. But we are unwilling to crush them by the weight of his name, until we have satisfactorily disposed of the objections themselves. I deny, therefore, that sin ought to be the less imputed because it is necessary; and, on the other hand, I deny the inference that sin may be avoided because it is voluntary. If any one will dispute with God, and endeavor to evade his judgment, by pretending that he could not have done otherwise, the answer already given is sufficient that it is owing not to creation, but the corruption of nature, that man has become the slave of sin, and can will nothing but evil. For whence that impotence of which the wicked so readily avail themselves as an excuse, but just because Adam voluntarily subjected himself to the tyranny of the devil? Hence the corruption by which we are held bound as with chains, originated in the first man's revolt from his Maker. If all men are justly held guilty of this revolt, let them not think themselves excused by a necessity in which they see the clearest cause of their condemnation. But this I have fully explained above; and in the case of the devil himself, have given an example of one who sins not less voluntarily that he sins necessarily. I have also shown, in the case of the elect angels, that though their will cannot decline from good, it does not therefore cease to be will. This Bernard shrewdly explains when he says (Serm. 81, in *Cantica*), that we are the more miserable in this, that the necessity is voluntary; and yet this necessity so binds us who are subject to it that we are the slaves of sin, as we have already observed. The second step in the reasoning is vicious, because it leaps from voluntary to free; whereas we have proved above that a thing may be done voluntarily, though not subject to free choice.

2. They add that unless virtue and vice proceed from free choice, it is absurd either to punish man or reward him. Although this argument is taken from Aristotle, I admit that it is also used by Chrysostom

and Jerome. Jerome, however, does not disguise that it was familiar to
the Pelagians. He even quotes their words, "If grace acts in us, grace,
and not we who do the work, will be crowned" (Hieron. in Ep. *ad
Ctesiphont.* et Dialog. 1) With regard to punishment, I answer, that it
is properly inflicted on those by whom the guilt is contracted. What
matters it whether you sin with a free or an enslaved judgment, so
long as you sin voluntarily, especially when man is proved to be a
sinner because he is under the bondage of sin? In regard to the rewards of righteousness, is there any great absurdity in acknowledging
that they depend on the kindness of God rather than our own merits? How often do we meet in Augustine with this expression "God
crowns not our merits but his own gifts; and the name of reward
is given not to what is due to our merits, but to the recompense of
grace previously bestowed?" Some seem to think there is acuteness in
the remark, that there is no place at all for the mind, if good works
do not spring from free will as their proper source; but in thinking
this so very unreasonable they are widely mistaken. Augustine does
not hesitate uniformly to describe as necessary the very thing which
they count it impious to acknowledge. Thus he asks, "What is human
merit? He who came to bestow not due recompense but free grace,
though himself free from sin, and the giver of freedom, found all men
sinners" (Augustin. *in Psal. 31*). Again, "If you are to receive your due,
you must be punished. What then is done? God has not rendered you
due punishment, but bestows upon you unmerited grace. If you wish
to be an alien from grace, boast your merits" (in Psal. 70). Again, "You
are nothing in yourself, sin is yours, merit God's. Punishment is your
due; and when the reward shall come, God shall crown his own gifts,
not your merits" (Ep. 52). To the same effect he elsewhere says (*De
Verb. Apostol.* Serm. 15), that grace is not of merit, but merit of grace.
And shortly after he concludes that God by his gifts anticipates all
our merit that he may thereby manifest his own merit, and give what
is absolutely free, because he sees nothing in us that can be a ground

of salvation. But why extend the list of quotations, when similar sentiments are ever and anon recurring in his works? The abettors of this error would see a still better refutation of it, if they would attend to the source from which the apostle derives the glory of the saints: "Moreover, whom he did predestinate, them he also called; and whom he called, them he also justified; and whom he justified, them he also glorified" (Rom. 8:30). On what ground, then, the apostle being judge (2 Tim. 4:8), are believers crowned? Because by the mercy of God, not their own exertions, they are predestinated, called, and justified. Away, then, with the vain fear that unless free will stand, there will no longer be any merit! It is most foolish to take alarm, and recoil from that which Scripture inculcates. "If thou didst receive it, why dost thou glory as if thou hadst not received it?" (1 Cor. 4:7). You see how everything is denied to free will, for the very purpose of leaving no room for merit. And yet, as the beneficence and liberality of God are manifold and inexhaustible, the grace which he bestows upon us, inasmuch as he makes it our own, he recompenses as if the virtuous acts were our own.

3. But it is added, in terms which seem to be borrowed from Chrysostom (Homil. 22, *in Genes.*), that if our will possesses not the power of choosing good or evil, all who are partakers of the same nature must be alike good or alike bad. A sentiment akin to this occurs in the work *De Vocatione Gentium* (lib. 4 c. 4), usually attributed to Ambrose, in which it is argued that no one would ever decline from faith, did not the grace of God leave us in a mutable state. It is strange that such men should have so blundered. How did it fail to occur to Chrysostom that it is divine election which distinguishes among men? We have not the least hesitation to admit what Paul strenuously maintains, that all, without exception, are depraved and given over to wickedness; but at the same time we add that through the mercy of God all do not continue in wickedness. Therefore, while we all labor naturally under the same disease, those only recover health to

whom the Lord is pleased to put forth his healing hand. The others whom, in just judgment, he passes over, pine and rot away till they are consumed. And this is the only reason why some persevere to the end, and others, after beginning their course, fall away. Perseverance is the gift of God, which he does not lavish promiscuously on all, but imparts to whom he pleases. If it is asked how the difference arises—why some steadily persevere, and others prove deficient in steadfastness, we can give no other reason than that the Lord, by his mighty power, strengthens and sustains the former, so that they perish not, while he does not furnish the same assistance to the latter, but leaves them to be monuments of instability.

4. Still it is insisted, that exhortations are vain, warnings superfluous, and rebukes absurd, if the sinner possesses not the power to obey. When similar objections were urged against Augustine, he was obliged to write his book, *De Correptione et Gratia*, where he has fully disposed of them. The substance of his answer to his opponents is this: "O, man! learn from the precept what you ought to do; learn from correction, that it is your own fault you have not the power; and learn in prayer, whence it is that you may receive the power." Very similar is the argument of his book, *De Spiritu et Litera*, in which he shows that God does not measure the precepts of his law by human strength, but, after ordering what is right, freely bestows on his elect the power of fulfilling it. The subject, indeed, does not require a long discussion. For we are not singular in our doctrine, but have Christ and all his apostles with us. Let our opponents, then, consider how they are to come off victorious in a contest which they wage with such antagonists. Christ declares, "without me ye can do nothing" (John 15:5). Does he the less censure and chastise those who, without him, did wickedly? Does he the less exhort every man to be intent on good works? How severely does Paul inveigh against the Corinthians for want of charity (1 Cor. 3:3); and yet at the same time, he prays that charity may be given them by the Lord. In the Epistle to the

Romans, he declares that "it is not of him that willeth, nor of him that runneth, but of God that showeth mercy" (Rom. 9:16). Still he ceases not to warn, exhort, and rebuke them. Why then do they not expostulate with God for making sport with men, by demanding of them things which he alone can give, and chastising them for faults committed through want of his grace? Why do they not admonish Paul to spare those who have it not in their power to will or to run, unless the mercy of God, which has forsaken them, precede? As if the doctrine were not founded on the strongest reason—reason which no serious inquirer can fail to perceive. The extent to which doctrine, and exhortation, and rebuke, are in themselves able to change the mind, is indicated by Paul when he says, "Neither is he that planteth any thing, neither he that watereth; but God that giveth the increase" (1 Cor 3:7) in like manner, we see that Moses delivers the precepts of the Law under a heavy sanction, and that the prophets strongly urge and threaten transgressors though they at the same time confess, that men are wise only when an understanding heart is given them; that it is the proper work of God to circumcise the heart, and to change it from stone into flesh; to write his law on their inward parts; in short, to renew souls so as to give efficacy to doctrine.

5. What purpose, then, is served by exhortations? It is this: as the wicked with obstinate heart despise them, they will be a testimony against them when they stand at the judgment-seat of God; nay, they even now strike and lash their consciences. For, however they may petulantly deride, they cannot disapprove them. But what, you will ask, can a miserable mortal do, when softness of heart, which is necessary to obedience, is denied him? I ask, in reply, why have recourse to evasion, since hardness of heart cannot be imputed to any but the sinner himself? The ungodly, though they would gladly evade the divine admonitions, are forced, whether they will or not, to feel their power. But their chief use is to be seen in the case of believers, in whom the Lord, while he always acts by his Spirit, also omits not

the instrumentality of his word, but employs it, and not without effect. Let this, then, be a standing truth, that the whole strength of the godly consists in the grace of God, according to the words of the prophet, "I will give them one heart, and I will put a new spirit within you; and I will take the stony heart out of their flesh, and will give them an heart of flesh, that they may walk in my statutes" (Ezek. 11:19-20). But it will be asked, why are they now admonished of their duty, and not rather left to the guidance of the Spirit? Why are they urged with exhortations when they cannot hasten any faster than the Spirit impels them? And why are they chastised, if at any time they go astray, seeing that this is caused by the necessary infirmity of the flesh? "O, man! who art thou that replies against God?" If, in order to prepare us for the grace which enables us to obey exhortation, God sees meet to employ exhortation, what is there in such an arrangement for you to carp and scoff at? Had exhortations and reprimands no other profit with the godly than to convince them of sin, they could not be deemed altogether useless. Now, when, by the Spirit of God acting within, they have the effect of inflaming their desire of good, of arousing them from lethargy, of destroying the pleasure and honeyed sweetness of sin, making it hateful and loathsome, who will presume to cavil at them as superfluous?

Should anyone wish a clearer reply, let him take the following— God works in his elect in two ways: inwardly, by his Spirit; outwardly, by his Word. By his Spirit illuminating their minds, and training their hearts to the practice of righteousness, he makes them new creatures, while by his Word he stimulates them to long and seek for this renovation. In both, he exerts the might of his hand in proportion to the measure in which he dispenses them. The Word, when addressed to the reprobate, though not effectual for their amendment, has another use. It urges their consciences now, and will render them more inexcusable on the day of judgment. Thus, our Savior, while declaring that none can come to him but those whom the Father draws, and that the elect come after they have heard and learned of the Father (John 6:44-45), does not lay aside the office of teacher, but carefully invites those who must be taught inwardly by the Spirit before they can make any profit. The reprobate, again, are admonished by Paul, that the doctrine is not in vain; because, while it is in them a savor of death unto death, it is still a sweet savor unto God (2 Cor. 2:16).

6. The enemies of this doctrine are at great pains in collecting passages of Scripture, as if, unable to accomplish anything by their weight, they were to overwhelm us by their number. But as in battle, when it is come to close quarters, an unwarlike multitude, how great soever the pomp and show they make, give way after a few blows, and take to flight, so we shall have little difficulty here in disposing of our opponents and their host. All the passages which they pervert in opposing us are very similar in their import; and hence, when they are arranged under their proper heads, one answer will suffice for several; it is not necessary to give a separate consideration to each. Precepts seem to be regarded as their stronghold. These they think so accommodated to our abilities, as to make it follow as a matter of course, that whatever they enjoin we are able to perform. Accordingly, they run over all the precepts, and by them fix the measure of our power. For, say they, when God enjoins meekness, submission, love, chastity, piety, and holiness, and when he forbids anger, pride, theft, uncleanness, idolatry, and the like, he either mocks us, or only requires things which are in our power.

All the precepts which they thus heap together may be divided into three classes. Some enjoin a first conversion unto God, others speak simply of the observance of the law, and others inculcate perseverance in the grace which has been received. We shall first treat of precepts in general, and then proceed to consider each separate class. That the abilities of man are equal to the precepts of the divine law, has long been a common idea, and has some show of plausibility. It is founded, however, on the grossest ignorance of the law. Those who deem it a kind of sacrilege to say, that the observance of the law is impossible, insist, as their strongest argument, that, if it is so, the Law has been given in vain (infra, Chap. 7 sec. 5). For they speak just as if Paul had never said anything about the Law. But what, pray, is meant by saying that the Law "was added because of transgressions;" "by the law is the knowledge of sin;" "I had not known sin but by the law;" "the law entered that the offense might abound?" (Gal. 3:19; Rom. 3:20; 7:7; 5:20). Is it meant that the Law was to be limited to our strength, lest it should be given in vain? Is it not rather meant that it was placed far above us, in order to convince us of our utter feebleness? Paul indeed declares, that charity is the end and fulfilling of the Law (1 Tim. 1:5). But when he prays that the minds of the Thessalonians may be filled with it, he clearly enough acknowledges that the Law sounds in our ears without profit, if God do not implant it thoroughly in our hearts (1 Thess. 3:12).

7. I admit, indeed, that if the Scripture taught nothing else on the subject than that the Law is a rule of life by which we ought to regulate our pursuits, I should at once assent to their opinion; but since it carefully and clearly explains that the use of the Law is manifold, the proper course is to learn from that explanation what the power of the Law is in man. In regard to the present question, while it explains what our duty is it teaches that the power of obeying it is derived from the goodness of God, and it accordingly urges us to pray that this power may be given us. If there were merely a command and no promise, it would be necessary to try whether our strength were sufficient to fulfill the command; but since promises are annexed, which proclaim not only that aid, but that our whole power is derived from divine grace, they at the same time abundantly testify that we are not only unequal to the observance of the Law, but mere fools in regard to it. Therefore, let us hear no more of a proportion between our ability and the divine precepts, as if the Lord had accommodated the standard of justice which he was to give in the Law to our feeble capacities. We should rather gather from the promises hove ill

provided we are, having in everything so much need of grace. But say they, who will believe that the Lord designed his Law for blocks and stones? There is no wish to make any one believe this. The ungodly are neither blocks nor stones when, taught by the Law that their lusts are offensive to God, they are proved guilty by their own confession; nor are the godly blocks or stones, when admonished of their powerlessness, they take refuge in grace. To this effect are the pithy sayings of Augustine, "God orders what we cannot do, that we may know what we ought to ask of him. There is a great utility in precepts, if all that is given to free will is to do greater honor to divine grace. Faith acquires what the Law requires; nay, the Law requires, in order that faith may acquire what is thus required; nay, more, God demands of us faith itself, and finds not what he thus demands, until by giving he makes it possible to find it." Again, he says, "Let God give what he orders, and order what he wills."

8. This will be more clearly seen by again attending to the three classes of precepts to which we above referred. Both in the Law and in the Prophets, God repeatedly calls upon us to turn to him. But, on the other hand, a prophet exclaims, "Turn thou me, and I shall be turned; for thou art the Lord my God. Surely after that I was turned, I repented." He orders us to circumcise the foreskins of our hearts; but Moses declares that that circumcision is made by his own hand. In many passages he demands a new heart, but in others he declares that he gives it. As Augustine says, "What God promises, we ourselves do not through choice or nature, but he himself does by grace." The same observation is made when, in enumerating the rules of Tichonius, he states the third in effect to be—that we distinguish carefully between the Law and the promises, or between the commands and grace (Augustin. *de Doctrine Christiana*, lib. 3). Let them now go and gather from precepts what man's power of obedience is, when they would destroy the divine grace by which the precepts themselves are accomplished. The precepts of the second class are simply those which enjoin us to worship God, to obey

and adhere to his will, to do his pleasure, and follow his teaching. But innumerable passages testify that every degree of purity, piety, holiness, and justices which we possess is his gift. Of the third class of precepts is the exhortation of Paul and Barnabas to the proselytes, as recorded by Luke; they "persuaded them to continue in the grace of God" (Acts 13:43). But the source from which this power of continuance must be sought is elsewhere explained by Paul, when he says, "Finally, my brethren, be strong in the Lord" (Eph. 6:10). In another passage he says, "Grieve not the Holy Spirit of God, whereby ye are sealed unto the day of redemption" (Eph. 4:30). But as the thing here enjoined could not be performed by man, he prays in behalf of the Thessalonians, that God would count them "worthy of this calling, and fulfill all the good pleasure of his goodness, and the work of faith with power" (2 Thess. 1:11). In the same way, in the Second Epistle to the Corinthians, when treating of alms, he repeatedly commends their good and pious inclination. A little farther on, however, he exclaims, "Thanks be to God, which put the same earnest care into the heart of Titus for you. For indeed he accepted the exhortation" (2 Cor. 8:16-17). If Titus could not even perform the office of being a mouth to exhort others, except in so far as God suggested, how could the others have been voluntary agents in acting, if the Lord Jesus had not directed their hearts?

9. Some, who would be thought more acute, endeavor to evade all these passages, by the quibble that there is nothing to hinder us from contributing our part, while God, at the same time, supplies our deficiencies. They, moreover, adduce passages from the Prophets, in which the work of our conversion seems to be shared between God and ourselves; "Turn ye unto me, saith the Lord of hosts, and I will turn unto you, saith the Lord of hosts" (Zech. 1:3). The kind of assistance which God gives us has been shown above (sect. 7-8), and need not now be repeated. One thing only I ask to be conceded to me, that it is vain to think we have a power of fulfilling the Law, merely because we are enjoined to obey it. Since, in order to our fulfilling the divine

precepts, the grace of the Lawgiver is both necessary, and has been promised to us, this much at least is clear, that more is demanded of us than we are able to pay. Nor can any cavil evade the declaration in Jeremiah that the covenant which God made with his ancient people was broken, because it was only of the letter—that to make it effectual, it was necessary for the Spirit to interpose and train the heart to obedience (Jer. 31:32). The opinion we now combat is not aided by the words, "Turn unto me, and I will turn unto you." The turning there spoken of is not that by which God renews the heart unto repentance; but that in which, by bestowing prosperity, he manifests his kindness and favor, just in the same way as he sometimes expresses his displeasure by sending adversity. The people complaining under the many calamities which befell them, that they were forsaken by God, he answers, that his kindness would not fail them, if they would return to a right course, and to himself, the standard of righteousness. The passage, therefore, is wrested from its proper meaning when it is made to countenance the idea that the work of conversion is divided between God and man (supra, Chap. 2 sec. 27). We have only glanced briefly at this subject, as the proper place for it will occur when we come to treat of the Law (Chap. 7 sec. 2 and 3).

10. The second class of objections is akin to the former. They allege the promises in which the Lord makes a paction with our will. Such are the following: "Seek good, and not evil, that ye may live" (Amos 5:14). "If ye be willing and obedient, ye shall eat the good of the land: but if ye refuse and rebel, ye shall be devoured with the sword; for the mouth of the Lord has spoken it" (Isaiah 1:19-20). "If thou wilt put away thine abominations out of my sight, then thou shalt not remove" (Jer. 4:1). "It shall come to pass, if thou shalt hearken diligently unto the voice of the Lord thy God, to observe and do all the commandments which I command thee this days that the Lord thy God will set thee on high above all nations of the earth" (Deut. 28:1). There are other similar passages (Lev. 26:3, &c). They think that the

blessings contained in these promises are offered to our will absurdly and in mockery, if it is not in our power to secure or reject them. It is, indeed, an easy matter to indulge in declamatory complaint on this subject, to say that we are cruelly mocked by the Lord, when he declares that his kindness depends on our wills if we are not masters of our wills—that it would be a strange liberality on the part of God to set his blessings before us, while we have no power of enjoying them—a strange certainty of promises, which, to prevent their ever being fulfilled, are made to depend on an impossibility. Of promises of this description, which have a condition annexed to them, we shall elsewhere speak, and make it plain that there is nothing absurd in the impossible fulfillment of them. In regard to the matter in hand, I deny that God cruelly mocks us when he invites us to merit blessings which he knows we are altogether unable to merit. The promises being offered alike to believers and to the ungodly have their use in regard to both. As God by his precepts stings the consciences of the ungodly, so as to prevent them from enjoying their sins while they have no remembrance of his judgments, so in his promises he in a manner takes them to witness how unworthy they are of his kindness. Who can deny that it is most just and most becoming in God to do good to those who worship him, and to punish with due severity those who despise his majesty? God, therefore, proceeds in due order when, though the wicked are bound by the fetters of sin, he lays down the law in his promises that he will do them good only if they depart from their wickedness. This would be right, though His only object were to let them understand that they are deservedly excluded from the favor due to his true worshipers. On the other hand, as he desires by all means to stir up believers to supplicate his grace, it surely should not seem strange that he attempts to accomplish by promises the same thing which, as we have shown, he to their great benefit accomplishes by means of precepts. Being taught by precepts what the will of God is, we are reminded of our wretchedness in being so completely at variance with that will, and, at the same time, are stimulated to invoke the aid of the Spirit to guide us into the right path. But as our indolence is not sufficiently aroused by precepts, promises are added that they may attract us by their sweetness, and produce a feeling of love for the precept. The greater our desire of righteousness, the greater will be our earnestness to obtain the grace of God. And thus it is, that in the protestations, if we be willing, if thou shalt hearken, the Lord neither attributes to us a full power of willing and hearkening, nor yet mocks us for our impotence.

11. The third class of objections is not unlike the other two. For they produce passages in which God upbraids his people for their ingratitude, intimating that it was not his fault that they did not obtain all kinds of favor from his indulgence. Of such passages, the following are examples: "The Amalekites and the Canaanites are before you, and ye shall fall by the sword: because ye are turned away from the Lord, therefore the Lord will not be with you" (Num. 14:43). "Because ye have done all these works, saith the Lord, and I spake unto you, rising up early and speaking, but ye heard not; and I called you, but ye answered not; therefore will I do unto this house, which is called by my name, wherein ye trust, and unto the place which I gave to you and to your fathers, as I have done to Shiloh" (Jer. 7:13-14). "They obeyed not thy voice, neither walked in thy law; they have done nothing of all that thou commandedst them to do: therefore thou hast caused all this evil to come upon them" (Jer. 32:23). How, they ask, can such upbraiding be directed against those who have it in their power immediately to reply—Prosperity was dear to us: we feared adversity; that we did not, in order to obtain the one and avoid the other, obey the Lord, and listen to his voice, is owing to its not being free for us to do so in consequence of our subjection to the dominion of sin; in vain, therefore, are we upbraided with evils which it was not in our power to escape. But to say nothing of the pretext of necessity, which is but a feeble and flimsy defense of their conduct, can they, I

ask, deny their guilt? If they are held convicted of any fault, the Lord
is not unjust in upbraiding them for having, by their own perverseness, deprived themselves of the advantages of his kindness. Let them
say, then, whether they can deny that their own will is the depraved
cause of their rebellion. If they find within themselves a fountain of
wickedness, why do they stand declaiming about extraneous causes,
with the view of making it appear that they are not the authors of
their own destruction? If it be true that it is not for another's faults
that sinners are both deprived of the divine favor, and visited with
punishment, there is good reason why they should hear these rebukes
from the mouth of God. If they obstinately persist in their vices, let
them learn in their calamities to accuse and detest their own wickedness, instead of charging God with cruelty and injustice. If they have
not manifested docility, let them, under a feeling of disgust at the
sins which they see to be the cause of their misery and ruin, return
to the right path, and, with serious contrition, confess the very thing
of which the Lord by his rebuke reminds them. Of what use those
upbraidings of the prophets above quoted are to believers, appears
from the solemn prayer of Daniel, as given in his ninth chapter. Of
their use in regard to the ungodly, we see an example in the Jews, to
whom Jeremiah was ordered to explain the cause of their miseries,
though the event could not be otherwise than the Lord had foretold.
"Therefore thou shalt speak these words unto them; but they will not
hearken unto thee: thou shalt also call unto them; but they will not
answer thee" (Jer. 7:27). Of what use, then, was it to talk to the deaf?
It was that even against their will they might understand that what
they heard was true, and that it was impious blasphemy to transfer
the blame of their wickedness to God, when it resided in themselves.

These few explanations will make it very easy for the reader to
disentangle himself from the immense heap of passages (containing
both precepts and reprimands) which the enemies of divine grace are
in the habit of piling up, that they may thereon erect their statue of

free will. The Psalmist upbraids the Jews as "a stubborn and rebellious generation; a generation that set not their heart aright" (Psalm 78:8); and in another passage, he exhorts the men of his time, "Harden not your heart" (Psalm 95:8). This implies that the whole blame of the rebellion lies in human depravity. But it is foolish thence to infer that the heart, the preparation of which is from the Lord, may be equally bent in either direction. The Psalmist says, "I have inclined my heart to perform thy statutes alway" (Psalm 119:112); meaning, that with willing and cheerful readiness of mind he had devoted himself to God. He does not boast, however, that he was the author of that disposition, for in the same psalm he acknowledges it to be the gift of God. We must, therefore, attend to the admonition of Paul, when he thus addresses believers, "Work out your own salvation with fear and trembling. For it is God which worketh in you both to will and to do of his good pleasure" (Phil. 2:12-13). He ascribes to them a part in acting that they may not indulge in carnal sloth, but by enjoining fear and trembling, he humbles them so as to keep them in remembrance, that the very thing which they are ordered to do is the proper work of God—distinctly intimating that believers act (if I may so speak) passively in as much as the power is given them from heaven, and cannot in any way be arrogated to themselves. Accordingly, when Peter exhorts us to "add to faith virtue" (2 Pet. 1:5), he does not concede to us the possession of a second place, as if we could do anything separately. He only arouses the sluggishness of our flesh, by which faith itself is frequently stifled. To the same effect are the words of Paul. He says, "Quench not the Spirit" (1 Thess. 5:19); because a spirit of sloth, if not guarded against, is ever and anon creeping in upon believers. But should any thence infer that it is entirely in their own power to foster the offered light, his ignorance will easily be refuted by the fact, that the very diligence which Paul enjoins is derived only from God (2 Cor. 7:1). We are often commanded to purge ourselves of all impurity, though the Spirit claims this as his peculiar office. In fine, that what properly belongs to God is transferred to us only by way of concession, is plain from the words of John, "He that is begotten of God keepeth himself" (1 John 5:18). The advocates of free will fasten upon the expression as if it implied, that we are kept partly by the power of God, partly by our own, whereas the very keeping of which the Apostle speaks is itself from heaven. Hence, Christ prays his Father to keep us from evil (John 17:15), and we know that believers, in their warfare against Satan, owe their victory to the armor of God. Accordingly, Peter, after saying, "Ye have purified your souls in obeying the truth," immediately adds by way of correction, "through the Spirit" (1 Pet. 1:22). In fine, the nothingness of human strength in the spiritual contest is briefly shown by John, when he says, that "Whosoever is born of God does not commit sin; for his seed remaineth in him" (1 John 3:9). He elsewhere gives the reasons "This is the victory that overcometh the world, even our faith" (1 John 5:4).

12. But a passage is produced from the Law of Moses, which seems very adverse to the view now given. After promulgating the Law, he takes the people to witness in these terms: "This commandment which I command thee this day, it is not hidden from thee, neither is it far off. It is not in heaven, that thou shouldst say, who shall go up for us to heaven, and bring it unto us, that we may hear it, and do it? But the word is very nigh unto thee, in thy mouth, and in thy heart, that thou mayest do it" (Deut. 30:11-12, 14). Certainly, if this is to be understood of mere precepts, I admit that it is of no little importance to the matter in hand. For, though it were easy to evade the difficulty by saying that the thing here treated of is not the observance of the law, but the facility and readiness of becoming acquainted with it, some scruple, perhaps, would still remain. The Apostle Paul, however, no mean interpreter, removes all doubt when he affirms that Moses here spoke of the doctrine of the Gospel (Rom. 10:8). If any one is so refractory as to contend that Paul violently wrested the words in applying them to the Gospel, though his hardihood is chargeable with impiety, we are

still able, independently of the authority of the Apostle, to repel the objection. For, if Moses spoke of precepts merely, he was only inflating the people with vain confidence. Had they attempted the observance of the law in their own strength, as a matter in which they should find no difficulty, what else could have been the result than to throw them headlong? Where, then, was that easy means of observing the law, when the only access to it was over a fatal precipice? Accordingly, nothing is more certain than that under these words is comprehended the covenant of mercy, which had been promulgated along with the demands of the law. A few verses before, he had said, "The Lord thy God will circumcise thine heart, and the heart of thy seed, to love the Lord thy God with all thine heart, and with all thy soul, that thou mayest live" (Deut. 30:6). Therefore, the readiness of which he imme-diately after speaks was placed not in the power of man, but in the pro-tection and help of the Holy Spirit, who mightily performs his own work in our weakness. The passage, however, is not to be understood of precepts simply, but rather of the Gospel promises, which, so far from proving any power in us to fulfill righteousness, utterly disprove it. This is confirmed by the testimony of Paul, when he observes that the Gospel holds forth salvation to us, not under the harsh, arduous, and impossible terms on which the law treats with us (namely, that those shall obtain it who fulfill all its demands), but on terms easy, expedi-tious, and readily obtained. This passage, therefore, tends in no degree to establish the freedom of the human will.

13. They are wont also to adduce certain passages in which God is said occasionally to try men by withdrawing the assistance of his grace, and to wait until they turn to him, as in Hosea, "I will go and return to my place, till they acknowledge their offense, and seek my face" (Hosea 5:15). It were absurd (say they) that the Lord should wait till Israel should seek his face, if their minds were not flexible, so as to turn in either direction of their own accord. As if anything were more common in the prophetical writings than for God to put

on the semblance of rejecting and casting off his people until they reform their lives. But what can our opponents extract from such threats? If they mean to maintain that a people, when abandoned by God, are able of themselves to think of turning unto him, they will do it in the very face of Scripture. On the other hand, if they admit that divine grace is necessary to conversion, why do they dispute with us? But while they admit that grace is so far necessary, they insist on reserving some ability for man. How do they prove it? Certainly not from this nor any similar passage; for it is one thing to withdraw from man, and look to what he will do when thus abandoned and left to himself, and another thing to assist his powers (whatever they may be), in proportion to their weakness. What, then, it will be asked, is meant by such expressions? I answer, just the same as if God were to say, since nothing is gained by admonishing, exhorting, rebuking this stubborn people, I will withdraw for a little, and silently leave them to be afflicted; I shall see whether, after long calamity, any remembrance of me will return, and induce them to seek my face. But by the departure of the Lord to a distance is meant the withdrawal of prophecy. By his waiting to see what men will do is meant that he, while silent, and in a manner hiding himself, tries them for a season with various afflictions. Both he does that he may humble us the more; for we shall sooner be broken than corrected by the strokes of adversity, unless his Spirit train us to docility. Moreover, when the Lord, offended and, as it were, fatigued with our obstinate perverseness, leaves us for a while (by withdrawing his word, in which he is wont in some degree to manifest his presence), and makes trial of what we will do in his absence, from this it is erroneously inferred that there is some power of free will, the extent of which is to be considered and tried, whereas the only end which he has in view is to bring us to an acknowledgment of our utter nothingness.

14. Another objection is founded on a mode of speaking which is constantly observed both in Scripture and in common discourse.

Good works are said to be ours, and we are said to do what is holy and acceptable to God, just as we are said to commit sin. But if sins are justly imputed to us, as proceeding from ourselves, for the same reason (say they) some share must certainly be attributed to us in works of righteousness. It could not be accordant with reason to say that we do those things which we are incapable of doing of our own motion, God moving us, as if we were stones. These expressions, therefore, it is said, indicate that while, in the matter of grace, we give the first place to God, a secondary place must be assigned to our agency. If the only thing here insisted on were that good works are termed ours, I, in my turn, would reply that the bread which we ask God to give us is also termed ours. What, then, can be inferred from the title of possession, but simply that by the kindness and free gift of Gods that becomes ours which in other respects is by no means due to us? Therefore let them either ridicule the same absurdity in the Lord's Prayer, or let them cease to regard it as absurd that good works should be called ours, though our only property in them is derived from the liberality of God. But there is something stronger in the fact, that we are often said in Scripture to worship God, do justice, obey the law, and follow good works. These being proper offices of the mind and will, how can they be consistently referred to the Spirit, and, at the same time, attributed to us, unless there be some concurrence on our part with the divine agency? This difficulty will be easily disposed of if we attend to the manner in which the Holy Spirit acts in the righteous. The similitude with which they invidiously assail us is foreign to the purpose; for who is so absurd as to imagine that movement in man differs in nothing from the impulse given to a stone? Nor can anything of the kind be inferred from our doctrine. To the natural powers of man we ascribe approving and rejecting, willing and not willing, striving and resisting—viz. approving vanity, rejecting solid good, willing evil and not willing good, striving for wickedness and resisting righteousness. What then does the Lord do? If he sees meet to employ depravity of this description as an instrument of his anger, he gives it whatever aim and direction he pleases, that by a guilty hand he may accomplish his own good work. A wicked man thus serving the power of God, while he is bent only on following his own lust, can we compare to a stone, which, driven by an external impulse, is borne along without motion, or sense, or will of its own? We see how wide the difference is. But how stands the case with the godly, as to whom chiefly the question is raised? When God erects his kingdom in them, he, by means of his Spirit, curbs their will, that it may not follow its natural bent and be carried hither and thither by vagrant lusts; bends, frames, trains, and guides it according to the rule of his justice, so as to incline it to righteousness and holiness, and establishes and strengthens it by the energy of his Spirit, that it may not stumble or fall. For which reason Augustine thus expresses himself (*De Corrept. et Gratia*, cap. 2), "It will be said we are therefore acted upon, and do not act. Nay, you act and are acted upon, and you then act well when you are acted upon by one that is good. The Spirit of God who actuates you is your helper in acting, and bears the name of helper, because you, too, do something." In the former member of this sentence, he reminds us that the agency of man is not destroyed by the motion of the Holy Spirit, because nature furnishes the will which is guided so as to aspire to good. As to the second member of the sentence, in which he says that the very idea of help implies that we also do something, we must not understand it as if he were attributing to us some independent power of action; but not to foster a feeling of sloth, he reconciles the agency of God with our own agency, by saying that to wish is from nature, to wish well is from grace. Accordingly, he had said a little before, "Did not God assist us, we should not only not be able to conquer, but not able even to fight."

15. Hence it appears that the grace of God (as this name is used when regeneration is spoken of) is the rule of the Spirit, in directing and governing the human will. Govern he cannot, without correcting,

reforming, renovating (hence we say that the beginning of regeneration consists in the abolition of what is ours); in like manner, he cannot govern without moving, impelling, urging, and restraining. Accordingly, all the actions which are afterwards done are truly said to be wholly his. Meanwhile, we deny not the truth of Augustine's doctrine that the will is not destroyed, but rather repaired, by grace—the two things being perfectly consistent—viz. that the human will may be said to be renewed when its vitiosity and perverseness being corrected, it is conformed to the true standard of righteousness and that, at the same time, the will may be said to be made new, being so vitiated and corrupted that its nature must be entirely changed. There is nothing then to prevent us from saying that our will does what the Spirit does in us, although the will contributes nothing of itself apart from grace. We must, therefore, remember what we quoted from Augustine, that some men labor in vain to find in the human will some good quality properly belonging to it. Any intermixture which men attempt to make by conjoining the effort of their own will with divine grace is corruption, just as when unwholesome and muddy water is used to dilute wine. But though every thing good in the will is entirely derived from the influence of the Spirit, yet, because we have naturally an innate power of willing, we are not improperly said to do the things of which God claims for himself all the praise; first, because every thing which his kindness produces in us is our own (only we must understand that it is not of ourselves); and, secondly, because it is our mind, our will, our study which are guided by him to what is good.

16. The other passages which they gather together from different quarters will not give much trouble to any person of tolerable understanding, who pays due attention to the explanations already given. They adduce the passage of Genesis, "Unto thee shall be his desire, and thou shalt rule over him" (Gen. 4:7). This they interpret of sin, as if the Lord were promising Cain that the dominion of sin should not

prevail over his mind, if he would labor in subduing it. We, however, maintain that it is much more agreeable to the context to understand the words as referring to Abel, it being there the purpose of God to point out the injustice of the envy which Cain had conceived against his brother. And this He does in two ways, by showing, first, that it was vain to think he could, by means of wickedness, surpass his brother in the favor of God, by whom nothing is esteemed but righteousness; and, secondly, how ungrateful he was for the kindness he had already received, in not being able to bear with a brother who had been subjected to his authority. But lest it should be thought that we embrace this interpretation because the other is contrary to our view, let us grant that God does here speak of sin. If so, his words contain either an order or a promise. If an order, we have already demonstrated that this is no proof of man's ability; if a promise, where is the fulfillment of the promise when Cain yielded to the sin over which he ought to have prevailed? They will allege a tacit condition in the promise, as if it were said that he would gain the victory if he contended. This subterfuge is altogether unavailing. For, if the dominion spoken of refers to sin, no man can have any doubt that the form of expression is imperative, declaring not what we are able, but what it is our duty to do, even if beyond our ability. Although both the nature of the case, and the rule of grammatical construction, require that it be regarded as a comparison between Cain and Abel, we think the only preference given to the younger brother was, that the elder made himself inferior by his own wickedness.

17. They appeal, moreover, to the testimony of the Apostle Paul, because he says, "It is not of him that willeth, nor of him that runneth, but of God that showeth mercy" (Rom. 9:15). From this they infer, that there is something in will and endeavor, which, though weak in themselves, still, being mercifully aided by God, are not without some measure of success. But if they would attend in sober earnest to the subject there handled by Paul, they would not so rashly pervert his

meaning. I am aware they can quote Origin and Jerome in support of this exposition. To these I might, in my turn, oppose Augustine. But it is of no consequence what they thought, if it is clear what Paul meant. He teaches that salvation is prepared for those only on whom the Lord is pleased to bestow his mercy—that ruin and death await all whom he has not chosen. He had proved the condition of the reprobate by the example of Pharaoh, and confirmed the certainty of gratuitous election by the passage in Moses, "I will have mercy on whom I will have mercy." Thereafter he concludes that it is not of him that wills, nor of him that runs, but of God that shows mercy. If these words are understood to mean that the will or endeavor are not sufficient, because unequal to such a task, the Apostle has not used them very appropriately. We must therefore abandon this absurd mode of arguing, "It is not of him that wills nor of him that runs;" therefore, there is some will, some running. Paul's meaning is more simple—there is no will nor running by which we can prepare the way for our salvation—it is wholly of the divine mercy. He indeed says nothing more than he says to Titus, when he writes, "After that the kindness and love of God our Savior toward man appeared, not by works of righteousness which we have done, but according to his mercy he saved us" (Titus 3:4-5). Those who argue that Paul insinuated there was some will and some running when he said, "It is not of him that willeth, nor of him that runneth," would not allow me to argue after the same fashion, that we have done some righteous works, because Paul says that we have attained the divine favor, "not by works of righteousness which we have done." But if they see a flaw in this mode of arguing, let them open their eyes, and they will see that their own mode is not free from a similar fallacy. The argument which Augustine uses is well founded, "If it is said, It is not of him that willeth, nor of him that runneth,' because neither will nor running are sufficient; it may, on the other hand, be retorted, it is not of God that showeth mercy,' because mercy does not act alone" (August. Ep. 170, *ad Vital.* See also *Enchirid. ad Laurent.* cap. 32). This second proposition being absurd, Augustine justly concludes the meaning of the words to be, that there is no good will in man until it is prepared by the Lord; not that we ought not to will and run, but that both are produced in us by God. Some, with equal unskillfulness, wrest the saying of Paul, "We are laborers together with God" (1 Cor. 3:9). There cannot be a doubt that these words apply to ministers only, who are called "laborers with God," not from bringing any thing of their own, but because God makes use of their instrumentality after he has rendered them fit, and provided them with the necessary endowments.

18. They appeal also to Ecclesiasticus, who is well known to be a writer of doubtful authority. But, though we might justly decline his testimony, let us see what he says in support of free will. His words are, "He himself made man from the beginning, and left him in the hand of his counsel; If thou will to keep the commandments and perform acceptable faithfulness. He has set fire and water before thee: stretch forth thy hand unto whether thou wilt. Before man is life and death; and whether him liketh shall be given him" (Ecclesiasticus 15:14-17). Grant that man received at his creation a power of acquiring life or death; what, then, if we, on the other hand, can reply that he has lost it? Assuredly I have no intention to contradict Solomon, who asserts that "God has made man upright;" that "they have sought out many inventions" (Eccl. 7:29). But since man, by degenerating, has made shipwreck of himself and all his blessings, it certainly does not follow that every thing attributed to his nature, as originally constituted, applies to it now when vitiated and degenerate. Therefore, not only to my opponents, but to the author of Ecclesiasticus himself (whoever he may have been), this is my answer: if you mean to tell man that in himself there is a power of acquiring salvation, your authority with us is not so great as, in the least degree, to prejudice the undoubted word of God; but if only wishing to curb the malignity of the fleshly which by transferring the blame of its own wickedness to God, is wont to catch at a vain defense, you say that rectitude was given to man, in

order to make it apparent he was the cause of his own destruction, I willingly assent. Only agree with me in this, that it is by his own fault he is stripped of the ornaments in which the Lord at first attired him, and then let us unite in acknowledging that what he now wants is a physician, and not a defender.

19. There is nothing more frequent in their mouths than the parable of the traveler who fell among thieves, and was left half dead (Luke 10:32). I am aware that it is a common idea with almost all writers that under the figure of the traveler is represented the calamity of the human race. Hence our opponents argue that man was not so mutilated by the robbery of sin and the devil as not to preserve some remains of his former endowments; because it is said he was left half dead. For where is the half living, unless some portion of right will and reason remain? First, were I to deny that there is any room for their allegory, what could they say? There can be no doubt that the Fathers invented it contrary to the genuine sense of the parable. Allegories ought to be carried no further than Scripture expressly sanctions: so far are they from forming a sufficient basis to found doctrines upon. And were I so disposed I might easily find the means of tearing up this fiction by the roots. The Word of God leaves no half life to man, but teaches, that, in regard to life and happiness, he has utterly perished. Paul, when he speaks of our redemption, says not that the half dead are cured (Eph. 2:5-6; 5:14) but that those who were dead are raised up. He does not call upon the half dead to receive the illumination of Christ, but upon those who are asleep and buried. In the same way our Lord himself says, "The hour is coming, and now is, when the dead shall hear the voice of the Son of God" (John 5:25). How can they presume to set up a flimsy allegory in opposition to so many clear statements? But be it that this allegory is good evidence, what can they extort out of it? Man is half dead, therefore there is some soundness in him. True! He has a mind capable of understanding, though incapable of attaining to heavenly and spiritual wisdom;

he has some discernment of what is honorable; he has some sense of the Divinity, though he cannot reach the true knowledge of God. But to what do these amount? They certainly do not refute the doctrine of Augustine—a doctrine confirmed by the common suffrages even of the Schoolmen, that after the fall, the free gifts on which salvation depends were withdrawn, and natural gifts corrupted and defiled (supra, chap. 2 sec. 2). Let it stand, therefore, as an indubitable truth, which no engines can shake, that the mind of man is so entirely alienated from the righteousness of God that he cannot conceive, desire, or design any thing but what is wicked, distorted, foul, impure, and iniquitous; that his heart is so thoroughly envenomed by sin that it can breathe out nothing but corruption and rottenness; that if some men occasionally make a show of goodness, their mind is ever interwoven with hypocrisy and deceit, their soul inwardly bound with the fetters of wickedness.

Study Guide Questions

Section 1
1. What is the first objection to Calvin's teaching on free will?
2. How do his opponents support this objection?
3. How does Calvin answer?

Section 2
1. What is the second objection to Calvin's teaching on free will?
2. How does Calvin answer?

Section 3
1. What is the third objection to Calvin's teaching on free will?
2. How does Calvin answer?

Section 4
1. What is the fourth objection to Calvin's teaching on free will?

2. How does Calvin answer?

Section 5
1. If an impious man scoffs at exhortations from God, what can he not do?
2. What rests entirely upon God's grace?
3. In what two ways does God work upon His elect?

Section 6
1. What is the central objection to Calvin's views of free will?
2. Do his opponents have no Scripture at all?
3. How does Calvin state this objection?

Section 7
1. If the law does not show what we ought to do and are able to do, what does it show?

Section 8
1. How has Calvin broken up this particular objection?
2. What does he then do with these categories?

Section 9
1. How is the work of conversion divided between God and man?
2. When God gives His law, what can we say about the grace of the Lawgiver?

Section 10
1. To whom are the promises offered?
2. What effect do the promises have on the impious?
3. What effect do the promises have on the believers?

Section 11

1. Why can unbelievers not find fault with God for His reproof of them?

Section 12

1. How does Calvin interpret Deuteronomy 30:11–12, 14?

2. And what interpretation is that?

Section 13

1. What is the next objection that Calvin deals with?

2. How does Calvin answer this?

Section 14

1. What objection is addressed in this section?

2. How does Calvin answer?

Section 15

1. In what sense are our good works ours, and in what sense God's?

Section 16

1. What is the next objection?

2. What is Calvin's view of this passage?

Section 17

1. What argument for free will is drawn from Romans 9:16?

2. What word does Calvin use in dismissing this argument?

Section 18

1. Does Calvin reject the author of Ecclesiasticus?

2. How does he handle this appeal?

3. What does man need instead of an advocate?

Section 19

1. How does Calvin handle the allegorical argument from the fact that the man beat up on the Jericho road was "half dead"?

2. What ought allegories not to be allowed to do, according to Calvin?

3. And how does Calvin handle the assertion that mankind has a "half life"?

CHAPTER 6

Redemption for man lost to be sought in Christ.

The parts of this chapter are:

I. The excellence of the doctrine of Christ the Redeemer—a doctrine always entertained by the Church, sec. 1.

II. Christ, the Mediator in both dispensations, was offered to the faith of the pious Israelites and people of old, as is plain from the institution of sacrifice, the calling of Abraham's family, and the elevation of David and his posterity, sec. 2.

III. Hence the consolation, strength, hope, and confidence of the godly under the Law, Christ being offered to them in various ways by their heavenly Father.

Outline:

1. The knowledge of God the Creator of no avail without faith in Christ the Redeemer. First reason. Second reason strengthened by the testimony of an Apostle. Conclusion. This doctrine entertained by the children of God in all ages from the beginning of the world. Error of throwing open heaven to the heathen, who know nothing of Christ. The pretexts for this refuted by passages of Scripture.

2. God never was propitious to the ancient Israelites without Christ the Mediator. First reason founded on the institution of sacrifice. Second reason founded on the calling of Abraham. Third reason founded on the elevation of David's family to regal dignity, and confirmed by striking passages of Scripture.

3. Christ the solace ever promised to the afflicted; the banner of faith and hope always erected. This confirmed by various passages of Scripture.

4. The Jews taught to have respect to Christ. This teaching sanctioned by our Savior himself. The common saying that God is the object of faith, requires to be explained and modified. Conclusion of this discussion concerning Christ. No saving knowledge of God in the heathen.

The whole human race having been undone in the person of Adam, the excellence and dignity of our origin, as already described, is so far from availing us, that it rather turns to our greater disgrace, until God, who does not acknowledge man when defiled and corrupted by sin as his own work, appear as a Redeemer in the person of his only begotten Son. Since our fall from life unto death, all that knowledge of God the Creator, of which we have discoursed, would be useless, were it not followed up by faith, holding forth God to us as a Father in Christ. The natural course undoubtedly was that the fabric of the world should be a school in which we might learn piety, and from it pass to eternal life and perfect felicity. But after looking at the perfection beheld wherever we turn our eye, above and below, we are met by the Divine malediction, which, while it involves innocent creatures in our fault, of necessity fills our own souls with despair. For although God is still pleased in many ways to manifest his paternal favor towards us, we cannot from a mere survey of the world infer that he is a Father. Conscience urging us within, and showing that sin is a just ground for our being forsaken, will not allow us to think that God accounts or treats us as sons. In addition to this are our sloth and ingratitude. Our minds are so blinded that they cannot perceive the truth, and all our senses are so corrupt that we wickedly rob God of his glory. Wherefore, we must conclude with Paul, "After that in the wisdom of God the world by wisdom knew not God, it pleased God by the foolishness of preaching to save them that believe" (1 Cor. 1:21). By the "wisdom of God," he designates this magnificent theatre of heaven and earth replenished with numberless wonders, the wise contemplation of which should have enabled us to know God. But this we do with little profit; and, therefore, he invites us to faith in Christ—faith which, by a semblance of foolishness, disgusts the unbeliever. Therefore, although the preaching of the cross is not in accordance with human wisdom, we must, however, humbly embrace it if we would return to God our Maker, from whom we are estranged, that he may again become our Father. It is certain that after the fall of our first parent, no knowledge of God without a Mediator was effectual to salvation. Christ speaks not of his own age merely, but embraces all ages, when he says "This is life eternal that they might know thee the only true God, and Jesus Christ, whom thou hast sent" (John 17:3). The more shameful therefore is the presumption of those who throw heaven open to the unbelieving and profane, in the absence of that grace which Scripture uniformly describes as the only door by which we enter into life. Should any confine our Savior's words to the period subsequent to the promulgation of the Gospel, the refutation is at hand; since on a ground common to all ages and nations, it is declared that those who are estranged from God, and as such are under the curse, the children of wrath, cannot be pleasing to God until they are reconciled. To this we may add the answer which our Savior gave to the Samaritan woman, "Ye worship ye know not what; we know what we worship: for salvation is of the Jews" (John 4:22). By these words, he both charges every Gentile religion with falsehood, and assigns the reason—viz. that under the Law the Redeemer was promised to the chosen people only, and that, consequently, no worship was ever pleasing to God in which respect was not had to Christ. Hence also Paul affirms that all the Gentiles were "without God," and deprived of the hope of life. Now, since John teaches that there was life in Christ from the beginning, and that the whole world had lost it (John 1:4), it is necessary to return to that fountain; and, accordingly, Christ declares that inasmuch as he is a propitiator, he is life. And, indeed, the inheritance of heaven belongs to none but the sons of God (John 15:6). Now, it were most incongruous to give the place and rank of sons to any who have not been engrafted into the body of the only begotten Son. And John distinctly testifies that those become the sons of God who believe in his name. But as it is not my intention at present formally to discuss the subject of faith in Christ, it is enough to have thus touched on it in passing.

2. Hence it is that God never showed himself propitious to his ancient people, nor gave them any hope of grace without a Mediator. I say nothing of the sacrifices of the Law, by which believers were plainly and openly taught that salvation was not to be found anywhere but in the expiation which Christ alone completed. All I maintain is that the prosperous and happy state of the Church was always founded in the person of Christ. For although God embraced the whole posterity of Abraham in his covenant, yet Paul properly argues (Gal. 3:16) that Christ was truly the seed in which all the nations of the earth were to be blessed, since we know that all who were born of Abraham, according to the flesh, were not accounted the seed. To omit Ishmael and others, how came it that of the two sons of Isaac, the twin brothers, Esau and Jacob, while yet in the womb, the one was chosen and the other rejected? Nay, how came it that the first-born was rejected, and the younger alone admitted? Moreover, how happens it that the majority are rejected? It is plain, therefore, that the seed of Abraham is considered chiefly in one head, and that the promised salvation is not attained without coming to Christ, whose office it is to gather

together those which were scattered abroad. Thus the primary adoption of the chosen people depended on the grace of the Mediator. Although it is not expressed in very distinct terms in Moses, it, however, appears to have been commonly known to all the godly. For before a king was appointed over the Israelites, Hannah, the mother of Samuel, describing the happiness of the righteous, speaks thus in her song, "He shall give strength unto his king, and exalt the horn of his anointed;" meaning by these words, that God would bless his Church. To this corresponds the prediction, which is afterwards added, "I will raise me up a faithful priest, and he shall walk before mine anointed for ever" (1 Sam. 2:10, 35). And there can be no doubt that our heavenly Father intended that a living image of Christ should be seen in David and his posterity. Accordingly, exhorting the righteous to fear Him, he bids them "Kiss the Son" (Psalm 2:12). Corresponding to this is the passage in the Gospel, "He that honoreth not the Son, honoreth not the Father" (John 5:23). Therefore, though the kingdom was broken up by the revolt of the ten tribes, yet the covenant which God had made in David and his successors behaved to stand, as is also declared by his Prophets, "Howbeit I will not take the whole kingdom out of his hand: but I will make him prince all the days of his life for David my servant's sake" (1 Kings 11:34). The same thing is repeated a second and third time. It is also expressly said, "I will for this afflict the seed of David, but not for ever" (1 Kings 11:39). Some time afterwards it was said, "Nevertheless, for David's sake did the Lord his God give him a lamp in Jerusalem, to set up his son after him, and to establish Jerusalem" (1 Kings 15:4). And when matters were bordering on destruction, it was again said, "Yet the Lord would not destroy Judah for David his servant's sake, as he had promised to give him alway a light, and to his children" (2 Kings 8:19).

The sum of the whole comes to this—David, all others being excluded, was chosen to be the person in whom the good pleasure of the Lord should dwell; as it is said elsewhere, "He forsook the tabernacle of Shiloh;" "Moreover, he refused the tabernacle of Joseph, and chose not the tribe of Ephraim;" "But chose the tribe of Judah, the mount Zion which he loved;" "He chose David also his servant, and took him from the sheep folds: from following the ewes great with young he brought him to feed Jacob his people, and Israel his inheritance" (Ps. 78:60, 67, 70-71). In fine, God, in thus preserving his Church, intended that its security and salvation should depend on Christ as its head. Accordingly, David exclaims, "The Lord is their strength, and he is the saving strength of his anointed;" and then prays "Save thy people, and bless thine inheritance;" intimating, that the safety of the Church was indissolubly connected with the government of Christ. In the same sense he elsewhere says, "Save, Lord: let the king hear us when we call" (Ps. 20:9). These words plainly teach that believers, in applying for the help of God, had their sole confidence in this— that they were under the unseen government of the King. This may be inferred from another psalm, "Save now, I beseech thee O Lord: Blessed be he that cometh in the name of the Lord" (Ps. 118:25-26). Here it is obvious that believers are invited to Christ, in the assurance that they will be safe when entirely in his hand. To the same effect is another prayer in which the whole Church implores the divine mercy "Let thy hand be upon the Man of thy right hand, upon the Son of man, whom thou madest strong (or best fitted) for thyself" (Ps. 80:17). For though the author of the psalm laments the dispersion of the whole nations he prays for its revival in him who is sole Head. After the people were led away into captivity, the land laid waste, and matters to appearance desperate, Jeremiah, lamenting the calamity of the Church, especially complains that by the destruction of the king-dom the hope of believers was cut off; "The breath of our nostrils, the anointed of the Lord, was taken in their pits, of whom we said, under his shadow we shall live among the heathen" (Lam. 4:20). From all this it is abundantly plain that as the Lord cannot be propitious to the human race without a Mediator, Christ was always held forth to the holy Fathers under the Law as the object of their faith.

3. Moreover when comfort is promised in affliction, especially when the deliverance of the Church is described, the banner of faith and hope in Christ is unfurled. "Thou wentest forth for the salvation of thy people, even for salvation with thine anointed," says Habakkuk (3:13). And whenever mention is made in the Prophets of the renovation of the Church, the people are directed to the promise made to David, that his kingdom would be for ever. And there is nothing strange in this, since otherwise there would have been no stability in the covenant. To this purpose is the remarkable prophecy in Isaiah 7:14. After seeing that the unbelieving king Ahab repudiated what he had testified regarding the deliverance of Jerusalem from siege and its immediate safety, he passes as it were abruptly to the Messiah, "Behold, a virgin shall conceive and bear a son, and shall call his name Emmanuel;" intimating indirectly that though the king and his people wickedly rejected the promise offered to them, as if they were bent on causing the faith of God to fail, the covenant would not be defeated—the Redeemer would come in his own time. In fine, all the prophets, to show that God was placable, were always careful to bring forward that kingdom of David on which redemption and eternal salvation depended. Thus in Isaiah it is said, "I will make an everlasting covenant with you, even the sure mercies of David. Behold, I have given him for a witness to the people" (Isa. 55:3-4); intimating, that believers, in calamitous circumstances, could have no hope, had they not this testimony that God would be ready to hear them. In the same way, to revive their drooping spirits, Jeremiah says, "Behold, the days come, saith the Lord, that I will raise unto David a righteous Branch, and a King shall reign and prosper, and shall execute judgment and justice in the earth. In his days Judah shall be saved, and Israel shall dwell safely" (Jer. 23:5-6). In Ezekiel also it is said, "I will set up one Shepherd over them, and he shall feed them, even my servant David;

he shall feed them, and he shall be their shepherd. And I the Lord will be their God, and my servant David a prince among them: I the Lord have spoken it. And I will make with them a covenant of peace" (Ezek. 34:23-25). And again, after discoursing of this wondrous renovation, he says, "David my servant shall be king over them: and they all shall have one shepherd." "Moreover, I will make a covenant of peace with them; it shall be an everlasting covenant with them" (Ezek. 37:24-26). I select a few passages out of many, because I merely wish to impress my readers with the fact that the hope of believers was ever treasured up in Christ alone. All the other prophets concur in this. Thus Hosea, "Then shall the children of Judah and the children of Israel be gathered together, and appoint themselves one head" (Hosea 1:11). This he afterwards explains in clearer terms, "Afterward shall the children of Israel return, and seek the Lord their God, and David their king" (Hosea 3:5). Micah, also speaking of the return of the people, says expressly, "Their king shall pass before them, and the Lord on the head of them" (Micah 2:13). So Amos, in predicting the renovation of the people, says "In that day will I raise up the tabernacle of David that is fallen, and close up the breaches thereof; and I will raise up the ruins, and I will build it as in the days of old" (Amos 9:11); in other words, the only banner of salvation was, the exaltation of the family of David to regal splendor, as fulfilled in Christ. Hence, too, Zechariah, as nearer in time to the manifestation of Christ, speaks more plainly, "Rejoice greatly, O daughter of Zion; shout, O daughter of Jerusalem: behold, thy King cometh unto thee: he is just, and having salvation" (Zech. 9:9). This corresponds to the passage already quoted from the Psalms, "The Lord is their strength, and he is the saving health of their anointed." Here salvation is extended from the head to the whole body.

4. By familiarizing the Jews with these prophecies, God intended to teach them that in seeking for deliverance, they should turn their eyes directly towards Christ. And though they had sadly degenerated,

they never entirely lost the knowledge of this general principle, that
God, by the hand of Christ, would be the deliverer of the Church, as
he had promised to David; and that in this way only the free covenant by which God had adopted his chosen people would be fulfilled.
Hence it was that on our Savior's entry into Jerusalem, shortly before his death, the children shouted, "Hosanna to the son of David"
(Matt. 21:9). For there seems to have been a hymn known to all, and
in general use, in which they sung that the only remaining pledge
which they had of the divine mercy was the promised advent of a
Redeemer. For this reason, Christ tells his disciples to believe in him,
in order that they might have a distinct and complete belief in God,
"Ye believe in God, believe also in me" (John 14:1). For although,
properly speaking, faith rises from Christ to the Father, he intimates,
that even when it leans on God, it gradually vanishes away, unless he
himself interpose to give it solid strength. The majesty of God is too
high to be scaled up to by mortals, who creep like worms on the earth.
Therefore, the common saying that God is the object of faith (Lac-
tantius, lib. 4 c. 16), requires to be received with some modification.
When Christ is called the image of the invisible God (Col. 1:15), the
expression is not used without cause, but is designed to remind us
that we can have no knowledge of our salvation, until we behold God
in Christ. For although the Jewish scribes had by their false glosses
darkened what the Prophets had taught concerning the Redeemer,
yet Christ assumed it to be a fact, received, as it were, with public
consent that there was no other remedy in desperate circumstances,
no other mode of delivering the Church than the manifestation of
the Mediator. It is true that the fact adverted to by Paul was not so
generally known as it ought to have been—viz. that Christ is the end
of the Law (Rom. 10:4), though this is both true, and clearly appears
both from the Law and the Prophets. I am not now, however, treating
of faith, as we shall elsewhere have a fitter place (Book 3 Chap. 2),
but what I wish to impress upon my readers in this way is that the

first step in piety is to acknowledge that God is a Father, to defend, govern, and cherish us, until he brings us to the eternal inheritance of his kingdom; that hence it is plain, as we lately observed, there is no having knowledge of God without Christ, and that, consequently, from the beginning of the world Christ was held forth to all the elect as the object of their faith and confidence. In this sense, Irenaeus says that the Father, who is boundless in himself, is bounded in the Son, because he has accommodated himself to our capacity, lest our minds should be swallowed up by the immensity of his glory (Irenaeus, lib. 4 cap. 8). Fanatics, not attending to this, distort a useful sentiment into an impious dream, as if Christ had only a share of the Godhead, as a part taken from a whole; whereas the meaning merely is, that God is comprehended in Christ alone. The saying of John was always true, "whosoever denieth the Son, the same has not the Father" (1 John 2:23). For though in old time there were many who boasted that they worshiped the Supreme Deity, the Maker of heaven and earth, yet as they had no Mediator, it was impossible for them truly to enjoy the mercy of God, so as to feel persuaded that he was their Father. Not holding the head, that is, Christ, their knowledge of God was evanescent; and hence they at length fell away to gross and foul superstitions betraying their ignorance, just as the Turks in the present day, who, though proclaiming, with full throat, that the Creator of heaven and earth is their God, yet by their rejection of Christ, substitute an idol in his place.

Study Guide Questions

Section 1

1. What illustration does Calvin use to describe heaven and earth?
2. What is our problem then?
3. What does God do for us in this situation?
4. Has any worship apart from Christ ever pleased God?

Section 2

1. Is the need for a Mediator revealed to us for the first time in the New Testament?

2. In order to be propitious toward the human race, what does God need?

Section 3

1. When is Christ prefigured in the Old Testament?

2. In the Old Testament, on what did our redemption and eternal salvation depend?

3. The hope of all the godly has always reposed where?

Section 4

1. What will happen to someone's faith in God without a Mediator?

2. Why can we not attain to God's majesty?

3. What teaching of Paul's should have been more commonly known among the Jews?

4. Are Muslims true theists because they worship one God?

CHAPTER 7

The law given, not to retain a people for itself, but to keep alive
the hope of salvation in Christ until his advent.

The divisions of this chapter are,
    I. The Moral and Ceremonial Law a schoolmaster to bring us
to Christ, sec. 1, 2.

II. This true of the Moral Law, especially its conditional promises.
These given for the best reasons. In what respect the observance of
the Moral Law is said to be impossible, sec. 3-5.

III. Of the threefold office and use of the Moral Law, sec. 6-12.
Antinomians refuted, sec. 13.

IV. What the abrogation of the Law, Moral and Ceremonial, sec.
14-17.

Outline:

The whole system of religion delivered by the hand of Moses, in
    many ways pointed to Christ. This exemplified in the case of
sacrifices, ablutions, and an endless series of ceremonies. This proved,
1. By the declared purpose of God; 2. By the nature of the ceremonies
themselves; 3. From the nature of God; 4. From the grace offered to
the Jews; 5. From the consecration of the priests.

2. Proof continued. 6. From a consideration of the kingdom erected in the family of David. 7. From the end of the ceremonies. 8. From the end of the Moral Law.

3. A more ample exposition of the last proof. The Moral Law leads believers to Christ. Showing the perfect righteousness required by God, it convinces us of our inability to fulfill it. It thus denies us life, adjudges us to death, and so urges us to seek deliverance in Christ.

4. The promises of the Law, though conditional, founded on the best reason. This reason explained.

5. No inconsistency in giving a law, the observance of which is impossible. This proved from reason, and confirmed by Scripture. Another confirmation from Augustine.

6. A consideration of the office and use of the Moral Law shows that it leads to Christ. The Law, while it describes the righteousness which is acceptable to God, proves that every man is unrighteous.

7. The Law fitly compared to a mirror, which shows us our wretchedness. This derogates not in any degree from its excellence.

8. When the Law discloses our guilt, we should not despond, but flee to the mercy of God. How this may be done.

9. Confirmation of the first use of the Moral Law from various passages in Augustine.

10. A second use of the Law is to curb sinners. This most necessary for the good of the community at large; and this in respect not only of the reprobate, but also of the elect, previous to regeneration. This confirmed by the authority of an Apostle.

11. The Law showing our wretchedness, disposes us to admit the remedy. It also tends to keep us in our duty. Confirmation from general experience.

12. The third and most appropriate use of the Law respects the elect. 1. It instructs and teaches them to make daily progress in doing the will of God. 2. Urges them by exhortation to obedience. Testimony of David. How he is to be reconciled with the Apostle.

13. The profane heresy of the Antinomians must be exploded. Argument founded on a passage in David, and another in Moses.

14. Last part of the chapter treating of the abrogation of the Law. In what respect any part of the Moral Law abrogated.

15. The curse of the Law how abrogated.

16. Of the abrogation of the Ceremonial Law in regard to the observance only.

17. The reason assigned by the Apostle applicable not to the Moral Law, but to ceremonial observances only. These abrogated, not only because they separated the Jews from the Gentiles, but still more because they were a kind of formal instruments to attest our guilt and impunity. Christ, by destroying these, is justly said to have taken away the handwriting that was against us, and nailed it to his cross.

From the whole course of the observations now made, we may infer that the Law was not superadded about four hundred years after the death of Abraham in order that it might lead the chosen people away from Christ, but, on the contrary, to keep them in suspense until his advent; to inflame their desire, and confirm their expectation, that they might not become dispirited by the long delay. By the Law, I understand not only the Ten Commandments, which contain a complete rule of life, but the whole system of religion delivered by the hand of Moses. Moses was not appointed as a Lawgiver, to do away with the blessing promised to the race of Abraham; nay, we see that he is constantly reminding the Jews of the free covenant which had been made with their fathers, and of which they were heirs; as if he had been sent for the purpose of renewing it. This is most clearly manifested by the ceremonies. For what could be more vain or frivolous than for men to reconcile themselves to God, by offering him the foul odor produced by burning the fat of beasts? Or to wipe away their own impurities by be sprinkling themselves with water or blood? In short, the whole legal worship (if considered by itself apart from the types and shadows of corresponding truth) is a mere mockery. Wherefore, both in Stephen's address (Acts 7:44), and in the Epistle to the Hebrews, great weight is justly given to the passage in which God says to Moses, "Look that thou make them after the pattern which was showed thee in the mount" (Exod. 25:40). Had there not been some spiritual end to which they were directed, the Jews, in the observance of them, would have deluded themselves as much as the Gentiles in their vanities. Profane men, who have never made religion their serious study, cannot bear without disgust to hear of such a multiplicity of rites. They not merely wonder why God fatigued his ancient people with such a mass of ceremonies, but they despise and ridicule them as childish toys. This they do, because they attend not to the end; from which, if the legal figures are separated, they cannot escape the charge of vanity. But the type shows that God did not enjoin sacrifice, in order that he might occupy his worshipers with earthly exercises, but rather that he might raise their minds to something higher. This is clear even from His own nature. Being a spirit, he is delighted only with spiritual worship. The same thing is testified by the many passages in which the Prophets accuse the Jews of stupidity, for imagining that mere sacrifices have any value in the sight of God. Did they by this mean to derogate in any respect from the Law? By no means; but as interpreters of its true meaning, they wished in this way to turn the attention of the people to the end which they ought to have had in view, but from which they generally wandered. From the grace offered to the Jews we may certainly infer that the law was not a stranger to Christ. Moses declared the end of the adoption of the Israelites to be that they should be "a kingdom of priests, and a holy nation" (Exod. 19:6). This they could not attain, without a greater and more excellent atonement than the blood of beasts. For what could be less in accordance with reason than that the sons of Adams who, from hereditary taint, are all born the slaves of sin, should be raised to royal dignity, and in this way made partakers of the glory of God, if the noble distinction were not derived from some other source? How, moreover, could the priestly office exist in vigor among those whose vices rendered them abominable in the sight of God, if they were not consecrated in a holy head? Wherefore, Peter elegantly transposes the words of Moses, teaching that the fullness of grace, of which the Jews had a foretaste under the Law, is exhibited in Christ, "Ye are a chosen generation, a royal priesthood" (1 Pet. 2:9). The transposition of the words intimates that those to whom Christ has appeared in the Gospel, have obtained more than their fathers, inasmuch as they are all endued with priestly and royal honor, and can, therefore, trusting to their Mediator, appear with boldness in the presence of God.

2. And it is to be observed, by the way, that the kingdom, which was at length erected in the family of David, is part of the Law, and is comprehended under the dispensation of Moses; whence it follows that as well in the whole tribe of Levi as in the posterity of David, Christ was exhibited to the eyes of the Israelites as in a double mirror. For, as I lately observed (sec. 1), in no other way could those who were the slaves of sin and death, and defiled with corruption, be either kings or priests. Hence appears the perfect truth of Paul's statement, "The law was our schoolmaster to bring us unto Christ," "till the seed should come to whom the promise was made" (Gal. 3:24, 19). For Christ not yet having been made familiarly known to the Jews, they were like children whose weakness could not bear a full knowledge of heavenly things. How they were led to Christ by the ceremonial law has already been adverted to, and may be made more intelligible by several passages in the Prophets. Although they were required, in order to appease God, to approach him daily with new sacrifices, yet Isaiah promises that all their sins would be expiated by one single sacrifice, and with this Daniel concurs (Isa. 53:5; Dan. 9:26-27). The priests appointed from the tribe of Levi entered the sanctuary, but it was once said of a single priest, "The Lord has sworn, and will not repent, Thou art a priest for ever, after the order of Melchizedek" (Ps.

110:4). The unction of oil was then visible, but Daniel in vision declares that there will be another unction. Not to dwell on this, the author of the Epistle to the Hebrews proves clearly, and at length, from the fourth to the eleventh chapter, that ceremonies were vain and of no value, unless as bringing us to Christ. In regard to the Ten Commandments, we must in like manner attend to the statement of Paul that "Christ is the end of the law for righteousness to every one that believeth" (Rom. 10:4); and, again, that ministers of the new testament were "not of the letter, but of the spirit: for the letter killeth, but the split giveth life" (2 Cor. 3:6). The former passage intimates, that it is in vain to teach righteousness by precept, until Christ bestow it by free imputation, and the regeneration of the Spirit. Hence he properly calls Christ the end or fulfilling of the Law, because it would avail us nothing to know what God demands did not Christ come to the succor of those who are laboring, and oppressed under an intolerable yoke and burden. In another place, he says that the Law "was added because of transgressions" (Gal. 3:19), that it might humble men under a sense of their condemnation. Moreover, inasmuch as this is the only true preparation for Christ, the statements, though made in different words, perfectly agree with each other. But because he had to dispute with perverse teachers who pretended that men merited justification by the works of the Law, he was sometimes obliged, in refuting their error, to speak of the Law in a more restricted sense, merely as law, though, in other respects, the covenant of free adoption is comprehended under it.

3. But in order that a sense of guilt may urge us to seek for pardon, it is of importance to know how our being instructed in the Moral Law renders us more inexcusable. If it is true that a perfect righteousness is set before us in the Law, it follows that the complete observance of it is perfect righteousness in the sight of God; that is, a righteousness by which a man may be deemed and pronounced righteous at the divine tribunal. Wherefore Moses, after promulgating the Law,

hesitates not to call heaven and earth to witness, that he had set life and death, good and evil, before the people. Nor can it be denied, that the reward of eternal salvation, as promised by the Lord, awaits the perfect obedience of the Law (Deut. 30:19). Again, however, it is of importance to understand in what way we perform that obedience for which we justly entertain the hope of that reward. For of what use is it to see that the reward of eternal life depends on the observance of the Law, unless it moreover appears whether it be in our power in that way to attain to eternal life? Herein, then, the weakness of the Law is manifested; for in none of us is that righteousness of the Law manifested, and therefore, being excluded from the promises of life, we again fall under the curse. I state not only what happens, but what must necessarily happen. The doctrine of the Law transcending our capacity, a man may indeed look from a distance at the promises held forth, but he cannot derive any benefit from them. The only thing, therefore, remaining for him is from their excellence to form a better estimate of his own misery, while he considers that the hope of salvation is cut off, and he is threatened with certain death. On the other hand, those fearful denunciations which strike not at a few individuals, but at every individual without exceptions rise up; rise up, I say, and, with inexorable severity, pursue us; so that nothing but instant death is presented by the Law.

4. Therefore, if we look merely to the Law, the result must be despondency, confusion, and despair, seeing that by it we are all cursed and condemned, while we are kept far away from the blessedness which it holds forth to its observers. Is the Lord, then, you will ask, only sporting with us? Is it not the next thing to mockery, to hold out the hope of happiness, to invite and exhort us to it, to declare that it is set before us, while all the while the entrance to it is precluded and quite shut up? I answer, although the promises, in so far as they are conditional, depend on a perfect obedience of the Law, which is nowhere to be found, they have not, however, been given in vain. For when we have learned that

the promises would be fruitless and unavailing, did not God accept us of his free goodness, without any view to our works, and when, having so learned, we by faith embrace the goodness thus offered in the gospel, the promises, with all their annexed conditions, are fully accomplished. For God, while bestowing all things upon us freely, crowns his goodness by not disdaining our imperfect obedience; forgiving its deficiencies, accepting it as if it were complete, and so bestowing upon us the full amount of what the Law has promised. But as this point will be more fully discussed in treating of justification by faith, we shall not follow it further at present.

5. What has been said as to the impossible observance of the Law, it will be proper briefly to explain and confirm, the general opinion being that nothing can be more absurd. Hence Jerome has not hesitated to denounce anathema against it. What Jerome thought, I care not; let us inquire what is the truth. I will not here enter into a long and intricate discussion on the various kinds of possibility. By impossible, I mean that which never was, and, being prevented by the ordination and decree of God, never will be. I say that if we go back to the remotest period, we shall not find a single saint who, clothed with a mortal body, ever attained to such perfection as to love the Lord with all his heart, and soul, and mind, and strength; and, on the other hand, not one who has not felt the power of concupiscence. Who can deny this? I am aware, indeed, of a kind of saint whom a foolish superstition imagines and whose purity the angels of heaven scarcely equal. This, however, is repugnant both to Scripture and experience. But I say further that no saint ever will attain to perfection, so long as he is in the body. Scripture bears clear testimony to this effect: "There is no man that sinneth not," saith Solomon (1 Kings 8:46). David says, "In thy sight shall no man living be justified" (Psalm 143:2). Job also, in numerous passages, affirms the same thing. But the clearest of all is Paul, who declares that "the flesh lusteth against the Spirit, and the Spirit against the flesh" (Gal. 5:17). And he proves that "as many as are of the

works of the law are under the curse," for the simple reason that it is written, "Cursed is every one that continueth not in all things which are written in the book of the law to do them" (Gal. 3:10; Deut. 27:26); intimating, or rather assuming it as confessed, that none can so continue. But whatever has been declared by Scripture must be regarded as perpetual, and hence necessary. The Pelagians annoyed Augustine with the sophism that it was insulting to God to hold that he orders more than believers are able, by his grace, to perform; and he, in order to evade it, acknowledged that the Lord was able, if he chose, to raise a mortal man to angelic purity; but that he had never done, and never would do it, because so the Scripture had declared (Augustine, *lib. de Nat. et Grat.*). This I deny not: but I add that there is no use in absurdly disputing concerning the power of God in opposition to his truth; and therefore there is no ground for caviling, when it is said that that thing cannot be, which the Scriptures declare will never be. But if it is the word that is objected to, I refer to the answer which our Savior gave to his disciples when they asked, "Who then can be saved?" "With men," said he, "this is impossible; but with God all things are possible" (Matt. 19:25). Augustine argues in the most convincing manner that, while in the flesh, we never can give God the love which we owe him. "Love so follows knowledge, that no man can perfectly love God who has not previously a full comprehension of his goodness" (Augustin. *de Spiritu et Litera*, towards the end, and elsewhere). So long as we are pilgrims in the world, we see through a glass darkly, and therefore our love is imperfect. Let it therefore be held incontrovertible, that, in consequence of the feebleness of our nature, it is impossible for us, so long as we are in the flesh, to fulfill the law. This will also be proved elsewhere from the writings of Paul (Rom. 8:3).

6. That the whole matter may be made clearer, let us take a succinct view of the office and use of the Moral Law. Now this office and use seems to me to consist of three parts. First, by exhibiting the righteousness of God—in other words, the righteousness which alone is

acceptable to God—it admonishes every one of his own unrighteous-ness, certiorates, convicts, and finally condemns him. This is necessary, in order that man, who is blind and intoxicated with self-love, may be brought at once to know and to confess his weakness and impurity. For until his vanity is made perfectly manifest, he is puffed up with infatuated confidence in his own powers, and never can be brought to feel their feebleness so long as he measures them by a standard of his own choice. So soon, however, as he begins to compare them with the requirements of the Law, he has something to tame his pre-sumption. How high soever his opinion of his own powers may be, he immediately feels that they pant under the heavy load, then totter and stumble, and finally fall and give way. He, then, who is schooled by the Law, lays aside the arrogance which formerly blinded him. In like manner must he be cured of pride, the other disease under which we have said that he labors. So long as he is permitted to appeal to his own judgment, he substitutes a hypocritical for a real righteous-ness, and, contented with this, sets up certain factitious observances in opposition to the grace of God. But after he is forced to weigh his conduct in the balance of the Law, renouncing all dependence on this fancied righteousness, he sees that he is at an infinite distance from holiness, and, on the other hand, that he teems with innumerable vices of which he formerly seemed free. The recesses in which concu-piscence lies hid are so deep and tortuous that they easily elude our view; and hence the Apostle had good reason for saying, "I had not known lust, except the law had said, 'Thou shalt not covet.'" For, if it be not brought forth from its lurking-places, it miserably destroys in secret before its fatal sting is discerned.

7. Thus the Law is a kind of mirror. As in a mirror we discover any stains upon our face, so in the Law we behold, first, our impotence; then, in consequence of it, our iniquity; and, finally, the curse, as the consequence of both. He who has no power of following righteous-ness is necessarily plunged in the mire of iniquity, and this iniquity

is immediately followed by the curse. Accordingly, the greater the transgression of which the Law convicts us, the severer the judgment to which we are exposed. To this effect is the Apostle's declaration, that "by the law is the knowledge of sin" (Rom. 3:20). By these words, he only points out the first office of the Law as experienced by sinners not yet regenerated. In conformity to this, it is said, "the law entered that the offense might abound;" and, accordingly, that it is "the ministration of death;" that it "worketh wrath" and kills (Rom. 5:20; 2 Cor. 3:7; Rom. 4:15). For there cannot be a doubt that the clearer the consciousness of guilt, the greater the increase of sin; because then to transgression a rebellious feeling against the Lawgiver is added. All that remains for the Law is to arm the wrath of God for the destruction of the sinner; for by itself it can do nothing but accuse, condemn, and destroy him. Thus Augustine says, "If the Spirit of grace be absent, the law is present only to convict and slay us." But to say this neither insults the law, nor derogates in any degree from its excellence. Assuredly, if our whole will were formed and disposed to obedience, the mere knowledge of the law would be sufficient for salvation; but since our carnal and corrupt nature is at enmity with the Divine law, and is in no degree amended by its discipline, the consequence is, that the law which, if it had been properly attended to, would have given life, becomes the occasion of sin and death. When all are convicted of transgression, the more it declares the righteousness of God, the more, on the other hand, it discloses our iniquity; the more certainly it assures us that life and salvation are treasured up as the reward of righteousness, the more certainly it assures us that the unrighteous will perish. So far, however, are these qualities from throwing disgrace on the Law that their chief tendency is to give a brighter display of the divine goodness. For they show that it is only our weakness and depravity that prevents us from enjoying the blessedness which the law openly sets before us. Hence additional sweetness is given to divine grace, which comes to our aid without the law, and additional

loveliness to the mercy which confers it, because they proclaim that
God is never weary in doing good, and in loading us with new gifts.

8. But while the unrighteousness and condemnation of all are attested by the law, it does not follow (if we make the proper use of it)
that we are immediately to give up all hope and rush headlong on
despair. No doubt, it has some such effect upon the reprobate, but
this is owing to their obstinacy. With the children of God the effect
is different. The Apostle testifies that the law pronounces its sentence
of condemnation in order "that every mouth may be stopped, and all
the world may become guilty before God" (Rom. 3:19). In another
place, however, the same Apostle declares, that "God has concluded them all in unbelief;" not that he might destroy all, or allow all
to perish, but that "he might have mercy upon all" (Rom. 11:32); in
other words, that divesting themselves of an absurd opinion of their
own virtue, they may perceive how they are wholly dependent on the
hand of God; that feeling how naked and destitute they are, they may
take refuge in his mercy, rely upon it, and cover themselves up entirely
with it; renouncing all righteousness and merit, and clinging to mercy
alone, as offered in Christ to all who long and look for it in true faith.
In the precepts of the law, God is seen as the rewarder only of perfect righteousness (a righteousness of which all are destitute), and, on
the other hand, as the stern avenger of wickedness. But in Christ his
countenance beams forth full of grace and gentleness towards poor
unworthy sinners.

9. There are many passages in Augustine, as to the utility of the law
in leading us to implore Divine assistance. Thus he writes to Hilary,
"The law orders, that we, after attempting to do what is ordered and
so feeling our weakness under the law, may learn to implore the help
of grace." In like manner, he writes to Asellius, "The utility of the
law is that it convinces man of his weakness, and compels him to
apply for the medicine of grace, which is in Christ." In like manner,
he says to Innocentius Romanus, "The law orders; grace supplies the

power of acting." Again, to Valentinus, "God enjoins what we cannot do, in order that we may know what we have to ask of him." Again, "The law was given that it might make you guilty—being made guilty might fear; fearing, might ask indulgence, not presume on your own strength." Again, "The law was given, in order to convert a great into a little man—to show that you have no power of your own for righteousness; and might thus, poor, needy, and destitute, flee to grace." He afterwards thus addresses the Almighty, "So do, O Lord, so do, O merciful Lord; command what cannot be fulfilled; nay, command what cannot be fulfilled, unless by thy own grace: so that when men feel they have no strength in themselves to fulfill it, every mouth may be stopped, and no man seem great in his own eyes. Let all be little ones; let the whole world become guilty before God." But I am forgetting myself in producing so many passages, since this holy man wrote a distinct treatise, which he entitled *De Spiritu et Litera*. The other branch of this first use he does not describe so distinctly, either because he knew that it depended on the former, or because he was not so well aware of it, or because he wanted words in which he might distinctly and clearly explain its proper meaning. But even in the reprobate themselves, this first office of the law is not altogether wanting. They do not, indeed, proceed so far with the children of God as, after the flesh is cast down, to be renewed in the inner man, and revive again, but stunned by the first terror, give way to despair. Still it tends to manifest the equity of the Divine judgment, when their consciences are thus heaved upon the waves. They would always willingly carp at the judgment of God; but now, though that judgment is not manifested, still the alarm produced by the testimony of the law and of their conscience bespeaks their deserts.

10. The second office of the Law is by means of its fearful denunciations and the consequent dread of punishment to curb those who, unless forced, have no regard for rectitude and justice. Such persons are curbed not because their mind is inwardly moved and affected,

but because, as if a bridle were laid upon them, they refrain their hands from external acts, and internally check the depravity which would otherwise petulantly burst forth. It is true, they are not on this account either better or more righteous in the sight of God. For although restrained by terror or shame, they dare not proceed to what their mind has conceived, nor give full license to their raging lust, their heart is by no means trained to fear and obedience. Nay, the more they restrain themselves, the more they are inflamed, the more they rage and boil, prepared for any act or outbreak whatsoever were it not for the terror of the law. And not only so, but they thoroughly detest the law itself, and execrate the Lawgiver; so that if they could, they would most willingly annihilate him, because they cannot bear either his ordering what is right, or his avenging the despisers of his Majesty. The feeling of all who are not yet regenerate, though in some more, in others less lively, is that, in regard to the observance of the law, they are not led by voluntary submission, but dragged by the force of fear. Nevertheless, this forced and extorted righteousness is necessary for the good of society, its peace being secured by a provision but for which all things would be thrown into tumult and confusion. Nay, this tuition is not without its use, even to the children of God, who, previous to their effectual calling, being destitute of the Spirit of holiness, freely indulge the lusts of the flesh. When, by the fear of Divine vengeance, they are deterred from open outbreakings, though from not being subdued in mind, they profit little at present, still they are in some measure trained to bear the yoke of righteousness, so that when they are called, they are not like mere novices, studying a discipline of which previously they had no knowledge. This office seems to be especially in the view of the Apostle, when he says that "the law is not made for a righteous man, but for the lawless and disobedient, for the ungodly and for sinners, for unholy and profane, for murderers of fathers and murderers of mothers, for manslayers, for whoremongers, for them that defile themselves with mankind, for men-stealers, for liars, for perjured persons, and if there be any other thing that is contrary to sound doctrine" (1 Tim. 1:9-10). He thus indicates that it is a restraint on unruly lusts that would otherwise burst all bonds.

11. To both may be applied the declaration of the Apostle in another place, that "the law was our schoolmaster to bring us unto Christ" (Gal. 3:24); since there are two classes of persons whom by its training it leads to Christ. Some (of whom we spoke in the first place) from excessive confidence in their own virtue or righteousness are unfit to receive the grace of Christ, until they are completely humbled. This the law does by making them sensible of their misery, and so disposing them to long for what they previously imagined they did not want. Others have need of a bridle to restrain them from giving full scope to their passions, and thereby utterly losing all desire after righteousness. For where the Spirit of God rules not, the lusts sometimes so burst forth as to threaten to drown the soul subjected to them in forgetfulness and contempt of God; and so they would, did not God interpose with this remedy. Those, therefore, whom he has destined to the inheritance of his kingdom, if he does not immediately regenerate, he, through the works of the law, preserves in fear, against the time of his visitation, not, indeed, that pure and chaste fear which his children ought to have, but a fear useful to the extent of instructing them in true piety according to their capacity. Of this we have so many proofs, that there is not the least need of an example. For all who have remained for some time in ignorance of God will confess, as the result of their own experience, that the law had the effect of keeping them in some degree in the fear and reverence of God, till, being regenerated by his Spirit, they began to love him from the heart.

12. The third use of the Law (being also the principal use, and more closely connected with its proper end) has respect to believers in whose hearts the Spirit of God already flourishes and reigns. For although the Law is written and engraven on their hearts by the finger of God, that

is, although they are so influenced and actuated by the Spirit that they desire to obey God, there are two ways in which they still profit in the Law. For it is the best instrument for enabling them daily to learn with greater truth and certainty what that will of the Lord is which they aspire to follow, and to confirm them in this knowledge; just as a servant who desires with all his soul to approve himself to his master must still observe and be careful to ascertain his master's dispositions, that he may comport himself in accommodation to them. Let none of us deem ourselves exempt from this necessity, for none have as yet attained to such a degree of wisdom, as that they may not, by the daily instruction of the Law, advance to a purer knowledge of the Divine will. Then, because we need not doctrine merely, but exhortation also, the servant of God will derive this further advantage from the Law: by frequently meditating upon it, he will be excited to obedience, and confirmed in it, and so drawn away from the slippery paths of sin. In this way must the saints press onward, since, however great the alacrity with which, under the Spirit, they hasten toward righteousness, they are retarded by the sluggishness of the flesh, and make less progress than they ought. The Law acts like a whip to the flesh, urging it on as men do a lazy sluggish ass. Even in the case of a spiritual man, inasmuch as he is still burdened with the weight of the flesh, the Law is a constant stimulus, pricking him forward when he would indulge in sloth. David had this use in view when he pronounced this high eulogium on the Law, "The law of the Lord is perfect, converting the soul: the testimony of the Lord is sure, making wise the simple. The statutes of the Lord are right, rejoicing the heart: the commandment of the Lord is pure, enlightening the eyes" (Ps. 19:7-8). Again, "Thy word is a lamp unto my feet, and a light unto my path" (Ps. 119:105). The whole psalm abounds in passages to the same effect. Such passages are not inconsistent with those of Paul, which show not the utility of the law to the regenerate, but what it is able of itself to bestow. The object of the Psalmist is to celebrate the advantages which the Lord, by means of his law, bestows on those whom he inwardly inspires with a love of obedience. And he adverts not to the mere precepts, but also to the promise annexed to them, which alone makes that sweet which in itself is bitter. For what is less attractive than the law when, by its demands and threatening, it overawes the soul and fills it with terror? David specially shows that in the law he saw the Mediator, without whom it gives no pleasure or delight.

13. Some unskillful persons, from not attending to this, boldly discard the whole law of Moses, and do away with both its Tables, imagining it unchristian to adhere to a doctrine which contains the ministration of death. Far from our thoughts be this profane notion. Moses has admirably shown that the Law, which can produce nothing but death in sinners, ought to have a better and more excellent effect upon the righteous. When about to die, he thus addressed the people, "Set your hearts unto all the words which I testify among you this day, which ye shall command your children to observe to do, all the words of this law. For it is not a vain thing for you; because it is your life" (Deut. 32:46-47). If it cannot be denied that it contains a perfect pattern of righteousness, then, unless we ought not to have any proper rule of life, it must be impious to discard it. There are not various rules of life, but one perpetual and inflexible rule; and, therefore, when David describes the righteous as spending their whole lives in meditating on the Law (Psalm 1:2), we must not confine to a single age, an employment which is most appropriate to all ages, even to the end of the world. Nor are we to be deterred or to shun its instructions, because the holiness which it prescribes is stricter than we are able to render, so long as we bear about the prison of the body. It does not now perform toward us the part of a hard taskmaster, who will not be satisfied without full payment; but, in the perfection to which it exhorts us, points out the goal at which, during the whole course of our lives, it is not less our interest than our duty to aim. It is well if we thus press onward. Our whole life is a race, and after we

have finished our course, the Lord will enable us to reach that goal to which, at present, we can only aspire in wish.

14. Since, in regard to believers, the law has the force of exhortation, not to bind their consciences with a curse, but by urging them, from time to time to shake off sluggishness and chastise imperfection—many, when they would express this exemption from the curse, say that in regard to believers the Law (I still mean the Moral Law) is abrogated: not that the things which it enjoins are no longer right to be observed, but only that it is not to believers what it formerly was; in other words, that it does not, by terrifying and confounding their consciences, condemn and destroy. It is certainly true that Paul shows, in clear terms, that there is such an abrogation of the Law. And that the same was preached by our Lord appears from this, that he would not have refuted the opinion of his destroying the Law, if it had not been prevalent among the Jews. Since such an opinion could not have arisen at random without some pretext, there is reason to presume that it originated in a false interpretation of his doctrine, in the same way in which all errors generally arise from a perversion of the truth. But lest we should stumble against the same stone, let us distinguish accurately between what has been abrogated in the Law, and what still remains in force. When the Lord declares that he came not to destroy the Law, but to fulfill (Matt. 5:17); that until heaven and earth pass away, not one jot or tittle shall remain unfulfilled; he shows that his advent was not to derogate, in any degree, from the observance of the Law. And justly, since the very end of his coming was to remedy the transgression of the Law. Therefore, the doctrine of the Law has not been infringed by Christ, but remains, that by teaching, admonishing, rebuking, and correcting, it may fit and prepare us for every good work.

15. What Paul says, as to the abrogation of the Law, evidently applies not to the Law itself, but merely to its power of constraining the conscience. For the Law not only teaches, but also imperiously demands. If obedience is not yielded, nay, if it is omitted in any degree,

it thunders forth its curse. For this reason, the Apostle says, that "as many as are of the works of the law are under the curse: for it is written, 'Cursed is every one that continueth not in all things which are written in the book of the law to do them'" (Gal. 3:10; Deut. 27:26). Those he describes as under the works of the Law, who do not place righteousness in that forgiveness of sins by which we are freed from the rigor of the Law. He therefore shows that we must be freed from the fetters of the Law, if we would not perish miserably under them. But what fetters? Those of rigid and austere exaction, which remits not one iota of the demand, and leaves no transgression unpunished. To redeem us from this curse, Christ was made a curse for us: for it is written, "Cursed is everyone that hangs on a tree" (Deut. 21:23, compared with Gal. 3:13, 4:4). In the following chapter, indeed, he says, that "Christ was made under the law, in order that he might redeem those who are under the law;" but the meaning is the same. For he immediately adds, "That we might receive the adoption of sons." What does this mean? That we might not be, all our lifetime, subject to bondage, having our consciences oppressed with the fear of death. Meanwhile, it must ever remain an indubitable truth that the Law has lost none of its authority, but must always receive from us the same respect and obedience.

16. The case of ceremonies is different, these having been abrogated not in effect but in use only. Though Christ by his advent put an end to their use, so far is this from derogating from their sacredness, that it rather commends and illustrates it. For as these ceremonies would have given nothing to God's ancient people but empty show, if the power of Christ's death and resurrection had not been prefigured by them—so, if the use of them had not ceased, it would, in the present day, be impossible to understand for what purpose they were instituted. Accordingly, Paul, in order to prove that the observance of them was not only superfluous, but pernicious also, says that they "are a shadow of things to come; but the body is of Christ" (Col. 2:17). We

see, therefore, that the truth is made clearer by their abolition than if Christ, who has been openly manifested, were still figured by them as at a distance, and as under a veil. By the death of Christ, the veil of the temple was rent in vain, the living and express image of heavenly things, which had begun to be dimly shadowed forth, being now brought fully into view, as is described by the author of the Epistle to the Hebrews (Heb. 10:1). To the same effect, our Savior declares, that "the law and the prophets were until John: since that time the kingdom of God is preached, and every man presseth into it" (Luke 16:16); not that the holy fathers were left without the preaching of the hope of salvation and eternal life, but because they only saw at a distance, and under a shadow, what we now behold in full light. Why it behaved the Church to ascend higher than these elements, is explained by John the Baptist, when he says, "The law was given by Moses, but grace and truth came by Jesus Christ" (John 1:17). For though it is true that expiation was promised in the ancient sacrifices, and the ark of the covenant was a sure pledge of the paternal favor of God, the whole would have been delusory had it not been founded on the grace of Christ, wherein true and eternal stability is found. It must be held as a fixed point, that though legal rites ceased to be observed, their end serves to show more clearly how great their utility was before the advent of Christ, who, while he abolished the use, sealed their force and effect by his death.

17. There is a little more difficulty in the following passage of Paul: "You, being dead in your sins and the uncircumcision of your flesh, has he quickened together with him, having forgiven you all trespasses; blotting out the handwriting of ordinances that was against us, which was contrary to us, and took it out of the way, nailing it to his cross," &c. (Col. 2:13-14). He seems to extend the abolition of the Law considerably farther, as if we had nothing to do with its injunctions. Some err in interpreting this simply of the Moral Law, as implying the abolition not of its injunctions, but of its inexorable rigor.

Others examining Paul's words more carefully, see that they properly apply to the Ceremonial Law, and show that Paul repeatedly uses the term ordinance in this sense. He thus writes to the Ephesians: "He is our peace, who has made both one, and has broken down the middle wall of partition between us; having abolished in his flesh the enmity, even the law of commandments contained in ordinances; for to make in himself of twain one new man" (Eph. 2:14). There can be no doubt that he is there treating of ceremonies, as he speaks of "the middle wall of partition" which separated Jews and Gentiles. I therefore hold that the former view is erroneous; but, at the same time, it does not appear to me that the latter comes fully up to the Apostle's meaning. For I cannot admit that the two passages are perfectly parallel. As his object was to assure the Ephesians that they were admitted to fellowship with the Jews, he tells them that the obstacle which formerly stood in the way was removed. This obstacle was in the ceremonies. For the rites of ablution and sacrifice, by which the Jews were consecrated to the Lord, separated them from the Gentiles. But who sees not that, in the Epistle to the Colossians, a sublimer mystery is adverted to? No doubt, a question is raised there as to the Mosaic observances, to which false apostles were endeavoring to bind the Christian people. But as in the Epistle to the Galatians he takes a higher view of this controversy, and in a manner traces it to its fountain, so he does in this passage also. For if the only thing considered in rites is the necessity of observing them, of what use was it to call it a handwriting which was contrary to us? Besides, how could the bringing in of it be set down as almost the whole sum of redemption? Wherefore, the very nature of the case clearly shows that reference is here made to something more internal. I cannot doubt that I have ascertained the genuine interpretation, provided I am permitted to assume what Augustine has somewhere most truly affirmed, nay, derived from the very words of the Apostle—viz. that in the Jewish ceremonies there was more a confession than an expiation of sins. For what more was done in sacrifice by those who substituted purifications instead of themselves, than to confess that they were conscious of deserving death? What did these purifications testify but that they themselves were impure? By these means, therefore, the handwriting both of their guilt and impurity was ever and anon renewed. But the attestation of these things was not the removal of them. Wherefore, the Apostle says that Christ is "the mediator of the new testament—by means of death, for the redemption of the transgressions that were under the first testament" (Heb. 9:15). Justly, therefore, does the Apostle describe these handwritings as against the worshipers, and contrary to them, since by means of them their impurity and condemnation were openly sealed. There is nothing contrary to this in the fact that they were partakers of the same grace with ourselves. This they obtained through Christ, and not through the ceremonies which the Apostle there contrasts with Christ, showing that by the continued use of them the glory of Christ was obscured. We perceive how ceremonies, considered in themselves, are elegantly and appositely termed handwritings, and contrary to the salvation of man, in as much as they were a kind of formal instruments which attested his liability. On the other hand, when false apostles wished to bind them on the Christian Church, Paul, entering more deeply into their signification, with good reason warned the Colossians how seriously they would relapse if they allowed a yoke to be in that way imposed upon them. By so doing, they, at the same time, deprived themselves of all benefit from Christ, who, by his eternal sacrifice once offered, had abolished those daily sacrifices, which were indeed powerful to attest sin, but could do nothing to destroy it.

Study Guide Questions

Section 1

1. What does Calvin mean when he uses the word "law"?
2. What was the basic reason for giving the law?

Section 2

1. What should we remember with regard to the Ten Commandments?

2. The righteousness taught by the commandments is all in vain until what happens?

Section 3

1. What else does the law do?

2. How many men are affected by the law in this way?

Section 4

1. Are the promises attached to the law all in vain because of our disobedience?

Section 5

1. What does Calvin mean by the impossibility of obedience?

2. What has plagued every human being?

3. What ought we not pit against one another?

Section 6

1. Without seeing ourselves in the mirror of God's law, what happens to us?

2. When we stand on our own judgment, what do we tend to do?

Section 7

1. The law is compared to what?

2. As we grow tired under the burden of sin, what does God never tire of?

Section 8

1. Does the first use of the law apply to unbelievers only?

Section 9

1. When we are condemned by the law, what does this make us want to do?

Section 10

1. What is the second use of the law?

2. Is their conformity to this law true righteousness?

Section 11

1. The law of God restrains us externally until what time?

Section 12

1. What is the third use of the law, according to Calvin?

2. Is this a minor use of the law?

3. How does the law help the believer?

4. Is this use dependent upon precept alone?

Section 13

1. What do certain ignorant persons do?

Section 14

1. In what two ways has the law been abrogated?

Section 15

1. What part of the law is abrogated to liberate the conscience?

2. How would that curse work on the conscience?

Section 16

1. Have the ceremonies been abrogated the same way?

2. In what way have the ceremonies been abrogated?

Section 17

1. What does Calvin do with the "handwriting of ordinances" of Colossians 2:13–14?

CHAPTER 8

Exposition of the moral law

This chapter consists of four parts.

I. Some general observations necessary for the understanding of the subject are made by way of preface, sec. 1-5.

II. Three things always to be attended to in ascertaining and expounding the meaning of the Moral Law, sec. 6-12.

III. Exposition of the Moral Law, or the Ten Commandments, sec. 13-15.

IV. The end for which the whole Law is intended—viz. to teach not only elementary principles, but perfection, sec. 51, to the end of the chapter.

Outline:

1. The Law was committed to writing, in order that it might teach more fully and perfectly that knowledge, both of God and of ourselves, which the law of nature teaches meagerly and obscurely. Proof of this from an enumeration of the principal parts of the Moral Law; and also from the dictate of natural law, written on the hearts of all, and, in a manner, effaced by sin.

2. Certain general maxims. 1. From the knowledge of God, furnished by the Law, we learn that God is our Father and Ruler. Righteousness is pleasing, iniquity is an abomination in his sight. Hence, how weak soever we may be, our duty is to cultivate the one, and shun the other.

3. From the knowledge of ourselves, furnished by the Law, we learn to discern our own utter powerlessness, we are ashamed; and seeing it is in vain to seek for righteousness in ourselves, are induced to seek it elsewhere.

4. Hence, God has annexed promises and threatening to his promises. These not limited to the present life, but embrace things heavenly and eternal. They, moreover, attest the spotless purity of God, his love of righteousness, and also his kindness towards us.

5. The Law shows, moreover, that there is nothing more acceptable to God than obedience. Hence, all superstitious and hypocritical modes of worship are condemned. A remedy against superstitious worship and human presumption.

6. The second part of the chapter, containing three observations or rules. First rule, our life must be formed by the Law, not only to external honesty, but to inward and spiritual righteousness. In this respect, the Law of God differs from civil laws, he being a spiritual Lawgiver, man not. This rule of great extent, and not sufficiently attended to.

7. This first rule confirmed by the authority of Christ, and vindicated from the false dogma of Sophists, who say that Christ is only another Moses.

8. Second observation or rule to be carefully attended to—viz. that the end of the command must be inquired into, until it is ascertained what the Lawgiver approves or disapproves. Example. Where the Law approves, its opposite is condemned, and vice versa.

9. Full explanation of this latter point. Example.

10. The Law states what is most impious in each transgression, in order to show how heinous the transgression is. Example.

11. Third observation or rule regards the division of the Law into Two Tables: the former comprehending our duty to God; the latter, our duty to our neighbor. The connection between these necessary and inseparable. Their invariable order. Sum of the Law.

12. Division of the Law into Ten Commandments. Various distinctions made with regard to them, but the best distinction that which divides them into Two Tables. Four commandments belong to the First, and six to the Second Table.

13. The third part of the chapter, containing an exposition of the Decalogue. The preface vindicates the authority of the Law. This it does in three ways. First, by a declaration of its majesty.

14. The preface to the Law vindicates its authority. Secondly, by calling to mind God's paternal kindness.

15. Thirdly, by calling to mind the deliverance out of the land of Egypt. Why God distinguishes himself by certain epithets. Why mention is made of the deliverance from Egypt. In what way, and how far, the remembrance of this deliverance should still affect us.

16. Exposition of the First Commandment. Its end. What it is to have God, and to have strange gods. Adoration due to God, trust, invocation, thanksgiving, and also true religion, required by the Commandment. Superstition, Polytheism, and Atheism, forbidden. What meant by the words, "before me."

17. Exposition of the Second Commandment. The end and sum of it. Two parts. Short enumeration of forbidden shapes.

18. Why a threatening is added. Four titles applied to God, to make a deeper impression. He is called Mighty, Jealous, an Avenger, Merciful. Why said to be jealous. Reason drawn from analogy.

19. Exposition of the threatening which is added. First, as to visiting the iniquity of the fathers upon the children. A misinterpretation on this head refuted, and the genuine meaning of the threatening explained.

20. Whether this visiting of the sins of parents inconsistent with the divine justice. Apparently conflicting passages reconciled.

21. Exposition of the latter part—viz. the showing mercy to thousands. The use of this promise. Consideration of an exception of frequent occurrence. The extent of this blessing.

22. Exposition of the Third Commandment. The end and sum of it. Three parts. These considered. What it is to use the name of God in vain. Swearing. Distinction between this commandment and the Ninth.

23. An oath defined. It is a species of divine worship. This explained.

24. Many modes in which this commandment is violated. 1. By taking God to witness what we know is false. The insult thus offered.

25. Modes of violation continued. 2. Taking God to witness in trivial matters. Contempt thus shown. When and how an oath should be used. 3. Substituting the servants of God instead of himself when taking an oath.

26. The Anabaptists, who condemn all oaths, refuted. 1. By the authority of Christ, who cannot be opposed in anything to the Father. A passage perverted by the Anabaptists explained. The design of our Savior in the passage. What meant by his there prohibiting oaths.

27. The lawfulness of oaths confirmed by Christ and the apostles. Some approve of public, but not of private oaths. The lawfulness of the latter proved both by reason and example. Instances from Scripture.

28. Exposition of the Fourth Commandment. Its end. Three purposes.

29. Explanation of the first purpose—viz. a shadowing forth of spiritual rest. This the primary object of the precept. God is therein set forth as our sanctifier; and hence we must abstain from work, that the work of God in us may not be hindered.

30. The number seven denoting perfection in Scripture, this commandment may, in that respect, denote the perpetuity of the Sabbath, and its completion at the last day.

31. Taking a simpler view of the commandment, the number is of no consequence, provided we maintain the doctrine of a perpetual

rest from all our works, and, at the same time, avoid a superstitious observance of days. The ceremonial part of the commandment abolished by the advent of Christ.

32. The second and third purposes of the Commandment explained. These twofold and perpetual. This confirmed. Of religious assemblies.

33. Of the observance of the Lord's day, in answer to those who complain that the Christian people are thus trained to Judaism. Objection.

34. Ground of this institution. There is no kind of superstitious necessity. The sum of the Commandment.

35. The Fifth Commandment (the first of the Second Table), expounded. Its end and substance. How far honor due to parents. To whom the term father applies.

36. It makes no difference whether those to whom this honor is required are worthy or unworthy. The honor is claimed especially for parents. It consists of three parts. 1. Reverence.

37. Honor due to parents continued. 2. Obedience. 3. Gratitude. Why a promise added. In what sense it is to be taken. The present life a testimony of divine blessing. The reservation considered and explained.

38. Conversely a curse denounced on disobedient children. How far obedience due to parents, and those in the place of parents.

39. Sixth Commandment expounded. Its end and substance. God, as a spiritual Lawgiver, forbids the murder of the heart, and requires a sincere desire to preserve the life of our neighbor.

40. A twofold ground for this Commandment. 1. Man is the image of God. 2. He is our flesh.

41. Exposition of the Seventh Command. The end and substance of it. Remedy against fornication.

42. Continence an excellent gift, when under the control of God only. Altogether denied to some; granted only for a time to others. Argument in favor of celibacy refuted.

43. Each individual may refrain from marriage so long as he is fit to observe celibacy. True celibacy, and the proper use of it. Any man

not gifted with continence wars with God and with nature, as constituted by him, in remaining unmarried. Chastity defined.

44. Precautions to be observed in married life. Everything repugnant to chastity here condemned.

45. Exposition of the Eighth Commandment. Its end and substance. Four kinds of theft. The bad acts condemned by this Commandment. Other peculiar kinds of theft.

46. Proper observance of this Commandment. Four heads. Application. 1. To the people and the magistrate. 2. To the pastors of the Church and their flocks. 3. To parents and children. 4. To the old and the young. 5. To servants and masters. 6. To individuals.

47. Exposition of the ninth Commandment. Its end and substance. The essence of the Commandment—detestation of falsehood, and the pursuit of truth. Two kinds of falsehood. Public and private testimony. The equity of this Commandment.

48. How numerous the violations of this Commandment. 1. By detraction. 2. By evil speaking—a thing contrary to the offices of Christian charity. 3. By scurrility or irony. 4. By prying curiosity, and proneness to harsh judgments.

49. Exposition of the Tenth Commandment. Its end and substance. What meant by the term Covetousness. Distinction between counsel and the covetousness here condemned.

50. Why God requires so much purity. Objection. Answer. Charity toward our neighbor here principally commended. Why house, wife, man-servant, maid-servant, ox, and ass, &c., are mentioned. Improper division of this Commandment into two.

51. The last part of the chapter. The end of the Law. Proof. A summary of the Ten Commandments. The Law delivers not merely rudiments and first principles, but a perfect standard of righteousness, modeled on the divine purity.

52. Why, in the Gospels and Epistles, the latter table only mentioned, and not the first. The same thing occurs in the Prophets.

53. An objection to what is said in the former section removed.

54. A conduct duly regulated by the divine Law, characterized by charity toward our neighbor. This subverted by those who give the first place to self-love. Refutation of their opinion.

55. Who our neighbor. Double error of the Schoolmen on this point.

56. This error consists, I. In converting precepts into counsels to be observed by monks.

57. Refutation of this error from Scripture and the ancient Theologians. Sophistical objection obviated.

58. Error of the Schoolmen consists, II. In calling hidden impiety and covetousness venial sins. Refutation drawn, 1. From a consideration of the whole Decalogue. 2. The testimony of an Apostle. 3. The authority of Christ. 4. The nature and majesty of God. 5. The sentence pronounced against sin. Conclusion.

59. Refutation drawn, 1. From a consideration of the whole Decalogue. 2. The testimony of an Apostle. 3. The authority of Christ. 4. The nature and majesty of God. 5. The sentence pronounced against sin. Conclusion.

I believe it will not be out of place here to introduce the Ten Commandments of the Law, and give a brief exposition of them. In this way it will be made more clear that the worship which God originally prescribed is still in force (a point to which I have already adverted); and then a second point will be confirmed—viz. that the Jews not only learned from the law wherein true piety consisted, but from feeling their inability to observe it were overawed by the fear of judgments and so drawn, even against their will, towards the Mediator. In giving a summary of what constitutes the true knowledge of God, we showed that we cannot form any just conception of the character of God, without feeling overawed by his majesty, and bound to do him service. In regard to the knowledge of ourselves, we showed that it principally consists in renouncing all idea of our own strength, and divesting ourselves of all confidence in our own righteousness, while, on the other hand, under a full consciousness of our wants, we learn true humility and self-abasement. Both of these the Lord accomplishes by his Law: first, when, in assertion of the right which he has to our obedience, he calls us to reverence his majesty, and prescribes the conduct by which this reverence is manifested; and, secondly, when by promulgating the rule of his justice (a rule to the rectitude of which our nature, from being depraved and perverted, is continually opposed, and to the perfection of which our ability, from its infirmity and nervelessness for good, is far from being able to attain), he charges us both with impotence and unrighteousness. Moreover, the very things contained in the two tables are, in a manner, dictated to us by that internal law, which, as has been already said, is in a manner written and stamped on every heart. For conscience, instead of allowing us to stifle our perceptions, and sleep on without interruption, acts as an inward witness and monitor, reminds us of what we owe to God, points out the distinction between good and evil, and thereby convicts us of departure from duty. But man, being immured in the darkness of error, is scarcely able, by means of that natural law, to form any tolerable idea of the worship which is acceptable to God. At all events, he is very far from forming any correct knowledge of it. In addition to this, he is so swollen with arrogance and ambition, and so blinded with self-love, that he is unable to survey and, as it were, descend into himself that he may so learn to humble and abase himself, and confess his misery. Therefore, as a necessary remedy, both for our dullness and our contumacy, the Lord has given us his written Law, which by its sure attestations removes the obscurity of the law of nature, and also by shaking off our lethargy makes a more lively and permanent impression on our minds.

2. It is now easy to understand the doctrine of the law—viz. that God, as our Creator, is entitled to be regarded by us as a Father and Master, and should, accordingly, receive from us fear, love, reverence,

and glory; nay, that we are not our own, to follow whatever course passion dictates, but are bound to obey him implicitly, and to acquiesce entirely in his good pleasure. Again, the Law teaches that justice and rectitude are a delight, injustice an abomination to him, and, therefore, as we would not with impious ingratitude revolt from our Maker, our whole life must be spent in the cultivation of righteousness. For if we manifest becoming reverence only when we prefer his will to our own, it follows that the only legitimate service to him is the practice of justice, purity, and holiness. Nor can we plead as an excuse that we want the power, and, like debtors, whose means are exhausted, are unable to pay. We cannot be permitted to measure the glory of God by our ability; whatever we may be, he ever remains like himself, the friend of righteousness, the enemy of unrighteousness, and whatever his demands from us may be, as he can only require what is right, we are necessarily under a natural obligation to obey. Our inability to do so is our own fault. If lust, in which sin has its dominion, so enthralls us that we are not free to obey our Father, there is no ground for pleading necessity as a defense, since this evil necessity is within, and must be imputed to ourselves.

3. When under the guidance of the Law we have advanced thus far, we must under the same guidance proceed to descend into ourselves. In this way, we at length arrive at two results: first, contrasting our conduct with the righteousness of the Law, we see how very far it is from being in accordance with the will of God, and, therefore, how unworthy we are of holding our place among his creatures, far less of being accounted his sons; and, secondly, taking a survey of our powers, we see that they are not only unequal to fulfill the Law, but are altogether null. The necessary consequence must be to produce distrust of our own ability, and also anxiety and trepidation of mind. Conscience cannot feel the burden of its guilt without forthwith turning to the judgment of God, while the view of this judgment cannot fail to excite a dread of death. In like manner, the proofs of our

utter powerlessness must instantly beget despair of our own strength. Both feelings are productive of humility and abasement, and hence the sinner, terrified at the prospect of eternal death (which he sees justly impending over him for his iniquities), turns to the mercy of God as the only haven of safety. Feeling his utter inability to pay what he owes to the Law, and thus despairing of himself, he rethinks him of applying and looking to some other quarter for help.

4. But the Lord does not count it enough to inspire a reverence for his justice. To imbue our hearts with love to himself, and, at the same time, with hatred to iniquity, he has added promises and threatening. The eye of our mind being too dim to be attracted by the mere beauty of goodness, our most merciful Father has been pleased, in his great indulgence, to allure us to love and long after it by the hope of reward. He accordingly declares that rewards for virtue are treasured up with him, that none who yield obedience to his commands will labor in vain. On the other hand, he proclaims not only that iniquity is hateful in his sight, but that it will not escape with impunity, because he will be the avenger of his insulted majesty. That he may encourage us in every way, he promises present blessings, as well as eternal felicity, to the obedience of those who shall have kept his commands, while he threatens transgressors with present suffering, as well as the punishment of eternal death. The promise, "Ye shall therefore keep my statutes, and my judgments; which if a man do, he shall live in them" (Lev. 18:5), and corresponding to this the threatening, "The souls that sinneth, it shall die" (Ezek. 18:4, 20); doubtless point to a future life and death, both without end. But though in every passage where the favor or anger of God is mentioned, the former comprehends eternity of life and the latter eternal destruction, the Law at the same time enumerates a long catalogue of present blessings and curses (Lev. 26:4; Deut. 28:1). The threatening attest the spotless purity of God, which cannot bear iniquity, while the promises attest at once his infinite love of righteousness (which he cannot leave unrewarded)

and his wondrous kindness. Being bound to do him homage with all that we have, he is perfectly entitled to demand everything which he requires of us as a debt; and as a debt, the payment is unworthy of reward. He therefore forgoes his right, when he holds forth reward for services which are not offered spontaneously, as if they were not due. The amount of these services, in themselves, has been partly described and will appear more clearly in its own place. For the present, it is enough to remember that the promises of the Law are no mean commendation of righteousness as they show how much God is pleased with the observance of them, while the threatening denounced are intended to produce a greater abhorrence of unrighteousness, lest the sinner should indulge in the blandishments of vice, and forget the judgment which the divine Lawgiver has prepared for him.

5. The Lord, in delivering a perfect rule of righteousness, has reduced it in all its parts to his mere will, and in this way has shown that there is nothing more acceptable to him than obedience. There is the more necessity for attending to this, because the human mind in its wantonness is ever and anon inventing different modes of worship as a means of gaining his favor. This irreligious affectation of religion being innate in the human mind has betrayed itself in every age, and is still doing so, men always longing to devise some method of procuring righteousness without any sanction from the Word of God. Hence in those observances which are generally regarded as good works, the precepts of the Law occupy a narrow space, almost the whole being usurped by this endless host of human inventions. But was not this the very license which Moses meant to curb, when, after the promulgation of the Law, he thus addressed the people: "Observe and hear all these words which I command thee, that it may go well with thee, and with thy children after thee for ever, when thou does that which is good and right in the sight of the Lord thy God." "What thing soever I command you, observe to do it: thou shalt not add thereto, nor diminish from it" (Deut 12:28-32). Previously, after

asking "what nation is there so great, that has statutes and judgments so righteous as all this law, which I set before you this day?" he had added, "Only take heed to thyself, and keep thy soul diligently, lest thou forget the things which thine eyes have seen, and lest they depart from thy heart all the days of thy life" (Deut. 4:8-9). God foreseeing that the Israelites would not rest, but after receiving the Law, would, unless sternly prohibited give birth to new kinds of righteousness, declares that the Law comprehended a perfect righteousness. This ought to have been a most powerful restraint, and yet they desisted not from the presumptuous course so strongly prohibited. How do we act? We are certainly under the same obligation as they were; for there cannot be a doubt that the claim of absolute perfection which God made for his Law is perpetually in force. Not contented with it, however, we labor prodigiously in feigning and coining an endless variety of good works, one after another. The best cure for this vice would be a constant and deep-seated conviction that the Law was given from heaven to teach us a perfect righteousness; that the only righteousness so taught is that which the divine will expressly enjoins; and that it is, therefore, vain to attempt, by new forms of worship, to gain the favor of God, whose true worship consists in obedience alone; or rather, that to go a wandering after good works which are not prescribed by the Law of God, is an intolerable violation of true and divine righteousness. Most truly does Augustine say in one place that the obedience which is rendered to God is the parent and guardian; in another, that it is the source of all the virtues.

6. After we shall have expounded the Divine Law, what has been previously said of its office and use will be understood more easily, and with greater benefit. But before we proceed to the consideration of each separate commandment, it will be proper to take a general survey of the whole. At the outset, it was proved that in the Law human life is instructed not merely in outward decency but in inward spiritual righteousness. Though none can deny this, yet very few duly

attend to it, because they do not consider the Lawgiver, by whose character that of the Law must also be determined. Should a king issue an edict prohibiting murder, adultery, and theft, the penalty, I admit, will not be incurred by the man who has only felt a longing in his mind after these vices, but has not actually committed them. The reason is that a human lawgiver does not extend his care beyond outward order, and, therefore, his injunctions are not violated without outward acts. But God, whose eye nothing escapes, and who regards not the outward appearance so much as purity of heart, under the prohibition of murder, adultery, and thefts includes wrath, hatred, lust, covetousness, and all other things of a similar nature. Being a spiritual Lawgiver, he speaks to the soul not less than the body. The murder which the soul commits is wrath and hatred; the theft, covetousness and avarice; and the adultery, lust. It may be alleged that human laws have respect to intentions and wishes, and not fortuitous events. I admit this but then these must manifest themselves externally. They consider the animus with which the act was done, but do not scrutinize the secret thoughts. Accordingly, their demand is satisfied when the hand merely refrains from transgression. On the contrary, the law of heaven being enacted for our minds, the first thing necessary to a due observance of the Law is to put them under restraint. But the generality of men, even while they are most anxious to conceal their disregard of the Law, only frame their hands and feet and other parts of their body to some kind of observance, but in the meanwhile keep the heart utterly estranged from everything like obedience. They think it enough to have carefully concealed from man what they are doing in the sight of God. Hearing the commandments, "Thou shalt not kill," "Thou shalt not commit adultery," "Thou shalt not steal," they do not unsheathe their sword for slaughter, nor defile their bodies with harlots, nor put forth their hands to other men's goods. So far well; but with their whole soul they breathe out slaughter, boil with lust, cast a greedy eye at their neighbor's property, and in wish

devour it. Here the principal thing which the Law requires is wanting. Whence then, this gross stupidity, but just because they lose sight
of the Lawgiver, and form an idea of righteousness in accordance
with their own disposition? Against this Paul strenuously protests,
when he declares that the "law is spiritual" (Rom. 7:14); intimating
that it not only demands the homage of the soul, and mind, and will,
but requires an angelic purity, which, purified from all filthiness of the
flesh, savors only of the Spirit.

7. In saying that this is the meaning of the Law, we are not introducing a new interpretation of our own; we are following Christ, the
best interpreter of the Law (Matt. 5:22, 28, 44). The Pharisees having
instilled into the people the erroneous idea that the Law was fulfilled
by everyone who did not in external act do anything against the Law,
he pronounces this a most dangerous delusion, and declares that an
immodest look is adultery, and that hatred of a brother is murder.
"Whosoever is angry with his brother without a cause, shall be in
danger of the judgment;" whosoever by whispering or murmuring
gives indication of being offended, "shall be in danger of the council;"
whosoever by reproaches and evil-speaking gives way to open anger,
"shall be in danger of hell-fire." Those who have not perceived this,
have pretended that Christ was only a second Moses, the giver of an
evangelical, to supply the deficiency of the Mosaic Law. Hence the
common axiom as to the perfection of the Evangelical Law, and its
great superiority to that of Moses. This idea is in many ways most
pernicious. For it will appear from Moses himself, when we come
to give a summary of his precepts, that great indignity is thus done
to the Divine Law. It certainly insinuates that the holiness of the fathers under the Law was little else than hypocrisy, and leads us away
from that one unvarying rule of righteousness. It is very easy, however, to confute this error, which proceeds on the supposition that
Christ added to the Law, whereas he only restored it to its integrity

by maintaining and purifying it when obscured by the falsehood, and defiled by the leaven of the Pharisees.

8. The next observation we would make is that there is always more in the requirements and prohibitions of the Law than is expressed in words. This, however, must be understood so as not to convert it into a kind of Lesbian code; and thus, by licentiously wresting the Scriptures, make them assume any meaning that we please. By taking this excessive liberty with Scripture, its authority is lowered with some, and all hope of understanding it abandoned by others. We must therefore, if possible, discover some path which may conduct us with direct and firm step to the will of God. We must consider, I say, how far interpretation can be permitted to go beyond the literal meaning of the words, still making it apparent that no appending of human glosses is added to the Divine Law, but that the pure and genuine meaning of the Lawgiver is faithfully exhibited. It is true that, in almost all the commandments, there are elliptical expressions, and that therefore, any man would make himself ridiculous by attempting to restrict the spirit of the Law to the strict letter of the words. It is plain that a sober interpretation of the Law must go beyond these, but how far is doubtful, unless some rule be adopted. The best rule, in my opinion, would be to be guided by the principle of the commandment—viz. to consider in the case of each what the purpose is for which it was given. For example, every commandment either requires or prohibits; and the nature of each is instantly discerned when we look to the principle of the commandment as its end. Thus, the end of the Fifth Commandment is to render honor to those on whom God bestows it. The sum of the commandment, therefore, is that it is right in itself and pleasing to God to honor those on whom he has conferred some distinction; that to despise and rebel against such persons is offensive to Him. The principle of the First Commandment is that God only is to be worshiped. The sum of the commandment, therefore, is that true piety, in other words, the worship of the Deity,

is acceptable, and impiety is an abomination to him. So in each of the commandments we must first look to the matter of which it treats, and then consider its end, until we discover what it properly is that the Lawgiver declares to be pleasing or displeasing to him. Only we must reason from the precept to its contrary in this way: if this pleases God, its opposite displeases; if that displeases, its opposite pleases: if God commands this, he forbids the opposite; if he forbids that, he commands the opposite.

9. What is now touched on somewhat obscurely will become perfectly clear as we proceed and get accustomed to the exposition of the Commandments. It is sufficient thus to have adverted to the subject; but perhaps our concluding statement will require to be briefly confirmed, as it might otherwise not be understood, or, though understood mighty perhaps, at the outset appear unsound. There is no need of proving that when good is ordered the evil which is opposed to it is forbidden. This every one admits. It will also be admitted, without much difficulty, that when evil is forbidden, its opposite is enjoined. Indeed, it is a common saying that censure of vice is commendation of virtue. We, however, demand somewhat more than is commonly understood by these expressions. When the particular virtue opposed to a particular vice is spoken of, all that is usually meant is abstinence from that vice. We maintain that it goes farther, and means opposite duties and positive acts. Hence the commandment, "Thou shalt not kill," the generality of men will merely consider as an injunction to abstain from all injury and all wish to inflict injury. I hold that it moreover means that we are to aid our neighbor's life by every means in our power. And not to assert without giving my reasons I prove it thus: God forbids us to injure or hurt a brother, because he would have his life to be dear and precious to us; and, therefore, when he so forbids, he, at the same time, demands all the offices of charity which can contribute to his preservation.

10. But why did God thus deliver his commandments, as it were, by halves, using elliptical expressions with a larger meaning than that actually expressed? Other reasons are given, but the following seems to me the best: as the flesh is always on the alert to extenuate the heinousness of sin (unless it is made, as it were, perceptible to the touch), and to cover it with specious pretexts, the Lord sets forth by way of example, whatever is foulest and most iniquitous in each species of transgression, that the delivery of it might produce a shudder in the hearer and impress his mind with a deeper abhorrence of sin. In forming an estimate of sins, we are often imposed upon by imagining that the more hidden the less heinous they are. This delusion the Lord dispels by accustoming us to refer the whole multitude of sins to particular heads, which admirably show how great a degree of heinousness there is in each. For example, wrath and hatred do not seem so very bad when they are designated by their own names; but when they are prohibited under the name of murder, we understand better how abominable they are in the sight of God, who puts them in the same class with that horrid crime. Influenced by his judgment, we accustom ourselves to judge more accurately of the heinousness of offenses which previously seemed trivial.

11. It will now be proper to consider what is meant by the division of the Divine law into Two Tables. It will be judged by all men of sense from the formal manner in which these are sometimes mentioned, that it has not been done at random, or without reason. Indeed, the reason is so obvious as not to allow us to remain in doubt with regard to it. God thus divided his Law into two parts, containing a complete rule of righteousness, that he might assign the first place to the duties of religion which relate especially to His worship, and the second to the duties of charity which have respect to man. The first foundation of righteousness undoubtedly is the worship of God. When it is subverted, all the other parts of righteousness, like a building rent asunder, and in ruins, are racked and scattered. What kind of

righteousness do you call it, not to commit theft and rapine, if you, in the meantime, with impious sacrilege, rob God of his glory? Or not to defile your body with fornication, if you profane his holy name with blasphemy? Or not to take away the life of man, if you strive to cut off and destroy the remembrance of God? It is vain, therefore, to talk of righteousness apart from religion. Such righteousness has no more beauty than the trunk of a body deprived of its head. Nor is religion the principal part merely: it is the very soul by which the whole lives and breathes. Without the fear of God, men do not even observe justice and charity among themselves. We say, then, that the worship of God is the beginning and foundation of righteousness; and that wherever it is wanting, any degree of equity, or continence, or temperance, existing among men themselves, is empty and frivolous in the sight of God. We call it the source and soul of righteousness, in as much as men learn to live together temperately, and without injury, when they revere God as the judge of right and wrong. In the First Table, accordingly, he teaches us how to cultivate piety, and the proper duties of religion in which his worship consists; in the second, he shows how, in the fear of his name, we are to conduct ourselves towards our fellow-men. Hence, as related by the Evangelists (Matt. 22:37; Luke 10:27), our Savior summed up the whole Law in two heads—viz. to love the Lord with all our heart, with all our soul, and with all our strength, and our neighbor as ourselves. You see how, of the two parts under which he comprehends the whole Law, he devotes the one to God, and assigns the other to mankind.

12. But although the whole Law is contained in two heads, yet, in order to remove every pretext for excuse, the Lord has been pleased to deliver more fully and explicitly in Ten Commandments, everything relating to his own honor, fear, and love, as well as everything relating to the charity which, for his sake, he enjoins us to have towards our fellowmen. Nor is it an unprofitable study to consider the division of the commandments, provided we remember that it is one of those

matters in which every man should have full freedom of judgment, and on account of which difference of opinion should not lead to contention. We are, indeed, under the necessity of making this observation, lest the division which we are to adopt should excite the surprise or derision of the reader, as novel or of recent invention.

There is no room for controversy as to the fact that the Law is divided into ten heads since this is repeatedly sanctioned by divine authority. The question, therefore, is not as to the number of the parts, but the method of dividing them. Those who adopt a division which gives three commandments to the First Table, and throws the remaining seven into the Second Table, expunge the commandment concerning images from the list, or at least conceal it under the first, though there cannot be a doubt that it was distinctly set down by the Lord as a separate commandment; whereas the tenth, which prohibits the coveting of what belongs to our neighbor, they absurdly break down into two. Moreover, it will soon appear that this method of dividing was unknown in a purer age. Others count four commandments in the First Table as we do, but for the first set down the introductory promise, without adding the precept. But because I must hold, unless I am convinced by clear evidence to the contrary, that the "ten words" mentioned by Moses are Ten Commandments and because I see that number arranged in most admirable order, I must, while I leave them to hold their own opinion, follow what appears to me better established—viz. that what they make to be the first commandment is of the nature of a preface to the whole Law, that thereafter follow four commandments in the First Table, and six in the Second, in the order in which they will here be reviewed. This division Origin adopts without discussion, as if it had been everywhere received in his day. It is also adopted by Augustine, in his book addressed to Boniface, where, in enumerating the commandments, he follows this order: Let one God be religiously obeyed, let no idol be worshiped, let the name of God be not used in vain; while previously he had made separate mention of the typical commandment of the Sabbath. Elsewhere, indeed, he expresses approbation of the first division, but on too slight grounds, because, by the number three (making the First Table consist of three commandments), the mystery of the Trinity would be better manifested. Even here, however, he does not disguise his opinion that in other respects our division is more to his mind. Besides these, we are supported by the author of an unfinished work on Matthew. Josephus, no doubt with the general consent of his age, assigns five commandments to each table. This, while repugnant to reason, inasmuch as it confounds the distinction between piety and charity, is also refuted by the authority of our Savior, who in Matthew places the command to honor parents in the list of those belonging to the Second Table (Matt. 19:19). Let us now hear God speaking in his own words.

First Commandment.

I AM THE LORD THY GOD, WHICH BROUGHT THEE OUT OF THE LAND OF EGYPT, OUT OF THE HOUSE OF BONDAGE. THOU SHALT HAVE NO OTHER GODS BEFORE ME.

13. Whether you take the former sentence as a part of the commandment, or read it separately is to me a matter of indifference, provided you grant that it is a kind of preface to the whole Law. In enacting laws, the first thing to be guarded against is their being forthwith abrogated by contempt. The Lord, therefore, takes care in the first place that this shall not happen to the Law about to be delivered, by introducing it with a triple sanction. He claims to himself power and authority to command, that he may impress the chosen people with the necessity of obedience; he holds forth a promise of favor, as a means of alluring them to the study of holiness; and he reminds them of his kindness, that he may convict them of ingratitude, if they fail to make a suitable return. By the name, Lord, are denoted power and lawful dominion. If all things are from him, and by him

consist, they ought in justice to bear reference to him, as Paul says (Rom. 11:36). This name, therefore, is in itself sufficient to bring us under the authority of the divine majesty: for it were monstrous for us to wish to withdraw from the dominion of him, out of whom we cannot even exist.

14. After showing that he has a right to command, and to be obeyed, he next, in order not to seem to drag men by mere necessity, but to allure them, graciously declares that he is the God of the Church. For the mode of expression implies that there is a mutual relation included in the promise, "I will be their God, and they shall be my people" (Jer. 31:33). Hence Christ infers the immortality of Abraham, Isaac, and Jacob from the fact that God had declared himself to be their God (Matt. 22:32). It is, therefore, the same as if he had said, I have chosen you to myself, as a people to whom I shall not only do good in the present life, but also bestow felicity in the life to come. The end contemplated in this is adverted to in the Law, in various passages. For when the Lord condescends in mercy to honor us so far as to admit us to partnership with his chosen people, he chooses us, as Moses says, "to be a holy people," "a peculiar people unto himself," to "keep all his commandments" (Deut. 7:6; 14:2; 26:18). Hence the exhortation, "Ye shall be holy; for I the Lord your God am holy" (Lev. 19:2). These two considerations form the ground of the remonstrance, "A son honoreth his father, and a servant his master; if then I be a father, where is mine honor? and if I be a master, where is my fear? saith the Lord of hosts" (Mal. 1:6).

15. Next follows a commemoration of his kindness, which ought to produce upon us an impression strong in proportion to the detestation in which ingratitude is held even among men. It is true, indeed, he was reminding Israel of a deliverance then recent, but one which, on account of its wondrous magnitude, was to be for ever memorable to the remotest posterity. Moreover, it is most appropriate to the matter in hand. For the Lord intimates that they were delivered from

miserable bondage that they might learn to yield prompt submission and obedience to him as the author of their freedom. In like manners to keep us to his true worship, he often describes himself by certain epithets which distinguish his sacred Deity from all idols and fictitious gods. For, as I formerly observed, such is our proneness to vanity and presumption, that as soon as God is named, our minds, unable to guard against error, immediately fly off to some empty delusion. In applying a remedy to this disease, God distinguishes his divinity by certain titles, and thus confines us, as it were, within distinct boundaries, that we may not wander hither and thither, and feign some new deity for ourselves, abandoning the living God, and setting up an idol. For this reason, whenever the Prophets would bring him properly before us, they invest, and, as it were, surround him with those characters under which he had manifested himself to the people of Israel. When he is called the God of Abraham, or the God of Israel, when he is stationed in the temple of Jerusalem, between the Cherubim, these, and similar modes of expression, do not confine him to one place or one people, but are used merely for the purpose of fixing our thoughts on that God who so manifested himself in the covenant which he made with Israel, as to make it unlawful on any account to deviate from the strict view there given of his character. Let it be understood, then, that mention is made of deliverance, in order to make the Jews submit with greater readiness to that God who justly claims them as his own. We again, instead of supposing that the matter has no reference to us, should reflect that the bondage of Israel in Egypt was a type of that spiritual bondage, in the fetters of which we are all bound, until the heavenly avenger delivers us by the power of his own arm, and transports us into his free kingdom. Therefore, as in old times, when he would gather together the scattered Israelites to the worship of his name, he rescued them from the intolerable tyranny of Pharaoh, so all who profess him now are delivered from the fatal tyranny of the devil, of which that of Egypt was only a type. There is no man, therefore, whose mind ought not to be aroused to give heed to the Law, which, as he is told, proceeded from the supreme King, from him who, as he gave all their being, justly destines and directs them to himself as their proper end. There is no man, I say, who should not hasten to embrace the Lawgiver, whose commands he knows he has been specially appointed to obey, from whose kindness he anticipates an abundance of all good, and even a blessed immortality, and to whose wondrous power and mercy he is indebted for deliverance from the jaws of death.

16. The authority of the Law being founded and established, God delivers his First Commandment—

THOU SHALT HAVE NO OTHER GODS BEFORE ME.

The purport of this commandment is that the Lord will have himself alone to be exalted in his people, and claims the entire possession of them as his own. That it may be so, he orders us to abstain from ungodliness and superstition of every kind, by which the glory of his divinity is diminished or obscured; and, for the same reason, he requires us to worship and adore him with truly pious zeal. The simple terms used obviously amount to this. For seeing we cannot have God without embracing everything which belongs to him, the prohibition against having strange gods means, that nothing which belongs to him is to be transferred to any other. The duties which we owe to God are innumerable, but they seem to admit of being not improperly reduced to four heads: Adoration, with its accessory spiritual submission of conscience, Trust, Invocation, Thanksgiving. By Adoration I mean the veneration and worship which we render to him when we do homage to his majesty; and hence I make part of it to consist in bringing our consciences into subjection to his Law. Trust is secure resting in him under a recognition of his perfections, when, ascribing to him all power, wisdom, justice, goodness, and truth, we consider ourselves happy in having been brought into intercourse with him. Invocation may be defined the retaking of ourselves to his promised aid as the only resource in every case of need. Thanksgiving is the gratitude which ascribes to him the praise of all our blessings. As the Lord does not allow these to be derived from any other quarter, so he demands that they shall be referred entirely to himself. It is not enough to refrain from other gods. We must, at the same time, devote ourselves wholly to him, not acting like certain impious despisers, who regard it as the shortest method, to hold all religious observance in derision. But here precedence must be given to true religion, which will direct our minds to the living God. When duly imbued with the knowledge of him, the whole aim of our lives will be to revere, fear, and worship his majesty, to enjoy a share in his blessings, to have recourse to him in every difficulty, to acknowledge, laud, and celebrate the magnificence of his works, to make him, as it were, the sole aim of all our actions. Next, we must beware of superstition, by which our minds are turned aside from the true God, and carried to and fro after a multiplicity of gods. Therefore, if we are contented with one God, let us call to mind what was formerly observed, that all fictitious gods are to be driven far away, and that the worship which he claims for himself is not to be mutilated. Not a particle of his glory is to be withheld: everything belonging to him must be reserved to him entire. The words, "before me," go to increase the indignity, God being provoked to jealousy whenever we substitute our fictions in his stead; just as an unfaithful wife stings her husband's heart more deeply when her adultery is committed openly before his eyes. Therefore, God having by his present power and grace declared that he had respect to the people whom he had chosen, now, in order to deter them from the wickedness of revolt, warns them that they cannot adopt strange gods without his being witness and spectator of the sacrilege. To the audacity of so doing is added the very great impiety of supposing that they can mock the eye of God with their evasions. Far from this the Lord proclaims that everything which we design, plan, or execute, lies open to his sight. Our conscience must, therefore, keep aloof from the most distant thought of revolt, if we would have our worship approved by the Lord. The glory of his Godhead must be maintained entire and incorrupt, not merely by external profession, but as under his eye, which penetrates the inmost recesses of his heart.

Second Commandment:

THOU SHALT NOT MAKE UNTO THEE ANY GRAVEN IMAGE, OR ANY LIKENESS OF ANYTHING THAT IS IN HEAVEN ABOVE, OR THAT IS IN THE EARTH BENEATH, OR THAT IS IN THE WATER UNDER THE EARTH: THOU SHALT NOT BOW DOWN THYSELF TO THEM, NOR SERVE THEM.

17. As in the first commandment the Lord declares that he is one, and that besides him no gods must be either worshiped or imagined, so he here more plainly declares what his nature is, and what the kind of worship with which he is to be honored, in order that we may not presume to form any carnal idea of him. The purport of the commandment, therefore, is that he will not have his legitimate worship profaned by superstitious rites. Wherefore, in general, he calls us entirely away from the carnal frivolous observances which our stupid minds are wont to devise after forming some gross idea of the divine nature, while at the same time he instructs us in the worship which is legitimate, namely, spiritual worship of his own appointment. The grossest vice here prohibited is external idolatry. This commandment consists of two parts. The former curbs the licentious daring which would subject the incomprehensible God to our senses, or represent him under any visible shape. The latter forbids the worship of images on any religious ground. There is, moreover, a brief enumeration of all the forms by which the Deity was usually represented by heathen and superstitious nations. By "any thing which is in heaven above" is meant the sun, the moon, and the stars, perhaps also birds, as in Deuteronomy, where the meaning is explained, there is mention of birds as well as stars (Deut. 4:15). I would not have made this observation, had I not seen that some

absurdly apply it to the angels. The other particulars I pass, as requiring no explanation. We have already shown clearly enough (Book 1. chap. 11-12) that every visible shape of Deity which man devises is diametrically opposed to the divine nature; and, therefore, that the moment idols appear, true religion is corrupted and adulterated.

18. The threatening subjoined ought to have no little effect in shaking off our lethargy. It is in the following terms:

I THE LORD THY GOD AM A JEALOUS GOD, VISITING THE INIQUITY OF THE FATHERS UPON THE CHILDREN UNTO THE THIRD AND FOURTH GENERATION OF THEM THAT HATE ME; AND SHEWING MERCY UNTO THOUSANDS OF THEM THAT LOVE ME, AND KEEP MY COMMANDMENTS.

The meaning here is the same as if he had said that our duty is to cleave to him alone. To induce us to this, he proclaims his authority which he will not permit to be impaired or despised with impunity. It is true, the word used is El, which means God; but as it is derived from a word meaning strength, I have had no hesitations in order to express the sense more fully, so to render it as inserted on the margin. Secondly, he calls himself jealous, because he cannot bear a partner. Thirdly, he declares that he will vindicate his majesty and glory, if any transfer it either to the creatures or to graven images; and that not by a simple punishment of brief duration, but one extending to the third and fourth generation of such as imitate the impiety of their progenitors. In like manner, he declares his constant mercy and kindness to the remote posterity of those who love him, and keep his Law. The Lord very frequently addresses us in the character of a husband; the union by which he connects us with himself, when he receives us into the bosom of the Church, having some resemblance to that of holy wedlock, because founded on mutual faith. As he performs all the offices of a true and faithful husband, so he stipulates for love and conjugal chastity from us; that is, that we do not prostitute our souls to Satan, to be defiled with foul carnal lusts. Hence, when he rebukes the Jews for their apostasy, he complains that they have cast off chastity, and polluted themselves with adultery. Therefore, as the purer and chaster the husband is, the more grievously is he offended when he sees his wife inclining to a rival; so the Lord, who has betrothed us to himself in truth, declares that he burns with the hottest jealousy whenever, neglecting the purity of his holy marriage, we defile ourselves with abominable lusts, and especially when the worship of his Deity, which ought to have been most carefully kept unimpaired, is transferred to another, or adulterated with some superstition; since, in this way, we not only violate our plighted troth, but defile the nuptial couch, by giving access to adulterers.

19. In the threatening we must attend to what is meant when God declares that he will visit the iniquity of the fathers upon the children unto the third and fourth generation. It seems inconsistent with the equity of the divine procedure to punish the innocent for another's fault; and the Lord himself declares that "the son shall not bear the iniquity of the father" (Ezek. 18:20). But still we meet more than once with a declaration as to the postponing of the punishment of the sins of fathers to future generations. Thus Moses repeatedly addresses the Lord as "visiting the iniquity of the fathers upon the children unto the third and fourth generation" (Num. 14:18). In like manner, Jeremiah, "Thou showest loving-kindness unto thousands, and recompenses the iniquity of the fathers into the bosom of their children after them" (Jer. 32:18). Some feeling sadly perplexed how to solve this difficulty think it is to be understood of temporal punishments only, which it is said sons may properly bear for the sins of their parents, because they are often inflicted for their own safety. This is indeed true; for Isaiah declared to Hezekiah that his children should be stripped of the kingdom, and carried away into captivity, for a sin which he had committed (Isa. 39:7); and the households of Pharaoh and Abimelech were made to suffer for an injury done to

Abraham (Gen. 12:17; 20:3-18). But the attempt to solve the question in this way is an evasion rather than a true interpretation. For the punishment denounced here and in similar passages is too great to be confined within the limits of the present life. We must therefore understand it to mean that a curse from the Lord righteously falls not only on the head of the guilty individual, but also on all his lineage. When it has fallen, what can be anticipated but that the father, being deprived of the Spirit of God, will live most flagitiously; that the son, being in like manner forsaken of the Lord, because of his father's iniquity, will follow the same road to destruction; and be followed in his turn by succeeding generations, forming a seed of evil-doers?

20. First, let us examine whether such punishment is inconsistent with the divine justice. If human nature is universally condemned, those on whom the Lord does not bestow the communication of his grace must be doomed to destruction; nevertheless, they perish by their own iniquity, not by unjust hatred on the part of God. There is no room to expostulate, and ask why the grace of God does not forward their salvation as it does that of others. Therefore, when God punishes the wicked and flagitious for their crimes, by depriving their families of his grace for many generations, who will dare to bring a charge against him for this most righteous vengeance? But it will be said, the Lord, on the contrary, declares, that the son shall not suffer for the father's sin (Ezek. 18:20). Observe the scope of that passage. The Israelites, after being subjected to a long period of uninterrupted calamities, had begun to say, as a proverb, that their fathers had eaten the sour grape, and thus set the children's teeth on edge; meaning that they, though in themselves righteous and innocent, were paying the penalty of sins committed by their parents, and this more from the implacable anger than the duly tempered severity of God. The prophet declares it was not so: that they were punished for their own wickedness; that it was not in accordance with the justice of God that a righteous son should suffer for the iniquity of a wicked father; and

that nothing of the kind was exemplified in what they suffered. For, if the visitation of which we now speak is accomplished when God withdraws from the children of the wicked the light of his truth and the other helps to salvation, the only way in which they are accursed for their fathers' wickedness is in being blinded and abandoned by God, and so left to walk in their parents' steps. The misery which they suffer in time, and the destruction to which they are finally doomed, are thus punishments inflicted by divine justice, not for the sins of others, but for their own iniquity.

21. On the other hand, there is a promise of mercy to thousands—a promise which is frequently mentioned in Scripture, and forms an article in the solemn covenant made with the Church—I will be "a God unto thee, and to thy seed after thee" (Gen. 17:7). With reference to this, Solomon says, "The just man walketh in his integrity: his children are blessed after him" (Prov. 20:7); not only in consequence of a religious education (though this certainly is by no means unimportant), but in consequence of the blessing promised in the covenant—viz. that the divine favor will dwell for ever in the families of the righteous. Herein is excellent consolation to believers, and great ground of terror to the wicked; for if, after death, the mere remembrance of righteousness and iniquity have such an influence on the divine procedure, that his blessing rests on the posterity of the righteous, and his curse on the posterity of the wicked, much more must it rest on the heads of the individuals themselves. Notwithstanding of this, however, the offspring of the wicked sometimes amends, while that of believers degenerates; because the Almighty has not here laid down an inflexible rule which might derogate from his free election. For the consolation of the righteous, and the dismay of the sinner, it is enough that the threatening itself is not vain or nugatory, although it does not always take effect. For as the temporal punishments inflicted on a few of the wicked are proofs of the divine wrath against sin, and of the future judgment that will ultimately overtake all sinners,

though many escape with impunity even to the end of their lives, so when the Lord gives one example of blessing a son for his father's sake, by visiting him in mercy and kindness, it is a proof of constant and unfailing favor to his worshipers. On the other hand, when in any single instance he visits the iniquity of the father on the son, he gives intimation of the judgment which awaits all the reprobate for their own iniquities. The certainty of this is the principal thing here taught. Moreover, the Lord, as it were by the way, commends the riches of his mercy by extending it to thousands, while he limits his vengeance to four generations.

Third Commandment.

THOU SHALT NOT TAKE THE NAME OF THE LORD THY GOD IN VAIN.

22. The purport of this Commandment is that the majesty of the name of God is to be held sacred. In sum, therefore, it means, that we must not profane it by using it irreverently or contemptuously. This prohibition implies a corresponding precept—viz. that it be our study and care to treat his name with religious veneration. Wherefore it becomes us to regulate our minds and our tongues, so as never to think or speak of God and his mysteries without reverence and great soberness, and never, in estimating his works, to have any feeling towards him but one of deep veneration. We must, I say, steadily observe the three following things: first, whatever our mind conceives of him, whatever our tongue utters, must bespeak his excellence, and correspond to the sublimity of his sacred name; in short, must be fitted to extol its greatness. Secondly, we must not rashly and preposterously pervert his sacred word and adorable mysteries to purposes of ambition, or avarice, or amusement, but, according as they bear the impress of his dignity, must always maintain them in due honor and esteem. Lastly, we must not detract from or throw obloquy upon his works, as miserable men are wont insultingly to do, but must laud every action which we attribute to him as wise, and just, and good. This

is to sanctify the name of God. When we act otherwise, his name is profaned with vain and wicked abuse, because it is applied to a purpose foreign to that to which it is consecrated. Were there nothing worse, in being deprived of its dignity it is gradually brought into contempt. But if there is so much evil in the rash and unseasonable employment of the divine name, there is still more evil in its being employed for nefarious purposes, as is done by those who use it in necromancy, cursing, illicit exorcisms, and other impious incantations. But the Commandment refers especially to the case of oaths, in which a perverse employment of the divine name is particularly detestable; and this it does the more effectually to deter us from every species of profanation. That the thing here commanded relates to the worship of God, and the reverence due to his name, and not to the equity which men are to cultivate towards each other, is apparent from this, that afterwards, in the Second Table, there is a condemnation of the perjury and false testimony by which human society is injured, and that the repetition would be superfluous, if, in this Commandment, the duty of charity were handled. Moreover, this is necessary even for distinction, because, as was observed, God has, for good reason, divided his Law into two tables. The inference then is, that God here vindicates his own right, and defends his sacred name, but does not teach the duties which men owe to men.

23. In the first place, we must consider what an oath is. An oath, then, is calling God to witness that what we say is true. Execrations being manifestly insulting to God are unworthy of being classed among oaths. That an oath, when duly taken, is a species of divine worship, appears from many passages of Scripture, as when Isaiah prophesies of the admission of the Assyrians and Egyptians to a participation in the covenant, he says, "In that day shall five cities in the land of Egypt speak the language of Canaan, and swear to the Lord of hosts" (Isaiah 19:18). Swearing by the name of the Lord here means that they will make a profession of religion. In like manner,

speaking of the extension of the Redeemer's kingdom, it is said, "He who blesseth himself in the earth shall bless himself in the God of truth: and he that sweareth in the earth shall swear by the God of truth" (Isaiah 65:16). In Jeremiah it is said, "If they will diligently learn the ways of my people, to swear by my name, 'The Lord liveth'; as they taught my people to swear by Baal; then shall they be built in the midst of my people" (Jer. 12:16). By appealing to the name of the Lord, and calling him to witness, we are justly said to declare our own religious veneration of him. For we thus acknowledge that he is eternal and unchangeable truth, inasmuch as we not only call upon him, in preference to others, as a fit witness to the truth, but as its only assertor, able to bring hidden things to light, a discerner of the hearts. When human testimony fails, we appeal to God as witness, especially when the matter to be proved lies hid in the conscience. For which reason, the Lord is grievously offended with those who swear by strange gods, and construes such swearing as a proof of open revolt, "Thy children have forsaken me, and sworn by them that are no gods" (Jer. 5:7). The heinousness of the offense is declared by the punishment denounced against it, "I will cut off them that swear by the Lord, and that swear by Malcham" (Zeph. 1:4-5).

24. Understanding that the Lord would have our oaths to be a species of divine worship, we must be the more careful that they do not, instead of worship, contain insult, or contempt and vilification. It is no slight insult to swear by him and do it falsely: hence in the Law this is termed profanation (Lev. 19:12). For if God is robbed of his truth, what is it that remains? Without truth he could not be God. But assuredly he is robbed of his truth when he is made the approver and attester of what is false. Hence, when Joshua is endeavoring to make Achan confess the truth, he says, "My son, give, I pray thee, glory to the Lord God of Israel" (Joshua 7:19); intimating that grievous dishonor is done to God when men swear by him falsely. And no wonder; for, as far as in them lies, his sacred name is in a manner branded with falsehood.

That this mode of expression was common among the Jews whenever anyone was called upon to take an oath is evident from a similar obtestation used by the Pharisees, as given in John (John 9:24); Scripture reminds us of the caution which we ought to use by employing such expressions as the following: "As the Lord liveth;" "God do so and more also;" "I call God for a record upon my soul." Such expressions intimate that we cannot call God to witness our statement without imprecating his vengeance for perjury if it is false.

25. The name of God is vulgarized and vilified when used in oaths, which, though true, are superfluous. This, too, is to take his name in vain. Wherefore, it is not sufficient to abstain from perjury, unless we at the same time remember that an oath is not appointed or allowed for passion or pleasure, but for necessity; and that, therefore, a licentious use is made of it by him who uses it on any other than necessary occasions. Moreover, no case of necessity can be pretended, unless where some purpose of religion or charity is to be served. In this matter, great sin is committed in the present day—sin the more intolerable in this, that its frequency has made it cease to be regarded as a fault, though it certainly is not accounted trivial before the judgment-seat of God. The name of God is everywhere profaned by introducing it indiscriminately in frivolous discourse; and the evil is disregarded, because it has been long and audaciously persisted in with impunity. The commandment of the Lord, however, stands; the penalty also stands, and will one day receive effect. Special vengeance will be executed on those who have taken the name of God in vain. Another form of violation is exhibited when with manifest impiety we in our oaths substitute the holy servants of God for God himself, thus conferring upon them the glory of his Godhead. It is not without cause the Lord has by a special commandment required us to swear by his name, and by a special prohibition forbidden us to swear by other gods. The Apostle gives a clear attestation to the same effect, when he says that "men verily swear by the greater;" but that "when

God made promise to Abraham, because he could swear by no greater, he sware by himself," (Heb. 6:16, 13).

26. The Anabaptists, not content with this moderate use of oaths, condemn all without exception on the ground of our Savior's general prohibition, "I say unto you, Swear not at all:" "Let your speech be Yea, yea; Nay, nay: for whatsoever is more than these cometh of evil" (Matt. 5:34; James 5:12). In this way, they inconsiderately make a stumbling-stone of Christ, setting him in opposition to the Father, as if he had descended into the world to annul his decrees. In the Law, the Almighty not only permits an oath as a thing that is lawful (this were amply sufficient), but in a case of necessity actually commands it (Exod. 22:11). Christ again declares that he and his Father are one; that he only delivers what was commanded of his Father; that his doctrine is not his own, but his that sent him (John 10:18, 30; 7:16). What then? Will they make God contradict himself, by approving and commanding at one time, what he afterwards prohibits and condemns? But as there is some difficulty in what our Savior says on the subject of swearing, it may be proper to consider it a little. Here, however, we shall never arrive at the true meaning unless we attend to the design of Christ and the subject of which he is treating. His purpose was neither to relax nor to curtail the Law, but to restore the true and genuine meaning which had been greatly corrupted by the false glosses of the Scribes and Pharisees. If we attend to this we shall not suppose that Christ condemned all oaths but those only which transgressed the rule of the Law. It is evident from the oaths themselves that the people were accustomed to think it enough if they avoided perjury, whereas the Law prohibits not perjury merely, but also vain and superfluous oaths. Therefore our Lord, who is the best interpreter of the Law, reminds them that there is a sin not only in perjury, but in swearing. How in swearing? Namely, by swearing vainly. Those oaths, however, which are authorized by the Law, he leaves safe and free. Those who condemn oaths think their argument invincible when

they fasten on the expression, not at all. The expression applies not to the word swear, but to the subjoined forms of oaths. For part of the error consisted in their supposing that when they swore by the heaven and the earth, they did not touch the name of God. The Lord, therefore, after cutting off the principal source of prevarication, deprives them of all subterfuges, warning them against supposing that they escape guilt by suppressing the name of God and appealing to heaven and earth. For it ought here to be observed in passing that although the name of God is not expressed, yet men swear by him in using indirect forms, as when they swear by the light of life, by the bread they eat, by their baptism, or any other pledges of the divine liberality towards them. Some erroneously suppose that our Savior, in that passage, rebukes superstition, by forbidding men to swear by heaven and earth and Jerusalem. He rather refutes the sophistical subtlety of those who thought it nothing vainly to utter indirect oaths, imagining that they thus spared the holy name of God, whereas that name is inscribed on each of his mercies. The case is different, when any mortal living or dead, or an angel, is substituted in the place of God, as in the vile form devised by flattery in heathen nations, "By the life or genius of the king"; for, in this case, the false apotheosis obscures and impairs the glory of the one God. But when nothing else is intended than to confirm what is said by an appeal to the holy name of God, although it is done indirectly, yet his majesty is insulted by all frivolous oaths. Christ strips this abuse of every vain pretext when he says "Swear not at all". To the same effect is the passage in which James uses the words of our Savior above quoted (James 5:12). For this rash swearing has always prevailed in the world, notwithstanding that it is a profanation of the name of God. If you refer the words, "not at all," to the act itself, as if every oath, without exception, were unlawful, what will be the use of the explanation which immediately follows: "Neither by heaven, neither by the earth," &c.? These words make it clear, that the object in view was to meet the cavils by which the Jews thought they could extenuate their fault.

27. Every person of sound judgment must now see that in that passage our Lord merely condemned those oaths which were forbidden by the Law. For he who in his life exhibited a model of the perfection which he taught, did not object to oaths whenever the occasion required them; and the disciples, who doubtless in all things obeyed their Master, followed the same rule. Who will dare to say that Paul would have sworn (Rom. 1:9; 2 Cor. 1:23) if an oath had been altogether forbidden? But when the occasion calls for it, he adjures without any scruple, and sometimes even imprecates. The question, however, is not yet disposed of. For some think that the only oaths exempted from the prohibition are public oaths, such as those which are administered to us by the magistrate, or independent states employ in ratifying treaties, or the people take when they swear allegiance to their sovereign, or the soldier in the case of the military oath, and others of a similar description. To this class they refer (and justly) those protestations in the writings of Paul, which assert the dignity of the Gospel; since the Apostles, in discharging their office, were not private individuals, but the public servants of God. I certainly deny not that such oaths are the safest because they are most strongly supported by passages of Scripture. The magistrate is enjoined, in a doubtful matter, to put the witness upon oath; and he in his turn to answer upon oath; and an Apostle says that in this way there is an end of all strife (Heb. 6:16). In this commandment, both parties are fully approved. Nay, we may observe that among the ancient heathens a public and solemn oath was held in great reverence, while those common oaths which were indiscriminately used were in little or no estimation, as if they thought that in regard to them the Deity did not interpose. Private oaths used soberly, sacredly, and reverently, on necessary occasions, it were perilous to condemn, supported as they are by reason and example. For if private individuals are permitted in

a grave and serious matter to appeal to God as a judge, much more may they appeal to him as a witness. Your brother charges you with perfidy. You, as bound by the duties of charity, labor to clear yourself from the charge. He will on no account be satisfied. If, through his obstinate malice, your good name is brought into jeopardy, you can appeal without offense to the judgment of God, that he may in time manifest your innocence. If the terms are weighed, it will be found that it is a less matter to call upon him to be witness; and I therefore see not how it can be called unlawful to do so. And there is no want of examples. If it is pretended that the oath which Abraham and Isaac made with Abimelech was of a public nature, that by which Jacob and Laban bound themselves in mutual league was private. Boaz, though a private man, confirmed his promise of marriage to Ruth in the same way. Obadiah too, a just man and one that feared God, though a private individual, in seeking to persuade Elijah asseverates with an oath. I hold, therefore, that there is no better rule than so to regulate our oaths that they shall neither be rash, frivolous, promiscuous, nor passionate, but be made to serve a just necessity; in other words, to vindicate the glory of God, or promote the edification of a brother. This is the end of the Commandment.

Fourth Commandment.

REMEMBER THE SABBATH DAY TO KEEP IT HOLY. SIX DAYS SHALT THOU LABOR AND DO ALL THY WORK: BUT THE SEVENTH DAY IS THE SABBATH OF THE LORD THY GOD. IN IT THOU SHALT NOT DO ANY WORK, &c.

28. The purport of the commandment is that being dead to our own affections and works, we meditate on the kingdom of God, and in order to such meditation, have recourse to the means which he has appointed. But as this commandment stands in peculiar circumstances apart from the others, the mode of exposition must be somewhat different. Early Christian writers are wont to call it typical, as containing

the external observance of a day which was abolished with the other types on the advent of Christ. This is indeed true; but it leaves the half of the matter untouched. Wherefore, we must look deeper for our exposition, and attend to three cases in which it appears to me that the observance of this commandment consists. First, under the rest of the seventh days the Divine Lawgiver meant to furnish the people of Israel with a type of the spiritual rest by which believers were to cease from their own works, and allow God to work in them. Secondly he meant that there should be a stated day on which they should assemble to hear the Law, and perform religious rites, or which at least they should specially employ in meditating on his works, and be thereby trained to piety. Thirdly, he meant that servants and those who lived under the authority of others should be indulged with a day of rest, and thus have some intermission from labor.

29. We are taught in many passages that this adumbration of spiritual rest held a primary place in the Sabbath. Indeed, there is no commandment the observance of which the Almighty more strictly enforces. When he would intimate by the Prophets that religion was entirely subverted, he complains that his Sabbaths were polluted, violated, not kept, not hallowed; as if, after it was neglected, there remained nothing in which he could be honored. The observance of it he eulogizes in the highest terms, and hence, among other divine privileges, the faithful set an extraordinary value on the revelation of the Sabbath. In Nehemiah, the Levites, in the public assembly, thus speak: "Thou madest known unto them thy holy sabbath, and commandedst them precepts, statutes, and laws, by the hand of Moses thy servant." You see the singular honor which it holds among all the precepts of the Law. All this tends to celebrate the dignity of the mystery, which is most admirably expressed by Moses and Ezekiel. Thus in Exodus: "Verily my Sabbaths shall ye keep: for it is a sign between me and you throughout your generations; that ye may know that I am the Lord that does sanctify you. Ye shall keep my sabbath therefore; for it

is holy unto you: every one that defileth it shall surely be put to death: for whosoever does any work therein, that soul shall be cut off from among his people. Six days may work be done; but in the seventh is the sabbath of rest, holy to the Lord: whosoever does any work in the sabbath day, he shall surely be put to death. Wherefore the children of Israel shall keep the sabbath; to observe the sabbath throughout their generations for a perpetual covenant. It is a sign between me and the children of Israel forever" (Exodus 31:13-17). Ezekiel is still more full, but the sum of what he says amounts to this: that the sabbath is a sign by which Israel might know that God is their sanctifier. If our sanctification consists in the mortification of our own will, the analogy between the external sign and the thing signified is most appropriate. We must rest entirely, in order that God may work in us; we must resign our own will, yield up our heart, and abandon all the lusts of the flesh. In short, we must desist from all the acts of our own mind, that God working in us, we may rest in him, as the Apostle also teaches (Heb. 3:13; 4:3, 9).

30. This complete cessation was represented to the Jews by the observance of one day in seven which, that it might be more religiously attended to, the Lord recommended by his own example. For it is no small incitement to the zeal of man to know that he is engaged in imitating his Creator. Should anyone expect some secret meaning in the number seven, this being in Scripture the number for perfection, it may have been selected, not without cause, to denote perpetuity. In accordance with this, Moses concludes his description of the succession of day and night on the same day on which he relates that the Lord rested from his works. Another probable reason for the number may be that the Lord intended that the Sabbath never should be completed before the arrival of the last day. We here begin our blessed rest in him, and daily make new progress in it; but because we must still wage an incessant warfare with the flesh, it shall not be consummated until the fulfillment of the prophecy of Isaiah: "From one new

moon to another, and from one sabbath to another, shall all flesh come to worship before me, saith the Lord" (Isaiah 66:23); in other words, when God shall be "all in all" (1 Cor. 15:28). It may seem, therefore, that by the seventh day the Lord delineated to his people the future perfection of his sabbath on the last day, that by continual meditation on the sabbath, they might throughout their whole lives aspire to this perfection.

31. Should these remarks on the number seem to any somewhat far-fetched, I have no objection to their taking it more simply: that the Lord appointed a certain day on which his people might be trained, under the tutelage of the Law, to meditate constantly on the spiritual rest, and fixed upon the seventh, either because he foresaw it would be sufficient, or in order that his own example might operate as a stronger stimulus; or, at least to remind men that the Sabbath was appointed for no other purpose than to render them conformable to their Creator. It is of little consequence which of these be adopted, provided we lose not sight of the principal thing delineated—viz. the mystery of perpetual resting from our works. To the contemplation of this, the Jews were every now and then called by the prophets, lest they should think a carnal cessation from labor sufficient. Beside the passages already quoted, there is the following: "If thou turn away thy foot from the sabbath, from doing thy pleasure on my holy day; and call the sabbath a delight, the holy of the Lord, honorable; and shalt honor him, not doing thine own ways, nor finding thine own pleasure, nor speaking thine own words: then shalt thou delight thyself in the Lord" (Isaiah 58:13-14). Still there can be no doubt that on the advent of our Lord Jesus Christ, the ceremonial part of the commandment was abolished. He is the truth at whose presence all the emblems vanish; the body, at the sight of which the shadows disappear. He, I say, is the true completion of the sabbath: "We are buried with him by baptism unto death: that like as Christ was raised up from the dead by the glory of the Father, even so we should walk

in newness of life" (Rom. 6:4). Hence, as the Apostle elsewhere says, "Let no man therefore judge you in meat, or in drink, or in respect of an holiday, or of the new moon, or of the sabbath days; which are a shadow of things to come; but the body is of Christ" (Col. 2:16-17); meaning by body the whole essence of the truth, as is well explained in that passage. This is not contented with one day, but requires the whole course of our lives, until being completely dead to ourselves, we are filled with the life of God. Christians, therefore, should have nothing to do with a superstitious observance of days.

32. The two other cases ought not to be classed with ancient shadows, but are adapted to every age. The sabbath being abrogated, there is still room among us, first, to assemble on stated days for the hearing of the Word, the breaking of the mystical bread, and public prayer; and, secondly, to give our servants and laborers relaxation from labor. It cannot be doubted that the Lord provided for both in the commandment of the Sabbath. The former is abundantly evinced by the mere practice of the Jews. The latter Moses has expressed in Deuteronomy in the following terms: "The seventh day is the sabbath of the Lord thy God: in it thou shalt not do any work, thou, nor thy son, nor thy daughter, nor thy man-servant, nor thy maid-servant; that thy man-servant and thy maid-servant may rest as well as thou" (Deut. 5:14). Likewise in Exodus, "That thine ox and thine ass may rest, and the son of thy handmaid, and the stranger, may be refreshed" (Exod. 23:12). Who can deny that both are equally applicable to us as to the Jews? Religious meetings are enjoined us by the word of God; their necessity, experience itself sufficiently demonstrates. But unless these meetings are stated, and have fixed days allotted to them, how can they be held? We must, as the apostle expresses it, do all things decently and in order (1 Cor. 14:40). So impossible, however, would it be to preserve decency and order without this politic arrangement that the dissolution of it would instantly lead to the disturbance and ruin of the Church. But if the reason for which the Lord appointed a

sabbath to the Jews is equally applicable to us, no man can assert that it is a matter with which we have nothing to do. Our most provident and indulgent Parent has been pleased to provide for our wants not less than for the wants of the Jews. Why, it may be asked, do we not hold daily meetings, and thus avoid the distinction of days? Would that we were privileged to do so! Spiritual wisdom undoubtedly deserves to have some portion of every day devoted to it. But if, owing to the weakness of many, daily meetings cannot be held, and charity will not allow us to exact more of them, why should we not adopt the rule which the will of God has obviously imposed upon us?

33. I am obliged to dwell a little longer on this because some restless spirits are now making an outcry about the observance of the Lord's day. They complain that Christian people are trained in Judaism, because some observance of days is retained. My reply is that those days are observed by us without Judaism, because in this matter we differ widely from the Jews. We do not celebrate it with most minute formality, as a ceremony by which we imagine that a spiritual mystery is typified, but we adopt it as a necessary remedy for preserving order in the Church. Paul informs us that Christians are not to be judged in respect of its observance, because it is a shadow of something to come (Col. 2:16); and, accordingly, he expresses a fear lest his labor among the Galatians should prove in vain, because they still observed days (Gal. 4:10-11). And he tells the Romans that it is superstitious to make one day differ from another (Rom. 14:5). But who, except those restless men, does not see what the observance is to which the Apostle refers? Those persons had no regard to that politic and ecclesiastical arrangement, but by retaining the days as types of spiritual things, they in so far obscured the glory of Christ, and the light of the Gospel. They did not desist from manual labor on the ground of its interfering with sacred study and meditation, but as a kind of religious observance; because they dreamed that by their cessation from labor, they were cultivating the mysteries which

had of old been committed to them. It was, I say, against this preposterous observance of days that the Apostle inveighs, and not against that legitimate selection which is subservient to the peace of Christian society. For in the churches established by him, this was the use for which the Sabbath was retained. He tells the Corinthians to set the first day apart for collecting contributions for the relief of their brethren at Jerusalem (1 Cor. 16:2). If superstition is dreaded, there was more danger in keeping the Jewish sabbath than the Lord's day as Christians now do. It being expedient to overthrow superstition, the Jewish holy day was abolished; and as a thing necessary to retain decency, order, and peace in the Church, another day was appointed for that purpose.

34. It was not, however, without a reason that the early Christians substituted what we call the Lord's day for the Sabbath. The resurrection of our Lord being the end and accomplishment of that true rest which the ancient sabbath typified, this day, by which types were abolished serves to warn Christians against adhering to a shadowy ceremony. I do not cling so to the number seven as to bring the Church under bondage to it, nor do I condemn churches for holding their meetings on other solemn days, provided they guard against superstition. This they will do if they employ those days merely for the observance of discipline and regular order. The whole may be thus summed up: as the truth was delivered typically to the Jews, so it is imparted to us without figure; first, that during our whole lives we may aim at a constant rest from our own works, in order that the Lord may work in us by his Spirit; secondly that every individual, as he has opportunity, may diligently exercise himself in private, in pious meditation on the works of God, and, at the same time, that all may observe the legitimate order appointed by the Church, for the hearing of the word, the administration of the sacraments, and public prayer: And, thirdly, that we may avoid oppressing those who are subject to us. In this way, we get quit of the trifling of the false prophets, who in

later times instilled Jewish ideas into the people, alleging that nothing was abrogated but what was ceremonial in the commandment (this they term in their language the taxation of the seventh day), while the moral part remains—viz. the observance of one day in seven. But this is nothing else than to insult the Jews, by changing the day, and yet mentally attributing to it the same sanctity; thus retaining the same typical distinction of days as had place among the Jews. And of a truth, we see what profit they have made by such a doctrine. Those who cling to their constitutions go thrice as far as the Jews in the gross and carnal superstition of sabbatism; so that the rebukes which we read in Isaiah (Isa. 1:13; 58:13) apply as much to those of the present day, as to those to whom the Prophet addressed them. We must be careful, however, to observe the general doctrine—viz. in order that religion may neither be lost nor languish among us, we must diligently attend on our religious assemblies, and duly avail ourselves of those external aids which tend to promote the worship of God.

Fifth Commandment.

HONOR THY FATHER AND THY MOTHER: THAT THY DAYS MAY BE LONG UPON THE LAND WHICH THE LORD THY GOD GIVETH THEE.

35. The end of this commandment is that since the Lord takes pleasure in the preservation of his own ordinance, the degrees of dignity appointed by him must be held inviolable. The sum of the commandment, therefore, will be that we are to look up to those whom the Lord has set over us, yielding them honor, gratitude, and obedience. Hence it follows that every thing in the way of contempt, ingratitude, or disobedience is forbidden. For the term honor has this extent of meaning in Scripture. Thus when the Apostle says, "Let the elders that rule well be counted worthy of double honor" (1 Tim. 5:17), he refers not only to the reverence which is due to them, but to the recompense to which their services are entitled. But as this command to submit is very repugnant to the perversity of the human mind (which

puffed up with ambitious longings will scarcely allow itself to be subject), that superiority which is most attractive and least invidious is set
forth as an example calculated to soften and bend our minds to habits
of submission. From that subjection which is most easily endured,
the Lord gradually accustoms us to every kind of legitimate subjection, the same principle regulating all. For to those whom he raises
to eminences he communicates his authority, in so far as necessary to
maintain their station. The titles of Father, God, and Lord all meet
in him alone and hence whenever any one of them is mentioned, our
mind should be impressed with the same feeling of reverence. Those,
therefore, to whom he imparts such titles, he distinguishes by some
small spark of his refulgence, so as to entitle them to honor, each in
his own place. In this way, we must consider that our earthly father
possesses something of a divine nature in him, because there is some
reason for his bearing a divine title, and that he who is our prince and
ruler is admitted to some communion of honor with God.

36. Wherefore, we ought to have no doubt that the Lord here lays
down this universal rule—viz. that knowing how every individual is
set over us by his appointment, we should pay him reverence, gratitude, obedience, and every duty in our power. And it makes no difference whether those on whom the honor is conferred are deserving or
not. Be they what they may, the Almighty, by conferring their station
upon them, shows that he would have them honored. The commandment specifies the reverence due to those to whom we owe our being.
This Nature herself should in some measure teach us. For they are
monsters, and not men, who petulantly and contumeliously violate
the paternal authority. Hence, the Lord orders all who rebel against
their parents to be put to death, they being, as it where, unworthy of
the light in paying no deference to those to whom they are indebted
for beholding it. And it is evident, from the various appendices to the
Law, that we were correct in stating that the honor here referred to
consists of three parts, reverence, obedience, and gratitude. The first

of these the Lord enforces, when he commands that whose curseth his father or his mother shall be put to death. In this way he avenges insult and contempt. The second he enforces, when he denounces the punishment of death on disobedient and rebellious children. To the third belongs our Savior's declaration that God requires us to do good to our parents (Matt. 15). And whenever Paul mentions this commandment, he interprets it as enjoining obedience.

37. A promise is added by way of recommendation, the better to remind us how pleasing to God is the submission which is here required. Paul applies that stimulus to rouse us from our lethargy, when he calls this the first commandment with promise; the promise contained in the First Table not being specially appropriated to any one commandment, but extended to the whole law. Moreover, the sense in which the promise is to be taken is as follows: the Lord spoke to the Israelites specially of the land which he had promised them for an inheritance. If, then, the possession of the land was an earnest of the divine favor, we cannot wonder if the Lord was pleased to testify his favor, by bestowing long life, as in this way they were able long to enjoy his kindness. The meaning therefore is: honor thy father and thy mother, that thou may be able, during the course of a long life, to enjoy the possession of the land which is to be given thee in testimony of my favor. But, as the whole earth is blessed to believers, we justly class the present life among the number of divine blessings. Whence this promise has, in like manner, reference to us also, inasmuch as the duration of the present life is a proof of the divine benevolence toward us. It is not promised to us, nor was it promised to the Jews, as if in itself it constituted happiness, but because it is an ordinary symbol of the divine favor to the pious. Wherefore, if anyone who is obedient to parents happens to be cut off before mature age (a thing which not infrequently happens), the Lord nevertheless adheres to his promise as steadily as when he bestows a hundred acres of land where he had promised only one. The whole lies in this: we must consider that long

life is promised only in so far as it is a blessing from God, and that it is a blessing only in so far as it is a manifestation of divine favor. This, however, he testifies and truly manifests to his servants more richly and substantially by death.

38. Moreover, while the Lord promises the blessing of present life to children who show proper respect to their parents, he at the same time intimates that an inevitable curse is impending over the rebellious and disobedient; and, that it may not fail of execution, he in his Law pronounces sentence of death upon them and orders it to be inflicted. If they escape the judgment, he, in some way or other, will execute vengeance. For we see how great a number of this description of individuals fall either in battle or in brawls; others of them are overtaken by unwonted disasters, and almost all are a proof that the threatening is not used in vain. But if any do escape till extreme old age, yet, because deprived of the blessing of God in this life, they only languish on in wickedness, and are reserved for severer punishment in the world to come, they are far from participating in the blessing promised to obedient children. It ought to be observed by the way, that we are ordered to obey parents only in the Lord. This is clear from the principle already laid down: for the place which they occupy is one to which the Lord has exalted them, by communicating to them a portion of his own honor. Therefore the submission yielded to them should be a step in our ascent to the Supreme Parent, and hence, if they instigate us to transgress the law, they deserve not to be regarded as parents, but as strangers attempting to seduce us from obedience to our true Father. The same holds in the case of rulers, masters, and superiors of every description. For it were unbecoming and absurd that the honor of God should be impaired by their exaltation—an exaltation which, being derived from him, ought to lead us up to him.

Sixth Commandment. THOU SHALT NOT KILL.

39. The purport of this commandment is that since the Lord has bound the whole human race by a kind of unity, the safety of all ought to be considered as entrusted to each. In general, therefore, all violence and injustice, and every kind of harm from which our neighbor's body suffers, is prohibited. Accordingly, we are required faithfully to do what in us lies to defend the life of our neighbor; to promote whatever tends to his tranquility, to be vigilant in warding off harm, and, when danger comes, to assist in removing it. Remembering that the Divine Lawgiver thus speaks, consider moreover that he requires you to apply the same rule in regulating your mind. It were ridiculous that he who sees the thoughts of the heart and has special regard to them should train the body only to rectitude. This commandment, therefore, prohibits the murder of the heart, and requires a sincere desire to preserve our brother's life. The hand, indeed, commits the murder, but the mind under the influence of wrath and hatred conceives it. How can you be angry with your brother, without passionately longing to do him harm? If you must not be angry with him, neither must you hate him, hatred being nothing but inveterate anger. However you may disguise the fact, or endeavor to escape from it by vain pretexts. Where either wrath or hatred is, there is an inclination to do mischief. If you still persist in tergiversation, the mouth of the Spirit has declared, that "whosoever hateth his brother is a murderer" (1 John 3:15); and the mouth of our Savior has declared, that "whosoever is angry with his brother without a cause shall be in danger of the judgment: and whosoever shall say to his brother, 'Raca,' shall be in danger of the council: but whosoever shall say, 'Thou fool,' shall be in danger of hell fire" (Matt. 5:22).

40. Scripture notes a twofold equity on which this commandment is founded. Man is both the image of God and our flesh. Wherefore, if we would not violate the image of God, we must hold the person of man sacred—if we would not divest ourselves of humanity we must cherish our own flesh. The practical inference to be drawn from the

redemption and gift of Christ will be elsewhere considered. The Lord has been pleased to direct our attention to these two natural considerations as inducements to watch over our neighbor's preservation— viz. to revere the Divine image impressed upon him and embrace our own flesh. To be clear of the crime of murder, it is not enough to refrain from shedding man's blood. If in act you perpetrate, if in endeavor you plot, if in wish and design you conceive what is adverse to another's safety, you have the guilt of murder. On the other hand, if you do not according to your means and opportunity study to defend his safety, by that inhumanity you violate the law. But if the safety of the body is so carefully provided for, we may hence infer how much care and exertion is due to the safety of the soul, which is of immeasurably higher value in the sight of God.

Seventh Commandment.

THOU SHALT NOT COMMIT ADULTERY.

41. The purport of this commandment is that as God loves chastity and purity, we ought to guard against all uncleanness. The substance of the commandment therefore is that we must not defile ourselves with any impurity or libidinous excess. To this corresponds the affirmative that we must regulate every part of our conduct chastely and continently. The thing expressly forbidden is adultery, to which lust naturally tends, that its filthiness (being of a grosser and more palpable form, in as much as it casts a stain even on the body) may dispose us to abominate every form of lust. As the law under which man was created was not to lead a life of solitude, but enjoy a help meet for him, and ever since he fell under the curse the necessity for this mode of life is increased; the Lord made the requisite provision for us in this respect by the institution of marriage, which, entered into under his authority, he has also sanctified with his blessing. Hence, it is evident that any mode of cohabitation different from marriage is cursed in his sight, and that the conjugal relation was ordained as a necessary means of preventing us from giving way to unbridled lust.

Let us beware, therefore, of yielding to indulgence, seeing we are assured that the curse of God lies on every man and woman cohabiting without marriage.

42. Now, since natural feeling and the passions unnamed by the fall make the marriage tie doubly necessary, save in the case of those whom God has by special grace exempted, let every individual consider how the case stands with himself. Virginity, I admit, is a virtue not to be despised; but since it is denied to some, and to others granted only for a season, those who are assailed by incontinence, and unable successfully to war against it, should retake themselves to the remedy of marriage, and thus cultivate chastity in the way of their calling. Those incapable of self-restraint, if they apply not to the remedy allowed and provided for intemperance, war with God and resist his ordinance. And let no man tell me (as many in the present day do) that he can do all things, God helping! The help of God is present with those only who walk in his ways (Ps. 91:14), that is, in his callings from which all withdraw themselves who, omitting the remedies provided by God, vainly and presumptuously strive to struggle with and surmount their natural feelings. That continence is a special gift from God, and of the class of those which are not bestowed indiscriminately on the whole body of the Church, but only on a few of its members, our Lord affirms (Matt. 19:12). He first describes a certain class of individuals who have made themselves eunuchs for the kingdom of heavenly sake; that is, in order that they may be able to devote themselves with more liberty and less restraint to the things of heaven. But lest anyone should suppose that such a sacrifice was in every man's power, he had shown a little before that all are not capable, but those only to whom it is specially given from above. Hence he concludes, "He that is able to receive it, let him receive it." Paul asserts the same thing still more plainly when he says, "Every man has his proper gift of God, one after this manner, and another after that" (1 Cor. 7:7).

43. Since we are reminded by an express declaration that it is not in every man's power to live chaste in celibacy although it may be his most strenuous study and aim to do so—that it is a special grace which the Lord bestows only on certain individuals, in order that they may be less encumbered in his service, do we not oppose God, and nature as constituted by him, if we do not accommodate our mode of life to the measure of our ability? The Lord prohibits fornication, therefore he requires purity and chastity. The only method which each has of preserving it is to measure himself by his capacity. Let no man rashly despise matrimony as a thing useless or superfluous to him; let no man long for celibacy unless he is able to dispense with the married state. Nor even here let him consult the tranquility or convenience of the flesh, save only that, freed from this tie, he may be the readier and more prepared for all the offices of piety. And since there are many on whom this blessing is conferred only for a time, let everyone, in abstaining from marriage, do it so long as he is fit to endure celibacy. If he has not the power of subduing his passion, let him understand that the Lord has made it obligatory on him to marry. The Apostle shows this when he enjoins: "Nevertheless, to avoid fornication, let every man have his own wife and let every woman have her own husband." "If they cannot contain, let them marry." He first intimates that the greater part of men are liable to incontinence; and then of those so liable, he orders all, without exception, to have recourse to the only remedy by which unchastity may be obviated. The incontinent, therefore, neglecting to cure their infirmity by this means, sin by the very circumstance of disobeying the Apostle's command. And let not a man flatter himself that because he abstains from the outward act he cannot be accused of unchastity. His mind may in the meantime be inwardly inflamed with lust. For Paul's definition of chastity is purity of mind, combined with purity of body. "The unmarried woman careth for the things of the Lord, that she may be holy both in body and spirit" (1 Cor. 7:34). Therefore when he gives a reason for the

former precept, he not only says that it is better to marry than to live in fornication, but that it is better to marry than to burn.

44. Moreover, when spouses are made aware that their union is blessed by the Lord, they are thereby reminded that they must not give way to intemperate and unrestrained indulgence. For though honorable wedlock veils the turpitude of incontinence, it does not follow that it ought forthwith to become a stimulus to it. Wherefore, let spouses consider that all things are not lawful for them. Let there be sobriety in the behavior of the husband toward the wife, and of the wife in her turn toward the husband; each so acting as not to do any thing unbecoming the dignity and temperance of married life. Marriage contracted in the Lord ought to exhibit measure and modesty—not run to the extreme of wantonness. This excess Ambrose censured gravely, but not undeservedly, when he described the man who shows no modesty or comeliness in conjugal intercourse as committing adultery with his wife. Lastly let us consider who the Lawgiver is that thus condemns fornication: even He who, as he is entitled to possess us entirely, requires integrity of body, soul, and spirit. Therefore, while he forbids fornication, he at the same time forbids us to lay snares for our neighbor's chastity by lascivious attire, obscene gestures, and impure conversation. There was reason in the remark made by Archelaus to a youth clothed effeminately and over-luxuriously, that it mattered not in what part his wantonness appeared. We must have respect to God, who abhors all contaminations whatever be the part of soul or body in which it appears. And that there may be no doubt about it, let us remember that what the Lord here commends is chastity. If he requires chastity, he condemns every thing which is opposed to it. Therefore, if you aspire to obedience, let not your mind burn within with evil concupiscence, your eyes wanton after corrupting objects, nor your body be decked for allurement; let neither your tongue by filthy speeches, nor your appetite by intemperance, entice the mind

to corresponding thoughts. All vices of this description are a kind of stains which despoil chastity of its purity.

Eighth Commandment.

THOU SHALT NOT STEAL.

45. The purport is that injustice being an abomination to God, we must render to every man his due. In substance, then, the commandment forbids us to long after other men's goods, and accordingly requires every man to exert himself honestly in preserving his own. For we must consider that what each individual possesses has not fallen to him by chance, but by the distribution of the sovereign Lord of all, that no one can pervert his means to bad purposes without committing a fraud on a divine dispensation. There are very many kinds of theft. One consists in violence, as when a man's goods are forcibly plundered and carried off; another in malicious imposture, as when they are fraudulently intercepted; a third in the more hidden craft which takes possession of them with a semblance of justice; and a fourth in sycophancy, which wiles them away under the pretense of donation. But not to dwell too long in enumerating the different classes, we know that all the arts by which we obtain possession of the goods and money of our neighbors, for sincere affection substituting an eagerness to deceive or injure them in any way, are to be regarded as thefts. Though they may be obtained by an action at law, a different decision is given by God. He sees the long train of deception by which the man of craft begins to lay nets for his more simple neighbor, until he entangles him in its meshes—sees the harsh and cruel laws by which the more powerful oppresses and crushes the feeble—sees the enticements by which the more wily baits the hook for the less wary, though all these escape the judgment of man, and no cognizance is taken of them. Nor is the violation of this commandment confined to money, or merchandise, or lands, but extends to every kind of right; for we defraud our neighbors to their hurt if we decline any of the duties which we are bound to perform towards them. If an agent or an indolent steward wastes the

substance of his employer, or does not give due heed to the management of his property; if he unjustly squanders or luxuriously wastes the means entrusted to him; if a servant holds his master in derision, divulges his secrets, or in any way is treacherous to his life or his goods; if, on the other hand, a master cruelly torments his household, he is guilty of theft before God; since everyone who, in the exercise of his calling, performs not what he owes to others, keeps back, or makes away with what does not belong to him.

46. This commandment, therefore, we shall duly obey if, contented with our own lot, we study to acquire nothing but honest and lawful gain; if we long not to grow rich by injustice, nor to plunder our neighbor of his goods, that our own may thereby be increased; if we hasten not to heap up wealth cruelly wrung from the blood of others; if we do not, by means lawful and unlawful, with excessive eagerness scrape together whatever may glut our avarice or meet our prodigality. On the other hand, let it be our constant aim faithfully to lend our counsel and aid to all so as to assist them in retaining their property; or if we have to do with the perfidious or crafty, let us rather be prepared to yield somewhat of our right than to contend with them. And not only so, but let us contribute to the relief of those whom we see under the pressure of difficulties, assisting their want out of our abundance. Lastly, let each of us consider how far he is bound in duty to others, and in good faith pay what we owe. In the same way, let the people pay all due honor to their rulers, submit patiently to their authority, obey their laws and orders, and decline nothing which they can bear without sacrificing the favor of God. Let rulers, again, take due charge of their people, preserve the public peace, protect the good, curb the bad, and conduct themselves throughout as those who must render an account of their office to God, the Judge of all. Let the ministers of churches faithfully give heed to the ministry of the word, and not corrupt the doctrine of salvation, but deliver it purely and sincerely to the people of God. Let them teach not merely

by doctrine, but by example; in short, let them act the part of good shepherds towards their flocks. Let the people, in their turn, receive them as the messengers and apostles of God, render them the honor which their Supreme Master has bestowed on them, and supply them with such things as are necessary for their livelihood. Let parents be careful to bring up, guide, and teach their children as a trust committed to them by God. Let them not exasperate or alienate them by cruelty, but cherish and embrace them with the levity and indulgence which becomes their character. The regard due to parents from their children has already been adverted to. Let the young respect those advanced in years as the Lord has been pleased to make that age honorable. Let the aged also, by their prudence and their experience (in which they are far superior), guide the feebleness of youth, not assailing them with harsh and clamorous invectives but tempering strictness with ease and affability. Let servants show themselves diligent and respectful in obeying their masters, and this not with eye-service, but from the heart, as the servants of God. Let masters also not be stern and disobliging to their servants, nor harass them with excessive asperity, nor treat them with insult, but rather let them acknowledge them as brethren and fellow-servants of our heavenly Master, whom, therefore, they are bound to treat with mutual love and kindness. Let everyone, I say, thus consider what in his own place and order he owes to his neighbors, and pay what he owes. Moreover, we must always have a reference to the Lawgiver, and so remember that the law requiring us to promote and defend the interest and convenience of our fellow-men, applies equally to our minds and our hands. Ninth Commandment.

THOU SHALT NOT BEAR FALSE WITNESS AGAINST THY NEIGHBOR.

47. The purport of the commandment is since God, who is truth, abhors falsehood, we must cultivate unfeigned truth towards each other. The sum, therefore, will be that we must not by calumnies and

false accusations injure our neighbor's name, or by falsehood impair his fortunes; in fine, that we must not injure any one from petulance, or a love of evil-speaking. To this prohibition corresponds the command that we must faithfully assist every one, as far as in us lies, in asserting the truth, for the maintenance of his good name and his estate. The Lord seems to have intended to explain the commandment in these words: "Thou shalt not raise a false report: put not thine hand with the wicked to be an unrighteous witness." "Keep thee far from a false matter" (Exod. 23:1, 7). In another passage, he not only prohibits that species of falsehood which consists in acting the part of tale-bearers among the people, but says, "Neither shalt thou stand against the blood of thy neighbor" (Lev. 19:16). Both transgressions are distinctly prohibited. Indeed, there can be no doubt, that as in the previous commandment he prohibited cruelty unchastity, and avarice, so here he prohibits falsehood, which consists of the two parts to which we have adverted. By malignant or vicious detraction, we sin against our neighbor's good name: by lying, sometimes even by casting a slur upon him, we injure him in his estate. It makes no difference whether you suppose that formal and judicial testimony is here intended, or the ordinary testimony which is given in private conversation. For we must always recur to the consideration that for each kind of transgression one species is set forth by way of example, that to it the others may be referred, and that the species chiefly selected is that in which the turpitude of the transgression is most apparent. It seems proper, however, to extend it more generally to calumny and sinister insinuations by which our neighbors are unjustly aggrieved. For falsehood in a court of justice is always accompanied with perjury. But against perjury, in so far as it profanes and violates the name of God, there is a sufficient provision in the third commandment. Hence the legitimate observance of this precept consists in employing the tongue in the maintenance of truth, so as to promote both the good name and the prosperity of our neighbor. The equity of this is perfectly clear. For if a good name is more precious than riches, a man, in being robbed of his good name, is no less injured than if he were robbed of his goods; while, in the latter case, false testimony is sometimes not less injurious than rapine committed by the hand.

48. And yet it is strange with what supine security men everywhere sin in this respect. Indeed, very few are found who do not notoriously labor under this disease: such is the envenomed delight we take both in prying into and exposing our neighbor's faults. Let us not imagine it is a sufficient excuse to say that on many occasions our statements are not false. He who forbids us to defame our neighbor's reputation by falsehood, desires us to keep it untarnished in so far as truth will permit. Though the commandment is only directed against false-hood, it intimates that the preservation of our neighbor's good name is recommended. It ought to be a sufficient inducement to us to guard our neighbor's good name, that God takes an interest in it. Where-fore, evil-speaking in general is undoubtedly condemned. Moreover, by evil-speaking, we understand not the rebuke which is administered with a view of correcting; not accusation or judicial decision, by which evil is sought to be remedied; not public censure, which tends to strike terror into other offenders; not the disclosure made to those whose safety depends on being forewarned, lest unawares they should be brought into danger, but the odious crimination which springs from a malicious and petulant love of slander. Nay, the commandment extends so far as to include that scurrilous affected urbanity, instinct with invec-tive, by which the failings of others, under an appearance of sportive-ness, are bitterly assailed, as some are wont to do, who court the praise of wit, though it should call forth a blush or inflict a bitter pang. By petulance of this description, our brethren are sometimes grievously wounded. But if we turn our eye to the Lawgiver, whose just authority extends over the ears and the mind, as well as the tongue, we cannot fail to perceive that eagerness to listen to slander, and an unbecoming proneness to censorious judgments are here forbidden. It were absurd

to suppose that God hates the disease of evil-speaking in the tongue, and yet disapproves not of its malignity in the mind. Wherefore, if the true fear and love of God dwell in us, we must endeavor, as far as is lawful and expedient, and as far as charity admits, neither to listen nor give utterance to bitter and acrimonious charges, nor rashly entertain sinister suspicions. As just interpreters of the words and the actions of other men, let us candidly maintain the honor due to them by our judgment, our ear, and our tongue.

Tenth Commandment.

THOU SHALT NOT COVET THY NEIGHBOR'S HOUSE, THOU SHALT NOT COVET THY NEIGHBOR'S WIFE NOR HIS MAN-SERVANT, NOR HIS MAID-SERVANT, NOR HIS OX NOR HIS ASS, NOR ANYTHING THAT IS THY NEIGHBOR'S.

49. The purport is: since the Lord would have the whole soul pervaded with love, any feeling of an adverse nature must be banished from our minds. The sum, therefore, will be that no thought be permitted to insinuate itself into our minds and inhale them with a noxious concupiscence tending to our neighbor's loss. To this corresponds the contrary precept, that every thing which we conceive, deliberate, will, or design, be conjoined with the good and advantage of our neighbor. But here it seems we are met with a great and perplexing difficulty. For if it was correctly said above, that under the words adultery and theft, lust and an intention to injure and deceive are prohibited, it may seem superfluous afterwards to employ a separate commandment to prohibit a covetous desire of our neighbor's goods. The difficulty will easily be removed by distinguishing between design and covetousness. Design, such as we have spoken of in the previous commandments, is a deliberate consent of the will, after passion has taken possession of the mind. Covetousness may exist without such deliberation and assent, when the mind is only stimulated and tickled by vain and perverse objects. As, therefore, the Lord

previously ordered that charity should regulate our wishes, studies, and actions, so he now orders us to regulate the thoughts of the mind in the same way, that none of them may be depraved and distorted, so as to give the mind a contrary bent. Having forbidden us to turn and incline our mind to wrath, hatred, adultery, theft, and falsehood, he now forbids us to give our thoughts the same direction.

50. Nor is such rectitude demanded without reason. For who can deny the propriety of occupying all the powers of the mind with charity? If it ceases to have charity for its aim, who can question that it is diseased? How comes it that so many desires of a nature hurtful to your brother enter your mind, but just because, disregarding him, you think only of yourself? Were your mind wholly imbued with charity, no portion of it would remain for the entrance of such thoughts. In so far, therefore, as the mind is devoid of charity, it must be under the influence of concupiscence. Someone will object that those fancies which casually rise up in the mind, and forthwith vanish away, cannot properly be condemned as concupiscences, which have their seat in the heart. I answer that the question here relates to a description of fancies which while they present themselves to our thoughts, at the same time impress and stimulate the mind with cupidity, since the mind never thinks of making some choice, but the heart is excited and tends towards it. God therefore commands a strong and ardent affection, an affection not to be impeded by any portion, however minute, of concupiscence. He requires a mind so admirably arranged as not to be prompted in the slightest degree contrary to the law of love. Lest you should imagine that this view is not supported by any grave authority, I may mention that it was first suggested to me by Augustine. But although it was the intention of God to prohibit every kind of perverse desire, he by way of example sets before us those objects which are generally regarded as most attractive: thus leaving no room for cupidity of any kind, by the interdiction of those things in which it especially delights and loves to revel. Such, then, is the Second Table

of the Law, in which we are sufficiently instructed in the duties which
we owe to man for the sake of God, on a consideration of whose
nature the whole system of love is founded. It were vain, therefore, to
inculcate the various duties taught in this table, without placing your
instructions on the fear and reverence to God as their proper foundation. I need not tell the considerate reader that those who make two
precepts out of the prohibition of covetousness, perversely split one
thing into two. There is nothing in the repetition of the words, "Thou
shalt not covet." The "house" being first put down, its different parts
are afterwards enumerated, beginning with the "wife;" and hence it
is clear that the whole ought to be read consecutively, as is properly
done by the Jews. The sum of the whole commandment, therefore,
is that whatever each individual possesses remain entire and secure,
not only from injury, or the wish to injure, but also from the slightest
feeling of covetousness which can spring up in the mind.

51. It will not now be difficult to ascertain the general end contemplated by the whole Law—viz. the fulfillment of righteousness, that
man may form his life on the model of the divine purity. For therein
God has so delineated his own character, that anyone exhibiting in
action what is commanded, would in some measure exhibit a living
image of God. Wherefore Moses, when he wished to fix a summary
of the whole in the memory of the Israelites, thus addressed them,
"And now, Israel, what does the Lord thy God require of thee, but
to fear the Lord thy God, to walk in all his ways, and to love him,
and to serve the Lord thy God with all thy heart, and with all thy
soul, to keep the commandments of the Lord and his statutes which
I command thee this day for thy good?" (Deut. 10:12-13). And he
ceased not to reiterate the same thing, whenever he had occasion to
mention the end of the Law. To this the doctrine of the Law pays so
much regard that it connects man, by holiness of life, with his God;
and, as Moses elsewhere expresses it (Deut. 6:5; 11:13), and makes
him cleave to him. Moreover, this holiness of life is comprehended

under the two heads above mentioned. "Thou shalt love the Lord thy God with all thy heart, and with all thy soul, and with all thy mind, and with all thy strength, and thy neighbor as thyself." First, our mind must be completely filled with love to God, and then this love must forthwith flow out toward our neighbor. This the Apostle shows when he says, "The end of the commandment is charity out of a pure heart, and a good conscience, and of faith unfeigned" (1 Tim. 1:5). You see that conscience and faith unfeigned are placed at the head, in other words, true piety; and that from this charity is derived. It is a mistake then to suppose that merely the rudiments and first principles of righteousness are delivered in the Law, to form, as it were, a kind of introduction to good works, and not to guide to the perfect performance of them. For complete perfection, nothing more can be required than is expressed in these passages of Moses and Paul. How far, pray, would he wish to go, who is not satisfied with the instruction which directs man to the fear of God, to spiritual worship, practical obedience; in fine, purity of conscience, faith unfeigned, and charity? This confirms that interpretation of the Law which searches out, and finds in its precepts, all the duties of piety and charity. Those who merely search for dry and meager elements, as if it taught the will of God only by halves, by no means understand its end, the Apostle being witness.

52. As, in giving a summary of the Law, Christ and the Apostles sometimes omit the First Table, very many fall into the mistake of supposing that their words apply to both tables. In Matthew, Christ calls "judgment, mercy, and faith," the "weightier matters of the Law." I think it clear that by faith is here meant veracity towards men. But in order to extend the words to the whole Law, some take it for piety towards God. This is surely to no purpose. For Christ is speaking of those works by which a man ought to approve himself as just. If we attend to this, we will cease to wonder why, elsewhere, when asked by the young man, "What good thing shall I do, that I may have eternal

life?" he simply answers that he must keep the commandments, "Thou shalt do no murder, Thou shalt not commit adultery, Thou shalt not steal, Thou shalt not bear false witness, Honor thy father and thy mother: and, Thou shalt love thy neighbor as thyself" (Matt. 19:16, 18). For the obedience of the First Table consisted almost entirely either in the internal affection of the heart, or in ceremonies. The affection of the heart was not visible, and hypocrites were diligent in the observance of ceremonies; but the works of charity were of such a nature as to be a solid attestation of righteousness. The same thing occurs so frequently in the Prophets that it must be familiar to everyone who has any tolerable acquaintance with them. For, almost on every occasion, when they exhort men to repentance, omitting the First Table, they insist on faith, judgment, mercy, and equity. Nor do they, in this way, omit the fear of God. They only require a serious proof of it from its signs. It is well known, indeed, that when they treat of the Law, they generally insist on the Second Table, because therein the cultivation of righteousness and integrity is best manifested. There is no occasion to quote passages. Everyone can easily for himself perceive the truth of my observation.

53. Is it then true, you will ask, that it is a more complete summary of righteousness to live innocently with men, than piously towards God? By no means; but because no man, as a matter of course, observes charity in all respects, unless he seriously fear God, such observance is a proof of piety also. To this we may add that the Lord, well knowing that none of our good deeds can reach him (as the Psalmist declares, Psalm 16:2), does not demand from us duties towards himself, but exercises us in good works towards our neighbor. Hence the Apostle, not without cause, makes the whole perfection of the saints to consist in charity (Eph. 3:19; Col. 3:14). And in another passage, he not improperly calls it the "fulfilling of the law," adding, that "he that loveth another has fulfilled the law" (Rom. 13:8). And again, "All the law is fulfilled in this: Thou shalt love thy neighbor as thyself"

(Gal. 5:14). For this is the very thing which Christ himself teaches when he says, "All things whatsoever ye would that men should do to you, do ye even so to them: for this is the law and the prophets" (Matt. 7:12). It is certain that in the law and the prophets, faith, and whatever pertains to the due worship of God, holds the first place, and that to this charity is made subordinate; but our Lord means that in the Law the observance of justice and equity towards men is prescribed as the means which we are to employ in testifying a pious fear of God, if we truly possess it.

54. Let us therefore hold that our life will be framed in best accordance with the will of God, and the requirements of his Law, when it is in every respect most advantageous to our brethren. But in the whole Law, there is not one syllable which lays down a rule as to what man is to do or avoid for the advantage of his own carnal nature. And, indeed, since men are naturally prone to excessive self-love, which they always retain, how great soever their departure from the truth may be, there was no need of a law to inflame a love already existing in excess. Hence it is perfectly plain, that the observance of the Commandments consists not in the love of ourselves, but in the love of God and our neighbor; and that he leads the best and holiest life who as little as may be studies and lives for himself; and that none lives worse and more unrighteously than he who studies and lives only for himself, and seeks and thinks only of his own. Nay, the better to express how strongly we should be inclined to love our neighbor, the Lord has made self-love as it were the standard, there being no feeling in our nature of greater strength and vehemence. The force of the expression ought to be carefully weighed. For he does not (as some sophists have stupidly dreamed) assign the first place to self-love, and the second to charity. He rather transfers to others the love which we naturally feel for ourselves. Hence the Apostle declares, that charity "seeketh not her own" (1 Cor. 13:5). Nor is the argument worth a straw that the thing regulated must always be inferior to

the rule. The Lord did not make self-love the rule, as if love towards others was subordinate to it; but whereas, through natural depravity, the feeling of love usually rests on ourselves, he shows that it ought to diffuse itself in another direction—that we should be prepared to do good to our neighbor with no less alacrity, ardor, and solicitude, than to ourselves.

55. Our Savior having shown in the parable of the Samaritan (Luke 10:36) that the term neighbor comprehends the most remote stranger, there is no reason for limiting the precept of love to our own connections. I deny not that the closer the relation the more frequent our offices of kindness should be. For the condition of humanity requires that there be more duties in common between those who are more nearly connected by the ties of relationship, or friendship, or neighborhood. And this is done without any offense to God, by whose providence we are in a manner impelled to do it. But I say that the whole human race, without exception, are to be embraced with one feeling of charity: that here there is no distinction of Greek or Barbarian, worthy or unworthy, friend or foe, since all are to be viewed not in themselves, but in God. If we turn aside from this view, there is no wonder that we entangle ourselves in error. Wherefore, if we would hold the true course in love, our first step must be to turn our eyes not to man, the sight of whom might oftener produce hatred than love, but to God, who requires that the love which we bear to him be diffused among all mankind, so that our fundamental principle must ever be: let a man be what he may, he is still to be loved, because God is loved.

56. Wherefore, nothing could be more pestilential than the ignorance or wickedness of the Schoolmen in converting the precepts respecting revenge and the love of enemies (precepts which had formerly been delivered to all the Jews, and were then delivered universally to all Christians) into counsels which it was free to obey or disobey, confining the necessary observance of them to the monks, who were

made more righteous than ordinary Christians, by the simple circumstance of voluntarily binding themselves to obey counsels. The reason they assign for not receiving them as laws is that they seem too heavy and burdensome, especially to Christians, who are under the law of grace. Have they, indeed, the hardihood to remodel the eternal law of God concerning the love of our neighbor? Is there a page of the Law in which any such distinction exists; or rather do we not meet in every page with commands which, in the strictest terms, require us to love our enemies? What is meant by commanding us to feed our enemy if he is hungry, to bring back his ox or his ass if we meet it going astray, or help it up if we see it lying under its burden? (Prov. 25:21; Exod. 23:4). Shall we show kindness to cattle for man's sake, and have no feeling of good will to himself? What? Is not the word of the Lord eternally true: "Vengeance is mine, I will repay?" (Deut. 32:35). This is elsewhere more explicitly stated: "Thou shalt not avenge, nor bear any grudge against the children of thy people" (Lev. 19:18). Let them either erase these passages from the Law, or let them acknowledge the Lord as a Lawgiver, not falsely feign him to be merely a counselor.

57. And what, pray, is meant by the following passage, which they have dared to insult with this absurd gloss? "Love your enemies, bless them that curse you, do good to them that hate you, and pray for them which despitefully use you, and persecute you; that ye may be the children of your Father which is in heaven" (Matt. 5:44-45). Who does not here concur in the reasoning of Chrysostom (lib. *de Compunctione Cordis*, et *ad Rom.* 7) that the nature of the motive makes it plain that these are not exhortations, but precepts? For what is left to us if we are excluded from the number of the children of God? According to the Schoolmen, monks alone will be the children of our Father in heaven—monks alone will dare to invoke God as their Father. And in the meantime, how will it fare with the Church? By the same rule, she will be confined to heathens and publicans. For our Savior says, "If ye love them which love you, what reward have

ye? Do not even the publicans the same?" It will truly be well with us if we are left only the name of Christians, while we are deprived of the inheritance of the kingdom of heaven! Nor is the argument of Augustine less forcible: "When the Lord forbids adultery, he forbids it in regard to the wife of a foe not less than the wife of a friend; when he forbids theft, he does not allow stealing of any description, whether from a friend or an enemy" (August. *Lib. de Doctr. Christ*). Now, these two commandments, "Thou shalt not steal, Thou shalt not commit adultery," Paul brings under the rule of love; nay, he says that they are briefly comprehended in this saying, "Thou shalt love thy neighbor as thyself" (Rom. 13:9). Therefore, Paul must either be a false interpreter of the Law, or we must necessarily conclude that under this precept we are bound to love our enemies just as our friends. Those, then, show themselves to be in truth the children of Satan who thus licentiously shake off a yoke common to the children of God. It may be doubted whether in promulgating this dogma they have displayed greater stupidity or impudence. There is no ancient writer who does not hold it as certain that these are pure precepts. It was not even doubted in the age of Gregory, as is plain from his decided assertion; for he holds it to be incontrovertible that they are precepts. And how stupidly they argue! The burden, say they, were too difficult for Christians to hear! As if any thing could be imagined more difficult than to love the Lord with all the heart, and soul, and strength. Compared with this Law, there is none which may not seem easy, whether it be to love our enemy, or to banish every feeling of revenge from our minds. To our weakness, indeed, everything, even to the minutest tittle of the Law, is arduous and difficult. In the Lord we have strength. It is his to give what he orders, and to order what he wills. That Christians are under the law of grace means not that they are to wander unrestrained without law, but that they are engrafted into Christ, by whose grace they are freed from the curse of the Law, and by whose Spirit they have the Law written in their hearts. This grace Paul has termed, but not in the proper sense of the term, a law, alluding to the Law of God, with which he was contrasting it. The Schoolmen, laying hold of the term Law, make it the ground-work of their vain speculations.

58. The same must be said of their application of the term, venial sin, both to the hidden impiety which violates the First Table, and the direct transgression of the last commandment of the Second Table. They define venial sin to be desire unaccompanied with deliberate assent, and not remaining long in the heart. But I maintain that it cannot even enter the heart unless through a want of those things which are required in the Law. We are forbidden to have strange gods. When the mind, under the influence of distrust, looks elsewhere or is seized with some sudden desire to transfer its blessedness to some other quarter, whence are these movements, however evanescent, but just because there is some empty corner in the soul to receive such temptations? And, not to lengthen out the discussion, there is a precept to love God with the whole heart, and mind, and soul; and, therefore, if all the powers of the soul are not directed to the love of God, there is a departure from the obedience of the Law; because those internal enemies which rise up against the dominion of God, and countermand his edicts prove that his throne is not well established in our consciences. It has been shown that the last commandment goes to this extent. Has some undue longing sprung up in our mind? Then we are chargeable with covetousness, and stand convicted as transgressors of the Law. For the Law forbids us not only to meditate and plan our neighbor's loss, but to be stimulated and inflamed with covetousness. But every transgression of the Law lays us under the curse, and therefore even the slightest desires cannot be exempted from the fatal sentence. "In weighing our sins," says Augustine, "let us not use a deceitful balance, weighing at our own discretion what we will, and how we will, calling this heavy and that light: but let us use the divine balance of the Holy Scriptures, as taken from the treasury

of the Lord, and by it weigh every offense, nay, not weigh, but rather recognize what has been already weighed by the Lord" (August. *De Bapt. cont. Donatist.* Lib. 2 chap. 6). And what saith the Scripture? Certainly when Paul says, that "the wages of sin is death" (Rom. 6:23), he shows that he knew nothing of this vile distinction. As we are but too prone to hypocrisy, there was very little occasion for this sop to soothe our torpid consciences.

59. I wish they would consider what our Savior meant when he said, "Whosoever shall break one of these least commandments, and shall teach men so, he shall be called the least in the kingdom of heaven" (Matt. 5:19). Are they not of this number when they presume to extenuate the transgression of the Law, as if it were unworthy of death? The proper course had been to consider not simply what is commanded, but who it is that commands, because every least transgression of his Law derogates from his authority. Do they count it a small matter to insult the majesty of God in any one respect? Again, since God has explained his will in the Law, every thing contrary to the Law is displeasing to him. Will they feign that the wrath of God is so disarmed that the punishment of death will not forthwith follow upon it? He has declared plainly (if they could be induced to listen to his voice, instead of darkening his clear truth by their insipid subtleties), "The soul that sinneth it shall die" (Ezek. 18:20). Again, in the passage lately quoted, "The wages of sin is death." What these men acknowledge to be sin, because they are unable to deny it, they contend is not mortal. Having already indulged this madness too long, let them learn to repent; or, if they persist in their infatuation, taking no further notice of them, let the children of God remember that all sin is mortal, because it is rebellion against the will of God, and necessarily provokes his anger; and because it is a violation of the Law, against every violation of which without exception the judgment of God has been pronounced. The faults of the saints are indeed venial,

not, however, in their own nature, but because through the mercy of God they obtain pardon.

Study Guide Questions

Section 1

1. What is the written moral law?
2. What does God reprove us for through the law?
3. Why is the written law necessary?

Section 2

1. When do we render God the reverence due to Him?
2. In what way is God always like Himself?

Section 3

1. What does the law teach us about ourselves?

Section 4

1. Why has God added promises and threats to the law?
2. What deserves no reward?

Section 5

1. Nothing is more acceptable to God than what?
2. What religious affectation is rooted in man's nature?
3. What is an intolerable profanation of divine righteousness?

Section 6

1. If an earthly king forbids a particular action, what is not included?
2. How is this different from what God forbids?

Section 7

1. Who is the best interpreter of the law?
2. Did Christ add to the law?

Section 8

1. Does a refusal to go beyond the law require that we interpret the law woodenly?

2. What is our central duty with regard to each law?

Section 9

1. What is conceded by all?

2. What mistake is commonly made in this?

Section 10

1. Why does God rebuke sin so strongly in the law and put the worst possible light on our behavior? For example, why call hatred "murder"?

Section 11

1. How does Calvin divide the law given in the Ten Commandments?

2. What is vanity to attempt?

Section 12

1. Why do some number the commandments differently?

Section 13

1. How does Calvin take the preface to the Ten Commandments?

2. Why is the preface important?

Section 14

1. What is meant by "I am the Lord thy God"?

Section 15

1. What does Calvin identify as one of the greatest crimes?

2. Why does God reveal Himself through certain particular titles?

3. What did Israel's enslavement in Israel represent typologically?

Section 16

1. What does the first commandment reveal about God's authority?

2. What four things may we not transfer away from God to another?

Section 17

1. What is the grossest fault of a superstitious style of worship?

2. What happens whenever idols appear?

Section 18

1. Penalties for idolatry extend how far?

2. How far does His kindness extend to those who love Him and keep His word?

3. What is the act of bowing down to an image compared to?

Section 19

1. Does Calvin interpret the threat to "visit iniquity" to subsequent generations as a reference to temporal difficulties only?

Section 20

1. Why did Ezekiel tell the people to stop using the proverb about the father eating grapes and the children's teeth being set on edge?

2. What therefore descends to subsequent generations?

Section 21

1. How is this promise to be interpreted? As an absolute, or as a general rule?

Section 22

1. What does the third commandment require?

2. What three things constitute adherence to this command?

Section 23

1. What is an oath?

2. What is one way of identifying a man's religion?

Section 24

1. What is it when a man swears falsely in the true name?

Section 25

1. What renders God's name cheap and common?

2. When men swear unnecessarily, what are they doing?

Section 26

1. Who condemns all oaths whatever, and why?

2. Interpreting Christ's words as forbidding all oaths whatever does what to the relationship between Jesus and His Father?

3. What was Christ forbidding then?

4. What is the relationship of God's name to all His benefits?

Section 27

1. Did Paul interpret Jesus as forbidding all oaths?

Section 28

1. What did Calvin think about the early fathers who interpreted the Sabbath as a type of Christ?

2. What are the three elements of obedience to this command?

Section 29

1. What lesson occupied the chief place in the Sabbath?

2. When should we be at this place of spiritual rest?

Section 30

1. What does the number seven represent in Scripture?

Section 31

1. Can the Sabbath be kept merely by abstaining from physical labor?

2. What must Christians shun completely?

Section 32

1. For Calvin, the Sabbath has been abrogated in Christ. But what two things do we still need to do?

Section 33

1. Is there danger in Christian superstitious observance of the Lord's day?

Section 34

1. For Calvin, is the Lord's day a continuation of the Sabbath or a replacement of it?

2. Why was the first day chosen as that replacement?

3. Does Calvin condemn churches that have other solemn days?

Section 35

1. Who is encompassed under the fifth commandment?

2. Is honor a word with a narrow definition?

3. What do fathers, princes, and lords all have?

Section 36

1. Are we allowed to withhold honor based on the recipient's lack of merit?

2. What are the three components of honor?

Section 37

1. Does the promise attached to this commandment apply to us today?

2. With the "exceptions," is God breaking His word?

Section 38

1. Are there sanctions connected to this commandment?

Section 39

1. What is the purpose of this commandment?

2. What is hatred?

3. Does this command address heart attitudes?

Section 40

1. What are the two reasons we are to refrain from murder?

Section 41

1. Why should all uncleanness be far from us?

2. What effect does fornication have?

Section 42

1. What makes men doubly subject to women's society?

2. What two ways is the gift of celibacy given?

3. Why can men not count on God's help for any attempt at celibacy?

Section 43

1. Can celibacy be achieved by great zeal and effort?

2. If a man is not able to be celibate, what does God require of him?

3. Is it adequate for a man to control external sexual behavior?

Section 44

1. What can we say about sexual association within marriage?

2. What follows from this?

3. Is anything permitted, just so long as the couple is married?

Section 45

1. What is the eighth commandment?

2. What is prohibited in this commandment?

3. Does it matter if we figure out a way to do it legally?

Section 46

1. What sort of gain should we pursue?

2. What do greedy men look like?

3. What should we do if we have to contend with faithless and deceitful men?

Section 47

1. What is the ninth commandment?

2. What is the first form of this that Calvin mentions?

3. For Calvin, what are the two parts of this commandment?

Section 48

1. What peculiar temptation does everyone experience in this regard?

2. What is not included under this prohibition?

3. What else is excluded?

Section 49

1. What is the tenth commandment?

2. If the prohibitions of adultery and murder forbade heart intent, then how is this commandment not superfluous?

Section 50

1. What happens if we entertain any desirable object in our minds?

2. What does God require of our heart?

Section 51

1. What is the purpose of the whole law?

2. What is a mistake to believe concerning the law?

Section 52

1. Why is the keeping of the law sometimes summarized in the second table only?

2. What are the two indicators of keeping the first table?

3. Why is this inadequate for identifying true godliness?

Section 53

1. What is the fulfillment of the law?

Section 54

1. What life best conforms to God's will?

2. What stupid imagination did the Sophists advance?

3. How does Calvin refute this?

Section 55

1. Does Calvin resist the priorities we have for those closest to us?

2. Does love for a man depend on his character?

Section 56

1. What did the Schoolmen do with all these divine requirements?

2. How did Calvin respond?

Section 57

1. How was the command to love our enemies diluted by some?

2. What early church fathers did Calvin appeal to in rejecting this?

Section 58

1. What is the definition of venial sin that Calvin works with?

2. But how do these sins even get an opportunity within us?

3. So what does all sin deserve?

Section 59

1. Why is every sin deadly?

2. If those who distinguish mortal from venial sin "indulged this madness too long," what should we do?

3. What should the children of God hold?

CHAPTER 9

Christ, though known to the Jews under the law, yet only
manifested under the Gospel.

There are three principal heads in this chapter.
I. Preparatory to a consideration of the knowledge of Christ,
and the benefits procured by him; the 1st and 2nd sections are occupied with the dispensation of this knowledge, which, after the manifestation of Christ in the flesh, was more clearly revealed than under the Law.

II. A refutation of the profane dream of Servetus that the promises
are entirely abrogated, sec. 3. Likewise, a refutation of those who do
not properly compare the Law with the Gospel, sec. 4.

III. A necessary and brief exposition of the ministry of John Baptist, which occupies an intermediate place between the law and the Gospel. Sections.

Outline:

1. The holy fathers under the Law saw the day of Christ, though obscurely. He is more fully revealed to us under the Gospel. A reason for this, confirmed by the testimony of Christ and his Apostles.

2. The term Gospel, used in its most extensive sense, comprehends the attestations of mercy which God gave to the fathers. Properly, however, it means the promulgation of grace exhibited in the God-man Jesus Christ.

3. The notion of Servetus that the promises are entirely abolished, refuted. Why we must still trust to the promises of God. Another reason. Solution of a difficulty.

4. Refutation of those who do not properly compare the Law and the Gospel. Answer to certain questions here occurring. The Law and the Gospel briefly compared.

5. Third part of the chapter. Of the ministry of John the Baptist.

Since God was pleased (and not in vain) to testify in ancient times by means of expiations and sacrifices that he was a Father, and to set apart for himself a chosen people, he was doubtless known even then in the same character in which he is now fully revealed to us. Accordingly Malachi, having enjoined the Jews to attend to the Law of Moses (because after his death there was to be an interruption of the prophetical office), immediately after declares that the Sun of righteousness should arise (Mal. 4:2); thus intimating, that though the Law had the effect of keeping the pious in expectation of the coming Messiah, there was ground to hope for much greater light on his advent. For this reason, Peter, speaking of the ancient prophets, says, "Unto whom it was revealed, that not unto themselves, but unto us, they did minister the things which are now reported unto you by them that have preached the gospel unto you, with the Holy Ghost sent down from heaven" (1 Pet. 1:12). Not that the prophetical doctrine was useless to the ancient people, or unavailing to the prophets themselves, but that they did not obtain possession of the treasure which God has transmitted to us by their hands. The grace of which they testified is now set familiarly before our eyes. They had only a slight foretaste; to us is given a fuller fruition. Our Savior, accordingly, while he declares that Moses testified of him, extols the superior measure of grace bestowed upon us (John 5:46). Addressing his disciples, he says, "Blessed are your eyes, for they see, and your ears, for they hear. For verily I say unto you that many prophets and righteous men have desired to see those things which ye see, and have not seen them, and to hear those things which ye hear, and have not heard them" (Matt. 13:16; Luke 10:23). It is no small commendation of the gospel revelation that God has preferred us to holy men of old, so much distinguished for piety. There is nothing in this view inconsistent with another passage, in which our Savior says, "Your father Abraham rejoiced to see my day, and he saw it and was glad" (John 8:56). For though the event being remote, his view of it was obscure, he had full assurance that it would one day be accomplished; and hence the joy which the holy patriarch experienced even to his death. Nor does John Baptist, when he says, "No man has seen God at any time; the only begotten Son, which is in the bosom of the Father, he has declared him" (John 1:18), exclude the pious who had previously died from a participation in the knowledge and light which are manifested in the person of Christ; but comparing their condition with ours, he intimates that the mysteries which they only beheld dimly under shadows are made clear to us; as is well explained by the author of the Epistle to the Hebrews, in these words, "God, who at sundry times and in divers manners spake in time past unto the fathers by the prophets, has in these last days spoken unto us by his Son" (Heb. 1:1-2). Hence, although this only begotten Son, who is now to us the brightness of his Father's glory and the express image of his person, was formerly made known to the Jews, as we have elsewhere shown from Paul, that he was the Deliverer under the old dispensation; it is nevertheless true, as Paul himself elsewhere declares, that "God, who commanded the light to shine out of darkness, has shined in our hearts, to give the light of the knowledge of the glory of God in the face of Jesus Christ" (2 Cor. 4:6); because, when he appeared in this

his image, he in a manner made himself visible, his previous appearance having been shadowy and obscure. More shameful and more detestable, therefore, is the ingratitude of those who walk blindfold in this meridian light. Accordingly, Paul says that "the god of this world has blinded their minds, lest the light of the glorious gospel of Christ should shine unto them" (2 Cor. 4:4).

2. By the Gospel, I understand the clear manifestation of the mystery of Christ. I confess, indeed, that inasmuch as the term Gospel is applied by Paul to the doctrine of faith (2 Tim. 4:10), it includes all the promises by which God reconciles men to himself, and which occur throughout the Law. For Paul there opposes faith to those terrors which vex and torment the conscience when salvation is sought by means of works. Hence it follows that Gospel, taken in a large sense, comprehends the evidences of mercy and paternal favor which God bestowed on the Patriarchs. Still, by way of excellence, it is applied to the promulgation of the grace manifested in Christ. This is not only founded on general use, but has the sanction of our Savior and his Apostles. Hence it is described as one of his peculiar characteristics that he preached the Gospel of the kingdom (Matt. 4:23; 9:35; Mark 1:14). Mark, in his preface to the Gospel, calls it "the beginning of the Gospel of Jesus Christ." There is no use of collecting passages to prove what is already perfectly known. Christ at his advent "brought life and immortality to light through the Gospel" (2 Tim. 1:10). Paul does not mean by these words that the Fathers were plunged in the darkness of death before the Son of God became incarnate; but he claims for the Gospel the honorable distinction of being a new and extraordinary kind of embassy, by which God fulfilled what he had promised, these promises being realized in the person of the Son. For though believers have at all times experienced the truth of Paul's declaration, that "all the promises of God in him are yea and amen," inasmuch as these promises were sealed upon their hearts; yet because he has in his flesh completed all the parts of our salvation, this vivid manifestation of realities was justly

entitled to this new and special distinction. Accordingly, Christ says, "Hereafter ye shall see heaven open, and the angels of God ascending and descending upon the Son of man." For though he seems to allude to the ladder which the Patriarch Jacob saw in vision, he commends the excellence of his advent in this, that it opened the gate of heaven, and gave us familiar access to it.

3. Here we must guard against the diabolical imagination of Servetus, who, from a wish, or at least the pretense of a wish, to extol the greatness of Christ, abolishes the promises entirely, as if they had come to an end at the same time with the Law. He pretends that by the faith of the Gospel all the promises have been fulfilled; as if there was no distinction between us and Christ. I lately observed that Christ had not left any part of our salvation incomplete; but from this it is erroneously inferred that we are now put in possession of all the blessings purchased by him; thereby implying that Paul was incorrect in saying, "We are saved by hope" (Rom. 3:24). I admit, indeed, that by believing in Christ we pass from death unto life; but we must at the same time remember the words of John, that though we know we are "the sons of God," "it does not yet appear what we shall be: but we know that, when he shall appear, we shall be like him; for we shall see him as he is" (1 John 3:2). Therefore, although Christ offers us in the Gospel a present fullness of spiritual blessings, fruition remains in the keeping of hope, until we are divested of corruptible flesh and transformed into the glory of him who has gone before us. Meanwhile, in leaning on the promises, we obey the command of the Holy Spirit, whose authority ought to have weight enough with us to silence all the barkings of that impure dog. We have it on the testimony of Paul that "godliness is profitable unto all things, having promise of the life that now is, and of that which is to come" (1 Tim. 4:8); for which reason, he glories in being "an apostle of Jesus Christ, according to the promise of life which is in Christ Jesus" (2 Tim. 1:1). And he elsewhere reminds us, that we have the same promises which were given

to the saints in ancient time (2 Cor. 7:1). In fine, he makes the sum of our felicity consist in being sealed with the Holy Spirit of promise. Indeed we have no enjoyment of Christ, unless by embracing him as clothed with his own promises. Hence it is that he indeed dwells in our hearts and yet we are as pilgrims in regard to him, because "we walk by faith, not by sight" (2 Cor. 5:6-7). There is no inconsistency in the two things—viz. that in Christ we possess everything pertaining to the perfection of the heavenly life, and yet that faith is only a vision "of things not seen" (Heb. 11:1). Only there is this difference to be observed in the nature or quality of the promises, that the Gospel points with the finger to what the Law shadowed under types.

4. Hence, also, we see the error of those who, in comparing the Law with the Gospel, represent it merely as a comparison between the merit of works, and the gratuitous imputation of righteousness. The contrast thus made is by no means to be rejected, because by the term Law, Paul frequently understands that rule of holy living in which God exacts what is his due, giving no hope of life unless we obey in every respect; and, on the other hand, denouncing a curse for the slightest failure. This Paul does when showing that we are freely accepted of God, and accounted righteous by being pardoned, because that obedience of the Law to which the reward is promised is nowhere to be found. Hence he appropriately represents the righteousness of the Law and the Gospel as opposed to each other. But the Gospel has not succeeded the whole Law in such a sense as to introduce a different method of salvation. It rather confirms the Law, and proves that every thing which it promised is fulfilled. What was shadow, it has made substance. When Christ says that the Law and the Prophets were until John, he does not consign the fathers to the curse, which, as the slaves of the Law, they could not escape. He intimates that they were only imbued with the rudiments, and remained far beneath the height of the Gospel doctrine. Accordingly Paul, after calling the Gospel "the power of God unto salvation to everyone that

believeth," shortly after adds that it was "witnessed by the Law and the Prophets" (Rom. 1:16; 3:21). And in the end of the same Epistle, though he describes "the preaching of Jesus Christ" as "the revelation of the mystery which was kept secret since the world began," he modifies the expression by adding that it is "now made manifest" "by the scriptures of the prophets" (Rom. 16:25-26). Hence we infer, that when the whole Law is spoken of, the Gospel differs from it only in respect of clearness of manifestation. Still, on account of the inestimable riches of grace set before us in Christ, there is good reason for saying that by his advent the kingdom of heaven was erected on the earth (Matt. 12:28).

5. John stands between the Law and the Gospel, holding an intermediate office allied to both. For though he gave a summary of the Gospel when he pronounced Christ to be "the Lamb of God who taketh away the sin of the world," yet, inasmuch as he did not unfold the incomparable power and glory which shone forth in his resurrection, Christ says that he was not equal to the Apostles. For this is the meaning of the words: "Among them that are born of woman, there has not risen a greater than John the Baptist: notwithstanding, he that is least in the kingdom of heaven is greater than he" (Matt. 11:28). He is not there commending the persons of men, but after preferring John to all the Prophets, he gives the first place to the preaching of the Gospel, which is elsewhere designated by the kingdom of heaven. When John himself, in answer to the Jews, says that he is only "a voice" (John 1:23), as if he were inferior to the Prophets it is not in pretended humility but he means to teach that the proper embassy was not entrusted to him, that he only performed the office of a messenger, as had been foretold by Malachi, "Behold, I will send you Elijah the prophets before the coming of the great and dreadful day of the Lord" (Mal. 4:5). And, indeed, during the whole course of his ministry, he did nothing more than prepare disciples for Christ. He even proves from Isaiah that this was the office to which he was

divinely appointed. In this sense, he is said by Christ to have been "a burning and a shining light" (John 5:35), because full day had not yet appeared. And yet this does not prevent us from classing him among the preachers of the gospel, since he used the same baptism which was afterwards committed to the Apostles. Still, however, he only began that which had freer course under the Apostles, after Christ was taken up into the heavenly glory.

Study Guide Questions

Section 1

1. What did God attest through the Old Testament promises?
2. What did the teaching and ceremonies of the Old Testament point to?
3. Did this make this teaching valueless to the prophets themselves?

Section 2

1. Taken in a broad sense, what does the word "gospel" include?
2. Taken in the higher sense, what does it mean?

Section 3

1. Are the promises of the Old Testament abrogated with the law?

Section 4

1. For Calvin, is there a legitimate contrast between law and gospel?
2. Did the gospel bring a different way of salvation than the law, rightly understood?

Section 5

1. What kind of office did John the Baptist hold with regard to law and gospel?
2. What was his role with regard to the disciples?

CHAPTER 10

The resemblance between the Old Testament and the New.

This chapter consists of four parts.

I. The sum, utility, and necessity of this discussion, sec. 1.

II. A proof that, generally speaking, the old and new dispensations are in reality one, although differently administered. Three points in which the two dispensations entirely agree, sec. 2-4.

III. The Old Testament, as well as the New, had regard to the hope of immortality and a future life, whence two other resemblances or points of agreement follow—viz. that both were established by the free mercy of God, and confirmed by the intercession of Christ. This proved by many arguments, passages of Scripture, and examples, see. 5-23.

IV. Conclusion of the whole chapter, where, for fuller confirmation, certain passages of Scripture are produced. Refutation of the cavils of the Sadducees and other Jews. Sections.

Outline:

1. Introduction, showing the necessity of proving the similarity of both dispensations in opposition to Servetus and the Anabaptists.

2. This similarity in general. Both covenants truly one, though differently administered. Three things in which they entirely agree.

3. First general similarity, or agreement—viz. that the Old Testament, equally with the New, extended its promises beyond the present life, and held out a sure hope of immortality. Reason for this resemblance. Objection answered.

4. The other two points of resemblance—viz. that both covenants were established in the mercy of God, and confirmed by the mediation of Christ.

5. The first of these points of resemblance being the foundation of the other two, a lengthened proof is given of it. The first argument taken from a passage, in which Paul, showing that the sacraments of both dispensations had the same meaning, proves that the condition of the ancient church was similar to ours.

6. An objection from John 6:49—viz. that the Israelites ate manna in the wilderness and are dead, whereas Christians eat the flesh of Christ, and die not. Answer reconciling this passage of the Evangelist with that of the Apostle.

7. Another proof from the Law and the Prophets—viz. the power of the divine word in quickening souls before Christ was manifested. Hence the believing Jews were raised to the hope of eternal life.

8. Third proof from the form of the covenant, which shows that it was in reality one both before and after the manifestation of Christ in the flesh.

9. Confirmation of the former proof from the clear terms in which the form is expressed. Another confirmation derived from the former and from the nature of God.

10. Fourth proof from examples. Adam, Abel, and Noah, when tried with various temptations, neglecting the present, aspired with living faith and invincible hope to a better life. They, therefore, had the same aim as believers under the Gospel.

11. Continuation of the fourth proof from the example of Abraham, whose call and whole course of life shows that he ardently aspired to eternal felicity. Objection disposed of.

12. Continuation of the fourth proof from the examples of Isaac and Jacob.

13. Conclusion of the fourth proof. Adam, Abel, Noah, Abraham, Isaac, Jacob, and others under the Law, looked for the fulfillment of the divine promises not on the earth, but in heaven. Hence they termed this life an earthly pilgrimage, and desired to be buried in the land of Canaan, which was a figure of eternal happiness.

14. A fifth proof from Jacob's earnestness to obtain the birth-right. This shows a prevailing desire of future life. This perceived in some degree by Balaam.

15. A sixth proof from David, who expects such great things from the Lord, and yet declares the present life to be mere vanity.

16. A seventh proof also from David. His descriptions of the happiness of believers could only be realized in a future state.

17. An eighth proof from the common feeling and confession of all the pious who sought by faith and hope to obtain in heaven what they did not see in the present shadowy life.

18. A continuation and confirmation of the former proof from the exultation of the righteous, even amid the destruction of the world.

19. A ninth proof from Job, who spoke most distinctly of this hope. Two objections disposed of.

20. A tenth proof from the later Prophets, who taught that the happiness of the righteous was placed beyond the limits of the present life.

21. This clearly established by Ezekiel's vision of the dry bones, and a passage in Isaiah.

22. Last proof from certain passages in the Prophets, which clearly show the future immortality of the righteous in the kingdom of heaven.

23. Conclusion of the whole discussion concerning the similarity of both dispensations. For fuller confirmation, four passages of Scripture produced. Refutation of the error of the Sadducees and other Jews, who denied eternal salvation and the sure hope of the Church.

From what has been said above, it must now be clear that all whom from the beginning of the world God adopted as his peculiar people were taken into covenant with him on the same conditions, and under the same bond of doctrine, as ourselves; but as it is of no small importance to establish this point, I will here add it by way of appendix, and show, since the Fathers were partakers with us in the same inheritance, and hoped for a common salvation through the grace of the same Mediator, how far their condition in this respect was different from our own. For although the passages which we have collected from the Law and the Prophets for the purpose of proof, make it plain that there never was any other rule of piety and religion among the people of God; yet as many things are written on the subject of the difference between the Old and New Testaments in a manner which may perplex ordinary readers, it will be proper here to devote a special place to the better and more exact discussion of this subject. This discussion, which would have been most useful at any rate, has been rendered necessary by that monstrous miscreant, Servetus, and some madmen of the sect of the Anabaptists, who think of the people of Israel just as they would do of some herd of swine, absurdly imagining that the Lord gorged them with temporal blessings here, and gave them no hope of a blessed immortality. Let us guard pious minds against this pestilential error, while we at the same time remove all the difficulties which are wont to start up when mention is made of the difference between the Old and the New Testaments. By the way also, let us consider what resemblance and what difference there is between the covenant which the Lord made with the Israelites before the advent of Christ, and that which he has made with us now that Christ is manifested.

2. It is possible, indeed, to explain both in one word. The covenant made with all the fathers is so far from differing from ours in reality and substance that it is altogether one and the same: still the administration differs. But because this brief summary is insufficient to give any one a full understanding of the subject, our explanation to be useful must extend to greater length. It were superfluous, however, in showing the similarity, or rather identity, of the two dispensations, again to treat of the particulars which have already been discussed, as it were unseasonable to introduce those which are still to be considered elsewhere. What we propose to insist upon here may be reduced to three heads: first, that temporal opulence and felicity was not the goal to which the Jews were invited to aspire, but that they were admitted to the hope of immortality, and that assurance of this adoption was given by immediate communications, by the Law and by the Prophets. Secondly, that the covenant by which they were reconciled to the Lord was founded on no merits of their own, but solely on the mercy of God, who called them; and, thirdly, that they both had and knew Christ the Mediator, by whom they were united to God, and made capable of receiving his promises. The second of these, as it is not yet perhaps sufficiently understood, will be fully considered in its own place (Book 3 chap. 15-18). For we will prove by many clear passages in the Prophets that all which the Lord has ever given or promised to his people is of mere goodness and indulgence. The third also has, in various places, been not obscurely demonstrated. Even the first has not been left unnoticed.

3. As the first is most pertinent to the present subject, and is most controverted, we shall enter more fully into the consideration of it, taking care, at the same time, where any of the others requires explanations to supply it by the way, or afterwards add it in its proper place. The Apostle, indeed, removes all doubt when he says that the Gospel

which God gave concerning his Son, Jesus Christ, "he had promised aforetime by his prophets in the holy Scriptures" (Rom. 1:2). And again that "the righteousness of God without the law is manifested, being witnessed by the law and the prophets" (Rom. 3:21). For the Gospel does not confine the hearts of men to the enjoyment of the present life, but raises them to the hope of immortality; does not fix them down to earthly delights, but announcing that there is a treasure laid up in heaven, carries the heart thither also. For in another place he thus explains, "After that ye believed [the Gospel,] ye were sealed with that Holy Spirit of promise, which is the earnest of our inheritance unto the redemption of the purchased possession" (Eph. 1:13-14). Again, "Since we heard of your faith in Christ Jesus, and of the love which ye have to all the saints, for the hope which is laid up for you in heaven, whereof ye heard before in the word of the truth of the Gospel" (Col. 1:4). Again, "Whereunto he called you by our Gospel to the obtaining of the glory of our Lord Jesus Christ" (2 Thess. 2:14). Whence also it is called the word of salvation and the power of God, with salvation to every one that believes, and the kingdom of heaven. But if the doctrine of the Gospel is spiritual, and gives access to the possession of incorruptible life, let us not suppose that those to whom it was promised and declared altogether neglected the care of the soul, and lived stupidly like cattle in the enjoyment of bodily pleasures. Let no one here quibble and say that the promises concerning the Gospel, which are contained in the Law and the Prophets, were designed for a new people. For Paul, shortly after making that statement concerning the Gospel promised in the Law, adds that "whatsoever things the law saith, it saith to those who are under the law." I admit, indeed, he is there treating of a different subject, but when he said that every thing contained in the Law was directed to the Jews, he was not so oblivious as not to remember what he had said a few verses before of the Gospel promised in the Law. Most clearly, therefore, does the Apostle demonstrate that the Old Testament had special reference to the future life, when he says that the promises of the Gospel were comprehended under it.

4. In the same way we infer that the Old Testament was both established by the free mercy of God and confirmed by the intercession of Christ. For the preaching of the Gospel declares nothing more than that sinners, without any merit of their own, are justified by the paternal indulgence of God. It is wholly summed up in Christ. Who, then, will presume to represent the Jews as destitute of Christ, when we know that they were parties to the Gospel covenant, which has its only foundation in Christ? Who will presume to make them aliens to the benefit of gratuitous salvation, when we know that they were instructed in the doctrine of justification by faith? And not to dwell on a point which is clear, we have the remarkable saying of our Lord, "Your father Abraham rejoiced to see my day, and he saw it and was glad" (John 8:56). What Christ here declares of Abraham, an apostle shows to be applicable to all believers, when he says that Jesus Christ is the "same yesterday, today, and forever" (Heb. 13:8). For he is not there speaking merely of the eternal divinity of Christ, but of his power, of which believers had always full proof. Hence both the blessed Virgin and Zachariah in their hymns say that the salvation revealed in Christ was a fulfillment of the mercy promised "to our fathers, to Abraham, and to his seed forever" (Luke 1:55, 72). If, by manifesting Christ, the Lord fulfilled his ancient oath, it cannot be denied that the subject of that oath must ever have been Christ and eternal life.

5. Nay, the Apostle makes the Israelites our equals, not only in the grace of the covenant, but also in the signification of the Sacraments. For employing the example of those punishments, which the Scripture states to have been of old inflicted on the Jews, in order to deter the Corinthians from falling into similar wickedness, he begins with premising that they have no ground to claim for themselves any privilege which can exempt them from the divine vengeance which overtook the Jews, since the Lord not only visited them with the same

mercies, but also distinguished his grace among them by the same symbols; as if he had said, if you think you are out of danger because the Baptism which you received and the Supper of which you daily partake, have excellent promises, and if, in the meantime, despising the goodness of God, you indulge in licentiousness, know that the Jews on whom the Lord inflicted his severest judgments possessed similar symbols. They were baptized in passing through the sea and in the cloud which protected them from the burning heat of the sun. It is said that this passage was a carnal baptism, corresponding in some degree to our spiritual baptism. But if so, there would be a want of conclusiveness in the argument of the Apostle, whose object is to prevent Christians from imagining that they excelled the Jews in the matter of baptism. Besides, the cavil cannot apply to what immediately follows—viz. that they did "all eat the same spiritual meat; and did all drink the same spiritual drink: for they drank of that spiritual Rock that followed them: and that Rock was Christ" (1 Cor. 10:3-4).

6. To take off the force of this passage of Paul, an objection is founded on the words of our Savior, "Your fathers did eat manna in the wilderness, and are dead." "If any man eat of this bread, he shall live forever" (John 6:49, 51). There is no difficulty in reconciling the two passages. The Lord, as he was addressing hearers who only desired to be filled with earthly food, while they cared not for the true food of the soul, in some degree adapts his speech to their capacity, and in particular to meet their carnal view, draws a comparison between manna and his own body. They called upon him to prove his authority by performing some miracle, such as Moses performed in the wilderness when he obtained manna from heaven. In this manna they saw nothing but a relief of the bodily hunger from which the people were then suffering; they did not penetrate to the sublimer mystery to which Paul refers. Christ, therefore, to demonstrate that the blessing which they ought to expect from him was more excellent than the lauded one which Moses had bestowed upon their fathers, draws this comparison: if, in

your opinion, it was a great and memorable miracle when the Lord, by Moses, supplied his people with heavenly food that they might be supported for a season, and not perish in the wilderness from famine; from this infer how much more excellent is the food which bestows immortality. We see why our Lord omitted to mention what was of principal virtue in the manna, and mentioned only its meanest use. Since the Jews had, as it were by way of upbraiding, cast up Moses to him as one who had relieved the necessity of the people by means of manna, he answers that he was the minister of a much larger grace, one compared with which the bodily nourishment of the people, on which they set so high a value, ought to be held worthless. Paul, again, knowing that the Lord, when he rained manna from heaven had not merely supplied their bodies with food, but had also dispensed it as containing a spiritual mystery to typify the spiritual quickening which is obtained in Christ, does not overlook that quality which was most deserving of consideration. Wherefore it is surely and clearly proved that the same promises of celestial and eternal life which the Lord now gives to us were not only communicated to the Jews, but also sealed by truly spiritual sacraments. This subject is copiously discussed by Augustine in his work against Faustus the Manichee.

7. But if my readers would rather have passages quoted from the Law and the Prophets, from which they may see, as we have already done from Christ and the Apostles, that the spiritual covenant was common also to the Fathers, I will yield to the wish, and the more willingly, because opponents will thus be more surely convinced that henceforth there will be no room for evasion. And I will begin with a proof which, though I know it will seem futile and almost ridiculous to supercilious Anabaptists, will have very great weight with the docile and sober-minded. I take it for granted that the word of God has such an inherent efficacy that it quickens the souls of all whom he is pleased to favor with the communication of it. Peter's statement has ever been true, that it is an incorruptible seed, "which liveth and abideth for ever"

(1 Peter 1:23), as he infers from the words of Isaiah (Is. 40:6). Now when God, in ancient times, bound the Jews to him by this sacred bond, there cannot be a doubt that he separated them unto the hope of eternal life. When I say that they embraced the word which brought them nearer to God, I refer not to that general method of communication which is diffused through heaven and earth, and all the creatures of the world, and which, though it quickens all things, each according to its nature, rescues none from the bondage of corruption. I refer to that special mode of communication by which the minds of the pious are both enlightened in the knowledge of God, and in a manner linked to him. Adam, Abel, Noah, Abraham, and the other patriarchs, having been united to God by this illumination of the word, I say there cannot be the least doubt that entrance was given them into the immortal kingdom of God. They had that solid participation in God which cannot exist without the blessing of everlasting life.

8. If the point still seems somewhat involved, let us pass to the form of the covenant, which will not only satisfy calm thinkers, but sufficiently establish the ignorance of gainsayers. The covenant which God always made with his servants was this, "I will walk among you, and will be your God, and ye shall be my people" (Lev. 26:12). These words, even as the prophets are wont to expound them, comprehend life and salvation, and the whole sum of blessedness. For David repeatedly declares, and with good reason, "Happy is that people whose God is the Lord." "Blessed is the nation whose God is the Lord; and the people whom he has chosen for his own inheritance" (Psalm 144:15; 33:12); and this not merely in respect of earthly happiness, but because he rescues from death, constantly preserves, and, with eternal mercy, visits those whom he has adopted for his people. As is said in other prophets, "Art not thou from everlasting, O Lord my God, mine Holy One? we shall not die." "The Lord is our judge, the Lord is our lawgiver, the Lord is our king; he will save us" "Happy art thou, O Israel: who is like unto thee, O people saved by the Lord?" (Hab. 1:12; Isaiah 33:22;

Deut. 33:29). But not to labor superfluously, the prophets are constantly reminding us that no good thing and, consequently, no assurance of salvation, is wanting, provided the Lord is our God. And justly.
For if his face, the moment it hath shone upon us, is a perfect pledge of
salvation, how can he manifest himself to any one as his God, without
opening to him the treasures of salvation? The terms on which God
makes himself ours is to dwell in the midst of us, as he declared by
Moses (Lev. 26:11). But such presence cannot be enjoyed without life
being, at the same time, possessed along with it. And though nothing
more had been expressed, they had a sufficiently clear promise of spiritual life in these words, "I am your God" (Exod. 6:7). For he declared
that he would be a God not to their bodies only, but specially to their
souls. Souls, however, if not united to God by righteousness, remain
estranged from him in death. On the other hand, that union, wherever
it exists, will bring perpetual salvation with it.

9. To this we may add that he not only declared he was, but also
promised that he would be their God. By this their hope was extended beyond present good, and stretched forward into eternity. Moreover, that this observance of the future had the effect appears from the
many passages in which the faithful console themselves not only in
their present evils, but also for the future, by calling to mind that God
was never to desert them. Moreover, in regard to the second part of
the promise—viz. the blessing of God, its extending beyond the limits
of the present life was still more clearly confirmed by the words, I will
be the God of your seed after you (Gen. 17:7). If he was to manifest
his favor to the dead by doing good to their posterity, much less would
he deny his favor to themselves. God is not like men, who transfer
their love to the children of their friends, because the opportunity of
bestowing kind offices as they wished upon themselves is interrupted
by death. But God, whose kindness is not impeded by death, does not
deprive the dead of the benefit of his mercy, which, on their account,
he continues to a thousand generations. God, therefore, was pleased to

give a striking proof of the abundance and greatness of his goodness which they were to enjoy after death, when he described it as overflowing to all their posterity (Exod. 20:6). The truth of this promise was sealed, and in a manner completed, when, long after the death of Abraham, Isaac, and Jacob, he called himself their God (Exod. 20:6). And why? Was not the name absurd if they had perished? It would have been just the same as if he had said, I am the God of men who exist not. Accordingly, the Evangelists relate that by this very argument our Savior refuted the Sadducees (Matt. 22:23; Luke 20:32), who were, therefore, unable to deny that the resurrection of the dead was attested by Moses, inasmuch as he had taught them that all the saints are in his hand (Deut. 33:3). Whence it is easy to infer that death is not the extinction of those who are taken under the tutelage, guardianship, and protection of him who is the disposer of life and death.

10. Let us now see (and on this the controversy principally turns) whether or not believers themselves were so instructed by the Lord, as to feel that they had elsewhere a better life, and to aspire to it while disregarding the present. First, the mode of life which heaven had imposed upon them made it a constant exercise, by which they were reminded that if in this world only they had hope, they were of all men the most miserable. Adam, most unhappy even in the mere remembrance of his lost felicity, with difficulty supplies his wants by anxious labors; and that the divine curse might not be restricted to bodily labor, his only remaining solace becomes a source of the deepest grief: of two sons, the one is torn from him by the parricidal hand of his brother; while the other, who survives, causes detestation and horror by his very look. Abel, cruelly murdered in the very flower of his days, is an example of the calamity which had come upon man. While the whole world are securely living in luxury, Noah, with much fatigue, spends a great part of his life in building an ark. He escapes death, but by greater troubles than a hundred deaths could have given. Besides his ten months' residence in the ark, as in a kind of sepulcher,

nothing could have been more unpleasant than to have remained so long pent up among the filth of beasts. After escaping these difficulties he falls into a new cause of sorrow. He sees himself mocked by his own son, and is forced, with his own mouth, to curse one whom, by the great kindness of God, he had received safe from the deluge.

11. Abraham alone ought to be to us equal to tens of thousands if we consider his faith, which is set before us as the best model of believing, to whose race also we must be held to belong in order that we may be the children of God. What could be more absurd than that Abraham should be the father of all the faithful, and not even occupy the meanest corner among them? He cannot be denied a place in the list; nay, he cannot be denied one of the most honorable places in it, without the destruction of the whole Church. Now, as regards his experience in life, the moment he is called by the command of God, he is torn away from friends, parents, and country, objects in which the chief happiness of life is deemed to consist, as if it had been the fixed purpose of the Lord to deprive him of all the sources of enjoyment. No sooner does he enter the land in which he was ordered to dwell, than he is driven from it by famine. In the country to which he retires to obtain relief, he is obliged for his personal safety to expose his wife to prostitution. This must have been more bitter than many deaths. After returning to the land of his habitation, he is again expelled by famine. What is the happiness of inhabiting a land where you must so often suffer from hunger, nay, perish from famine, unless you flee from it? Then, again, with Abimelech, he is reduced to the same necessity of saving his head by the loss of his wife (Gen. 12:12). While he wanders up and down uncertain for many years, he is compelled, by the constant quarreling of servants to part with his nephew, who was to him as a son. This departure must doubtless have cost him a pang something like the cutting off of a limb. Shortly after, he learns that his nephew is carried off captive by the enemy. Wherever he goes, he meets with savage-hearted neighbors who will not even

allow him to drink of the wells which he has dug with great labor. For he would not have purchased the use from the king of Gerar if he had not been previously prohibited. After he had reached the verge of life, he sees himself childless (the bitterest and most unpleasant feeling to old age), until beyond expectation Ishmael is born; and yet he pays dearly for his birth in the reproaches of Sarah, as if he was the cause of domestic disturbance by encouraging the contumacy of a female slave. At length Isaac is born, but in return, the first-born Ishmael is displaced, and almost hostilely driven forth and abandoned. Isaac remains alone, and the good man, now worn out with age, has his heart upon him, when shortly after he is ordered to offer him up in sacrifice. What can the human mind conceive more dreadful than for the father to be the murderer of his son? Had he been carried off by disease, who would not have thought the old man much to be pitied in having a son given to him in mockery, and in having his grief for being childless doubled to him? Had he been slain by some stranger, this would, indeed, have been much worse than natural death. But all these calamities are little compared with the murder of him by his father's hand. Thus, in fine, during the whole course of his life, he was harassed and tossed in such a way, that any one desirous to give a picture of a calamitous life could not find one more appropriate. Let it not be said that he was not so very distressed, because he at length escaped from all these tempests. He is not said to lead a happy life who, after infinite difficulties during a long period, at last laboriously works out his escape, but he who calmly enjoys present blessings without any alloy of suffering.

12. Isaac is less afflicted, but he enjoys very few of the sweets of life. He also meets with those vexations which do not permit a man to be happy on the earth. Famine drives him from the land of Canaan; his wife is torn from his bosom; his neighbors are ever and anon annoying and vexing him in all kinds of ways, so that he is even obliged to fight for water. At home, he suffers great annoyance

from his daughters-in-law; he is stung by the dissension of his sons, and has no other cure for this great evil than to send the son whom he had blessed into exile (Gen. 26:27); Jacob, again, is nothing but a striking example of the greatest wretchedness. His boyhood is passed most uncomfortably at home amidst the threats and alarms of his elder brother, and to these he is at length forced to give way (Gen. 27:28); a fugitive from his parents and his native soil, in addition to the hardships of exile, the treatment he receives from his uncle Laban is in no respect milder and more humane (Gen. 29). As if it had been little to spend seven years of hard and rigorous servitude, he is cheated in the matter of a wife. For the sake of another wife, he must undergo a new servitude, during which, as he himself complains, the heat of the sun scorches him by day, while in frost and cold he spends the sleepless night (Gen. 31:40-41). For twenty years he spends this bitter life, and daily suffers new injuries from his father-in-law. Nor is he quiet at home, which he sees disturbed and almost broken up by the hatreds, quarrels, and jealousies of his wives. When he is ordered to return to his native land, he is obliged to take his departure in a manner resembling an ignominious flight. Even then he is unable to escape the injustice of his father-in-law, but in the midst of his journey is assailed by him with contumely and reproach (Gen. 31:20). By and bye a much greater difficulty befalls him (Gen. 32-33). For as he approaches his brother, he has as many forms of death in prospect as a cruel foe could invent. Hence, while waiting for his arrival, he is distracted and excruciated by direful terrors; and when he comes into his sight, he falls at his feet like one half dead, until he perceives him to be more placable than he had ventured to hope. Moreover, when he first enters the land, he is bereaved of Rachel his only beloved wife. Afterwards he hears that the son whom she had borne him, and whom he loved more than all his other children, is devoured by a wild beast (Gen. 37:33). How deep the sorrow caused by his death he himself evinces, when, after long tears, he obstinately refuses to be comforted, declaring that he will go down to the grave to his son mourning. In the meantime, what vexation, anxiety, and grief, must he have received from the carrying off and dishonor of his daughter, and the cruel revenge of his sons, which not only brought him into bad odor with all the inhabitants of the country, but exposed him to the greatest danger of extermination? (Gen. 34) Then follows the horrid wickedness of Reuben his first-born, wickedness than which none could be committed more grievous (Gen. 36:22). The dishonor of a wife being one of the greatest of calamities, what must be said when the atrocity is perpetrated by a son? Some time after, the family is again polluted with incest (Gen. 38:18). All these disgraces might have crushed a mind otherwise the most firm and unbroken by misfortune. Towards the end of his life, when he seeks relief for himself and his family from famine, he is struck by the announcement of a new misfortune, that one of his sons is detained in prison, and that to recover him he must entrust to others his dearly beloved Benjamin (Gen. 42-43). Who can think that in such a series of misfortunes, one moment was given him in which he could breathe secure? Accordingly, his own best witness, he declares to Pharaoh, "Few and evil have the days of the years of my life been" (Gen. 47:9). In declaring that he had spent his life in constant wretchedness, he denies that he had experienced the prosperity which had been promised him by the Lord. Jacob, therefore, either formed a malignant and ungrateful estimate of the Lord's favor, or he truly declared that he had lived miserable on the earth. If so, it follows that his hope could not have been fixed on earthly objects.

13. If these holy Patriarchs expected a happy life from the hand of God (and it is indubitable that they did), they viewed and contemplated a different happiness from that of a terrestrial life. This is admirably shown by an Apostle: "By faith he [Abraham] sojourned in the land of promise, as in a strange country, dwelling in tabernacles with Isaac and Jacob, the heirs with him of the same promise: for he looked for a city

which has foundations, whose builder and maker is God." "These all died in faith, not having received the promises, but having seen them afar off, and were persuaded of them, and embraced them, and confessed that they were strangers and pilgrims on the earth. For they that say such things declare plainly that they seek a country. And truly, if they had been mindful of that country from whence they came out, they might have had opportunity to have returned. But now they desire a better country, that is, a heavenly: wherefore God is not ashamed to be called their God: for he has prepared for them a city" (Heb. 11:9-10, 13-16). They had been duller than blocks in so pertinaciously pursuing promises, no hope of which appeared upon the earth, if they had not expected their completion elsewhere. The thing which the Apostle specially urges, and not without reason, is, that they called this world a pilgrimage, as Moses also relates (Gen. 47:9). If they were pilgrims and strangers in the land of Canaan, where is the promise of the Lord which appointed them heirs of it? It is clear, therefore, that the promise of possession which they had received looked farther. Hence, they did not acquire a foot breadth in the land of Canaan, except for sepulture; thus testifying that they hoped not to receive the benefit of the promise till after death. And this is the reason why Jacob set so much value on being buried there, that he took Joseph bound by oath to see it done; and why Joseph wished that his bones should some ages later, long after they had moldered into dust, be carried thither (Gen. 47:29-30; 50:25).

14. In short, it is manifest that in the whole course of their lives, they had an eye to future blessedness. Why should Jacob have aspired so earnestly to primogeniture, and intrigued for it at so much risk, if it was to bring him only exile and destitution, and no good at all, unless he looked to some higher blessing? And that this was his feeling, he declared in one of the last sentences he uttered, "I have waited for thy salvation, O God" (Gen. 49:18). What salvation could he have waited for, when he felt himself breathing his last, if he did not see in death the beginning of a new life? And why talk of saints and the children

of God, when even one, who otherwise strove to resist the truth, was not devoid of some similar impression? For what did Balaam mean when he said, "Let me die the death of the righteous, and let my last end be like his" (Num. 23:10), unless he felt convinced of what David afterward declares, "Precious in the sight of the Lord is the death of his saints?" (Ps. 116:15; 34:12). If death were the goal and ultimate limit, no distinction could be observed between the righteous and the wicked. The true distinction is the different lot which awaits them after death.

15. We have not yet come farther down than the books of Moses, whose only office according to our opponents was to induce the people to worship God by setting before them the fertility of the land, and its general abundance; and yet to everyone who does not voluntarily shun the light, there is clear evidence of a spiritual covenant. But if we come down to the Prophets, the kingdom of Christ and eternal life are there exhibited in the fullest splendor. First, David, as earlier in time, in accordance with the order of the Divine procedure, spoke of heavenly mysteries more obscurely than they, and yet with what clearness and certainty does he point to it in all he says. The value he put upon his earthly habitation is attested by these words, "I am a stranger with thee, and a sojourner, as all my fathers were. Verily every man at his best estate is altogether vanity. Surely every man walketh in a vain show. And now, Lord, what wait I for? My hope is in thee" (Ps. 39:12, 5-7). He who confesses that there is nothing solid or stable on the earth, and yet firmly retains his hope in God, undoubtedly contemplates a happiness reserved for him elsewhere. To this contemplation he is wont to invite believers whenever he would have them to be truly comforted. For, in another passages after speaking of human life as a fleeting and evanescent show, he adds, "The mercy of the Lord is from everlasting to everlasting upon them that fear him" (Ps. 103:17). To this there is a corresponding passage in another psalm, "Of old thou hast laid the foundation of the earth; and the heavens are the work of thy hands. They shall perish, but thou shalt endure; yea, all of them

shall wax old like a garment; as a vesture shalt thou change them, and they shall be changed; but thou art the same, and thy years shall have no end. The children of thy servants shall continue, and their seed shall be established before thee" (Ps. 102:25-28). If, notwithstanding of the destruction of the heavens and the earth, the godly cease not to be established before God, it follows that their salvation is connected with his eternity. But this hope could have no existence, if it did not lean upon the promise as expounded by Isaiah, "The heavens shall vanish away like smoke, and the earth shall wax old like a garment, and they that dwell therein shall die in like manner; but my salvation shall be for ever, and my righteousness shall not be abolished" (Isa. 51:6). Perpetuity is here attributed to righteousness and salvation, not as they reside in God, but as they are experienced by men.

16. Nor can those things which are everywhere said as to the prosperous success of believers be understood in any other sense than as referring to the manifestation of celestial glory. Of this nature are the following passages: "He preserveth the souls of his saints; he delivereth them out of the hand of the wicked. Light is sown for the righteous, and gladness for the upright in heart." "His righteousness endureth for ever; his horn shall be exalted with honor—the desire of the wicked shall perish." "Surely the righteous shall give thanks unto thy name; the upright shall dwell in thy presence." "The righteous shall be in everlasting remembrance." "The Lord redeemeth the soul of his servants." But the Lord often leaves his servants, not only to be annoyed by the violence of the wicked, but to be lacerated and destroyed; allows the good to languish in obscurity and squalid poverty, while the ungodly shine forth, as it were, among the stars; and even by withdrawing the light of his countenance does not leave them lasting joy. Wherefore, David by no means disguises the fact that if believers fix their eyes on the present condition of the world, they will be grievously tempted to believe that with God integrity has neither favor nor reward; so much does impiety prosper and flourish, while the godly

are oppressed with ignominy, poverty, contempt, and every kind of cross. The Psalmist says, "But as for me, my feet were almost gone; my steps had well nigh slipped. For I was envious of the foolish, when I saw the prosperity of the wicked." At length, after a statement of the case, he concludes, "When I thought to know this, it was too painful for me: until I went into the sanctuary of God; then understood I their end" (Ps. 73:2-3, 16-17).

17. Therefore, even from this confession of David, let us learn that the holy fathers under the Old Testament were not ignorant that in this world God seldom or never gives his servants the fulfillment of what is promised them, and therefore has directed their minds to his sanctuary, where the blessings not exhibited in the present shadowy life are treasured up for them. This sanctuary was the final judgment of God, which, as they could not at all discern it by the eye, they were contented to apprehend by faith. Inspired with this confidence, they doubted not that whatever might happen in the world, a time would at length arrive when the divine promises would be fulfilled. This is attested by such expressions as these: "As for me, I will behold thy face in righteousness: I shall be satisfied, when I awake, with thy likeness" (Psalm 17:15). "I am like a green olive tree in the house of God" (Psalm 52:8). Again, "The righteous shall flourish like the palm tree: he shall grow like a cedar in Lebanon. Those that be planted in the house of the Lord shall flourish in the courts of our God. They shall still bring forth fruit in old age; they shall be fat and flourishing" (Psalm 92:12-14). He had exclaimed a little before "O Lord, how great are thy works! and thy thoughts are very deep." "When the wicked spring as the grass, and when all the workers of iniquity do flourish: it is that they shall be destroyed for ever." Where was this splendor and beauty of the righteous, unless when the appearance of this world was changed by the manifestation of the heavenly kingdom? Lifting their eyes to the eternal world, they despised the momentary hardships and calamities of the present life, and confidently

broke out into these exclamations: "He shall never suffer the righteous to be moved. But thou, O God, shalt bring them down into the pit of destruction: bloody and deceitful men shall not live out half their days" (Psalm 55:22-23). Where in this world is there a pit of eternal destruction to swallow up the wicked, of whose happiness it is elsewhere said, "They spend their days in wealth, and in a moment go down to the grave?" (Job 21:13). Where, on the other hand, is the great stability of the saints, who, as David complains, are not only disturbed, but everywhere utterly bruised and oppressed? It is here. He set before his eyes not merely the unstable vicissitudes of the world, tossed like a troubled sea, but what the Lord is to do when he shall one day sit to fix the eternal constitution of heaven and earth, as he in another place elegantly describes: "They that trust in their wealth, and boast themselves in the multitude of their riches; none of them can by any means redeem his brother, nor give to God a ransom for him." "For he sees that wise men die, likewise the fool and the brutish person perish, and leave their wealth to others. Their inward thought is, that their houses shall continue for ever, and their dwelling-places to all generations; they call their lands after their own names. Nevertheless, man being in honor abideth not: he is like the beasts that perish. This their way is their folly: yet their posterity approve their sayings. Like sheep they are laid in the grave; death shall feed on them; and the upright shall have dominion over them in the morning; and their beauty shall consume in the grave from their dwelling" (Psalm 49:6-7, 10-14). By this derision of the foolish for resting satisfied with the slippery and fickle pleasures, of the world, he shows that the wise must seek for a very different felicity. But he more clearly unfolds the hidden doctrine of the resurrection when he sets up a kingdom to the righteous after the wicked are cast down and destroyed. For what, pray, are we to understand by the "morning," unless it be the revelation of a new life, commencing when the present comes to an end?

18. Hence the consideration which believers employed as a solace for their sufferings, and a remedy for their patience: "His anger endureth but a moment: in his favor is life" (Psalm 30:5). How did their afflictions, which continued almost throughout the whole course of life, terminate in a moment? Where did they see the long duration of the divine benignity, of which they had only the slightest taste? Had they clung to earth, they could have found nothing of the kind; but looking to heaven, they saw that the period during which the Lord afflicted his saints was but a moment, and that the mercies with which he gathers them are everlasting: on the other hand, they foresaw that for the wicked, who only dreamed of happiness for a day, there was reserved an eternal and never-ending destruction. Hence those expressions: "The memory of the just is blessed, but the name of the wicked shall rot" (Prov. 10:7). "Precious in the sight of the Lord is the death of his saints" (Psalm 116:15). Again in Samuel: "The Lord will keep the feet of his saints, and the wicked shall be silent in darkness" (1 Sam. 2:9); showing they knew well, that however much the righteous might be tossed about, their latter end was life and peace; that how pleasant soever the delights of the wicked, they gradually lead down to the chambers of death. They accordingly designated the death of such persons as the death "of the uncircumcised," that is, persons cut off from the hope of resurrection (Ezek. 28:10; 31:18). Hence David could not imagine a greater curse than this: "Let them be blotted out of the book of the living, and not be written with the righteous" (Psalm 69:28).

19. The most remarkable passage of all is that of Job: "I know that my Redeemer liveth, and that he shall stand at the latter day upon the earth: and though after my skin worms destroy this body, yet in my flesh shall I see God: whom I shall see for myself, and mine eyes shall behold, and not another" (Job 19:25-27). Those who would make a display of their acuteness, pretend that these words are to be understood not of the last resurrection, but of the day when Job expected

that God would deal more gently with him. Granting that this is partly meant, we shall, however, compel them, whether they will or not, to admit that Job never could have attained to such fullness of hope if his thoughts had risen no higher than the earth. It must, therefore, be confessed that he who saw that the Redeemer would be present with him when lying in the grave, must have raised his eyes to a future immortality. To those who think only of the present life, death is the extremity of despair; but it could not destroy the hope of Job. "Though he slay me," said he, "yet will I trust in him" (Job 13:15). Let no trifler here burst in with the objection that these are the sayings of a few, and do not by any means prove that there was such a doctrine among the Jews. To this my instant answer is that these few did not in such passages give utterance to some hidden wisdom, to which only distinguished individuals were admitted privately and apart from others, but that having been appointed by the Holy Spirit to be the teachers of the people, they openly promulgated the mysteries of God, which all in common behaved to learn as the principles of public religion. When, therefore, we hear that those passages in which the Holy Spirit spoke so distinctly and clearly of the spiritual life were public oracles in the Jewish Church, it were intolerably perverse to confine them entirely to a carnal covenant relating merely to the earth and earthly riches.

20. When we descend to the later prophets, we have it in our power to expatiate freely as in our own field. If, when David, Job, and Samuel, were in question, the victory was not difficult, much easier is it here; for the method and economy which God observed in administering the covenant of his mercy was that the nearer the period of its full exhibition approached, the greater the additions which were daily made to the light of revelation. Accordingly, at the beginning, when the first promise of salvation was given to Adam (Gen. 3:15), only a few slender sparks beamed forth: additions being afterwards made, a greater degree of light began to be displayed, and continued

gradually to increase and shine with greater brightness, until at length all the clouds being dispersed, Christ the Sun of righteousness arose, and with full refulgence illumined all the earth (Mal. 4). In appealing to the Prophets, therefore, we can have no fear of any deficiency of proof; but as I see an immense mass of materials which would occupy us much longer than compatible with the nature of our present work (the subject, indeed, would require a large volume), and as I trust, that by what has already been said, I have paved the way so that every reader of the very least discernment may proceed without stumbling, I will avoid a prolixity for which at present there is little necessity; only reminding my readers to facilitate the entrance by means of the key which was formerly put into their hands (supra, Chap. 4 sec. 3-4); namely, that whenever the Prophets make mention of the happiness of believers (a happiness of which scarcely any vestiges are discernible in the present life), they must have recourse to this distinction: that the better to commend the Divine goodness to the people, they used temporal blessings as a kind of lineaments to shadow it forth, and yet gave such a portrait as might lift their minds above the earth, the elements of this world, and all that will perish, and compel them to think of the blessedness of a future and spiritual life.

21. One example will suffice. When the Israelites were carried away to Babylon, their dispersion seemed to be the next thing to death, and they could scarcely be dissuaded from thinking that Ezekiel's prophecy of their restoration (Ezek. 37:4) was a mere fable, because it seemed to them the same thing as if he had prophesied that putrid caresses would be raised to life. The Lord, in order to show that, even in that case, there was nothing to prevent him from making room for his kindness, set before the prophet in vision a field covered with dry bones, to which, by the mere power of his word, he in one moment restored life and strength. The vision served, indeed, to correct the unbelief of the Jews at the time, but it also reminded them how much farther the power of the Lord extended than to the bringing back

of the people, since by a single nod it could so easily give life to dry scattered bones. Wherefore, the passage may be fitly compared with one in Isaiah, "Thy dead men shall live, together with my dead body shall they arise. Awake and sing, ye that dwell in dust: for thy dew is as the dew of herbs, and the earth shall cast out the dead. Come, my people, enter thou into thy chambers, and shut thy doors about thee: hide thyself as it were for a little moment, until the indignation be overpast. For, behold, the Lord cometh out of his place to punish the inhabitants of the earth for their iniquity: the earth also shall disclose her blood, and shall no more cover her slain" (Isa. 26:19-21).

22. It were absurd however to interpret all the passages on a similar principle; for there are several which point without any veil to the future immortality which awaits believers in the kingdom of heaven. Some of them we have already quoted, and there are many others, but especially the following two. The one is in Isaiah, "As the new heavens and the new earth, which I will make, shall remain before me, saith the Lord, so shall your seed and your name remain. And it shall come to pass that from one new moon to another, and from one sabbath to another, shall all flesh come to worship before me, saith the Lord. And they shall go forth, and look upon the carcasses of the men that have transgressed against me: for their worm shall not die, neither shall their fire be quenched; and they shall be an abhorring unto all flesh" (Isa. 66:22-24). The other passage is in Daniel. "At that time shall Michael stand up, the great prince which standeth for the children of thy people: and there shall be a time of trouble, such as there never was since there was a nation even to that same time: and at that time thy people shall be delivered, every one shall be found written in the book. And many of them that sleep in the dust of the earth shall awake, some to everlasting life, and some to shame and everlasting contempt" (Dan. 12:1-2).

23. In proving the two remaining points—viz. that the Patriarchs had Christ as the pledge of their covenant, and placed all their hope of

blessing in him, as they are clearer, and not so much controverted, I will be less particular. Let us then lay it down confidently as a truth which no engines of the devil can destroy—that the Old Testament or covenant which the Lord made with the people of Israel was not confined to earthly objects, but contained a promise of spiritual and eternal life, the expectation of which behaved to be impressed on the minds of all who truly consented to the covenant. Let us put far from us the senseless and pernicious notion that the Lord proposed nothing to the Jews, or that they sought nothing but full supplies of food, carnal delights, abundance of wealth, external influence, a numerous offspring, and all those things which our animal nature deems valuable. For, even now, the only kingdom of heaven which our Lord Jesus Christ promises to his followers is one in which they may sit down with Abraham, and Isaac and Jacob (Matt. 8:11); and Peter declared of the Jews of his day that they were heirs of gospel grace because they were the sons of the prophets, and comprehended in the covenant which the Lord of old made with his people (Acts 3:25). And that this might not be attested by words merely, our Lord also approved it by act (Matt. 27:52). At the moment when he rose again, he deigned to make many of the saints partakers of his resurrection, and allowed them to be seen in the city; thus giving a sure earnest, that every thing which he did and suffered in the purchase of eternal salvation belonged to believers under the Old Testament, just as much as to us. Indeed, as Peter testifies, they were endued with the same spirit of faith by which we are regenerated to life (Acts 15:8). When we hear that that spirit, which is, as it were, a kind of spark of immortality in us (whence it is called the "earnest" of our inheritance, Eph. 1:14), dwelt in like manner in them, how can we presume to deny them the inheritance? Hence, it is the more wonderful how the Sadducees of old fell into such a degree of sottishness as to deny both the resurrection and the substantive existence of spirits, both of which where attested to them by so many striking passages of Scripture. Nor would the stupidity of the whole nation in the present day, in expecting an earthly reign of the Messiah, be less wonderful, had not the Scriptures foretold this long before as the punishment which they were to suffer for rejecting the Gospel, God, by a just judgment, blinding minds which voluntarily invite darkness, by rejecting the offered light of heaven. They read, and are constantly turning over the pages of Moses, but a veil prevents them from seeing the light which beams forth in his countenance (2 Cor. 3:14); and thus to them he will remain covered and veiled until they are converted to Christ, between whom and Moses they now study, as much as in them lies, to maintain a separation.

Study Guide Questions

Section 1

1. What point does Calvin believe is very important to make?
2. What was said concerning the Jews by Calvin's opponents?

Section 2

1. How much alike are the various covenants that God has made with men?
2. Are these covenants similar?
3. What are the three points Calvin makes here?

Section 3

1. According to the Bible, what were the Old Testament saints looking forward to?
2. What was the Old Testament particularly concerned with?

Section 4

1. What notable saying of the Lord does Calvin use in this discussion?
2. In passing, what does Calvin call the Lord's mother?

Section 5

1. Does Calvin contrast the Jews in the wilderness with the Corinthians?
2. If the Jews' baptism into Moses was carnal only, would Paul's argument have worked?

Section 6

1. Does Calvin believe that manna was sacramental food?
2. How does he answer the objection from John 6:49, 54?

Section 7

1. In arguing for the spiritual benefits enjoyed by the Old Testament saints, what does Calvin point to in this section as their possession?

Section 8

1. What else did they possess?

Section 9

1. What is Calvin's next argument for the spiritual blessedness of the Old Testament saints?

Section 10

1. What is another reason for saying that they were not enjoying all the heaven they were going to get here on earth?

Section 11

1. Who was a preeminent example of this?

Section 12

1. Did Isaac live as troubled a life as Abraham?
2. What about Jacob?
3. What are the implications of this?

Section 13

1. What Scripture settles the issue?

2. What would the patriarchs have been if God had promised them earthly blessing which they did not receive?

Section 14

1. Did they ever express this hope openly?

Sections 15–16

1. What does David habitually call believers back to?

2. And what does he allude to throughout the Psalms?

Section 17

1. How often did Calvin believe that promises of blessedness were fulfilled in this life for Old Testament saints?

2. Did this cause these saints to despair of the fulfillment?

Section 18

1. Did the wicked ever receive "blessings" in this life?

Section 19

1. Did Job expect a future life?

2. Was this an esoteric insight for just him?

Section 20

1. If for Calvin the doctrine of the resurrection was clear in the earlier portions of the Old Testament, what happened later?

Section 21

1. How does Calvin interpret the valley of dry bones?

Section 22

1. Which two prophets does Calvin cite here to reinforce this point?
Isaiah and Daniel.

Section 23

1. What was the first of Calvin's two remaining points?
2. The second?
3. So what doctrine falls to the ground?

CHAPTER 11

The difference between the two Testaments.

This chapter consists principally of three parts.

I. Five points of difference between the Old and the New Testament, sec. 1-11.

II. The last of these points being that the Old Testament belonged to the Jews only, whereas the New Testament belongs to all; the calling of the Gentiles is shortly considered, sec. 12.

III. A reply to two objections usually taken to what is here taught concerning the difference between the Old and the New Testaments, sec. 13-14.

Outline:

1. Five points of difference between the Old and the New Testaments. These belong to the mode of administration rather than the substance. First difference. In the Old Testament the heavenly inheritance is exhibited under temporal blessings; in the New, aids of this description are not employed.

2. Proof of this first difference from the simile of an heir in pupillarity, as in Gal. 4:1.

3. This the reason why the Patriarchs, under the Law, set a higher value on this life and the blessings of it, and dreaded the punishments, these being even more striking. Why severe and sudden punishments existed under the Law.

4. A second difference. The Old Testament typified Christ under ceremonies. The New exhibits the immediate truth and the whole body. The scope of the Epistle to the Hebrews in explaining this difference. Definition of the Old Testament.

5. Hence the Law our Schoolmaster to bring us unto Christ.

6. Notwithstanding, among those under the Law, some of the strongest examples of faith are exhibited, their equals being scarcely to be found in the Christian Church. The ordinary method of the divine dispensation to be here attended to. These excellent individuals placed under the Law, and aided by ceremonies, that they might behold and hail Christ afar off.

7. Third difference. The Old Testament is literal, the New spiritual. This difference considered first generally.

8. Next treated specially, on a careful examination of the Apostle's text. A threefold antithesis. The Old Testament is literal, deadly, temporary. The New is spiritual, quickening, eternal. Difference between the letter and the spirit.

9. Fourth difference. The Old Testament belongs to bondage, the New to liberty. This confirmed by three passages of Scripture. Two objections answered.

10. Distinction between the three last differences and the first. Confirmation of the above from Augustine. Condition of the patriarchs under the Old Testament.

11. Fifth difference. The Old Testament belonged to one people only, the New to all.

12. The second part of the chapter depending on the preceding section. Of the calling of the Gentiles. Why the calling of the Gentiles scented to the Apostles so strange and new.

13. The last part of the chapter. Two objections considered. 1. God being immutable, cannot consistently disapprove what he once ordered. Answer confirmed by a passage of Scripture.

14. Objections. 2. God could at first have transacted with the Jews as he now does with Christians. Answer, showing the absurdity of this objection. Another answer founded on a just consideration of the divine will and the dispensation of grace.

W hat, then? You will say, is there no difference between the Old and the New Testaments? What is to become of the many passages of Scripture in which they are contrasted as things differing most widely from each other? I readily admit the differences which are pointed out in Scripture, but still hold that they derogate in no respect from their established unity, as will be seen after we have considered them in their order. These differences (so far as I have been able to observe them and can remember) seem to be chiefly four, or, if you choose to add a fifth, I have no objections. I hold and think I will be able to show, that they all belong to the mode of administration rather than to the substance. In this way, there is nothing in them to prevent the promises of the Old and New Testament from remaining the same, Christ being the foundation of both. The first difference then is that though in old time the Lord was pleased to direct the thoughts of his people, and raise their minds to the heavenly inheritance, yet that their hope of it might be the better maintained, he held it forth, and in a manner gave a foretaste of it under earthly blessings, whereas the gift of future life, now more clearly and lucidly revealed by the Gospel, leads our minds directly to meditate upon it, the inferior mode of exercise formerly employed in regard to the Jews being now laid aside. Those who attend not to the divine purpose in this respect suppose that God's ancient people ascended no higher than the blessings which were promised to the body. They hear the land of Canaan so often named as the special and as it were the only reward of the Divine

Law to its worshipers; they hear that the severest punishment which the Lord denounces against the transgressors of the Law is expulsion from the possession of that land and dispersion into other countries; they see that this forms almost the sum of the blessings and curses declared by Moses; and from these things they confidently conclude that the Jews were separated from other nations not on their own account, but for another reason—viz. that the Christian Church might have an emblem in whose outward shape might be seen an evidence of spiritual things. But since the Scripture sometimes demonstrates that the earthly blessings thus bestowed were intended by God himself to guide them to a heavenly hope, it shows great unskillfulness, not to say dullness, not to attend to this mode of dispensation. The ground of controversy is this: our opponents hold that the land of Canaan was considered by the Israelites as supreme and final happiness, and now, since Christ was manifested, typifies to us the heavenly inheritance; whereas we maintain that, in the earthly possession which the Israelites enjoyed, they beheld, as in a mirror, the future inheritance which they believed to be reserved for them in heaven.

2. This will better appear from the similitude which Paul uses in Galatians (Gal. 4:1). He compares the Jewish nation to an heir in pupillarity, who, as yet unfit to govern himself, follows the direction of a tutor or guide to whose charge he has been committed. Though this simile refers especially to ceremonies, there is nothing to prevent us from applying it most appropriately here also. The same inheritance was destined to them as to us, but from nonage they were incapable of entering to it and managing it. They had the same Church, though it was still in puerility. The Lord, therefore kept them under this tutelage, giving them spiritual promises, not clear and simple, but typified by earthly objects. Hence, when he chose Abraham, Isaac, and Jacob, and their posterity, to the hope of immortality, he promised them the land of Canaan for an inheritance, not that it might be the limit of their hopes, but that the view of it might train and confirm them in the

hope of that true inheritance, which as yet appeared not. And to guard against delusion, they received a better promise, which attested that this earth was not the highest measure of the divine kindness. Thus, Abraham is not allowed to keep down his thoughts to the promised land; by a greater promise his views are carried upward to the Lord. He is thus addressed, "Fear not, Abram: I am thy shield, and thy exceeding great reward" (Gen. 15:1). Here we see that the Lord is the final reward promised to Abraham that he might not seek a fleeting and evanescent reward in the elements of this world, but look to one which was incorruptible. A promise of the land is afterwards added for no other reason than that it might be a symbol of the divine benevolence, and a type of the heavenly inheritance, as the saints declare their understanding to have been. Thus David rises from temporal blessings to the last and highest of all, "My flesh and my heart faileth: but God is the strength of my heart, and my portion for ever." "My heart and my flesh crieth out for the living God" (Ps. 73:26; 84:2). Again, "The Lord is the portion of mine inheritance and of my cup: thou maintainest my lot" (Ps. 16:5). Again "I cried unto thee O Lord: I said Thou art my refuge and my portion in the land of the living" (Ps. 142:5). Those who can venture to speak thus, assuredly declare that their hope rises beyond the world and worldly blessings. This future blessedness, however, the prophets often describe under a type which the Lord had taught them. In this way are to be understood the many passages in Job (Job 18:17) and Isaiah, to the effect that the righteous shall inherit the earth, that the wicked shall be driven out of it, that Jerusalem will abound in all kinds of riches, and Zion overflow with every species at abundance. In strict propriety, all these things obviously apply not to the land of our pilgrimage, nor to the earthly Jerusalem, but to the true country, the heavenly city of believers, in which the Lord has commanded blessing and life for evermore (Ps. 133:3).

3. Hence the reason why the saints under the Old Testament set a higher value on this mortal life and its blessings than would now be

meet. For, though they well knew that in their race they were not to halt at it as the goal, yet perceiving that the Lord in accommodation to their feebleness had there imprinted the lineaments of his favor, it gave them greater delight than it could have done if considered only in itself. For, as the Lord, in testifying his good will towards believers by means of present blessings, then exhibited spiritual felicity under types and emblems, so on the other hand by temporal punishments he gave proofs of his judgment against the reprobate. Hence by earthly objects the favor of the Lord was displayed, as well as his punishment inflicted. The unskillful, not considering this analogy and correspondence (if I may so speak) between rewards and punishments, wonder that there is so much variance in God that those who in old time were suddenly visited for their faults with severe and dreadful punishments, he now punishes much more rarely and less severely, as if he had laid aside his former anger, and for this reason they can scarcely help imagining like the Manichees that the God of the Old Testament was different from that of the New. But we shall easily disencumber ourselves of such doubts if we attend to that mode of divine administration to which I have adverted—that God was pleased to indicate and typify both the gift of future and eternal felicity by terrestrial blessings, as well as the dreadful nature of spiritual death by bodily punishments, at that time when he delivered his covenant to the Israelites as under a kind of veil.

4. Another distinction between the Old and New Testaments is in the types, the former exhibiting only the image of truth, while the reality was absent, the shadow instead of the substance, the latter exhibiting both the full truth and the entire body. Mention is usually made of this whenever the New Testament is contrasted with the Old, but it is nowhere so fully treated as in the Epistle to the Hebrews (chap. 7-10). The Apostle is there arguing against those who thought that the observances of the Mosaic Law could not be abolished without producing the total ruin of religion. In order to refute this error, he

adverts to what the Psalmist had foretold concerning the priesthood of Christ (Ps. 110:4). Seeing that an eternal priesthood is assigned to him, it is clear that the priesthood in which there was a daily succession of priests is abolished. And he proves that the institution of this new Priest must prevail, because confirmed by an oath. He afterwards adds, that a change of the priest necessarily led to a change of the covenant. And the necessity of this he confirms by the reason that the weakness of the law was such that it could make nothing perfect. He then goes on to show in what this weakness consists, namely that it had external carnal observances which could not render the worshipers perfect in respect of conscience, because its sacrifices of beasts could neither take away sins nor procure true holiness. He therefore concludes that it was a shadow of good things to come, and not the very image of the things, and accordingly had no other office than to be an introduction to the better hope which is exhibited in the Gospel.

Here we may see in what respect the legal is compared with the evangelical covenant, the ministry of Christ with that of Moses. If the comparison referred to the substance of the promises, there would be a great repugnance between the two covenants; but since the nature of the case leads to a different view, we must follow it in order to discover the truth. Let us therefore bring forward the covenant which God once ratified as eternal and unending. Its completion, whereby it is fixed and ratified, is Christ. Till such completion takes place, the Lord, by Moses, prescribes ceremonies which are, as it were formal symbols of confirmation. The point brought under discussion was whether or not the ceremonies ordained in the Law behaved to give way to Christ. Although these were merely accidents of the covenant, or at least additions and appendages and, as they are commonly called, accessories, yet because they were the means of administering it, the name of covenant is applied to them, just as is done in the case of other sacraments. Hence, in general, the Old Testament is the name given to the solemn method of confirming the covenant comprehended under ceremonies and sacrifices. Since there is nothing substantial in it until we look beyond it, the Apostle contends that it behaved to be annulled and become antiquated (Heb. 7:22), to make room for Christ, the surety and mediator of a better covenant, by whom the eternal sanctification of the elect was once purchased, and the transgressions which remained under the Law wiped away. But if you prefer it, take it thus: the covenant of the Lord was old, because veiled by the shadowy and ineffectual observance of ceremonies; and it was therefore temporary, being as it were in suspense until it received a firm and substantial confirmation. Then only did it become new and eternal when it was consecrated and established in the blood of Christ. Hence the Savior, in giving the cup to his disciples in the last supper, calls it the cup of the new testament in his blood; intimating that the covenant of God was truly realized, made new, and eternal, when it was sealed with his blood.

5. It is now clear in what sense the Apostle said (Gal. 3:24; 4:1), that by the tutelage of the Law the Jews were conducted to Christ, before he was exhibited in the flesh. He confesses that they were sons and heirs of God, though on account of nonage they were placed under the guardianship of a tutor. It was fit, the Sun of Righteousness not yet having risen, that there should neither be so much light of revelation nor such clear understanding. The Lord dispensed the light of his word, so that they could behold it at a distance, and obscurely. Accordingly, this slender measure of intelligence is designated by Paul by the term childhood, which the Lord was pleased to train by the elements of this world, and external observances, until Christ should appear. Through him the knowledge of believers was to be matured. This distinction was noted by our Savior himself when he said that the Law and the Prophets were until John, that from that time the gospel of the kingdom was preached (Matt. 11:13). What did the Law and the Prophets deliver to the men of their time? They gave a foretaste of that wisdom which was one day to be clearly manifested,

and showed it afar off. But where Christ can be pointed to with the finger, there the kingdom of God is manifested. In him are contained all the treasures of wisdom and understanding, and by these we penetrate almost to the very shrine of heaven.

6. There is nothing contrary to this in the fact that in the Christian Church scarcely one is to be found who in excellence of faith can be compared to Abraham, and that the Prophets were so distinguished by the power of the Spirit that even in the present day they give light to the whole world. For the question here is not what grace the Lord conferred upon a few, but what was the ordinary method which he followed in teaching the people, and which even was employed in the case of those very prophets who were endued with special knowledge above others. For their preaching was both obscure as relating to distant objects, and was included in types. Moreover, however wonderful the knowledge displayed in them, as they were under the necessity of submitting to the tutelage common to all the people, they must also be ranked among children. Lastly, none of them ever had such a degree of discernment as not to savor somewhat of the obscurity of the age. Whence the words of our Savior, "Many kings and prophets have desired to see the things which you see, and have not seen them, and to hear the things which ye hear, and have not heard them. Blessed are your eyes, for they see, and your ears, for they hear" (Matt. 13:17). And it was right that the presence of Christ should have this distinguishing feature, that by means of it the revelation of heavenly mysteries should be made more transparent. To the same effect is the passage which we formerly quoted from the First Epistle of Peter, that to them it was revealed that their labor should be useful not so much to themselves as to our age.

7. I proceed to the third distinction, which is thus expressed by Jeremiah: "Behold, the days come, saith the Lord, that I will make a new covenant with the house of Israel, and with the house of Judah; not according to the covenant that I made with their fathers, in the

day that I took them by the hand, to bring them out of the land
of Egypt; (which my covenant they brake, although I was an husband unto them, saith the Lord); but this shall be the covenant that
I will make with the house of Israel; after those days, saith the Lord,
I will put my law in their inward parts, and write it in their hearts;
and will be their God, and they shall be my people. And they shall
teach no more every man his neighbor, and every man his brother,
saying, know the Lord: for they shall all know me, from the least of
them unto the greatest of them" (Jer. 31:31-34). From these words,
the Apostle took occasion to institute a comparison between the Law
and the Gospel, calling the one a doctrine of the letter, the other a
doctrine of the spirit; describing the one as formed on tables of stone,
the other on tables of the heart; the one the preaching of death, the
other of life; the one of condemnation, the other of justification; the
one made void, the other permanent (2 Cor. 3:5-6). The object of the
Apostle being to explain the meaning of the Prophet, the worlds of
the one furnish us with the means of ascertaining what was understood by both. And yet there is some difference between them. For
the Apostle speaks of the Law more disparagingly than the Prophet.
This he does not simply in respect of the Law itself, but because there
were some false zealots of the Law who, by a perverse zeal for ceremonies, obscured the clearness of the Gospel, he treats of the nature
of the Law with reference to their error and foolish affection. It will,
therefore, be proper to attend to this peculiarity in Paul. Both, however, as they are contrasting the Old and New Testament, consider
nothing in the Law but what is peculiar to it. For example, the Law
everywhere contains promises of mercy; but as these are adventitious
to it, they do not enter into the account of the Law as considered only
in its own nature. All which is attributed to it is, that it commands
what is right, prohibits crimes, holds forth rewards to the cultivators
of righteousness, and threatens transgressors with punishment, while

at the same time it neither changes nor amends that depravity of heart which is naturally inherent in all.

8. Let us now explain the Apostle's contrast step by step. The Old Testament is literal because promulgated without the efficacy of the Spirit: the New spiritual, because the Lord has engraven it on the heart. The second antithesis is a kind of exposition of the first. The Old is deadly, because it can do nothing but involve the whole human race in a curse; the New is the instrument of life, because those who are freed from the curse it restores to favor with God. The former is the ministry of condemnation, because it charges the whole sons of Adam with transgression; the latter the ministry of righteousness, because it unfolds the mercy of God, by which we are justified. The last antithesis must be referred to the Ceremonial Law. Being a shadow of things to come, it behaved in time to perish and vanish away; whereas the Gospel, inasmuch as it exhibits the very body, is firmly established for ever. Jeremiah indeed calls the Moral Law also a weak and fragile covenant; but for another reason—namely, because it was immediately broken by the sudden defection of an ungrateful people; but as the blame of such violation is in the people themselves, it is not properly alleged against the covenant. The ceremonies, again, inasmuch as through their very weakness they were dissolved by the advent of Christ, had the cause of weakness from within. Moreover, the difference between the spirit and the letter must not be understood as if the Lord had delivered his Law to the Jews without any good result; i.e. as if none had been converted to him. It is used comparatively to commend the riches of the grace with which the same Lawgivers assuming, as it were a new characters honored the preaching of the Gospel. When we consider the multitude of those whom by the preaching of the Gospel he has regenerated by his Spirit and gathered out of all nations into the communion of his Church, we may say that those of ancient Israel who with sincere and heartfelt affections embraced the covenant of

the Lord were few or none, though the number is great when they are
considered in themselves without comparison.

9. Out of the third distinction a fourth arises. In Scripture, the
term bondage is applied to the Old Testaments because it begets fear,
and the term freedom to the New, because productive of confidence
and security. Thus Paul says to the Romans, "Ye have not received
the spirit of bondage again to fear; but ye have received the Spirit of
adoption whereby we cry, Abba, Father" (Rom. 8:15). To the same
effect is the passage in the Hebrews, "For ye are not come unto the
mount that might be touched, and that burned with fire, nor unto
blackness, and darkness, and tempest, and the sound of a trumpet,
and the voice of words; which voice they that heard entreated that
the word should not be spoken to them anymore (for they could
not endure that which was commanded: 'And if so much as a beast
touch the mountain, it shall be stoned, or thrust through with a dart,'
and so terrible was the sight that Moses said, 'I exceedingly fear and
quake'); but ye are come unto mount Zion, and unto the city of the
living God, the heavenly Jerusalem," &c. (Heb. 12:18-22). What Paul
briefly touches on in the passage which we have quoted from the Romans, he explains more fully in the Epistles to the Galatians, where
he makes an allegory of the two sons of Abraham in this way: "Hagar
is Mount Sinai in Arabia, and answereth to Jerusalem which now is,
and is in bondage with her children. But Jerusalem which is above is
free, which is the mother of us all" (Gal. 4:25-26). As the offspring of
Hagar was born in slavery, and could never attain to the inheritances
while that of Sara was free and entitled to the inheritance, so by the
Law we are subjected to slavery, and by the Gospel alone regenerated
into liberty. The sum of the matter comes to this: the Old Testament
filled the conscience with fear and trembling; the New inspires it with
gladness. By the former the conscience is held in bondage, by the
latter it is manumitted and made free. If it be objected, that the holy
fathers among the Israelites, as they were endued with the same spirit

of faith, must also have been partakers of the same liberty and joy, we answer that neither was derived from the Law; but feeling that by the Law they were oppressed like slaves, and vexed with a disquieted conscience, they fled for refuge to the gospel; and, accordingly, the peculiar advantage of the Gospel was that, contrary to the common rule of the Old Testament, it exempted those who were under it from those evils. Then again we deny that they did possess the spirit of liberty and security in such a degree as not to experience some measure of fear and bondage. For however they might enjoy the privilege which they had obtained through the grace of the Gospel, they were under the same bonds and burdens of observances as the rest of their nation. Therefore, seeing they were obliged to the anxious observance of ceremonies (which were the symbols of a tutelage bordering on slavery, and handwritings by which they acknowledged their guilt, but did not escape from it), they are justly said to have been, comparatively, under a covenant of fear and bondage, in respect of that common dispensation under which the Jewish people were then placed.

10. The three last contrasts to which we have adverted (sec. 4, 7, 9) are between the Law and the Gospel, and hence in these the Law is designated by the name of the Old, and the Gospel by that of the New Testament. The first is of wider extent (sec. 1), comprehending under it the promises which were given even before the Law. When Augustine maintained that these were not to be included under the name of the Old Testament (August. *ad Bonifac.* lib. 3 c. 14), he took a most correct view, and meant nothing different from what we have now taught; for he had in view those passages of Jeremiah and Paul in which the Old Testament is distinguished from the word of grace and mercy. In the same passage, Augustine with great shrewdness remarks that from the beginning of the world the sons of promise, the divinely regenerated, who through faith working by love obeyed the commandments, belonged to the New Testament; entertaining the hope not of carnal, earthly, temporal, but spiritual, heavenly, and

eternal blessings, believing especially in a Mediator, by whom they doubted not both that the Spirit was administered to them, enabling them to do good, and pardon imparted as often as they sinned. The thing which he thus intended to assert was, that all the saints mentioned in Scripture, from the beginning of the world, as having been specially selected by God, were equally with us partakers of the blessing of eternal salvation. The only difference between our division and that of Augustine is that ours (in accordance with the words of our Savior, "All the prophets and the law prophesied until John," Matt. 11:13) distinguishes between the gospel light and that more obscure dispensation of the word which preceded it, while the other division simply distinguishes between the weakness of the Law and the strength of the Gospel. And here also, with regard to the holy fathers, it is to be observed that though they lived under the Old Testament, they did not stop there, but always aspired to the New and so entered into sure fellowship with it. Those who, contented with existing shadows, did not carry their thoughts to Christ, the Apostle charges with blindness and malediction. To say nothing of other matters, what greater blindness can be imagined than to hope for the expiation of sin from the sacrifice of a beast, or to seek mental purification in external washing with water, or to attempt to appease God with cold ceremonies, as if he were greatly delighted with them? Such are the absurdities into which those fall who cling to legal observances, without respect to Christ.

11. The fifth distinction which we have to add consists in this: that until the advent of Christ the Lord set apart one nation, to which he confined the covenant of his grace. Moses says, "When the Most High divided to the nations their inheritance, when he separated the sons of Adam, he set the bounds of the people according to the number of the children of Israel. For the Lord's portion is his people; Jacob is the lot of his inheritance" (Deut. 32:8-9). In another passage he thus addresses the people: "Behold, the heaven and the heaven of

heavens is the Lord's thy God, the earth also, with all that therein is. Only the Lord had a delight in thy fathers to love them, and he chose their seed, after them, even you, above all people, as it is this day" (Deut. 10:14-15). That people, therefore, as if they had been the only part of mankind belonging to him he favored exclusively with the knowledge of his name, depositing his covenant, as it were, in their bosom, manifesting to them the presence of his divinity and honoring them with all privileges. But to say nothing of other favors, the only one here considered is his binding them to him by the communion of his word, so that he was called and regarded as their God. Meanwhile, other nations, as if they had had no kind of intercourse with him, he allowed to wander in vanity not even supplying them with the only means of preventing their destructions—viz. the preaching of his word. Israel was thus the Lord's favorite child the others were aliens. Israel was known and admitted to trust and guardianship, the others left in darkness; Israel was made holy, the others were profane; Israel was honored with the presence of God, the others kept far aloof from him. But on the fullness of the time destined to renew all things, when the Mediator between God and man was manifested the middle wall of partition, which had long kept the divine mercy within the confines of Israel, was broken down, peace was preached to them who were afar off, as well as to those who were nigh, that being, together reconciled to God, they might unite as one people. Wherefore, there is now no respect of Jew or Greek, of circumcision or uncircumcision, but Christ is all and in all. To him the heathen have been given for his inheritance, and the uttermost parts of the earth for his possession (Ps. 2:8), that he may rule without distinction "from sea to sea, and from the river unto the ends of the earth" (Ps. 72:8).

12. The calling of the Gentiles, therefore, is a distinguishing feature illustrative of the superiority of the New over the Old Testament. This, it is true, had been previously declared by the prophets, in passages both numerous and clear, but still the fulfillment of it was deferred to

the reign of the Messiah. Even Christ did not acknowledge it at the very outset of his ministry, but delayed it until having completed the whole work of redemption in all its parts, and finished the period of his humiliation, he received from the Father "a name which is above every name, that at the name of Jesus every knee should bow" (Phil. 2:9-10). Hence the period being not yet completed, he declared to the woman of Canaan, "I am not sent but unto the lost sheep of the house of Israel" (Matt. 15:24). Nor in his first commission to the Apostles does he permit them to pass the same limits, "Go not into the way of the Gentiles, and into any city of the Samaritans enter ye not: but go rather to the lost sheep of the house of Israel" (Matt. 10:5-6). However plainly the thing may have been declared in numerous passages, when it was announced to the Apostles, it seemed to them so new and extraordinary that they were horrified at it as something monstrous. At length, when they did act upon it, it was timorously, and not without reluctance. Nor is this strange; for it seemed by no means in accordance with reason that the Lord, who for so many ages had selected Israel from the rest of the nations should suddenly, as it were, change his purpose and abandon his choice. Prophecy, indeed, had foretold it, but they could not be so attentive to prophecies as not to be somewhat startled by the novel spectacle thus presented to their eye. It was not enough that God had in old times given specimens of the future calling of the Gentiles. Those whom he had so called were very few in number, and, moreover, he in a manner adopted them into the family of Abraham before allowing them to approach his people. But by this public call, the Gentiles were not only made equal to the Jews, but seemed to be substituted into their place, as if the Jews had been dead. We may add that any strangers whom God had formerly admitted into the body of the Church had never been put on the same footing with the Jews. Wherefore, it is not without cause that Paul describes it as the mystery which has been hid from ages and from generations, but now is made manifest to his saints (Col. 1:26).

13. The whole difference between the Old and New Testaments has, I think, been fully and faithfully explained under these four or five heads in so far as requisite for ordinary instruction. But since this variety in governing the Church, this diversity in the mode of teaching, this great change in rites and ceremonies, is regarded by some as an absurdity, we must reply to them before passing to other matters. And this can be done briefly, because the objections are not so strong as to require a very careful refutation. It is unreasonable, they say, to suppose that God who is always consistent with himself permitted such a change as afterwards to disapprove what he had once ordered and commended. I answer that God ought not to be deemed mutable because he adapts different forms to different ages, as he knows to be expedient for each. If the husband-man prescribes one set of duties to his household in winter, and another in summer, we do not therefore charge him with fickleness or think he deviates from the rules of good husbandry which depends on the regular course of nature. In like manner, if a father of a family in educating, governing, and managing his children, pursues one course in boyhood, another in adolescence, and another in manhood, we do not therefore say that he is fickle or abandons his opinions. Why then do we charge God with inconstancy when he makes fit and congruous arrangements for diversities of times? The latter similitude ought to be completely satisfactory. Paul likens the Jews to children, and Christians to grown men (Gal. 4:1). What irregularity is there in the Divine arrangement, which confined them to the rudiments which were suitable to their age, and trains us by a firmer and more manly discipline? The constancy of God is conspicuous in this, that he delivered the same doctrine to all ages, and persists in requiring that worship of his name which he commanded at the beginning. His changing the external form and manner does not show that he is liable to change. In so far he has only accommodated himself to the mutable and diversified capacities of man.

14. But it is said, whence this diversity, save that God chose to make it? Would it not have been as easy for him from the first, as after the advent of Christ, to reveal eternal life in clear terms without any figures, to instruct his people by a few clear sacraments, to bestow his Holy Spirit, and diffuse his grace over the whole globe? This is very much the same as to bring a charge against God, because he created the world at so late a period, when he could have done it at the first, or because he appointed the alternate changes of summer and winter, of day and night. With the feeling common to every pious mind, let us not doubt that every thing which God has done has been done wisely and justly, although we may be ignorant of the cause which required that it should be so done. We should arrogate too much to ourselves were we not to concede to God that he may have reasons for his counsel, which we are unable to discern. It is strange, they say, that he now repudiates and abominates the sacrifices of beasts, and the whole apparatus of that Levitical priesthood in which he formerly delighted. As if those external and transient matters could delight God, or affect him in any way! It has already been observed that he appointed none of these things on his own account, but instituted them all for the salvation of men. If a physician, adopting the best method, effects a cure upon a youth, and afterwards, when the same individual has grown old, and is again subject to the same disease, employs a different method of cure, can it be said that he repudiates the method which he formerly approved? Nay, continuing to approve of it, he only adapts himself to the different periods of life. In like manner, it was necessary in representing Christ in his absence, and predicting his future advent, to employ a different set of signs from those which are employed, now that his actual manifestation is exhibited. It is true that since the advent of Christ the calling of God is more widely addressed to all nations, and the graces of the Spirit more liberally bestowed than they had previously been. But who, I ask, can deny the right of God to have the free and uncontrolled disposal of his gifts, to

select the nations which he may be pleased to illuminate, the places which he may be pleased to illustrate by the preaching of his word, and the mode and measure of progress and success which he may be pleased to give to his doctrine—to punish the world for its ingratitude by withdrawing the knowledge of his name for certain ages, and again, when he so pleases, to restore it in mercy? We see, then, that in the calumnies which the ungodly employ in this matter, to perplex the minds of the simple, there is nothing that ought to throw doubt either on the justice of God or the veracity of Scripture.

Study Guide Questions

Section 1

1. How many differences are there between the Old and New Testaments?
2. What is the first of these differences?
3. How did this differ from what Calvin's opponents said?

Section 2

1. Calvin reapplies an image that Paul used in Galatians. What is that image?

Section 3

1. What did Calvin believe about benefits and punishments in the Old Testament era?
2. What purpose did that serve?

Section 4

1. What was the second difference between the two testaments?
2. What is the fulfillment of those figures?
3. When did the covenant become new and eternal?

Section 5

1. Was the truth understood clearly and distinctly in the time of the Old Testament?

2. What did the Law and the Prophets point to, then?

Section 6

1. Is this view consistent with understanding that few Christians if any measure up to Abraham's faith?

Section 7

1. According to Calvin, what is the third difference between the testaments?

2. What does Calvin mean by those particular words?

Section 8

1. Why is the New Testament spiritual?

2. What is the final contrast between the testaments?

3. What is the difference between the moral law and the ceremonial law in the Old Testament?

Section 9

1. What is the fourth contrast between the testaments?

2. How then were Old Testament saints saved?

3. Nevertheless, what did these true saints of the Old Testament still have to do?

Section 10

1. How did the holy patriarchs live under the Old Covenant?

Section 11

1. What is the fifth difference, which may be added?

Section 12

1. What is therefore a "distinguishing feature" of the excellence of the New Testament?

2. Had the Old Testament foretold this?

Section 13

1. Why did God change His manner of administration?

Section 14

1. What is Calvin's basic assumption about all God's dealings with man?

2. Is God doing all this for His own sake?

CHAPTER 12

Christ, to perform the office of Mediator, behooved to become a man.

The two divisions of this chapter are:

I. The reasons why our Mediator behooved to be very God, and to become man, sec. 1-3.

II. Disposal of various objections by some fanatics, and especially by Osiander, to the orthodox doctrine concerning the Mediator, sec. 4-7.

Outline:

1. Necessary, not absolutely but by divine decree, that the Mediator should be God, and become man. Neither man nor angel, though pure, could have sufficed. The Son of God behooved to come down. Man in innocence could not penetrate to God without a Mediator, much less could he after the fall.

2. A second reason why the Mediator behooved to be God and man—viz. that he had to convert those who were heirs of hell into children of God.

3. Third reason, that in our flesh he might yield a perfect obedience, satisfy the divine justice, and pay the penalty of sin. Fourth reason, regarding the consolation and confirmation of the whole Church.

4. First objection against the orthodox doctrine: Answer to it. Conformation from the sacrifices of the Law, the testimony of the Prophets, Apostles, Evangelists, and even Christ himself.

5. Second objection: Answer: Answer confirmed. Third objection: Answer. Fourth objection by Osiander: Answer.

6. Fifth objection, forming the basis of Osiander's errors on this subject: Answer. Nature of the divine image in Adam. Christ the head of angels and men.

7. Sixth objection: Answer. Seventh objection: Answer. Eighth objection: Answer. Ninth objection: Answer. Tenth objection: Answer. Eleventh objection: Answer. Twelfth objection: Answer. The sum of the doctrine.

It deeply concerned us that he who was to be our Mediator should be very God and very man. If the necessity be inquired into, it was not what is commonly termed simple or absolute, but flowed from the divine decree on which the salvation of man depended. What was best for us, our most merciful Father determined. Our iniquities, like a cloud intervening between Him and us, having utterly alienated us from the kingdom of heaven, none but a person reaching to him could be the medium of restoring peace. But who could thus reach to him? Could any of the sons of Adam? All of them, with their parents, shuddered at the sight of God. Could any of the angels? They had need of a head, by connection with which they might adhere to their God entirely and inseparably. What then? The case was certainly desperate, if the Godhead itself did not descend to us, it being impossible for us to ascend. Thus the Son of God behooved to become our Emmanuel, the God with us; and in such a way that by mutual union his divinity and our nature might be combined; otherwise, neither was the proximity near enough, nor the affinity strong enough, to give us hope that God would dwell with us; so great was the repugnance between our pollution and the spotless purity of God. Had man remained free from all taint, he was of too humble a condition to penetrate to God without a Mediator. What, then, must it have been, when by fatal ruin he was plunged into death and hell, defiled by so many stains, made loathsome by corruption; in fine, overwhelmed with every curse? It is not without cause, therefore, that Paul, when he would set forth Christ as the Mediator, distinctly declares him to be man. There is, says he, "one Mediator between God and man, the man Christ Jesus" (1 Tim. 2:5). He might have called him God, or at least, omitting to call him God he might also have omitted to call him man; but because the Spirit, speaking by his mouth, knew our infirmity, he opportunely provides for it by the most appropriate remedy, setting the Son of God familiarly before us as one of ourselves. That no one, therefore, may feel perplexed where to seek the Mediator, or by what means to reach him, the Spirit, by calling him man, reminds us that he is near, nay, contiguous to us, inasmuch as he is our flesh. And, indeed, he intimates the same thing in another place, where he explains at greater length that he is not a high priest who "cannot be touched with the feeling of our infirmities; but was in all points tempted like as we are, yet without sin" (Heb. 4:15).

2. This will become still clearer if we reflect that the work to be performed by the Mediator was of no common description: being to restore us to the divine favor, so as to make us, instead of sons of men, sons of God; instead of heirs of hell, heirs of a heavenly kingdom. Who could do this unless the Son of God should also become the Son of man, and so receive what is ours as to transfer to us what is his, making that which is his by nature to become ours by grace? Relying on this earnest, we trust that we are the sons of God, because the natural Son of God assumed to himself a body of our body, flesh of our flesh, bones of our bones, that he might be one with us; he declined not to take what was peculiar to us, that he might in his turn extend to us what was peculiarly his own, and thus might be in common with us both Son of God and Son of man. Hence that holy brotherhood which he

commends with his own lips, when he says, "I ascend to my Father, and your Father, to my God, and your God" (John 20:17). In this way, we have a sure inheritance in the heavenly kingdom, because the only Son of God, to whom it entirely belonged, has adopted us as his brethren; and if brethren, then partners with him in the inheritance (Rom. 8:17). Moreover, it was especially necessary for this cause also that he who was to be our Redeemer should be truly God and man. It was his to swallow up death: who but Life could do so? It was his to conquer sin: who could do so save Righteousness itself? It was his to put to flight the powers of the air and the world: who could do so but the mighty power superior to both? But who possesses life and righteousness, and the dominion and government of heaven, but God alone? Therefore, God, in his infinite mercy, having determined to redeem us, became himself our Redeemer in the person of his only begotten Son.

3. Another principal part of our reconciliation with God was that man, who had lost himself by his disobedience, should by way of remedy oppose to it obedience, satisfy the justice of God, and pay the penalty of sin. Therefore, our Lord came forth very man, adopted the person of Adam, and assumed his name, that he might in his stead obey the Father; that he might present our flesh as the price of satisfaction to the just judgment of God, and in the same flesh pay the penalty which we had incurred. Finally, since as God only he could not suffer, and as man only could not overcome death, he united the human nature with the divine, that he might subject the weakness of the one to death as an expiation of sin, and by the power of the other, maintaining a struggle with death, might gain us the victory. Those, therefore, who rob Christ of divinity or humanity either detract from his majesty and glory, or obscure his goodness. On the other hand, they are no less injurious to men, undermining and subverting their faith, which, unless it rest on this foundation, cannot stand. Moreover, the expected Redeemer was that son of Abraham and David whom God had promised in the Law and in the Prophets. Here believers

have another advantage. Tracing up his origin in regular series to David and Abraham, they more distinctly recognize him as the Messiah celebrated by so many oracles. But special attention must be paid to what I lately explained, namely, that a common nature is the pledge of our union with the Son of God; that, clothed with our flesh, he warred to death with sin that he might be our triumphant conqueror; that the flesh which he received of us he offered in sacrifice, in order that by making expiation he might wipe away our guilt, and appease the just anger of his Father.

4. He who considers these things with due attention, will easily disregard vague speculations, which attract giddy minds and lovers of novelty. One speculation of this class is that Christ, even though there had been no need of his interposition to redeem the human race, would still have become man. I admit that in the first ordering of creation, while the state of nature was entire, he was appointed head of angels and men; for which reason Paul designates him "the first-born of every creature" (Col. 1:15). But since the whole Scripture proclaims that he was clothed with flesh in order to become a Redeemer, it is presumptuous to imagine any other cause or end. We know well why Christ was at first promised—viz. that he might renew a fallen world, and succor lost man. Hence under the Law he was typified by sacrifices, to inspire believers with the hope that God would be propitious to them after he was reconciled by the expiation of their sins. Since from the earliest age, even before the Law was promulgated, there was never any promise of a Mediator without blood, we justly infer that he was destined in the eternal counsel of God to purge the pollution of man, the shedding of blood being the symbol of expiation. Thus, too, the prophets, in discoursing of him, foretold that he would be the Mediator between God and man. It is sufficient to refer to the very remarkable prophecy of Isaiah (Is. 53:4-5), in which he foretells that he was "smitten for our iniquities;" that "the chastisement of our peace was upon him;" that as a priest "he was made an offering for

sin;" "that by his stripes we are healed;" that as all "like lost sheep have gone astray," "it pleased the Lord to bruise him, and put him to grief," that he might "bear our iniquities." After hearing that Christ was divinely appointed to bring relief to miserable sinners, whose overleaps these limits gives too much indulgence to a foolish curiosity.

Then when he actually appeared, he declared the cause of his advent to be, that by appeasing God he might bring us from death unto life. To the same effect was the testimony of the Apostles concerning him (John 1:9; 10:14). Thus John, before teaching that the Word was made flesh, narrates the fall of man. But above all, let us listen to our Savior himself when discoursing of his office: "God so loved the world, that he gave his only begotten Son, that whosoever believeth in him should not perish, but have everlasting life." Again, "The hour is coming, and now is, when the dead shall hear the voice of the Son of God: and they that hear shall live." "I am the resurrection and the life: he that believeth in me, though he were dead, yet shall he live." "The Son of man is come to save that which was lost." Again, "They that be whole need not a physician." I should never have done were I to quote all the passages. Indeed, the Apostles, with one consent, lead us back to this fountain; and assuredly, if he had not come to reconcile God, the honor of his priesthood would fall, seeing it was his office as priest to stand between God and men, and "offer both gifts and sacrifices for sins" (Heb. 5:1); nor could he be our righteousness, as having been made a propitiation for us in order that God might not impute to us our sins (2 Cor. 5:19). In short, he would be stripped of all the titles with which Scripture invests him. Nor could Paul's doctrine stand "What the law could not do, in that it was weak through the flesh, God sending his own Son in the likeness of sinful flesh, and for sin, condemned sin in the flesh" (Rom. 8:3). Nor what he states in another passage: "The grace of God that bringeth salvation has appeared to all men" (Tit. 2:11). In fine, the only end which the Scripture uniformly assigns for the Son of God voluntarily assuming our nature, and even receiving it as a command from the Father, is that he might propitiate the Father to us by becoming a victim. "Thus it is written, and thus it behooved Christ to suffer;" "and that repentance and remission of sins should be preached in his name." "Therefore does my Father love me, because I lay down my life, that I might take it again." "This commandment have I received of my Father." "As Moses lifted up the serpent in the wilderness, even so must the Son of man be lifted up." "Father, save me from this hour, but for this cause came I unto this hour. Father, glorify thy name." Here he distinctly assigns as the reason for assuming our nature, that he might become a propitiatory victim to take away sin. For the same reason Zacharias declares (Luke 1:79) that he came "to perform the mercy promised to our fathers," "to give light to them that sit in darkness, and in the shadow of death." Let us remember that all these things are affirmed of the Son of God, in whom, as Paul elsewhere declares, were "hid all the treasures of wisdom and knowledge," and save whom it was his determination "not to know any thing" (Col. 2:3; 1 Cor. 2:2).

5. Should anyone object that in this there is nothing to prevent the same Christ who redeemed us when condemned from also testifying his love to us when safe by assuming our nature, we have the brief answer that when the Spirit declares that by the eternal decree of God the two things were connected together—viz. that Christ should be our Redeemer, and, at the same time, a partaker of our nature, it is unlawful to inquire further. He who is tickled with a desire of knowing something more, not contented with the immutable ordination of God, shows also that he is not even contented with that Christ who has been given us as the price of redemption. And, indeed, Paul not only declares for what end he was sent, but rising to the sublime mystery of predestination, seasonably represses all the wantonness and prurience of the human mind. "He has chosen us in him before the foundation of the world, that we should be holy and without blame before him in love: having predestinated us unto the adoption of children by Jesus Christ

to himself, according to the good pleasure of his will, to the praise of
the glory of his grace, wherein he has made us accepted in the Beloved,
in whom we have redemption through his blood" (Eph. 1:4-7). Here
certainly the fall of Adam is not presupposed as anterior in point of
time, but our attention is directed to what God predetermined before
all ages, when he was pleased to provide a cure for the misery of the
human race. If, again, it is objected that this counsel of God depended
on the fall of man, which he foresaw, to me it is sufficient and more
to reply, that those who propose to inquire, or desire to know more of
Christ than God predestinated by his secret decree, are presuming with
impious audacity to invent a new Christ. Paul, when discoursing of the
proper office of Christ, justly prays for the Ephesians that God would
strengthen them "by his Spirit in the inner man," that they might "be
able to comprehend with all saints what is the breadth and length, and
depth and height; and to know the love of Christ which passeth knowledge" (Eph. 3:16, 18); as if he intended of set purpose to set barriers
around our minds, and prevent them from declining one iota from the
gift of reconciliation whenever mention is made of Christ. Wherefore,
seeing it is as Paul declares it to be, "a faithful saying, and worthy of
all acceptation, that Christ Jesus came into the world to save sinners"
(1 Tim. 1:15), in it I willingly acquiesce. And since the same Apostle
elsewhere declares that the grace which is now manifested by the Gospel "was given us in Christ Jesus before the world began" (2 Tim. 1:9),
I am resolved to adhere to it firmly even to the end. This moderation
is unjustly vituperated by Osiander, who has unhappily in the present
day again agitated this question, which a few had formerly raised. He
brings a charge of overweening confidence against those who deny that
the Son of God would have appeared in the flesh if Adam had not fall-
en, because this notion is not repudiated by any passage of Scripture. As
if Paul did not lay a curb on perverse curiosity when after speaking of
the redemption obtained by Christ, he bids us "avoid foolish questions"
(Tit. 3:9). To such insanity have some proceeded in their preposterous

eagerness to seem acute, that they have made it a question whether the Son of God might not have assumed the nature of an ass. This blasphemy, at which all pious minds justly shudder with detestation, Osiander excuses by the pretext that it is no where distinctly refuted in Scripture; as if Paul, when he counted nothing valuable or worth knowing "save Jesus Christ and him crucified" (1 Cor. 2:2) were admitting that the author of salvation is an ass. He who elsewhere declares that Christ was by the eternal counsel of the Father appointed "head over all things to the church," would never have acknowledged another to whom no office of redemption had been assigned.

6. The principle on which Osiander founds is altogether frivolous. He will have it that man was created in the image of God, inasmuch as he was formed on the model of the future Messiah, in order to resemble him whom the Father had already determined to clothe with flesh. Hence he infers that though Adam had never fallen from his first and pure original, Christ would still have been man. How silly and distorted this view is, all men of sound judgment at once discern; still he thinks he was the first to see what the image of God was, namely, that not only did the divine glory shine forth in the excellent endowments with which he was adorned, but God dwelt in him essentially. But while I grant that Adam bore the image of God, inasmuch as he was united to God (this being the true and highest perfection of dignity), yet I maintain that the likeness of God is to be sought for only in those marks of superiority with which God has distinguished Adam above the other animals. And likewise, with one consent, acknowledge that Christ was even then the image of God, and, accordingly, whatever excellence was engraven on Adam had its origin in this, that by means of the only begotten Son he approximated to the glory of his Maker. Man, therefore, was created in the image of God (Gen. 1:27), and in him the Creator was pleased to behold, as in a mirror, his own glory. To this degree of honor he was exalted by the kindness of the only begotten Son. But I add that as

the Son was the common head both of men and angels, so the dignity which was conferred on man belonged to the angels also. For when we hear them called the sons of God (Ps. 82:6), it would be incongruous to deny that they were endued with some quality in which they resembled the Father. But if he was pleased that his glory should be represented in men and angels, and made manifest in both natures, it is ignorant trifling in Osiander to say that angels were postponed to men because they did not bear the image of Christ. They could not constantly enjoy the immediate presence of God if they were not like to him; nor does Paul teach (Col. 3:10) that men are renewed in the image of God in any other way than by being associated with angels, that they may be united together under one head. In fine, if we believe Christ, our felicity will be perfected when we shall have been received into the heavens, and made like the angels. But if Osiander is entitled to infer that the primary type of the image of God was in the man Christ, on the same ground may anyone maintain that Christ behooved to partake of the angelic nature, seeing that angels also possess the image of God.

7. Osiander has no reason to fear that God would be found a liar, if the decree to incarnate the Son was not previously immutably fixed in his mind. Even had Adam not lost his integrity, he would, with the angels, have been like to God; and yet it would not therefore have been necessary that the Son of God should become either a man or an angel. In vain does he entertain the absurd fear that unless it had been determined by the immutable counsel of God, before man was created, that Christ should be born, not as the Redeemer, but as the first man, he might lose his precedence, since he would not have been born, except for an accidental circumstance, namely, that he might restore the lost race of man; and in this way would have been created in the image of Adam. For why should he be alarmed at what the Scripture plainly teaches, that "he was in all points tempted like as we are, yet without sin?" (Heb. 4:15). Hence Luke, also, hesitates

not to reckon him in his genealogy as a son of Adam (Luke 3:38). I should like to know why Christ is termed by Paul the second Adam (1 Cor. 15:47), unless it be that a human condition was decreed him, for the purpose of raising up the ruined posterity of Adam. For if in point of order, that condition was antecedent to creation, he ought to have been called the first Adam. Osiander confidently affirms that because Christ was in the purpose of God foreknown as man, men were formed after him as their model. But Paul, by calling him the second Adam, gives that revolt which made it necessary to restore nature to its primitive condition an intermediate place between its original formation and the restitution which we obtain by Christ: hence it follows that it was this restitution which made the Son of God be born, and thereby become man. Moreover, Osiander argues ill and absurdly that as long as Adam maintained his integrity, he would have been the image of himself, and not of Christ. I maintain, on the contrary, that although the Son of God had never become incarnate, nevertheless the image of God was conspicuous in Adam, both in his body and his soul; in the rays of this image it always appeared that Christ was truly head, and had in all things the preeminence. In this way we dispose of the futile sophism put forth by Osiander, that the angels would have been without this head, had not God purposed to clothe his Son with flesh, even independent of the sin of Adam. He inconsiderately assumes what no rational person will grant, that Christ could have had no supremacy over the angels, so that they might enjoy him as their prince, unless in so far as he was man. But it is easy to infer from the words of Paul (Col. 1:15), that inasmuch as he is the eternal Word of God, he is the first-born of every creature, not because he is created, or is to be reckoned among the creatures, but because the entire structure of the world, such as it was from the beginning, when adorned with exquisite beauty had no other beginning; then, inasmuch as he was made man, he is the first-born from the dead. For in one short passage (Col. 1:16-18), the Apostle calls

our attention to both views: that by the Son all things were created, so
that he has dominion over angels; and that he became man in order
that he might begin to be a Redeemer. Owing to the same ignorance,
Osiander says that men would not have had Christ for their king unless he had been a man; as if the kingdom of God could not have been
established by his eternal Son, though not clothed with human flesh,
holding the supremacy while angels and men were gathered together
to participate in his celestial life and glory. But he is always deluded,
or imposes upon himself by this false principle, that the church would
have been *akephalon*—without a head—had not Christ appeared in
the flesh. In the same way as angels enjoyed him for their head, could
he not by his divine energy preside over men, and by the secret virtue
of his Spirit quicken and cherish them As his body, until they were
gathered into heaven to enjoy the same life with the angels? The absurdities which I have been refuting, Osiander regards as infallible
oracles. Taking an intoxicating delight in his own speculations, his
wont is to extract ridiculous plans out of nothing. He afterwards says
that he has a much stronger passage to produce, namely, the prophecy
of Adam, who, when the woman was brought to him, said, "This is
now bone of my bone, and flesh of my flesh" (Gen. 2:23). But how
does he prove it to be a prophecy? Because in Matthew Christ attributes the same expression to God! As if every thing which God
has spoken by man contained a prophecy. On the same principle, as
the law proceeded from God, let Osiander in each precept find a
prophecy. Add that our Savior's exposition would have been harsh
and groveling, had he confined himself to the literal meaning. He was
not referring to the mystical union with which he has honored the
Church, but only to conjugal fidelity, and states, that the reason why
God declared man and wife to be one flesh was to prevent anyone
from violating that indissoluble tie by divorce. If this simple meaning
is too low for Osiander, let him censure Christ for not leading his
disciples to the hidden sense, by interpreting his Father's words with

more subtlety. Paul gives no countenance to Osiander's dream, when after saying that "we are members of his body, of his flesh, and of his bones," he immediately adds, "This is a great mystery" (Eph. 5:30-32). For he meant not to refer to the sense in which Adam used the words, but sets forth, under the figure and similitude of marriage, the sacred union which makes us one with Christ. His words have this meaning; for reminding us that he is speaking of Christ and the Church, he, by way of correction, distinguishes between the marriage tie and the spiritual union of Christ with his Church. Wherefore, this subtlety vanishes at once. I deem it unnecessary to discuss similar absurdities: for from this very brief refutation, the vanity of them all will be discovered. Abundantly sufficient for the solid nurture of the children of God is this sober truth, that "when the fullness of the time was come, God sent forth his Son, made of a woman, made under the law, to redeem them who were under the law" (Gal. 4:4-5).

Study Guide Questions

Section 1

1. What was of the greatest importance?
2. Where did this necessity come from?
3. Why did God have to descend to us?

Section 2

1. What were the children of men to become?
2. The heirs of Gehenna were to become what?
3. Christ took our nature upon Him ungrudgingly in order to do what?

Section 3

1. The Incarnation was necessary how?

Section 4

1. What "speculation" does Calvin address next?

2. What does Calvin think of those who "overleap these limits"?

Section 5

1. Who is Calvin addressing in this section?

2. Does Calvin believe that Adam's fall precedes God's decree in time?

Section 6

1. What is the basis of Osiander's teaching?

Section 7

1. What is Calvin's reply concerning Christ's "precedence"?

2. Does Calvin believe that Christ could have been "Head" of the human race without the Incarnation?

CHAPTER 13

Christ clothed with the true substance of human nature.

The heads of this chapter are:
I. The orthodoxy doctrine as to the true humanity of our Savior, proved from many passages of Scripture, sec. 1.

II. Refutation of the impious objections of the Marcionites, Manichees, and similar heretics, sec. 2-4. Sections.

Outline:

1. Proof of the true humanity of Christ, against the Manichees and Marcionites.

2. Impious objections of heretics further discussed. Six objections answered.

3. Other eight objections answered.

4. Other three objections answered.

Of the divinity of Christ, which has elsewhere been established by clear and solid proofs, I presume it were superfluous again to treat. It remains, therefore, to see how, when clothed with our flesh, he fulfilled the office of Mediator. In ancient times, the reality of his human nature was impugned by the Manichees and Marcionites, the latter figuring to themselves a phantom instead of the body of Christ, and the former dreaming of his having been invested with celestial flesh. The passages of Scripture contradictory to both are numerous and strong. The blessing is not promised in a heavenly seed, or the mask of a man, but the seed of Abraham and Jacob; nor is the everlasting throne promised to an aerial man, but to the Son of David, and the fruit of his loins. Hence, when manifested in the flesh, he is called the Son of David and Abraham, not because he was born of a virgin, and yet created in the air, but because, as Paul explains, he was "made of the seed of David, according to the flesh" (Rom. 1:3), as the same apostle elsewhere says, that he came of the Jews (Rom. 9:5). Wherefore, our Lord himself not contented with the name of man, frequently calls himself the Son of man, wishing to express more clearly that he was a man by true human descent. The Holy Spirit having so often, by so many organs, with so much care and plainness, declared a matter which in itself is not abstruse, who could have thought that mortals would have had the effrontery to darken it with their glosses? Many other passages are at hand, were it wished to produce more: for instance, that one of Paul, that "God sent forth his Son, made of a woman" (Gal. 4:4), and innumerable others, which show that he was subject to hunger, thirst, cold, and the other infirmities of our nature. But from the many we must chiefly select those which may conduce to build up our minds in true faith, as when it is said, "Verily, he took not on him the nature of angels, but he took on him the seed of Abraham," "that through death he might destroy him that had the power of death" (Heb. 2:16, 14). Again, "Both he that sanctifieth and they who are sanctified are all of one: for which cause he is not ashamed to call them brethren." "Wherefore in all things it behooved him to be made like unto his brethren, that he might be a merciful and faithful high priest." (Heb. 2:11, 17). Again "We have not an high priest which cannot be touched with the feeling of our infirmities" (Heb. 4:15), and the like. To the same effect is the passage to which we lately referred, in which Paul distinctly declares, that the sins of the world behooved to be expiated in our flesh (Rom. 8:3). And certainly every thing which the Father conferred on Christ pertains to us for this reason, that "he is the head," that from him the whole body is "fitly joined together, and compacted by that which every joint supplieth" (Eph. 4:16). Nay, in no other way could it hold true as is said, that the Spirit was given to him without measure (John 1:16), and that out of his fullness have all we received; since nothing could be more absurd than that God, in his own essence, should be enriched by an adventitious gift. For this reason also, Christ himself elsewhere says, "For their sakes I sanctify myself" (John 17:19).

2. The passages which they produce in confirmation of their error are absurdly wrested, nor do they gain any thing by their frivolous subtleties when they attempt to do away with what I have now adduced in opposition to them. Marcion imagines that Christ, instead of a body, assumed a phantom, because it is elsewhere said, that he was made in the likeness of man, and found in fashion as a man. Thus he altogether overlooks what Paul is then discussing (Phil. 2:7). His object is not to show what kind of body Christ assumed, but that, when he might have justly asserted his divinity he was pleased to exhibit nothing but the attributes of a mean and despised man. For, in order to exhort us to submission by his example, he shows, that when as God he might have displayed to the world the brightness of his glory, he gave up his right, and voluntarily emptied himself; that he assumed the form of a servant, and, contented with that humble condition, suffered his divinity to be concealed under a veil of flesh. Here, unquestionably, he explains not what Christ was, but in what way he acted. Nay, from the whole context it is easily gathered, that it was in the true nature of man that Christ humbled himself. For what is meant by the words, he was "found in fashion as a man," but that for a time, instead of being resplendent with divine glory, the human

form only appeared in a mean and abject condition? Nor would the words of Peter, that he was "put to death in the flesh, but quickened by the Spirit" (1 Pet. 3:18) hold true, unless the Son of God had become weak in the nature of man. This is explained more clearly by Paul, when he declares that "he was crucified through weakness" (2 Cor. 13:4). And hence his exaltation; for it is distinctly said that Christ acquired new glory after he humbled himself. This could fitly apply only to a man endued with a body and a soul. Manes dreams of an aerial body because Christ is called the second Adam, the Lord from heaven. But the apostle does not there speak of the essence of his body as heavenly, but of the spiritual life which derived from Christ quickens us (1 Cor. 15:47). This life Paul and Peter, as we have seen, separate from his flesh. Nay, that passage admirably confirms the doctrine of the orthodox, as to the human nature of Christ. If his body were not of the same nature with ours, there would be no soundness in the argument which Paul pursues with so much earnestness: if Christ is risen we shall rise also; if we rise not, neither has Christ risen. Whatever be the cavils by which the ancient Manichees or their modern disciples endeavor to evade this, they cannot succeed. It is a frivolous and despicable evasion to say that Christ is called the Son of Man, because he was promised to men; it being obvious that, in the Hebrew idiom, the Son of Man means a true man: and Christ, doubtless, retained the idiom of his own tongue. Moreover, there cannot be a doubt as to what is to be understood by the sons of Adam. Not to go farther, a passage in the eighth psalm, which the apostles apply to Christ, will abundantly suffice: "What is man, that thou art mindful of him? and the son of man, that thou visitest him?" (Ps 8:4). Under this figure is expressed the true humanity of Christ. For although he was not immediately descended of an earthly father, yet he originally sprang from Adam. Nor could it otherwise be said in terms of the passage which we have already quoted, "Forasmuch, then, as the children are partakers of flesh and blood, he also himself likewise took part of the same;" these words plainly proving that he was an associate and partner in the same nature with ourselves. In this sense also it is said that "both he that sanctifieth and they who are sanctified are all of one." The context proves that this refers to a community of nature; for it is immediately added, "For which cause he is not ashamed to call them brethren" (Heb. 2:11). Had he said at first that believers are of God, where could there have been any ground for being ashamed of persons possessing such dignity? But when Christ of his boundless grace associates himself with the mean and ignoble, we see why it was said that "he is not ashamed." It is vain to object that in this way the wicked will be the brethren of Christ; for we know that the children of God are not born of flesh and blood, but of the Spirit through faith. Therefore, flesh alone does not constitute the union of brotherhood. But although the Apostle assigns to believers only the honor of being one with Christ, it does not however follow, that unbelievers have not the same origin according to the flesh; just as when we say that Christ became man that he might make us sons of God, the expression does not extend to all classes of persons; the intervention of faith being necessary to our being spiritually ingrafted into the body of Christ. A dispute is also ignorantly raised as to the term first-born. It is alleged that Christ ought to have been the first son of Adam, in order that he might be the first-born among the brethren (Rom. 8:29). But primogeniture refers not to age, but to degree of honor and preeminence of virtue. There is just as little color for the frivolous assertion that Christ assumed the nature of man, and not that of angels (Heb. 2:16), because it was the human race that he restored to favor. The Apostle, to magnify the honor which Christ has conferred upon us, contrasts us with the angels, to whom we are in this respect preferred. And if due weight is given to the testimony of Moses (Gen. 3:15), when he says that the seed of the woman would bruise the head of the serpent, the dispute is at an end. For the words there used refer not to Christ alone, but to the whole human race.

Since the victory was to be obtained for us by Christ, God declares generally that the posterity of the woman would overcome the devil. From this it follows that Christ is a descendant of the human race, the purpose of God in thus addressing Eve being to raise her hopes, and prevent her from giving way to despair.

3. The passages in which Christ is called the seed of Abraham, and the fruit of the loins of David, those persons, with no less folly than wickedness, wrap up in allegory. Had the term seed been used allegorically, Paul surely would not have omitted to notice it, when he affirms clearly, and without figure, that the promise was not given "to seeds, as of many; but as of one, And to thy seed, which is Christ" (Gal. 3:16). With similar absurdity they pretend that he was called the Son of David for no other reason but because he had been promised, and was at length in due time manifested. For Paul, after he had called him the Son of David, by immediately subjoining "according to the flesh," certainly designates his nature. So also (Rom. 9:5), while declaring him to be "God blessed for ever," he mentions separately that, "as concerning the flesh, he was descended from the Jews." Again if he had not been truly begotten of the seed of David, what is the meaning of the expression, that he is the "fruit of his loins;" or what the meaning of the promise, "Of the fruit of thy body will I set upon thy throne?" (Ps. 132:11). Moreover their mode of dealing with the genealogy of Christ, as given by Matthew, is mere sophistry; for though he reckons up the progenitors not of Mary, but of Joseph, yet as he was speaking of a matter then generally understood, he deems it enough to show that Joseph was descended from the seed of David, since it is certain that Mary was of the same family. Luke goes still farther, showing that the salvation brought by Christ is common to the whole human race, inasmuch as Christ, the author of salvation, is descended from Adam, the common father of us all. I confess, indeed, that the genealogy proves Christ to be the Son of David only as being descended of the Virgin; but the new Marcionites, for the purpose of giving a gloss

to their heresy, namely to prove that the body which Christ assumed was unsubstantial, too confidently maintain that the expression as to seed is applicable only to males, thus subverting the elementary principles of nature. But as this discussion belongs not to theology, and the arguments which they adduce are too futile to require any labored refutation, I will not touch on matters pertaining to philosophy and the medical art. It will be sufficient to dispose of the objection drawn from the statement of Scripture, that Aaron and Jehoiadah married wives out of the tribe of Judah, and that thus the distinction of tribes was confounded, if proper descent could come through the female. It is well known that in regard to civil order, descent is reckoned through the male; and yet the superiority on his part does not prevent the female from having her proper share in the descent. This solution applies to all the genealogies. When Scripture gives a list of individuals, it often mentions males only. Must we therefore say that females go for nothing? Nay, the very children know that they are classified with men. For this reasons wives are said to give children to their husbands, the name of the family always remaining with the males. Then, as the male sex has this privilege, that sons are deemed of noble or ignoble birth, according to the condition of their fathers, so, on the other hand, in slavery, the condition of the child is determined by that of the mother, as lawyers say, *partus sequitur ventrem*. Whence we may infer, that offspring is partly procreated by the seed of the mother. According to the common custom of nations, mothers are deemed progenitors, and with this the Divine law agrees, which could have had no ground to forbid the marriage of the uncle with the niece, if there was no consanguinity between them. It would also be lawful for a brother and sister uterine to intermarry, when their fathers are different. But while I admit that the power assigned to the woman is passive, I hold that the same thing is affirmed indiscriminately of her and of the male. Christ is not said to have been made by a woman, but of a woman (Gal. 4:4). But some of this herd, laying aside all shame, publicly ask whether we mean to maintain that Christ was procreated of the proper seed of a Virgin. I, in my turn, ask whether they are not forced to admit that he was nourished to maturity in the Virgin's womb. Justly, therefore, we infer from the words of Matthew that Christ, inasmuch as he was begotten of Mary, was procreated of her seed; as a similar generation is denoted when Boaz is said to have been begotten of Rahab (Matt. 1:5, 16). Matthew does not here describe the Virgin as the channel through which Christ flowed, but distinguishes his miraculous from an ordinary birth, in that Christ was begotten by her of the seed of David. For the same reason for which Isaac is said to be begotten of Abraham, Joseph of Jacob, Solomon of David, is Christ said to have been begotten of his mother. The Evangelist has arranged his discourse in this way. Wishing to prove that Christ derives his descent from David, he deems it enough to state, that he was begotten of Mary. Hence it follows, that he assumed it as an acknowledged fact, that Mary was of the same lineage as Joseph.

4. The absurdities which they wish to fasten upon us are mere puerile calumnies. They reckon it base and dishonoring to Christ to have derived his descent from men; because, in that case, he could not be exempted from the common law which includes the whole offspring of Adam, without exception, under sin. But this difficulty is easily solved by Paul's antithesis, "As by one man sin entered into the world, and death by sin"; "even so by the righteousness of one the free gift came upon all men unto justification of life" (Rom. 5:12, 18). Corresponding to this is another passage, "The first man is of the earth, earthy: the second man is the Lord from heaven" (1 Cor. 15:47). Accordingly, the same apostle, in another passage, teaching that Christ was sent "in the likeness of sinful flesh, that the righteousness of the law might be fulfilled in us," distinctly separates him from the common lot, as being true man, and yet without fault and corruption (Rom. 8:3). It is childish trifling to maintain, that if Christ is free from all taint, and was begotten of the seed of Mary, by the

secret operation of the Spirit, it is not therefore the seed of the woman that is impure, but only that of the man. We do not hold Christ to be free from all taint, merely because he was born of a woman unconnected with a man, but because he was sanctified by the Spirit, so that the generation was pure and spotless, such as it would have been before Adam's fall. Let us always bear in mind, that wherever Scripture adverts to the purity of Christ, it refers to his true human nature, since it were superfluous to say that God is pure. Moreover, the sanctification of which John speaks in his seventeenth chapter is inapplicable to the divine nature. This does not suggest the idea of a twofold seed in Adam, although no contamination extended to Christ, the generation of man not being in itself vicious or impure, but an accidental circumstance of the fall. Hence, it is not strange that Christ, by whom our integrity was to be restored, was exempted from the common corruption. Another absurdity which they obtrude upon us—viz. that if the Word of God became incarnate, it must have been enclosed in the narrow tenement of an earthly body, is sheer petulance. For although the boundless essence of the Word was united with human nature into one person, we have no idea of any enclosing. The Son of God descended miraculously from heaven, yet without abandoning heaven, was pleased to be conceived miraculously in the Virgin's womb, to live on the earth, and hang upon the cross, and yet always filled the world as from the beginning.

Study Guide Questions

Section 1

1. In this part of the *Institutes*, Calvin is answering three groups. Who are they?

2. What were the two options suggested by these groups for the "body of Christ"?

Section 2

1. What does Calvin say Paul is not doing in Philippians 2:5–7?

2. What is the basic approach to answering these heresies?

Section 3

1. According to Calvin, the genealogy in Matthew was whose?

2. Although the male line is the basis for reckoning in the political order, does this exclude women?

3. What does Calvin argue concerning Mary engendering Christ from her seed?

Section 4

1. When the Word in His immeasurable essence was united with the nature of man into one person, did He leave heaven?

CHAPTER 14

How two natures constitute the person of the Mediator.

This chapter contains two principal heads:

I. A brief exposition of the doctrine of Christ's two natures in one person, sec. 1-4.

II. A refutation of the heresies of Servetus, which destroy the distinction of natures in Christ, and the eternity of the divine nature of the Son.

Outline:

1. Proof of two natures in Christ—a human and a divine. Illustrated by analogy, from the union of body and soul. Illustration applied.

2. Proof from passages of Scripture which distinguish between the two natures. Proof from the communication of properties.

3. Proof from passages showing the union of both natures. A rule to be observed in this discussion.

4. Utility and use of the doctrine concerning the two natures. The Nestorians. The Eutychians. Both justly condemned by the Church.

When it is said that the Word was made flesh, we must not understand it as if he were either changed into flesh, or confusedly intermingled with flesh, but that he made choice of the Virgin's womb as a temple in which he might dwell. He who was the Son of God became the Son of man, not by confusion of substance, but by unity of person. For we maintain that the divinity was so conjoined and united with the humanity, that the entire properties of each nature remain entire, and yet the two natures constitute only one Christ. If, in human affairs, anything analogous to this great mystery can be found, the most apposite similitude seems to be that of man, who obviously consists of two substances, neither of which however is so intermingled with the other as that both do not retain their own properties. For neither is soul body, nor is body soul. Wherefore that is said separately of the soul which cannot in any way apply to the body; and that, on the other hand, of the body which is altogether inapplicable to the soul; and that, again, of the whole man, which cannot be affirmed without absurdity either of the body or of the soul separately. Lastly, the properties of the soul are transferred to the body, and the properties of the body to the soul, and yet these form only one man, not more than one. Such modes of expression intimate both that there is in man one person formed of two compounds, and that these two different natures constitute one person. Thus the Scriptures speak of Christ. They sometimes attribute to him qualities which should be referred specially to his humanity and sometimes qualities applicable peculiarly to his divinity, and sometimes qualities which embrace both natures, and do not apply specially to either. This combination of a twofold nature in Christ they express so carefully, that they sometimes communicate them with each other, a figure of speech which the ancients termed *idiomaton koinonia* (a communication of properties).

2. Little dependence could be placed on these statements, were it not proved by numerous passages throughout the sacred volume that none of them is of man's devising. What Christ said of himself, "Before Abraham was I am" (John 8:58) was very foreign to his humanity. I am not unaware of the cavil by which erroneous spirits distort this passage—viz. that he was before all ages, inasmuch as he was foreknown as the Redeemer, as well in the counsel of the Father as in the minds of believers. But seeing he plainly distinguishes the period of his manifestation from his eternal existence, and professedly founds on his ancient government, to prove his precedence to Abraham, he undoubtedly claims for himself the peculiar attributes of divinity. Paul's assertion that he is "the first-born of every creature," that "he is before all things, and by him all things consist" (Col. 1:15, 17); his own declaration, that he had glory with the Father before the world was, and that he worketh together with the Father, are equally inapplicable to man. These and similar properties must be specially assigned to his divinity. Again, his being called the servant of the Father, his being said to grow in stature, and wisdom, and favor with God and man, not to seek his own glory, not to know the last day, not to speak of himself, not to do his own will, his being seen and handled, apply entirely to his humanity; since, as God, he cannot be in any respect said to grow, works always for himself, knows every thing, does all things after the counsel of his own will, and is incapable of being seen or handled. And yet he not merely ascribes these things separately to his human nature, but applies them to himself as suitable to his office of Mediator. There is a communication of *idiomata*, or properties, when Paul says that God purchased the Church "with

his own blood" (Acts 20:28), and that the Jews crucified the Lord of glory (1 Cor. 2:8). In like manner, John says that the Word of God was "handled." God certainly has no blood, suffers not, cannot be touched with hands; but since that Christ, who was true God and true man, shed his blood on the cross for us, the acts which were performed in his human nature are transferred improperly, but not ceaselessly, to his divinity. We have a similar example in the passage where John says that God laid down his life for us (1 John 3:16). Here a property of his humanity is communicated with his other nature. On the other hand, when Christ, still living on the earth, said, "No man has ascended up to heaven but he that came down from heaven, even the Son of man, which is in heaven" (John 3:13), certainly regarded as man in the flesh which he had put on, he was not then in heaven, but inasmuch as he was both God and man, he, on account of the union of a twofold nature, attributed to the one what properly belonged to the other.

3. But, above all, the true substance of Christ is most clearly declared in those passages which comprehend both natures at once. Numbers of these exist in the Gospel of John. What we there read as to his having received power from the Father to forgive sins; as to his quickening whom he will; as to his bestowing righteousness, holiness, and salvation; as to his being appointed judge both of the quick and the dead; as to his being honored even as the Father, are not peculiar either to his Godhead or his humanity, but applicable to both. In the same way he is called the Light of the world, the good Shepherd, the only Door, the true Vine. With such prerogatives the Son of God was invested on his manifestation in the flesh, and though he possessed the same with the Father before the world was created, still it was not in the same manner or respect; neither could they be attributed to one who was a man and nothing more. In the same sense we ought to understand the saying of Paul that at the end Christ shall deliver up "the kingdom to God, even the Father" (1 Cor. 15:24). The kingdom

of God assuredly had no beginning and will have no end; but because he was hid under a humble clothing of flesh, and took upon himself the form of a servant, and humbled himself (Phil. 2:8), and, laying aside the insignia of majesty, became obedient to the Father; and after undergoing this subjection was at length crowned with glory and honor (Heb. 2:7), and exalted to supreme authority, that at his name every knee should bow (Phil. 2:10); so at the end he will subject to the Father both the name and the crown of glory, and whatever he received of the Father, that God may be all in all (1 Cor. 15:28). For what end were that power and authority given to him, save that the Father might govern us by his hand? In the same sense, also, he is said to sit at the right hand of the Father. But this is only for a time, until we enjoy the immediate presence of his Godhead. And here we cannot excuse the error of some ancient writers, who, by not attending to the office of Mediator, darken the genuine meaning of almost the whole doctrine which we read in the Gospel of John, and entangle themselves in many snares. Let us, therefore, regard it as the key of true interpretation that those things which refer to the office of Mediator are not spoken of the divine or human nature simply. Christ, therefore, shall reign until he appear to judge the world, inasmuch as, according to the measure of our feeble capacity, he now connects us with the Father. But when, as partakers of the heavenly glory, we shall see God as he is, then Christ, having accomplished the office of Mediator, shall cease to be the vicegerent of the Father, and will be content with the glory which he possessed before the world was. Nor is the name of Lord specially applicable to the person of Christ in any other respect than in so far as he holds a middle place between God and us. To this effect are the words of Paul, "To us there is but one God, the Father, of whom are all things, and we in him; and one Lord Jesus Christ, by whom are all things, and we by him" (1 Cor. 8:6); that is, to the latter a temporary authority has been committed by the Father until his divine majesty shall be beheld face to face. His giving up of the kingdom to the Father, so far from impairing his majesty, will give a brighter manifestation of it. God will then cease to be the head of Christ, and Christ's own Godhead will then shine forth of itself, whereas it is now in a manner veiled.

4. This observation, if the readers apply it properly, will be of no small use in solving a vast number of difficulties. For it is strange how the ignorant, nay, some who are not altogether without learning, are perplexed by these modes of expression which they see applied to Christ, without being properly adapted either to his divinity or his humanity, not considering their accordance with the character in which he was manifested as God and man, and with his office of Mediator. It is very easy to see how beautifully they accord with each other, provided they have a sober interpreter, one who examines these great mysteries with the reverence which is meet. But there is nothing which furious and frantic spirits cannot throw into confusion. They fasten on the attributes of humanity to destroy his divinity; and, on the other hand, on those of his divinity to destroy his humanity, while those which, spoken conjointly of the two natures, apply to neither, they employ to destroy both. But what else is this than to contend that Christ is not man because he is God, not God because he is man, and neither God nor man because he is both at once. Christ, therefore, as God and man, possessing natures which are united, but not confused, we conclude that he is our Lord and the true Son of God, even according to his humanity, though not by means of his humanity. For we must put far from us the heresy of Nestorius, who, presuming to dissect rather than distinguish between the two natures, devised a double Christ. But we see the Scripture loudly protesting against this, when the name of the Son of God is given to him who is born of a Virgin, and the Virgin herself is called the mother of our Lord (Luke 1:32, 43). We must beware also of the insane fancy of Eutyches, lest, when we would demonstrate the unity of person, we destroy the two natures. The many passages we have already quoted, in which the divinity is distinguished

from the humanity, and the many other passages existing throughout Scripture, may well stop the mouth of the most contentious. I will shortly add a few observations, which will still better dispose of this fiction. For the present, one passage will suffice—Christ would not have called his body a temple (John 2:19), had not the Godhead distinctly dwelt in it. Wherefore, as Nestorius had been justly condemned in the Council of Ephesus, so afterwards was Eutyches in those of Constantinople and Chalcedony, it being not more lawful to confound the two natures of Christ than to divide them.

5. But in our age, also, has arisen a not less fatal monster, Michael Servetus, who for the Son of God has substituted a figment composed of the essence of God, spirit, flesh, and three untreated elements. First, indeed, he denies that Christ is the Son of God, for any other reason than because he was begotten in the womb of the Virgin by the Holy Spirit. The tendency of this crafty device is to make out, by destroying the distinction of the two natures, that Christ is somewhat composed of God and man, and yet is not to be deemed God and man. His aim throughout is to establish that before Christ was manifested in the flesh there were only shadowy figures in God, the truth or effect of which existed for the first time, when the Word who had been destined to that honor truly began to be the Son of God. We indeed acknowledge that the Mediator who was born of the Virgin is properly the Son of God. And how could the man Christ be a mirror of the inestimable grace of God, had not the dignity been conferred upon him both of being and of being called the only-begotten Son of God? Meanwhile, however, the definition of the Church stands unmoved that he is accounted the Son of God, because the Word begotten by the Father before all ages assumed human nature by hypostatic union—a term used by ancient writers to denote the union which of two natures constitutes one person, and invented to refute the dream of Nestorius, who pretended that the Son of God dwelt in the flesh in such a manner as not to be at

the same time man. Servetus calumniously charges us with making the Son of God double, when we say that the eternal Word before he was clothed with flesh was already the Son of God, as if we said anything more than that he was manifested in the flesh. Although he was God before he became man, he did not therefore begin to be a new God. Nor is there any greater absurdity in holding that the Son of God, who by eternal generation ever had the property of being a Son, appeared in the flesh. This is intimated by the angel's word to Mary: "That holy thing which shall be born of thee shall be called the Son of God" (Luke 1:35); as if he had said that the name of Son, which was more obscure under the law, would become celebrated and universally known. Corresponding to this is the passage of Paul, that being now the sons of God by Christ, we "have received the Spirit of adoption, whereby we cry, Abba, Father" (Rom. 8:15). Were not also the holy patriarchs of old reckoned among the sons of God? Yea, trusting to this privilege, they invoked God as their Father. But because ever since the only-begotten Son of God came forth into the world, his celestial paternity has been more clearly manifested, Paul assigns this to the kingdom of Christ as its distinguishing feature. We must, however, constantly hold that God never was a Father to angels and men save in respect of his only-begotten Son; that men, especially, who by their iniquity were rendered hateful to God, are sons by gratuitous adoption, because he is a Son by nature. Nor is there anything in the assertion of Servetus that this depends on the filiation which God had decreed with himself. Here we deal not with figures, as expiation by the blood of beasts was shown to be; but since they could not be the sons of God in reality, unless their adoption was founded in the head, it is against all reason to deprive the head of that which is common to the members. I go farther: since the Scripture gives the name of sons of God to the angels, whose great dignity in this respect depended not on the future redemption, Christ must in order take precedence of them that he may reconcile the Father to them. I will again briefly repeat and add the same thing concerning the human race. Since angels as well as men were at first created on the condition that God should be the common Father of both; if it is true, as Paul says, that Christ always was the head, "the first-born of every creature—that in all things he might have the preeminence" (Col. 1:15, 18), I think I may legitimately infer that he existed as the Son of God before the creation of the world.

6. But if his filiation (if I may so express it) had a beginning at the time when he was manifested in the flesh, it follows that he was a Son in respect of human nature also. Servetus, and others similarly frenzied, hold that Christ who appeared in the flesh is the Son of God, inasmuch as but for his incarnation he could not have possessed this name. Let them now answer me, whether, according to both natures, and in respect of both, he is a Son? So indeed they prate; but Paul's doctrine is very different. We acknowledge, indeed, that Christ in human nature is called a Son, not like believers by gratuitous adoption merely, but the true, natural, and, therefore, only Son, this being the mark which distinguishes him from all others. Those of us who are regenerated to a new life God honors with the name of sons; the name of true and only-begotten Son he bestows on Christ alone. But how is he an only Son in so great a multitude of brethren, except that he possesses by nature what we acquire by gift? This honor we extend to his whole character of Mediator, so that He who was born of a Virgin, and on the cross offered himself in sacrifice to the Father, is truly and properly the Son of God; but still in respect of his Godhead: as Paul teaches when he says, that he was "separated unto the gospel of God (which he had promised afore by his prophets in the Holy Scriptures), concerning his Son Jesus Christ our Lord, which was made of the seed of David according to the flesh; and declared to be the Son of God with power" (Rom. 1:1-4). When distinctly calling him the Son of David according to the flesh, why should he also say that he was "declared to be the Son of God," if he meant not to

intimate that this depended on something else than his incarnation? For in the same sense in which he elsewhere says, that "though he was crucified through weakness, yet he liveth by the power of God" (2 Cor. 13:4), so he now draws a distinction between the two natures. They must certainly admit, that as on account of his mother he is called the Son of David, so on account of his Father he is the Son of God, and that in some respect differing from his human nature. The Scripture gives him both names, calling him at one time the Son of God, at another the Son of Man. As to the latter, there can be no question that he is called a Son in accordance with the phraseology of the Hebrew language, because he is of the offspring of Adam. On the other hand, I maintain that he is called a Son on account of his Godhead and eternal essence, because it is no less congruous to refer to his divine nature his being called the Son of God than to refer to his human nature his being called the Son of Man. In fine, in the passage which I have quoted, Paul does not mean that he who according to the flesh was begotten of the seed of David was declared to be the Son of God in any other sense than he elsewhere teaches that Christ, who descended of the Jews according to the flesh, is "over all, God blessed for ever" (Rom. 9:5). But if in both passages the distinction of two natures is pointed out, how can it be denied that he who according to the flesh is the Son of Man, is also in respect of his divine nature the Son of God?

7. They indeed find a blustering defense of their heresy in its being said that "God spared not his own Son," and in the communication of the angel that He who was to be born of the Virgin should be called the "Son of the Highest" (Rom. 8:32; Luke 1:32). But before pluming themselves on this futile objection, let them for a little consider with us what weight there is in their argument. If it is legitimately concluded that at conception he began to be the Son of God, because he who has been conceived is called a son, it will follow that he began to be the Word after his manifestation in the flesh, because

John declares that the Word of life of which he spoke was that which "our hands have handled" (1 John 1:1). In like manner we read in the prophet, "Thou, Bethlehem Ephratha, though thou be little among the thousands of Israel, yet out of thee shall he come forth that is to be a ruler in Israel; whose goings forth have been from of old, from everlasting" (Mic. 5:2). How will they be forced to interpret if they will follow such a method of arguing? I have declared that we by no means assent to Nestorius, who imagined a twofold Christ, when we maintain that Christ by means of brotherly union made us sons of God with himself, because in the flesh which he took from us he is the only-begotten Son of God. And Augustine wisely reminds us that he is a bright mirror of the wonderful and singular grace of God, because as man he obtained honor which he could not merit. With this distinction, therefore, according to the flesh, was Christ honored even from the womb—viz. to be the Son of God. Still, in the unity of person we are not to imagine any intermixture which takes away from the Godhead what is peculiar to it. Nor is it more absurd that the eternal Word of God and Christ, uniting the two natures in one person, should in different ways be called the Son of God, than that he should in various respects be called at one time the Son of God, at another the Son of Man. Nor are we more embarrassed by another cavil of Servetus—viz. that Christ, before he appeared in the flesh, is nowhere called the Son of God, except under a figure. For though the description of him was then more obscure, yet it has already been clearly proved that he was not otherwise the eternal God, than as he was the Word begotten of the eternal Father. Nor is the name applicable to the office of Mediator which he undertook, except in that he was God manifest in the flesh. Nor would God have thus from the beginning been called a Father, had there not been even then a mutual relation to the Son, "of whom the whole family in heaven and earth is named" (Eph. 3:15). Hence it is easy to infer that under the Law and the Prophets he was the Son of God before this name was celebrated in the Church. But if we are to dispute about the word merely, Solomon, speaking of the incomprehensibility of God, affirms that his Son is like himself, incomprehensible: "What is his name, and what is his Son's name, if thou canst tell?" (Prov. 30:4). I am well aware that with the contentious this passage will not have sufficient weight; nor do I found much upon it, except as showing the malignant cavils of those who affirm that Christ is the Son of God only in so far as he became man. We may add that all the most ancient writers, with one mouth and consent, testified the same thing so plainly, that the effrontery is no less ridiculous than detestable, which dares to oppose us with Irenaeus and Tertullian, both of whom acknowledge that He who was afterwards visibly manifested was the invisible Son of God.

8. But although Servetus heaped together a number of horrid dogmas, to which, perhaps, others would not subscribe, you will find that all who refuse to acknowledge the Son of God except in the flesh, are obliged, when urged more closely, to admit that he was a Son, for no other reason than because he was conceived in the womb of the Virgin by the Holy Spirit; just like the absurdity of the ancient Manichees that the soul of man was derived by transfusion from God, from its being said that he breathed into Adam's nostrils the breath of life (Gen. 2:7). For they lay such stress on the name of Son that they leave no distinction between the natures, but babblingly maintain that the man Christ is the Son of God, because, according to his human nature, he was begotten of God. Thus, the eternal generation of Wisdom, celebrated by Solomon (Prov. 8:22ff) is destroyed, and no kind of Godhead exists in the Mediator, or a phantom is substituted instead of a man. The grosser delusions of Servetus, by which he imposed upon himself and some others, it were useful to refute, that pious readers might be warned by the example, to confine themselves within the bounds of soberness and modesty; however, I deem it superfluous here, as I have already done it in a special treatise. The whole comes to this, that the Son of God was from the beginning an idea,

and was even then a preordained man, who was to be the essential image of God. Nor does he acknowledge any other Word of God except in external splendor. The generation he interprets to mean that from the beginning a purpose of generating the Son was begotten in God, and that this purpose extended itself by act to creation. Meanwhile, he confounds the Spirit with the Word, saying that God arranged the invisible Word and Spirit into flesh and soul. In short, in his view the typifying of Christ occupies the place of generation; but he says that he who was then in appearance a shadowy Son, was at length begotten by the Word, to which he attributes a generating power. From this it will follow that dogs and swine are not less sons of God, because created of the original seed of the Divine Word. But although he compounds Christ of three untreated elements, that he may be begotten of the essence of God, he pretends that he is the first-born among the creatures, in such a sense that, according to their degree, stones have the same essential divinity. But lest he should seem to strip Christ of his Deity, he admits that his flesh is *omoousion*, of the same substance with God, and that the Word was made man, by the conversion of flesh into Deity. Thus, while he cannot comprehend that Christ was the Son of God, until his flesh came forth from the essence of God and was converted into Deity, he reduces the eternal personality (*hypostasis*) of the Word to nothing, and robs us of the Son of David, who was the promised Redeemer. It is true, he repeatedly declares that the Son was begotten of God by knowledge and predestination, but that he was at length made man out of that matter which, from the beginning, shone with God in the three elements, and afterwards appeared in the first light of the world, in the cloud and pillar of fire. How shamefully inconsistent with himself he ever and anon becomes, it were too tedious to relate. From this brief account sound readers will gather, that by the subtle ambiguities of this infatuated man, the hope of salvation was utterly extinguished. For if the flesh were the Godhead itself, it would cease to be its temple.

Now, the only Redeemer we can have is He who being begotten of the seed of Abraham and David according to the flesh, truly became man. But he erroneously insists on the expression of John, "The Word was made flesh." As these words refute the heresy of Nestorius, so they give no countenance to the impious fiction of which Eutyches was the inventor, since all that the Evangelist intended was to assert a unity of person in two natures.

Study Guide Questions

Section 1

1. What two things must we not attribute to the two natures of Christ?

2. How then did the Son of God become the Son of Man?

3. What illustration of this does Calvin use?

Section 2

1. How do we know that this doctrine was not "of man's devising"?

2. Can we ever speak of the attributes of one nature in terms of the other?

Section 3

1. When we speak of the office of Mediator, which way do we speak?

Section 4

1. Those who stumble over the question of Christ's two natures do not consider what?

2. What does it mean when Christ calls His body a temple?

Section 5

1. How does Calvin define the hypostatic union?

Sections 6–8

1. What did Servetus teach about this?

2. Does Calvin struggle in answering the arguments of Servetus?

3. What is Calvin's summary of Servetus' position?

CHAPTER 15

Three things briefly to be regarded in Christ—viz., His offices of
prophet, king, and priest.

The principal parts of this chapter are—
I. Of the Prophetical Office of Christ, its dignity and use,
sec. 1-2.

II. The nature of the Kingly power of Christ, and the advantage
we derive from it, sec. 3-5. III. Of the Priesthood of Christ, and the
efficacy of it, sec. 6. Sections.

Outline:

1. Among heretics and false Christians, Christ is found in name
only; but by those who are truly and effectually called of God, he is
acknowledged as a Prophet, King, and Priest. In regard to the Prophetical Office, the Redeemer of the Church is the same from whom
believers under the Law hoped for the full light of understanding.

2. The unction of Christ, though it has respect chiefly to the Kingly
Office, refers also to the Prophetical and Priestly Offices. The dignity,
necessity, and use of this unction.

3. From the spirituality of Christ's kingdom its eternity is inferred. This twofold, referring both to the whole body of the Church, and to its individual members.

4. Benefits from the spiritual kingdom of Christ. 1. It raises us to eternal life. 2. It enriches us with all things necessary to salvation. 3. It makes us invincible by spiritual foes. 4. It animates us to patient endurance. 5. It inspires confidence and triumph. 6. It supplies fortitude and love.

5. The unction of our Redeemer heavenly. Symbol of this unction. A passage in the apostle reconciled with others previously quoted, to prove the eternal kingdom of Christ.

6. What necessary to obtain the benefit of Christ's Priesthood. We must set out with the death of Christ. From it follows, 1. His intercession for us. 2. Confidence in prayer. 3. Peace of conscience. 4. Through Christ, Christians themselves become priests. Grievous sin of the Papists in pretending to sacrifice Christ.

Though heretics pretend the name of Christ, truly does Augustine affirm (Enchir. ad Laurent. cap. 5), that the foundation is not common to them with the godly, but belongs exclusively to the Church: for if those things which pertain to Christ be diligently considered, it will be found that Christ is with them in name only, not in reality. Thus in the present day, though the Papists have the words, Son of God, Redeemer of the world, sounding in their mouths, yet, because contented with an empty name, they deprive him of his virtue and dignity; what Paul says of "not holding the head," is truly applicable to them (Col. 2:19). Therefore, that faith may find in Christ a solid ground of salvation, and so rest in him, we must set out with this principle, that the office which he received from the Father consists of three parts. For he was appointed both Prophet, King, and Priest; though little were gained by holding the names unaccompanied by a knowledge of the end and use. These too are spoken of in the Papacy, but frigidly, and with no great benefit, the full meaning comprehended under each title not being understood. We formerly observed, that though God, by supplying an uninterrupted succession of prophets, never left his people destitute of useful doctrine, such as might suffice for salvation; yet the minds of believers were always impressed with the conviction that the full light of understanding was to be expected only on the advent of the Messiah. This expectation, accordingly, had reached even the Samaritans, to whom the true religion had never been made known. This is plain from the expression of the woman, "I know that Messiah cometh, which is called Christ: when he is come, he will tell us all things" (John 4:25). Nor was this a mere random presumption which had entered the minds of the Jews. They believed what sure oracles had taught them. One of the most remarkable passages is that of Isaiah, "Behold, I have given him for a witness to the people, a leader and commander to the people" (Is. 55:4); that is, in the same way in which he had previously in another place styled him "Wonderful, Counselor" (Is. 9:6). For this reason, the apostle commending the perfection of gospel doctrine, first says that "God, at sundry times and in divers manners spake in times past unto the prophets," and then adds, that he "has in these last days spoken unto us by his Son" (Heb. 1:1-2). But as the common office of the prophets was to hold the Church in suspense, and at the same time support it until the advent of the Mediator; we read, that the faithful, during the dispersion, complained that they were deprived of that ordinary privilege. "We see not our signs: there is no more any prophet, neither is there among us any that knoweth how long" (Ps. 74:9). But when Christ was now not far distant, a period was assigned to Daniel "to seal up the vision and prophecy" (Daniel 9:24), not only that the authority of the prediction there spoken of might be established, but that believers might, for a time, patiently submit to the want of the prophets, the fulfillment and completion of all the prophecies being at hand.

2. Moreover, it is to be observed, that the name Christ refers to those three offices: for we know that under the law, prophets as well

as priests and kings were anointed with holy oil. Whence, also, the
celebrated name of Messiah was given to the promised Mediator. But
although I admit (as, indeed, I have elsewhere shown) that he was so
called from a view to the nature of the kingly office, still the prophetical and sacerdotal unctions have their proper place, and must not
be overlooked. The former is expressly mentioned by Isaiah in these
words: "The Spirit of the Lord God is upon me: because the Lord has
anointed me to preach good tidings unto the meek; he has sent me
to bind up the broken-hearted, to proclaim liberty to the captive, and
the opening of the prison to them that are bound; to proclaim the
acceptable year of the Lord" (Is. 60:1-2). We see that he was anointed
by the Spirit to be a herald and witness of his Father's grace, and not
in the usual way; for he is distinguished from other teachers who
had a similar office. And here, again, it is to be observed, that the
unction which he received, in order to perform the office of teacher, was not for himself, but for his whole body, that a corresponding
efficacy of the Spirit might always accompany the preaching of the
Gospel. This, however, remains certain, that by the perfection of doctrine which he brought, an end was put to all the prophecies, so that
those who, not contented with the Gospel, annex somewhat extraneous to it, derogate from its authority. The voice which thundered
from heaven, "This is my beloved Son, hear him" gave him a special
privilege above all other teachers. Then from him, as head, this unction is diffused through the members, as Joel has foretold, "Your sons
and your daughters shall prophesy, your old men shall dream dreams,
and your young men shall see visions" (Joel 2:28). Paul's expressions,
that he was "made unto us wisdom" (1 Cor. 1:30), and elsewhere, that
in him "are hid all the treasures of wisdom and knowledge" (Col. 2:3),
have a somewhat different meaning, namely, that out of him there is
nothing worth knowing, and that those who, by faith, apprehend his
true character, possess the boundless immensity of heavenly blessings.
For which reason, he elsewhere says, "I determined not to know any

thing among you, save Jesus Christ and him crucified" (1 Cor. 2:2). And most justly: for it is unlawful to go beyond the simplicity of the Gospel. The purpose of this prophetical dignity in Christ is to teach us, that in the doctrine which he delivered is substantially included a wisdom which is perfect in all its parts.

3. I come to the Kingly office, of which it were in vain to speak, without previously reminding the reader that its nature is spiritual; because it is from thence we learn its efficacy, the benefits it confers, its whole power and eternity. Eternity, moreover, which in Daniel an angel attributes to the office of Christ (Dan. 2:44), in Luke an angel justly applies to the salvation of his people (Luke 1:33). But this is also twofold, and must be viewed in two ways; the one pertains to the whole body of the Church the other is proper to each member. To the former is to be referred what is said in the Psalms, "Once have I sworn by my holiness, that I will not lie unto David. His seed shall endure for ever, and his throne as the sun before me. It shall be established for ever, as the moon, and as a faithful witness in heaven" (Ps. 89:35, 37). There can be no doubt that God here promises that he will be, by the hand of his Son, the eternal governor and defender of the Church. In none but Christ will the fulfillment of this prophecy be found; since immediately after Solomon's death the kingdom in n great measure lost its dignity, and, with ignominy to the family of David, was transferred to a private individual. Afterwards decaying by degrees, it at length came to a sad and dishonorable end. In the same sense are we to understand the exclamation of Isaiah, "Who shall declare his generation?" (Isaiah 53:8). For he asserts that Christ will so survive death as to be connected with his members. Therefore, as often as we hear that Christ is armed with eternal power, let us learn that the perpetuity of the Church is thus effectually secured; that amid the turbulent agitations by which it is constantly harassed, and the grievous and fearful commotions which threaten innumerable disasters, it still remains safe. Thus, when David derides the audacity of the enemy who

attempt to throw off the yoke of God and his anointed, and says, that kings and nations rage "in vain" (Ps. 2:2-4), because he who sitteth in the heaven is strong enough to repel their assaults, assuring believers of the perpetual preservation of the Church, he animates them to have good hope whenever it is occasionally oppressed. So, in another place, when speaking in the person of God, he says, "The Lord said unto my Lord, Sit thou at my right hand, until I make thine enemies thy footstool" (Ps. 110:1), he reminds us, that however numerous and powerful the enemies who conspire to assault the Church, they are not possessed of strength sufficient to prevail against the immortal decree by which he appointed his Son eternal King. Whence it follows that the devil, with the whole power of the world, can never possibly destroy the Church, which is founded on the eternal throne of Christ. Then in regard to the special use to be made by each believer, this same eternity ought to elevate us to the hope of a blessed immortality. For we see that every thing which is earthly, and of the world, is temporary, and soon fades away. Christ, therefore, to raise our hope to the heavens, declares that his kingdom is not of this world (John 18:36). In fine, let each of us, when he hears that the kingdom of Christ is spiritual, be roused by the thought to entertain the hope of a better life, and to expect that as it is now protected by the hand of Christ, so it will be fully realized in a future life.

4. That the strength and utility of the kingdom of Christ cannot, as we have said, be fully perceived without recognizing it as spiritual, is sufficiently apparent, even from this, that having during the whole course of our lives to war under the cross, our condition here is bitter and wretched. What then would it avail us to be ranged under the government of a heavenly King, if its benefits were not realized beyond the present earthly life? We must, therefore, know that the happiness which is promised to us in Christ does not consist in external advantages—such as leading a joyful and tranquil life, abounding in wealth, being secure against all injury, and having an affluence of

delights, such as the flesh is wont to long for—but properly belongs to the heavenly life. As in the world the prosperous and desirable condition of a people consists partly in the abundance of temporal good and domestic peace, and partly in the strong protection which gives security against external violence; so Christ also enriches his people with all things necessary to the eternal salvation of their souls and fortifies them with courage to stand unassailable by all the attacks of spiritual foes. Whence we infer, that he reigns more for us than for himself, and that both within us and without us; that being replenished, in so far as God knows to be expedient, with the gifts of the Spirit, of which we are naturally destitute, we may feel from their first fruits, that we are truly united to God for perfect blessedness; and then trusting to the power of the same Spirit, may not doubt that we shall always be victorious against the devil, the world, and every thing that can do us harm. To this effect was our Savior's reply to the Pharisees, "The kingdom of God is within you." "The kingdom of God cometh not with observation" (Luke 17:21-22). It is probable that on his declaring himself to be that King under whom the highest blessing of God was to be expected, they had in derision asked him to produce his insignia. But to prevent those who were already more than enough inclined to the earth from dwelling on its pomp, he bids them enter into their consciences, for "the kingdom of God" is "righteousness, and peace, and joy in the Holy Ghost" (Rom. 14:17). These words briefly teach what the kingdom of Christ bestows upon us. Not being earthly or carnal, and so subject to corruption, but spiritual, it raises us even to eternal life, so that we can patiently live at present under toil, hunger, cold, contempt, disgrace, and other annoyances; contented with this, that our King will never abandon us, but will supply our necessities until our warfare is ended, and we are called to triumph: such being the nature of his kingdom, that he communicates to us whatever he received of his Father. Since then he arms and equips us by his power, adorns us with splendor and magnificence, enriches us with wealth, we here find most abundant cause of glorying, and also are inspired with boldness, so that we can contend intrepidly with the devil, sin, and death. In fine, clothed with his righteousness, we can bravely surmount all the insults of the world: and as he replenishes us liberally with his gifts, so we can in our turn bring forth fruit unto his glory.

5. Accordingly, his royal unction is not set before us as composed of oil or aromatic perfumes; but he is called the Christ of God, because "the Spirit of the Lord" rested upon him; "the Spirit of wisdom and understanding, the Spirit of counsel and might, the Spirit of knowledge and of the fear of the Lord" (Isaiah 11:2). This is the oil of joy with which the Psalmist declares that he was anointed above his fellows (Ps. 45:7). For, as has been said, he was not enriched privately for himself, but that he might refresh the parched and hungry with his abundance. For as the Father is said to have given the Spirit to the Son without measure (John 3:34), so the reason is expressed, that we might all receive of his fullness, and grace for grace (John 1:16). From this fountain flows the copious supply (of which Paul makes mention, Eph. 4:7) by which grace is variously distributed to believers according to the measure of the gift of Christ. Here we have ample confirmation of what I said, that the kingdom of Christ consists in the Spirit, and not in earthly delights or pomp, and that hence, in order to be partakers with him, we must renounce the world. A visible symbol of this grace was exhibited at the baptism of Christ, when the Spirit rested upon him in the form of a dove. To designate the Spirit and his gifts by the term "unction" is not new, and ought not to seem absurd (see 1 John 2:20, 27), because this is the only quarter from which we derive life; but especially in what regards the heavenly life, there is not a drop of vigor in us save what the Holy Spirit instills, who has chosen his seat in Christ, that thence the heavenly riches, of which we are destitute, might flow to us in copious abundance. But because believers stand invincible in the strength of their King, and his spiritual

riches abound towards them, they are not improperly called Christians. Moreover, from this eternity of which we have spoken, there is nothing derogatory in the expression of Paul, "Then cometh the end, when he shall have delivered up the kingdom to God, even the Father" (1 Cor. 15:24); and also, "Then shall the Son also himself be subject unto him that put all things under him, that God may be all in and" (1 Cor. 15:28); for the meaning merely is, that, in that perfect glory, the administration of the kingdom will not be such as it now is. For the Father has given all power to the Son, that by his hand he may govern, cherish, sustain us, keep us under his guardianship, and give assistance to us. Thus, while we wander far as pilgrims from God, Christ interposes, that he may gradually bring us to full communion with God. And, indeed, his sitting at the right hand of the Father has the same meaning as if he was called the vicegerent of the Father, entrusted with the whole power of government. For God is pleased, mediately (so to speak) in his person to rule and defend the Church. Thus also his being seated at the right hand of the Father is explained by Paul, in the Epistle to the Ephesians, to mean, that "he is the head over all things to the Church, which is his body" (Eph. 1:20, 22). Nor is this different in purport from what he elsewhere teaches, that God has "given him a name which is above every name; that at the name of Jesus every knee shall bow, of things in heaven, and things in earth, and things under the earth, and that every tongue should confess that Jesus Christ is Lord, to the glory of God the Father" (Phil. 2:9-11). For in these words, also, he commends an arrangement in the kingdom of Christ, which is necessary for our present infirmity. Thus Paul rightly infers that God will then be the only Head of the Church, because the office of Christ, in defending the Church, shall then have been completed. For the same reason, Scripture throughout calls him Lord, the Father having appointed him over us for the express purpose of exercising his government through him. For though many lordships are celebrated in the world, yet Paul says, "To us there is but one God, the Father, of whom are all things, and we in him; and one Lord Jesus Christ, by whom are all things, and we by him" (1 Cor. 8:6). Whence it is justly inferred that he is the same God, who, by the mouth of Isaiah, declared, "The Lord is our Judge, the Lord is our Lawgiver, the Lord is our King: he will save us" (Isaiah 33:22). For though he every where describes all the power which he possesses as the benefit and gift of the Father, the meaning simply is, that he reigns by divine authority, because his reason for assuming the office of Mediator was, that descending from the bosom and incomprehensible glory of the Father, he might draw near to us. Wherefore there is the greater reason that we all should with one consent prepare to obey, and with the greatest alacrity yield implicit obedience to his will. For as he unites the offices of King and Pastor towards believers, who voluntarily submit to him, so, on the other hand, we are told that he wields an iron scepter to break and bruise all the rebellious like a potter's vessel (Ps. 2:9). We are also told that he will be the Judge of the Gentiles, that he will cover the earth with dead bodies, and level down every opposing height (Ps. 110:6). Of this examples are seen at present, but full proof will be given at the final judgment, which may be properly regarded as the last act of his reign.

6. With regard to his Priesthood, we must briefly hold its end and use to be, that as a Mediator, free from all taint, he may by his own holiness procure the favor of God for us. But because a deserved curse obstructs the entrance, and God in his character of Judge is hostile to us, expiation must necessarily intervene, that as a priest employed to appease the wrath of God, he may reinstate us in his favor. Wherefore, in order that Christ might fulfill this office, it behooved him to appear with a sacrifice. For even under the law of the priesthood it was forbidden to enter the sanctuary without blood, to teach the worshiper that however the priest might interpose to deprecate, God could not be propitiated without the expiation of sin. On this subject the Apostle discourses at length in the Epistle to the Hebrews, from

the seventh almost to the end of the tenth chapter. The sum comes to this, that the honor of the priesthood was competent to none but Christ, because, by the sacrifice of his death, he wiped away our guilt, and made satisfaction for sin. Of the great importance of this matter, we are reminded by that solemn oath which God uttered, and of which he declared he would not repent, "Thou art a priest forever, after the order of Melchizedek" (Ps. 110:4). For, doubtless, his purpose was to ratify that point on which he knew that our salvation chiefly hinged. For, as has been said, there is no access to God for us or for our prayers until the priest, purging away our defilements, sanctify us, and obtain for us that favor of which the impurity of our lives and hearts deprives us. Thus we see, that if the benefit and efficacy of Christ's priesthood is to reach us, the commencement must be with his death. Whence it follows, that he by whose aid we obtain favor, must be a perpetual intercessor. From this again arises not only confidence in prayer, but also the tranquility of pious minds, while they recline in safety on the paternal indulgence of God, and feel assured, that whatever has been consecrated by the Mediator is pleasing to him. But since God under the Law ordered sacrifices of beasts to be offered to him, there was a different and new arrangement in regard to Christ—viz. that he should be at once victim and priest, because no other fit satisfaction for sin could be found, nor was any one worthy of the honor of offering an only begotten son to God. Christ now bears the office of priest, not only that by the eternal law of reconciliation he may render the Father favorable and propitious to us, but also admit us into this most honorable alliance. For we though in ourselves polluted, in him being priests (Rev. 1:6), offer ourselves and our all to God, and freely enter the heavenly sanctuary, so that the sacrifices of prayer and praise which we present are grateful and of sweet odor before him. To this effect are the words of Christ, "For their sakes I sanctify myself" (John 17:19); for being clothed with his holiness, inasmuch as he has devoted us to the Father with himself (otherwise we were an abomination before him), we please him as if we were pure and clean, nay, even sacred. Hence that unction of the sanctuary of which mention is made in Daniel (Dan. 9:24). For we must attend to the contrast between this unction and the shadowy one which was then in use; as if the angel had said, that when the shadows were dispersed, there would be a clear priesthood in the person of Christ. The more detestable, therefore, is the fiction of those who, not content with the priesthood of Christ, have dared to take it upon themselves to sacrifice him, a thing daily attempted in the Papacy, where the mass is represented as an immolation of Christ.

Study Guide Questions

Section 1

1. According to Calvin, the office assigned to Christ consisted of what three parts?

2. Is it enough to acknowledge the right names of these offices?

Section 2

1. Which of the offices does the title Christ apply to?

2. Is the prophetic office extended to the Church?

3. What should be known outside Christ?

4. What is it not lawful to go beyond?

Section 3

1. What is the nature of Christ's kingship?

2. What basic responsibility of a king does Calvin begin with?

Section 4

1. How must we fight throughout our lives?

2. Where does Calvin locate our happiness?

3. In the midst of our trials here, what must we be content with?

Section 5

1. What was the oil of gladness that anointed Christ?

2. If Christ's kingdom does not lie in earthly pleasures or pomp, what does it lie in?

3. What can we not have one drop of apart from the Spirit?

Section 6

1. As priest, what does Christ do for us forever?

2. In this new and different order, what two roles did Christ play?

CHAPTER 16

How Christ performed the office of Redeemer in procuring our
salvation. The death, resurrection, and ascension of Christ.

This chapter contains four leading heads—

I. A general consideration of the whole subject, including a
discussion of a necessary question concerning the justice of God and
his mercy in Christ, sec. 1-4.

II. How Christ fulfilled the office of Redeemer in each of its parts,
sec. 5-17. His death, burial, descent to hell, resurrection, ascension to
heaven, seat at the right hand of the Father, and return to judgment.

III. A great part of the Creed being here expounded, a statement
is given of the view which ought to be taken of the Creed commonly
ascribed to the Apostles, sec. 18.

IV. Conclusion, setting forth the doctrine of Christ the Redeemer,
and the use of the doctrine, sec. 19.

Outline:

1. Every thing needful for us exists in Christ. How it is to be
obtained.

2. Question as to the mode of reconciling the justice with the mercy of God. Modes of expression used in Scripture to teach us how miserable our condition is without Christ.

3. Not used improperly; for God finds in us ground both of hatred and love.

4. This confirmed from passages of Scripture and from Augustine.

5. The second part of the chapter, treating of our redemption by Christ. First generally. Redemption extends to the whole course of our Savior's obedience, but is specially ascribed to his death. The voluntary subjection of Christ. His agony. His condemnation before Pilate. Two things observable in his condemnation. 1. That he was numbered among transgressors. 2. That he was declared innocent by the judge. Use to be made of this.

6. Why Christ was crucified. This hidden doctrine typified in the Law, and completed by the Apostles and Prophets. In what sense Christ was made a curse for us. The cross of Christ connected with the shedding of his blood.

7. Of the death of Christ. Why he died. Advantages from his death. Of the burial of Christ. Advantages.

8. Of the descent into hell. This article gradually introduced into the Church. Must not be rejected, nor confounded with the previous article respecting burial.

9. Absurd exposition concerning the *Limbus Patrum*. This fable refuted.

10. The article of the descent to hell more accurately expounded. A great ground of comfort.

11. Confirmation of this exposition from passages of Scripture and the works of ancient Theologians. An objection refuted. Advantages of the doctrine.

12. Another objection that Christ is insulted, and despair ascribed to him in its being said that he feared. Answer, from the statements of the Evangelists, that he did fear, was troubled in spirit, amazed,

and tempted in all respects as we are, yet without sin. Why Christ was pleased to become weak. His fear without sin. Refutation of another objection, with an answer to the question, Did Christ fear death, and why? When did Christ descend to hell, and how? What has been said refutes the heresy of Apollinaris and of the Monothelites.

13. Of the resurrection of Christ. The many advantages from it. 1. Our righteousness in the sight of God renewed and restored. 2. His life the basis of our life and hope, also the efficacious cause of new life in us. 3. The pledge of our future resurrection.

14. Of the ascension of Christ. Why he ascended. Advantages derived from it.

15. Of Christ's seat at the Father's right hand. What meant by it.

16. Many advantages from the ascension of Christ. 1. He gives access to the kingdom which Adam had shut up. 2. He intercedes for us with the Father. 3. His virtue being thence transfused into us, he works effectually in us for salvation.

17. Of the return of Christ to judgment. Its nature. The quick and dead who are to be judged. Passages apparently contradictory reconciled. Mode of judgment.

18. Advantages of the doctrine of Christ's return to judgment. Third part of the chapter, explaining the view to be taken of the Apostles' Creed. Summary of the Apostles' Creed.

19. Conclusion of the whole chapter, showing that in Christ the salvation of the elect in all its parts is comprehended.

All that we have hitherto said of Christ leads to this one result, that condemned, dead, and lost in ourselves, we must in him seek righteousness, deliverance, life and salvation, as we are taught by the celebrated words of Peter, "Neither is there salvation in any other: for there is none other name under heaven given among men whereby we must be saved" (Acts 4:12). The name of Jesus was not given him at random, or fortuitously, or by the will of man, but was brought from heaven by an angel, as the herald of the supreme decree; the reason also being added, "for he shall save his people from their sins" (Matt. 1:21). In these words attention should be paid to what we have elsewhere observed, that the office of Redeemer was assigned him in order that he might be our Savior. Still, however, redemption would be defective if it did not conduct us by an uninterrupted progression to the final goal of safety. Therefore, the moment we turn aside from him in the minutest degree, salvation, which resides entirely in him, gradually disappears; so that all who do not rest in him voluntarily deprive themselves of all grace. The observation of Bernard well deserves to be remembered: "The name of Jesus is not only light but food also, yea, oil, without which all the food of the soul is dry; salt, without which as a condiment whatever is set before us is insipid; in fine, honey in the mouth, melody in the ear, joy in the heart, and, at the same time, medicine; every discourse where this name is not heard is absurd" (Bernard in *Cantica.*, Serm. 15). But here it is necessary diligently to consider in what way we obtain salvation from him, that we may not only be persuaded that he is the author of it, but having embraced whatever is sufficient as a sure foundation of our faith, may eschew all that might make us waver. For seeing no man can descend into himself, and seriously consider what he is, without feeling that God is angry and at enmity with him, and therefore anxiously longing for the means of regaining his favor (this cannot be without satisfaction), the certainty here required is of no ordinary description—sinners, until freed from guilt, being always liable to the wrath and curse of God, who, as he is a just judge, cannot permit his law to be violated with impunity, but is armed for vengeance.

2. But before we proceed farther, we must see in passing, how can it be said that God, who prevents us with his mercy, was our enemy until he was reconciled to us by Christ. For how could he have given us in his only-begotten Son a singular pledge of his love, if he had not previously embraced us with free favor? As there thus arises some

appearance of contradiction, I will explain the difficulty. The mode in which the Spirit usually speaks in Scripture is that God was the enemy of men until they were restored to favor by the death of Christ (Rom. 5:10); that they were cursed until their iniquity was expiated by the sacrifice of Christ (Gal. 3:10, 13); that they were separated from God, until by means of Christ's body they were received into union (Col. 1:21-22). Such modes of expression are accommodated to our capacity, that we may the better understand how miserable and calamitous our condition is without Christ. For were it not said in clear terms that Divine wrath, and vengeance, and eternal death, lay upon us, we should be less sensible of our wretchedness without the mercy of God, and less disposed to value the blessing of deliverance. For example, let a person be told, 'Had God at the time you were a sinner hated you, and cast you off as you deserved, horrible destruction must have been your doom; but spontaneously and of free indulgence he retained you in his favor, not suffering you to be estranged from him, and in this way rescued you from danger—the person will indeed be affected, and made sensible in some degree how much he owes to the mercy of God.' But again, let him be told, as Scripture teaches, that he was estranged from God by sin, an heir of wrath, exposed to the curse of eternal death, excluded from all hope of salvation, a complete alien from the blessing of God, the slave of Satan, captive under the yoke of sin; in fine, doomed to horrible destruction, and already involved in it; that then Christ interposed, took the punishment upon himself and bore what by the just judgment of God was impending over sinners; with his own blood expiated the sins which rendered them hateful to God, by this expiation satisfied and duly propitiated God the Father, by this intercession appeased his anger, on this basis founded peace between God and men, and by this tie secured the Divine benevolence toward them; will not these considerations move him the more deeply, the more strikingly they represent the greatness of the calamity from which he was delivered?

In short, since our mind cannot lay hold of life through the mercy of God with sufficient eagerness, or receive it with becoming gratitude, unless previously impressed with fear of the Divine anger, and dismayed at the thought of eternal death, we are so instructed by divine truth, as to perceive that without Christ God is in a manner hostile to us, and has his arm raised for our destruction. Thus taught, we look to Christ alone for divine favor and paternal love.

3. Though this is said in accommodation to the weakness of our capacity, it is not said falsely. For God, who is perfect righteousness, cannot love the iniquity which he sees in all. All of us, therefore, have that within which deserves the hatred of God. Hence, in respect, first, of our corrupt nature; and, secondly, of the depraved conduct following upon it, we are all offensive to God, guilty in his sight, and by nature the children of hell. But as the Lord wills not to destroy in us that which is his own, he still finds something in us which in kindness he can love. For though it is by our own fault that we are sinners, we are still his creatures; though we have brought death upon ourselves he had created us for life. Thus, mere gratuitous love prompts him to receive us into favor. But if there is a perpetual and irreconcilable repugnance between righteousness and iniquity, so long as we remain sinners we cannot be completely received. Therefore, in order that all ground of offense may be removed, and he may completely reconcile us to himself, he, by means of the expiation set forth in the death of Christ, abolishes all the evil that is in us, so that we, formerly impure and unclean, now appear in his sight just and holy. Accordingly, God the Father, by his love, prevents and anticipates our reconciliation in Christ. Nay, it is because he first loves us that he afterwards reconciles us to himself. But because the iniquity, which deserves the indignation of God, remains in us until the death of Christ comes to our aid, and that iniquity is in his sight accursed and condemned, we are not admitted to full and sure communion with God, unless, in so far as Christ unites us. And, therefore, if we would indulge the hope of

having God placable and propitious to us, we must fix our eyes and minds on Christ alone, as it is to him alone it is owing that our sins, which necessarily provoked the wrath of God, are not imputed to us.

4. For this reason Paul says that God "has blessed us with all spiritual blessings in heavenly places in Christ: according as he has chosen us in him before the foundation of the world" (Eph. 1:3-4). These things are clear and conformable to Scripture, and admirably reconcile the passages in which it is said that "God so loved the world, that he gave his only begotten Son" (John 3:16); and yet that it was "when we were enemies we were reconciled to God by the death of his Son" (Rom. 5:10). But to give additional assurance to those who require the authority of the ancient Church, I will quote a passage of Augustine to the same effect: "Incomprehensible and immutable is the love of God. For it was not after we were reconciled to him by the blood of his Son that he began to love us, but he loved us before the foundation of the world, that with his only begotten Son we too might be sons of God before we were any thing at all. Our being reconciled by the death of Christ must not be understood as if the Son reconciled us, in order that the Father, then hating, might begin to love us, but that we were reconciled to him already, loving, though at enmity with us because of sin. To the truth of both propositions we have the attestation of the Apostle, God commendeth his love toward us, in that while we were yet sinners, Christ died for us,' (Rom. 5:8). Therefore he had this love towards us even when, exercising enmity towards him, we were the workers of iniquity. Accordingly in a manner wondrous and divine, he loved even when he hated us. For he hated us when we were such as he had not made us, and yet because our iniquity had not destroyed his work in every respect, he knew in regard to each one of us, both to hate what we had made, and love what he had made." Such are the words of Augustine (Tract in Jo. 110).

5. When it is asked then how Christ by abolishing sin removed the enmity between God and us, and purchased a righteousness which

made him favorable and kind to us, it may be answered generally that he accomplished this by the whole course of his obedience. This is proved by the testimony of Paul, "As by one man's disobedience many were made sinners, so by the obedience of one shall many be made righteous" (Rom. 5:19). And indeed he elsewhere extends the ground of pardon which exempts from the curse of the law to the whole life of Christ, "When the fullness of the time was come, God sent forth his Son, made of a woman, made under the law, to redeem them that were under the law" (Gal. 4:4-5). Thus even at his baptism he declared that a part of righteousness was fulfilled by his yielding obedience to the command of the Father. In short, from the moment when he assumed the form of a servant, he began, in order to redeem us, to pay the price of deliverance. Scripture, however, the more certainly to define the mode of salvation, ascribes it peculiarly and specially to the death of Christ. He himself declares that he gave his life a ransom for many (Matt. 20:28). Paul teaches that he died for our sins (Rom. 4:25). John Baptist exclaimed, "Behold the Lamb of God, which taketh away the sin of the world" (John 1:29). Paul in another passage declares, "that we are justified freely by his grace, through the redemption that is in Christ Jesus: whom God has set forth to be a propitiation through faith in his blood" (Rom. 3:25). "Again, being justified by his blood, we shall be saved from wrath through him" (Rom. 5:9). Again, "He has made him to be sin for us, who knew no sin; that we might be made the righteousness of God in him" (2 Cor. 5:21). I will not search out all the passages, for the list would be endless, and many are afterwards to be quoted in their order. In the Confession of Faith called the Apostles' Creed, the transition is admirably made from the birth of Christ to his death and resurrection, in which the completion of a perfect salvation consists. Still there is no exclusion of the other part of obedience which he performed in life. Thus Paul comprehends from the beginning even to the end his having assumed the form of a servant, humbled himself, and become obedient to death, even the death of the cross (Phil. 2:7). And, indeed, the first step in obedience was his voluntary subjection; for the sacrifice would have been unavailing to justification if not offered spontaneously. Hence our Lord, after testifying, "I lay down my life for the sheep," distinctly adds, "No man taketh it from me" (John 10:15, 18). In the same sense Isaiah says, "Like a sheep before her shearers is dumb, so he opened not his mouth" (Is. 53:7). The gospel history relates that he came forth to meet the soldiers; and in presence of Pilate, instead of defending himself, stood to receive judgment. This, indeed, he did not without a struggle, for he had assumed our infirmities also, and in this way it behooved him to prove that he was yielding obedience to his Father. It was no ordinary example of incomparable love towards us to struggle with dire terrors, and amid fearful tortures to cast away all care of himself that he might provide for us. We must bear in minds that Christ could not duly propitiate God without renouncing his own feelings and subjecting himself entirely to his Father's will. To this effect the Apostle appositely quotes a passage from the Psalms, "Lo, I come (in the volume of the book it is written of me) to do thy will, O God" (Heb. 10:5; Ps. 40:7-8). Thus, as trembling consciences find no rest without sacrifice and ablution by which sins are expiated, we are properly directed thither, the source of our life being placed in the death of Christ. Moreover, as the curse consequent upon guilt remained for the final judgment of God, one principal point in the narrative is his condemnation before Pontius Pilate, the governor of Judea, to teach us that the punishment to which we were liable was inflicted on that Just One. We could not escape the fearful judgment of God; and Christ, that he might rescue us from it, submitted to be condemned by a mortal, nay, by a wicked and profane man. For the name of Governor is mentioned not only to support the credibility of the narrative, but to remind us of what Isaiah says, that "the chastisement of our peace was upon him;" and that "with his stripes we are healed" (Is. 53:5). For, in order to remove our condemnation, it was not sufficient to endure any kind of death. To satisfy our ransom, it was necessary to select a mode of death in which he might deliver us, both by giving himself up to condemnations and undertaking our expiation. Had he been cut off by assassins, or slain in a seditious tumult, there could have been no kind of satisfaction in such a death. But when he is placed as a criminal at the bar, where witnesses are brought to give evidence against him, and the mouth of the judge condemns him to die, we see him sustaining the character of an offender and evildoer. Here we must attend to two points which had both been foretold by the prophets, and tend admirably to comfort and confirm our faith. When we read that Christ was led away from the judgment-seat to execution, and was crucified between thieves, we have a fulfillment of the prophecy which is quoted by the Evangelist, "He was numbered with the transgressors" (Is. 53:12; Mark 15:28). Why was it so? That he might bear the character of a sinner, not of a just or innocent person, inasmuch as he met death on account not of innocence, but of sin. On the other hand, when we read that he was acquitted by the same lips that condemned him (for Pilate was forced once and again to bear public testimony to his innocence), let us call to mind what is said by another prophet, "I restored that which I took not away" (Ps. 69:4). Thus we perceive Christ representing the character of a sinner and a criminal, while, at the same time, his innocence shines forth, and it becomes manifest that he suffers for another's and not for his own crime. He therefore suffered under Pontius Pilate, being thus, by the formal sentence of the judge, ranked among criminals, and yet he is declared innocent by the same judge, when he affirms that he finds no cause of death in him. Our acquittal is in this that the guilt which made us liable to punishment was transferred to the head of the Son of God (Is. 53:12). We must specially remember this substitution in order that we may not be all our lives in trepidation and anxiety, as if the just vengeance which the Son of God transferred to himself, were still impending over us.

6. The very form of the death embodies a striking truth. The cross was cursed not only in the opinion of men, but by the enactment of the Divine Law. Hence Christ, while suspended on it, subjects himself to the curse. And thus it behooved to be done, in order that the whole curse, which on account of our iniquities awaited us, or rather lay upon us, might be taken from us by being transferred to him. This was also shadowed in the Law, since *tomsha*, the word by which sin itself is properly designated, was applied to the sacrifices and expiations offered for sin. By this application of the term, the Spirit intended to intimate, that they were a kind of *katharmaton* (purifications), bearing, by substitutions the curse due to sin. But that which was represented figuratively in the Mosaic sacrifices is exhibited in Christ the archetype. Wherefore, in order to accomplish a full expiation, he made his soul *masha*, i.e., a propitiatory victim for sin (as the prophet says, Is. 53:5, 10), on which the guilt and penalty being in a manner laid, ceases to be imputed to us. The Apostle declares this more plainly when he says that "he made him to be sin for us, who knew no sin; that we might be made the righteousness of God in him" (2 Cor. 5:21). For the Son of God, though spotlessly pure, took upon him the disgrace and ignominy of our iniquities, and in return clothed us with his purity. To the same thing he seems to refer, when he says that he "condemned sin in the flesh" (Rom. 8:3), the Father having destroyed the power of sin when it was transferred to the flesh of Christ. This term, therefore, indicates that Christ, in his death, was offered to the Father as a propitiatory victim; that, expiation being made by his sacrifice, we might cease to tremble at the divine wrath. It is now clear what the prophet means when he says, that "the Lord has laid upon him the iniquity of us all" (Is. 53:6); namely, that as he was to wash away the pollution of sins, they were transferred to him by imputation. Of this the cross to which he was nailed was a symbol, as the Apostle declares, "Christ has redeemed us from the curse of the law, being made a curse for us: for it is written, 'Cursed is every one that

hangeth on a tree'; that the blessing of Abraham might come on the Gentiles through Jesus Christ" (Gal. 3:13-14). In the same way Peter says that he "bare our sins in his own body on the tree" (1 Peter 2:24), inasmuch as from the very symbol of the curse, we perceive more clearly that the burden with which we were oppressed was laid upon him. Nor are we to understand that by the curse which he endured he was himself overwhelmed, but rather that by enduring it he repressed broke, annihilated all its force. Accordingly, faith apprehends acquittal in the condemnation of Christ, and blessing in his curse. Hence it is not without cause that Paul magnificently celebrates the triumph which Christ obtained upon the cross, as if the cross, the symbol of ignominy, had been converted into a triumphal chariot. For he says that he blotted out the handwriting of ordinances that was against us, which was contrary to us, and took it out of the way, nailing it to his cross; that "having spoiled principalities and powers he made a show of them openly, triumphing over them in it" (Col. 2:14-15). Nor is this to be wondered at; for, as another Apostle declares, Christ, "through the eternal Spirit, offered himself without spot to God" (Heb. 9:14), and hence that transformation of the cross which were otherwise against its nature. But that these things may take deep root and have their seat in our inmost hearts, we must never lose sight of sacrifice and ablution. For, were not Christ a victim, we could have no sure conviction of his being *apolutrosis antilutron, kai ilasterion,* our substitute-ransom and propitiation. And hence mention is always made of blood whenever scripture explains the mode of redemption: although the shedding of Christ's blood was available not only for propitiation, but also acted as a laver to purge our defilements.

7. The Creed next mentions that he "was dead and buried". Here again it is necessary to consider how he substituted himself in order to pay the price of our redemption. Death held us under its yoke, but he in our place delivered himself into its power, that he might exempt us from it. This the Apostle means when he says, "that he tasted death for

every man" (Heb. 2:9). By dying he prevented us from dying; or (which is the same thing) he by his death purchased life for us (see Calvin in *Psychopann*). But in this he differed from us, that in permitting himself to be overcome of death, it was not so as to be engulfed in its abyss but rather to annihilate it, as it must otherwise have annihilated us; he did not allow himself to be so subdued by it as to be crushed by its power; he rather laid it prostrate, when it was impending over us, and exulting over us as already overcome. In fine, his object was, "that through death he might destroy him that had the power of death, that is, the devil, and deliver them who through fear of death were all their life-time subject to bondage" (Heb. 2:14-15). This is the first fruit which his death produced to us. Another is that by fellowship with him he mortifies our earthly members that they may not afterwards exert themselves in action, and kill the old man, that he may not hereafter be in vigor and bring forth fruit. An effect of his burials moreover is that we as his fellows are buried to sin. For when the Apostle says that we are ingrafted into the likeness of Christ's deaths and that we are buried with him unto sin, that by his cross the world is crucified unto us and we unto the world, and that we are dead with him, he not only exhorts us to manifest an example of his death, but declares that there is an efficacy in it which should appear in all Christians, if they would not render his death unfruitful and useless. Accordingly in the death and burial of Christ a twofold blessing is set before us—viz. deliverance from death, to which we were enslaved, and the mortification of our flesh (Rom. 6:5; Gal. 2:19, 6:14; Col. 3:3).

8. Here we must not omit the descent to hell, which was of no little importance to the accomplishment of redemption. For although it is apparent from the writings of the ancient Fathers that the clause which now stands in the Creed was not formerly so much used in the churches, still, in giving a summary of doctrine, a place must be assigned to it, as containing a matter of great importance which ought not by any means to be disregarded. Indeed, some of the ancient

Fathers do not omit it, and hence we may conjecture that having been inserted in the Creed after a considerable lapse of time, it came into use in the Church not immediately but by degrees. This much is uncontroverted, that it was in accordance with the general sentiment of all believers, since there is none of the Fathers who does not mention Christ's descent into hell, though they have various modes of explaining it. But it is of little consequence by whom and at what time it was introduced. The chief thing to be attended to in the Creed is that it furnishes us with a full and every way complete summary of faith, containing nothing but what has been derived from the infallible word of God. But should any still scruple to give it admission into the Creed, it will shortly be made plain that the place which it holds in a summary of our redemption is so important, that the omission of it greatly detracts from the benefit of Christ's death. There are some again who think that the article contains nothing new, but is merely a repetition in different words of what was previously said respecting burial, the word Hell (*Infernis*) being often used in Scripture for sepulcher. I admit the truth of what they allege with regard to the not infrequent use of the term *infernos* for sepulcher; but I cannot adopt their opinion, for two obvious reasons. First, what folly would it have been, after explaining a matter attended with no difficulty in clear and unambiguous terms, afterwards to involve rather than illustrate it by clothing it in obscure phraseology? When two expressions having the same meaning are placed together, the latter ought to be explanatory of the former. But what kind of explanation would it be to say, the expression, "Christ was buried," means that "he descended into hell"? My second reason is the improbability that a superfluous tautology of this description should have crept into this compendium, in which the principal articles of faith are set down summarily in the fewest possible number of words. I have no doubt that all who weigh the matter with some degree of care will here agree with me.

9. Others interpret differently—viz., that Christ descended to the souls of the Patriarchs who died under the law, to announce his accomplished redemption, and bring them out of the prison in which they were confined. To this effect they wrest the passage in the Psalms "He hath broken the gates of brass, and cut the bars of iron in sunder." (Ps. 107:16); and also the passage in Zechariah, "I have sent forth thy prisoners out of the pit wherein is no water" (Zech. 9:11). But since the psalm foretells the deliverance of those who were held captive in distant lands, and Zechariah comparing the Babylonish disaster into which the people had been plunged to a deep dry well or abyss, at the same time declares, that the salvation of the whole Church was an escape from a profound pit, I know not how it comes to pass that posterity imagined it to be a subterraneous cavern, to which they gave the name of Limbus. Though this fable has the countenance of great authors, and is now also seriously defended by many as truth, it is nothing but a fable. To conclude from it that the souls of the dead are in prison is childish. And what occasion was there that the soul of Christ should go down thither to set them at liberty? I readily admit that Christ illumined them by the power of his Spirit, enabling them to perceive that the grace of which they had only had a foretaste was then manifested to the world. And to this not improbably the passage of Peter may be applied, wherein he says that Christ "went and preached to the spirits that were in prison" (or rather "a watch-tower") (1 Pet. 3:19). The purport of the context is that believers who had died before that time were partakers of the same grace with ourselves: for he celebrates the power of Christ's death, in that he penetrated even to the dead, pious souls obtaining an immediate view of that visitation for which they had anxiously waited; while, on the other hand, the reprobate were more clearly convinced that they were completely excluded from salvation. Although the passage in Peter is not perfectly definite, we must not interpret as if he made no distinction between

the righteous and the wicked: he only means to intimate, that the death of Christ was made known to both.

10. But, apart from the Creed, we must seek for a surer exposition of Christ's descent to hell: and the word of God furnishes us with one not only pious and holy, but replete with excellent consolation. Nothing had been done if Christ had only endured corporeal death. In order to interpose between us and God's anger, and satisfy his righteous judgment, it was necessary that he should feel the weight of divine vengeance. Whence also it was necessary that he should engage, as it were, at close quarters with the powers of hell and the horrors of eternal death. We lately quoted from the Prophet that the "chastisement of our peace was laid upon him;" that he "was bruised for our iniquities;" that he "bore our infirmities;" expressions which intimate that, like a sponsor and surety for the guilty, and, as it were, subjected to condemnation, he undertook and paid all the penalties which must have been exacted from them, the only exception being that the pains of death could not hold him. Hence there is nothing strange in its being said that he descended to hell, seeing he endured the death which is inflicted on the wicked by an angry God. It is frivolous and ridiculous to object that in this way the order is perverted, it being absurd that an event which preceded burial should be placed after it. But after explaining what Christ endured in the sight of man, the Creed appropriately adds the invisible and incomprehensible judgment which he endured before God, to teach us that not only was the body of Christ given up as the price of redemption, but that there was a greater and more excellent price—that he bore in his soul the tortures of condemned and ruined man.

11. In this sense, Peter says that God raised up Christ, "having loosed the pains of death: because it was not possible he should be holden of it" (Acts 2:24). He does not mention death simply, but says that the Son of God endured the pains produced by the curse and wrath of God, the source of death. How small a matter had it

been to come forth securely, and as it were in sport to undergo death. Herein was a true proof of boundless mercy, that he shunned not the death he so greatly dreaded. And there can be no doubt that, in the Epistle to the Hebrews, the Apostle means to teach the same thing, when he says that he "was heard in that he feared" (Heb. 5:7). Some instead of "feared," use a term meaning reverence or piety, but how inappropriately is apparent both from the nature of the thing and the form of expression. Christ then praying in a loud voice, and with tears, is heard in that he feared, not so as to be exempted from death, but so as not to be swallowed up of it like a sinner, though standing as our representative. And certainly no abyss can be imagined more dreadful than to feel that you are abandoned and forsaken of God, and not heard when you invoke him, just as if he had conspired your destruction. To such a degree was Christ dejected that in the depth of his agony he was forced to exclaim, "My God, my God, why hast thou forsaken me?" The view taken by some, that he here expressed the opinion of others rather than his own conviction, is most improbable; for it is evident that the expression was wrung from the anguish of his inmost soul. We do not, however, insinuate that God was ever hostile to him or angry with him. How could he be angry with the beloved Son, with whom his soul was well pleased? or how could he have appeased the Father by his intercession for others if He were hostile to himself? But this we say, that he bore the weight of the divine anger, that, smitten and afflicted, he experienced all the signs of an angry and avenging God. Hence Hilary argues that to this descent we owe our exemption from death. Nor does he dissent from this view in other passages, as when he says, "The cross, death, hell, are our life." And again, "The Son of God is in hell, but man is brought back to heaven." And why do I quote the testimony of a private writer, when an Apostle asserts the same thing, stating it as one fruit of his victory that he delivered "them who through fear of death were all their lifetime subject to bondage?" (Heb. 2:15). He behooved therefore, to conquer the fear which incessantly vexes and agitates the breasts of all mortals; and this he could not do without a contest. Moreover it will shortly appear with greater clearness that his was no common sorrow, was not the result of a trivial cause. Thus by engaging with the power of the devil, the fear of death, and the pains of hell, he gained the victory, and achieved a triumph, so that we now fear not in death those things which our Prince has destroyed.

12. Here some miserable creatures, who, though unlearned, are however impelled more by malice than ignorance, cry out that I am offering an atrocious insult to Christ, because it were most incongruous to hold that he feared for the safety of his soul. And then in harsher terms they urge the calumnious charge that I attribute despair to the Son of God, a feeling the very opposite of faith. First, they wickedly raise a controversy as to the fear and dread which Christ felt, though these are openly affirmed by the Evangelists. For before the hour of his death arrived, he was troubled in spirit, and affected with grief; and at the very onset began to be exceedingly amazed. To speak of these feelings as merely assumed, is a shameful evasion. It becomes us, therefore (as Ambrose truly teaches), boldly to profess the agony of Christ, if we are not ashamed of the cross. And certainly had not his soul shared in the punishment, he would have been a Redeemer of bodies only. The object of his struggle was to raise up those who were lying prostrate; and so far is this from detracting from his heavenly glory, that his goodness, which can never be sufficiently extolled, becomes more conspicuous in this, that he declined not to bear our infirmities.

Hence also that solace to our anxieties and griefs which the Apostle sets before us: "We have not an high priest who cannot be touched with the feeling of our infirmities; but was in all respects tempted like as we are, yet without sin" (Heb. 4:15). These men pretend that a thing in its nature vicious is improperly ascribed to Christ; as if they were wiser than the Spirit of God, who in the same passage reconciles the two things—viz. that he was tempted in all respects like as we are, and yet was without sin. There is no reason, therefore, to take alarm at infirmity in Christ, infirmity to which he submitted not under the constraint of violence and necessity, but merely because he loved and pitied us. Whatever he spontaneously suffered, detracts in no degree from his majesty. One thing which misleads these detractors is, that they do not recognize in Christ an infirmity which was pure and free from every species of taint, inasmuch as it was kept within the limits of obedience. As no moderation can be seen in the depravity of our nature, in which all affections with turbulent impetuosity exceed their due bounds, they improperly apply the same standard to the Son of God. But as he was upright, all his affections were under such restraint as prevented every thing like excess. Hence he could resemble us in grief, fear, and dread, but still with this mark of distinction. Thus refuted, they fly off to another cavil, that although Christ feared death, yet he feared not the curse and wrath of God, from which he knew that he was safe. But let the pious reader consider how far it is honorable to Christ to make him more effeminate and timid than the generality of men. Robbers and other malefactors contumaciously hasten to death, many men magnanimously despise it, others meet it calmly. If the Son of God was amazed and terror-struck at the prospect of it, where was his firmness or magnanimity? We are even told, what in a common death would have been deemed most extraordinary, that in the depth of his agony his sweat was like great drops of blood falling to the ground. Nor was this a spectacle exhibited to the eyes of others, since it was from a secluded spot that he uttered his groans to his Father. And that no doubt may remain, it was necessary that angels should come down from heaven to strengthen him with miraculous consolation. How shamefully effeminate would it have been (as I have observed) to be so excruciated by the fear of an ordinary death as to sweat drops of blood, and not even be revived by the presence of angels? What? Does not that prayer, thrice repeated, "Father, if it be possible, let this cup pass from me" (Matt. 26:39), a prayer dictated by incredible bitterness of soul, show that Christ had a fiercer and more arduous struggle than with ordinary death?

Hence it appears that these triflers, with whom I am disputing, presume to talk of what they know not, never having seriously considered what is meant and implied by ransoming us from the justice of God. It is of consequence to understand aright how much our salvation cost the Son of God. If any one now ask, did Christ descend to hell at the time when he deprecated death? I answer that this was the commencement, and that from it we may infer how dire and dreadful were the tortures which he endured when he felt himself standing at the bar of God as a criminal in our stead. And although the divine power of the Spirit veiled itself for a moment, that it might give place to the infirmity of the flesh, we must understand that the trial arising from feelings of grief and fear was such as not to be at variance with faith. And in this was fulfilled what is said in Peter's sermon as to having been loosed from the pains of death, because "it was not possible he could be holden of it" (Acts 2:24). Though feeling, as it were, forsaken of God, he did not cease in the slightest degree to confide in his goodness. This appears from the celebrated prayer in which, in the depth of his agony, he exclaimed, "My God, my God, why hast thou forsaken me?" (Matt. 27:46). Amid all his agony he ceases not to call upon his God, while exclaiming that he is forsaken by him. This refutes the Apollinarian heresy as well as that of those who are called Monothelites. Apollinaris pretended that in Christ the eternal Spirit supplied the place of a soul, so that he was only half a man; as if he could have expiated our sins in any other way than by obeying the Father. But where does the feeling or desire of obedience reside but in the soul? And we know that his soul was troubled in order that ours, being free from trepidation, might obtain peace and quiet. Moreover, in opposition to the Monothelites, we see that in his human he felt a repugnance to what he willed in his divine nature. I say nothing of his subduing the fear of which we have spoken by a contrary affection.

This appearance of repugnance is obvious in the words, "Father, save me from this hour: but for this cause came I unto this hour. Father, glorify thy name" (John 12:27-28). Still, in this perplexity, there was no violent emotion, such as we exhibit while making the strongest endeavors to subdue our own feelings.

13. Next follows the resurrection from the dead, without which all that has hitherto been said would be defective. For seeing that in the cross, death, and burial of Christ, nothing but weakness appears, faith must go beyond all these, in order that it may be provided with full strength. Hence, although in his death we have an effectual completion of salvation, because by it we are reconciled to God, satisfaction is given to his justice, the curse is removed, and the penalty paid; still it is not by his death, but by his resurrection, that we are said to be begotten again to a living hope (1 Pet. 1:3); because, as he, by rising again, became victorious over death, so the victory of our faith consists only in his resurrection. The nature of it is better expressed in the words of Paul, "Who (Christ) was delivered for our offenses, and was raised again for our justification" (Rom. 4:25); as if he had said, by his death sin was taken away, by his resurrection righteousness was renewed and restored. For how could he by dying have freed us from death, if he had yielded to its power? How could he have obtained the victory for us, if he had fallen in the contest?

Our salvation may be thus divided between the death and the resurrection of Christ: by the former sin was abolished and death annihilated; by the latter righteousness was restored and life revived, the power and efficacy of the former being still bestowed upon us by means of the latter. Paul accordingly affirms that he was declared to be the Son of God by his resurrection (Rom. 1:4), because he then fully displayed that heavenly power which is both a bright mirror of his divinity, and a sure support of our faith; as he also elsewhere teaches, that "though he was crucified through weakness, yet he liveth by the power of God" (2 Cor. 13:4). In the same sense, in another passage, treating of perfection, he says, "That I may know him and the power of his resurrection" (Phil. 3:10). Immediately after he adds, "being made conformable unto his death." In perfect accordance with this is the passage in Peter, that God "raised him up from the dead, and gave him glory, that your faith and hope might be in God" (1 Pet. 1:21). Not that faith founded merely on his death is vacillating, but that the divine power by which he maintains our faith is most conspicuous in his resurrection. Let us remember, therefore, that when death only is mentioned, everything peculiar to the resurrection is at the same time included, and that there is a like synecdoche in the term resurrection, as often as it is used apart from death, everything peculiar to death being included. But as, by rising again, he obtained the victory, and became the resurrection and the life, Paul justly argues, "If Christ be not raised, your faith is vain; ye are yet in your sins" (1 Cor. 15:17). Accordingly, in another passage, after exulting in the death of Christ in opposition to the terrors of condemnation, he thus enlarges, "Christ that died, yea rather, that is risen again, who is even at the right hand of God, who also maketh intercession for us" (Rom. 8:34). Then, as we have already explained that the mortification of our flesh depends on communion with the cross, so we must also understand, that a corresponding benefit is derived from his resurrection. For as the Apostle says, "Like as Christ was raised up from the dead by the glory of the Father, even so we also should walk in newness of life" (Rom. 6:4). Accordingly, as in another passage, from our being dead with Christ, he inculcates, "Mortify therefore your members which are upon the earth" (Col. 3:5); so from our being risen with Christ he infers, "seek those things which are above, where Christ sitteth at the right hand of God" (Col. 3:1). In these words we are not only urged by the example of a risen Savior to follow newness of life, but are taught that by his power we are renewed unto righteousness. A third benefit derived from it is, that, like an earnest, it assures us of our own resurrection, of which it is certain that his is the surest representation.

This subject is discussed at length (1 Cor. 15). But it is to be observed in passing that when he is said to have "risen from the dead," these terms express the reality both of his death and resurrection, as if it had been said that he died the same death as other men naturally die, and received immortality in the same mortal flesh which he had assumed.

14. The resurrection is naturally followed by the ascension into heaven. For although Christ, by rising again, began fully to display his glory and virtue, having laid aside the abject and ignoble condition of a mortal life, and the ignominy of the cross, yet it was only by his ascension to heaven that his reign truly commenced. This the Apostle shows when he says he ascended "that he might fill all things" (Eph. 4:10), thus reminding us that under the appearance of contradiction, there is a beautiful harmony, inasmuch as though he departed from us, it was that his departure might be more useful to us than that presence which was confined in a humble tabernacle of flesh during his abode on the earth. Hence John, after repeating the celebrated invitation, "If any man thirst, let him come unto me and drink," immediately adds, "the Holy Ghost was not yet given; because that Jesus was not yet glorified" (John 7:37, 39). This our Lord himself also declared to his disciples, "It is expedient for you that I go away: for if I go not away the Comforter will not come unto you" (John 16:7). To console them for his bodily absence, he tells them that he will not leave them comfortless, but will come again to them in a manner invisible indeed, but more to be desired, because they were then taught by a surer experience that the government which he had obtained, and the power which he exercises would enable his faithful followers not only to live well, but also to die happily. And, indeed we see how much more abundantly his Spirit was poured out, how much more gloriously his kingdom was advanced, how much greater power was employed in aiding his followers and discomfiting his enemies. Being raised to heaven, he withdrew his bodily presence from our sight, not that he might cease to be with his followers, who are still pilgrims

on the earth, but that he might rule both heaven and earth more immediately by his power; or rather, the promise which he made to be with us even to the end of the world, he fulfilled by this ascension, by which, as his body has been raised above all heavens, so his power and efficacy have been propagated and diffused beyond all the bounds of heaven and earth. This I prefer to explain in the words of Augustine rather than my own: "Through death Christ was to go to the right hand of the Father, whence he is to come to judge the quick and the dead, and that in corporal presence, according to the sound doctrine and rule of faith. For, in spiritual presence, he was to be with them after his ascension" (August. *Tract. in Joann.* 109). In another passage he is more full and explicit: "In regard to ineffable and invisible grace, is fulfilled what he said, "Lo, I am with you always, even to the end of the world" (Matt. 28:20); but in regard to the flesh which the Word assumed in regard to his being born of a Virgin, in regard to his being apprehended by the Jews, nailed to the tree, taken down from the cross, wrapped in linen clothes, laid in the sepulcher, and manifested on his resurrection, it may be said, "Me ye have not always with you." Why? Because, in bodily presence, he conversed with his disciples forty days, and leading them out where they saw, but followed not, he ascended into heaven, and is not here, for there he sits at the right hand of the Father, and yet he is here, for the presence of his Godhead was not withdrawn. Therefore, as regards his divine presence, we have Christ always: as regards his bodily presence, it was truly said to the disciples, "Me ye have not always." For a few days the Church had him bodily present. Now, she apprehends him by faith, but sees him not by the eye" (August. *Tract.* 51).

15. Hence it is immediately added, that he "sitteth at the right hand of God the Father;" a similitude borrowed from princes, who have their assessors to whom they commit the office of ruling and issuing commands. Thus Christ, in whom the Father is pleased to be exalted, and by whose hand he is pleased to reign, is said to have

been received up, and seated on his right hand (Mark 16:19); as if it had been said that he was installed in the government of heaven and earth, and formally admitted to possession of the administration committed to him, and not only admitted for once, but to continue until he descend to judgment. For so the Apostle interprets, when he says, that the Father "set him at his own right hand in the heavenly places, far above all principality, and power, and might, and dominion, and every name that is named not only in this world, but also in that which is to come; and has put all things under his feet, and given him to be the head over all things to the Church." You see to what end he is so seated namely, that all creatures both in heaven and earth should reverence his majesty, be ruled by his hand, do him implicit homage, and submit to his power. All that the Apostles intends when they so often mention his seat at the Father's hand, is to teach, that every thing is placed at his disposal. Those, therefore, are in error, who suppose that his blessedness merely is indicated. We may observe, that there is nothing contrary to this doctrine in the testimony of Stephen, that he saw him standing (Acts 7:56), the subject here considered being not the position of his body, but the majesty of his empire, sitting meaning nothing more than presiding on the judgment-seat of heaven.

16. From this doctrine faith derives manifold advantages. First, it perceives that the Lord, by his ascension to heaven, has opened up the access to the heavenly kingdom, which Adam had shut. For having entered it in our flesh, as it were in our name, it follows, as the Apostle says, that we are in a manner now seated in heavenly places, not entertaining a mere hope of heaven, but possessing it in our head. Secondly, faith perceives that his seat beside the Father is not without great advantage to us. Having entered the temple not made with hands, he constantly appears as our advocate and intercessor in the presence of the Father; directs attention to his own righteousness, so as to turn it away from our sins; so reconciles him to us, as by his intercession

to pave for us a way of access to his throne, presenting it to miserable sinners, to whom it would otherwise be an object of dread, as replete with grace and mercy. Thirdly, it discerns his power, on which depend our strength, might, resources, and triumph over hell, "When he ascended up on high, he led captivity captive" (Eph. 4:8). Spoiling his foes, he gave gifts to his people, and daily loads them with spiritual riches. He thus occupies his exalted seat, that thence transferring his virtue unto us, he may quicken us to spiritual life, sanctify us by his Spirit, and adorn his Church with various graces, by his protection preserve it safe from all harm, and by the strength of his hand curb the enemies raging against his cross and our salvation; in fine, that he may possess all power in heaven and earth, until he have utterly routed all his foes, who are also ours and completed the structure of his Church. Such is the true nature of the kingdom, such the power which the Father has conferred upon him, until he arrive to complete the last act by judging the quick and the dead.

17. Christ, indeed, gives his followers no dubious proofs of present power, but as his kingdom in the world is in a manner veiled by the humiliation of a carnal condition, faith is most properly invited to meditate on the visible presence which he will exhibit on the last day. For he will descend from heaven in visible form, in like manner as he was seen to ascend, and appear to all, with the ineffable majesty of his kingdom, the splendor of immortality, the boundless power of divinity, and an attending company of angels. Hence we are told to wait for the Redeemer against that day on which he will separate the sheep from the goats and the elect from the reprobate, and when not one individual either of the living or the dead shall escape his judgment. From the extremities of the universe shall be heard the clang of the trumpet summoning all to his tribunal; both those whom that day shall find alive, and those whom death shall previously have removed from the society of the living. There are some who take the words, quick and dead, in a different sense; and, indeed, some ancient

writers appear to have hesitated as to the exposition of them; but our meaning being plain and clear, is much more accordant with the Creed which was certainly written for popular use. There is nothing contrary to it in the Apostle's declaration that it is appointed unto all men once to die. For though those who are surviving at the last day shall not die after a natural manner, yet the change which they are to undergo, as it shall resemble, is not improperly called death (Heb. 9:27). "We shall not all sleep, but we shall all be changed" (1 Cor. 15:51). What does this mean? Their mortal life shall perish and be swallowed up in one moment, and be transformed into an entirely new nature. Though no one can deny that that destruction of the flesh will be death, it still remains true that the quick and the dead shall be summoned to judgment (1 Thess. 4:16); for "the dead in Christ shall rise first; then we which are alive and remain shall be caught up together with them in the clouds to meet the lord in the air." Indeed, it is probable that these words in the Creed were taken from Peter's sermon as related by Luke (Acts 10:42), and from the solemn charge of Paul to Timothy (2 Tim. 4:1).

18. It is most consolatory to think that judgment is vested in him who has already destined us to share with him in the honor of judgment (Matt. 19:28); so far is it from being true that he will ascend the judgment-seat for our condemnation. How could a most merciful prince destroy his own people? How could the head disperse its own members? How could the advocate condemn his clients? For if the Apostle, when contemplating the interposition of Christ, is bold to exclaim, "Who is he that condemneth?" (Rom. 8:33), much more certain is it that Christ, the intercessor, will not condemn those whom he has admitted to his protection. It certainly gives no small security that we shall be sisted at no other tribunal than that of our Redeemer, from whom salvation is to be expected; and that he who in the Gospel now promises eternal blessedness, will then as judge ratify his promise. The end for which the Father has honored the Son

by committing all judgment to him (John 5:22) was to pacify the consciences of his people when alarmed at the thought of judgment. Hitherto I have followed the order of the Apostles' Creed, because it states the leading articles of redemption in a few words, and may thus serve as a tablet in which the points of Christian doctrine, most deserving of attention, are brought separately and distinctly before us. I call it the Apostles' Creed, though I am by no means solicitous as to its authorship. The general consent of ancient writers certainly does ascribe it to the Apostles, either because they imagined it was written and published by them for common use, or because they thought it right to give the sanction of such authority to a compendium faithfully drawn up from the doctrine delivered by their hands. I have no doubt that from the very commencement of the Church and, therefore, in the very days of the Apostles, it held the place of a public and universally received confession, whatever be the quarter from which it originally proceeded. It is not probable that it was written by some private individual, since it is certain that, from time immemorial, it was deemed of sacred authority by all Christians. The only point of consequence we hold to be incontrovertible—viz. that it gives, in clear and succinct order, a full statement of our faith, and in everything which it contains is sanctioned by the sure testimony of Scripture. This being understood, it were to no purpose to labor anxiously, or quarrel with any one as to the authorship, unless, indeed, we think it not enough to possess the sure truth of the Holy Spirit, without at the same time knowing by whose mouth it was pronounced, or by whose hand it was written.

19. When we see that the whole sum of our salvation and every single part of it are comprehended in Christ, we must beware of deriving even the minutest portion of it from any other quarter. If we seek salvation, we are taught by the very name of Jesus that he possesses it; if we seek any other gifts of the Spirit, we shall find them in his unction; strength in his government; purity in his conception; indulgence

in his nativity, in which he was made like us in all respects, in order that he might learn to sympathize with us; if we seek redemption, we shall find it in his passion; acquittal in his condemnation; remission of the curse in his cross; satisfaction in his sacrifice; purification in his blood; reconciliation in his descent to hell; mortification of the flesh in his sepulcher; newness of life in his resurrection; immortality also in his resurrection; the inheritance of a celestial kingdom in his entrance into heaven; protection, security, and the abundant supply of all blessings, in his kingdom; secure anticipation of judgment in the power of judging committed to him. In fine, since in him all kinds of blessings are treasured up, let us draw a full supply from him, and none from any other quarter. Those who, not satisfied with him alone, entertain various hopes from others, though they may continue to look to him chiefly, deviate from the right path by the simple fact that some portion of their thought takes a different direction. No distrust of this description can arise when once the abundance of his blessings is properly known.

Study Guide Questions

Section 1

1. Where did the name "Jesus" come from? .
2. What happens if we turn away from Christ, however slightly?

Section 2

1. What must happen before we can accept God's gift of life with the gratitude we owe?

Section 3

1. Does God love us before our salvation?
2. Can He just receive us that way?

Section 4

1. According to Calvin, did God love us before we were reconciled to Him?

2. Which church father does he cite in agreement with this?

Section 5

1. How did Christ accomplish salvation for us?

2. We are freed from the curse of the law by what?

3. What passage in Galatians does Calvin claim as support for this?

4. According to Calvin, was the means by which Christ died important?

Section 6

1. What happened to the curse that was on us?

2. What exchange did the Son of God make, even though He was utterly clean of all fault?

3. Christ cleansed our filth by what means?

4. Even though it was full of shame, what was the cross changed into?

Section 7

1. What two things did the death of Jesus accomplish?

Section 8

1. Does Calvin believe that the descent into hell belongs in the Creed?

Section 9

1. What traditional view does Calvin reject with regard to this article?

Section 10

1. If Calvin rejects the idea that Christ descended into the nether world, how does he take the phrase from the Creed?

2. Does the compiler of these study questions agree with this?

Section 11

1. How does Calvin undertake to prove this view?

Section 12

1. How does Calvin answer his critics on this point?

Section 13

1. What must faith do in order to attain its full strength?
2. What is the summary of the effects of the death and resurrection respectively?
3. What should we understand in Scripture when the benefits of His death or resurrection are spoken of singly?

Section 14

1. What did Christ's ascension do for His relation to all things?
2. The ascension of Christ's body did what to His power and energy?

Section 15

1. What is the central meaning of Christ's position at the right hand of God the Father?

Section 16

1. What did Jesus do for us by means of His ascent into heaven?
2. Do we look forward to heaven as with a "mere hope"?

Section 17

1. Despite His present power, where is Christ's kingdom now?
2. Will any escape His judgment when He returns?

Section 18

1. Who will share with Him in the work of judging?
2. What can a head not do?

3. What does the Son do with the judgment He has been given?

Section 19

1. What do we find in every clause of the Creed?

CHAPTER 17

Christ rightly and properly said to have merited grace and
salvation for us.

The three leading divisions of this chapter are—

I. A proof from reason and from Scripture that the grace of
God and the merit of Christ (the prince and author of our salvation)
are perfectly compatible, sec. 1 and 2.

II. Christ, by his obedience, even to the death of the cross (which
was the price of our redemption), merited divine favor for us, sec. 3-5.

III. The presumptuous rashness of the Schoolmen in treating this
branch of doctrine.

Outline:

1. Christ not only the minister, but also the author and prince of
salvation. Divine grace not obscured by this mode of expression. The
merit of Christ not opposed to the mercy of God, but depends upon it.

2. The compatibility of the two proved by various passages of
Scripture.

3. Christ by his obedience truly merited divine grace for us.

4. This grace obtained by the shedding of Christ's blood, and his
obedience even unto death.

5. In this way he paid our ransom.

6. The presumptuous manner in which the Schoolmen handle this subject.

A question must here be considered by way of supplement. Some men too much given to subtlety, while they admit that we obtain salvation through Christ, will not hear of the name of merit, by which they imagine that the grace of God is obscured; and therefore insist that Christ was only the instrument or minister, not the author or leader, or prince of life, as he is designated by Peter (Acts 3:15). I admit that were Christ opposed simply, and by himself, to the justice of God, there could be no room for merit, because there cannot be found in man a worth which could make God a debtor; nay, as Augustine says most truly, "The Savior, the man Christ Jesus, is himself the brightest illustration of predestination and grace: his character as such was not procured by any antecedent merit of works or faith in his human nature. Tell me, I pray, how that man, when assumed into unity of person by the Word, co-eternal with the Father, as the only begotten Son at God, could merit this." "Let the very fountain of grace, therefore, appear in our head, whence, according to the measure of each, it is diffused through all his members. Every man, from the commencement of his faith, becomes a Christian, by the same grace by which that man from his formation became Christ." Again, in another passage, "There is not a more striking example of predestination than the mediator himself. He who made him (without any antecedent merit in his will) of the seed of David a righteous man never to be unrighteous, also converts those who are members of his head from unrighteous into righteous," and so forth. Therefore when we treat of the merit of Christ, we do not place the beginning in him, but we ascend to the ordination of God as the primary cause, because of his mere good pleasure he appointed a Mediator to purchase salvation for us. Hence the merit of Christ is inconsiderately opposed to the mercy of God. It is a well known rule that principal and accessory are not incompatible, and therefore there is nothing to prevent the justification of man from being the gratuitous result of the mere mercy of God, and, at the same time, to prevent the merit of Christ from intervening in subordination to this mercy. The free favor of God is as fitly opposed to our works as is the obedience of Christ, both in their order: for Christ could not merit anything save by the good pleasure of God, but only inasmuch as he was destined to appease the wrath of God by his sacrifice, and wipe away our transgressions by his obedience: in one word, since the merit of Christ depends entirely on the grace of God (which provided this mode of salvation for us), the latter is no less appropriately opposed to all righteousness of men than is the former.

2. This distinction is found in numerous passages of Scripture: "God so loved the world, that he gave his only begotten Son, that whosoever believeth in him might not perish" (John 3:16). We see that the first place is assigned to the love of God as the chief cause or origin, and that faith in Christ follows as the second and more proximate cause. Should any one object that Christ is only the formal cause, he lessens his energy more than the words justify. For if we obtain justification by a faith which leans on him, the groundwork of our salvation must be sought in him. This is clearly proved by several passages: "Herein is love, not that we loved God, but that he loved us, and sent his Son to be the propitiation for our sins" (1 John 4:10). These words clearly demonstrate that God, in order to remove any obstacle to his love towards us, appointed the method of reconciliation in Christ. There is great force in this word "propitiation"; for in a manner which cannot be expressed, God, at the very time when he loved us, was hostile to us until reconciled in Christ. To this effect are all the following passages: "He is the propitiation for our sins;" "It pleased the Father that in him should all fullness dwell, and having made peace by the blood of his cross, by him to reconcile all things unto himself;" "God was in Christ reconciling the world unto himself,

not imputing their trespasses unto them;" "He has made us accepted in the Beloved," "That he might reconcile both into one body by the cross." The nature of this mystery is to be learned from the first chapter to the Ephesians, where Paul, teaching that we were chosen in Christ, at the same time adds that we obtained grace in him. How did God begin to embrace with his favor those whom he had loved before the foundation of the world, unless in displaying his love when he was reconciled by the blood of Christ? As God is the fountain of all righteousness, he must necessarily be the enemy and judge of man so long as he is a sinner. Wherefore, the commencement of love is the bestowing of righteousness, as described by Paul: "He has made him to be sin for us who knew no sin; that we might be made the righteousness of God in him" (2 Cor. 5:21). He intimates that by the sacrifice of Christ we obtain free justification, and become pleasing to God, though we are by nature the children of wrath, and by sin estranged from him. This distinction is also noted whenever the grace of Christ is connected with the love of God (2 Cor. 13:13); whence it follows that he bestows upon us of his own which he acquired by purchase. For otherwise there would be no ground for the praise ascribed to him by the Father, that grace is his, and proceeds from him.

3. That Christ, by his obedience, truly purchased and merited grace for us with the Father, is accurately inferred from several passages of Scripture. I take it for granted that if Christ satisfied for our sins, if he paid the penalty due by us, if he appeased God by his obedience; in fine, if he suffered the just for the unjust, salvation was obtained for us by his righteousness; which is just equivalent to meriting. Now, Paul's testimony is that we were reconciled, and received reconciliation through his death (Rom. 5:11). But there is no room for reconciliation unless where offense has preceded. The meaning, therefore, is that God, to whom we were hateful through sin, was appeased by the death of his Son and made propitious to us. And the antithesis which immediately follows is carefully to be observed, "As by one

man's disobedience many were made sinners, so by the obedience of one shall many be made righteous" (Rom. 5:19). For the meaning is— as by the sin of Adam we were alienated from God and doomed to destruction, so by the obedience of Christ we are restored to his favor as if we were righteous. The future tense of the verb does not exclude present righteousness, as is apparent from the context. For he had previously said, "the free gift is of many offenses unto justification."

4. When we say that grace was obtained for us by the merit of Christ, our meaning is that we were cleansed by his blood, that his death was an expiation for sin, "His blood cleanses us from all sin." "This is my blood, which is shed for the remission of sins" (1 John 1:7; Luke 22:20). If the effect of his shed blood is that our sins are not imputed to us, it follows that by that price the justice of God was satisfied. To the same effect are the Baptist's words, "Behold the Lamb of God, which taketh away the sin of the world" (John 1:29). For he contrasts Christ with all the sacrifices of the Law, showing that in him alone was fulfilled what these figures typified. But we know the common expression in Moses: iniquity shall be expiated, sin shall be wiped away and forgiven. In short, we are admirably taught by the ancient figures what power and efficacy there is in Christ's death. And the Apostle, skillfully proceeding from this principle, explains the whole matter in the Epistle to the Hebrews, showing that without shedding of blood there is no remission (Heb. 9:22). From this he infers that Christ appeared once for all to take away sin by the sacrifice of himself. Again, that he was offered to bear the sins of many (Heb. 9:12). He had previously said that not by the blood of goats or of heifers, but by his own blood, he had once entered into the holy of holies, having obtained eternal redemption for us. Now, when he reasons thus, "If the blood of bulls and of goats, and the ashes of an heifer sprinkling the unclean, sanctifieth to the purifying of the flesh: how much more shall the blood of Christ, who through the eternal Spirit offered himself to God, purge your consciences from dead works to

serve the living God?" (Heb. 9:13-14), it is obvious that too little effect is given to the grace of Christ, unless we concede to his sacrifice the power of expiating, appeasing, and satisfying: as he shortly after adds, "For this cause he is the mediator of the new testament, that by means of his death, for the redemption of the transgressions that were under the first testament, they which are called might receive the promise of eternal inheritance" (Heb. 9:15). But it is especially necessary to attend to the analogy which is drawn by Paul as to his having been made a curse for us (Gal. 3:13). It had been superfluous and therefore absurd that Christ should have been burdened with a curse, had it not been in order that by paying what others owed he might acquire righteousness for them. There is no ambiguity in Isaiah's testimony, "He was wounded for our transgressions, he was bruised for our iniquities: the chastisement of our peace was laid upon him; and with his stripes we are healed" (Is. 53:5). For had not Christ satisfied for our sins, he could not be said to have appeased God by taking upon himself the penalty which we had incurred. To this corresponds what follows in the same place, "for the transgression of my people was he stricken" (Is. 53:8). We may add the interpretation of Peter, who unequivocally declares that he "bare our sins in his own body on the tree" (1 Pet. 2:24), that the whole burden of condemnation, of which we were relieved, was laid upon him.

5. The Apostles also plainly declare that he paid a price to ransom us from death: "Being justified freely by his grace, through the redemption that is in Christ Jesus: whom God has set forth to be a propitiation through faith in his blood" (Rom. 3:24-25). Paul commends the grace of God, in that he gave the price of redemption in the death of Christ; and he exhorts us to flee to his blood that having obtained righteousness, we may appear boldly before the judgment-seat of God. To the same effect are the words of Peter: "Forasmuch as ye know that ye were not redeemed with corruptible things, as silver and gold," "but with the precious blood of Christ, as of a lamb without blemish and

without spot" (1 Pet. 1:18-19). The antithesis would be incongruous if he had not by this price made satisfaction for sins. For which reason Paul says, "Ye are bought with a price." Nor could it be elsewhere said, there is "one mediator between God and men, the man Christ Jesus; who gave himself a ransom for all" (1 Tim. 2:5-6), had not the punishment which we deserved been laid upon him. Accordingly, the same Apostle declares that "we have redemption through his blood, even the forgiveness of sins" (Col. 1:14); as if he had said that we are justified or acquitted before God, because that blood serves the purpose of satisfaction. With this another passage agrees—viz. that he blotted out "the handwriting of ordinances which was against us, which was contrary to us" (Col. 2:14). These words denote the payment or compensation which acquits us from guilt. There is great weight also in these words of Paul: "If righteousness come by the law, then Christ is dead in vain" (Gal. 2:21). For we hence infer that it is from Christ we must seek what the Law would confer on any one who fulfilled it; or, which is the same thing, that by the grace of Christ we obtain what God promised in the Law to our works: "If a man do, he shall live in them" (Lev. 18:5). This is no less clearly taught in the discourse at Antioch, when Paul declares, "That through this man is preached unto you the forgiveness of sins; and by him all that believe are justified from all things, from which ye could not be justified by the law of Moses" (Acts 13:38-39). For if the observance of the Law is righteousness, who can deny that Christ, by taking this burden upon himself, and reconciling us to God, as if we were the observers of the Law, merited favor for us? Of the same nature is what he afterwards says to the Galatians: "God sent forth his Son, made of a woman, made under the law, to redeem them that were under the law" (Gal. 4:4-5). For to what end that subjection, unless that he obtained justification for us by undertaking to perform what we were unable to pay? Hence that imputation of righteousness without works, of which Paul treats (Rom. 4:5), the righteousness found in Christ alone being accepted as if it were ours. And certainly the only reason why Christ is called our "meat" (John 6:55) is because we find in him the substance of life. And the source of this efficacy is just that the Son of God was crucified as the price of our justification; as Paul says, Christ "has given himself for us an offering and a sacrifice to God for a sweet-smelling savor" (Eph. 5:2); and elsewhere, he "was delivered for our offenses, and was raised again for our justification" (Rom. 4:25). Hence it is proved not only that salvation was given us by Christ, but that on account of him the Father is now propitious to us. For it cannot be doubted that in him is completely fulfilled what God declares by Isaiah under a figure, "I will defend this city to save it for mine own sakes and for my servant David's sake" (Isaiah 37:35). Of this the Apostle is the best witness when he says "Your sins are forgiven you for his name's sake" (1 John 2:12). For although the name of Christ is not expressed, John, in his usual manner, designates him by the pronoun "He" (αυτον). In the same sense also our Lord declares, "As the living Father has sent me, and I live by the Father: so he that eateth me, even he shall live by me" (John 6:57). To this corresponds the passage of Paul, "Unto you it is given in the behalf of Christ, not only to believe in him, but also to suffer for his sake" (Phil. 1:29).

6. To inquire, as Lombard and the Schoolmen do (*Sent.* Lib. 3 Dist. 18) whether he merited for himself is foolish curiosity. Equally rash is their decision when they answer in the affirmative. How could it be necessary for the only Son of God to come down in order to acquire some new quality for himself? The exposition which God gives of his own purpose removes all doubt. The Father is not said to have consulted the advantage of his Son in his services, but to have given him up to death, and not spared him, because he loved the world (Rom. 8). The prophetical expressions should be observed: "To us a Son is born;" "Rejoice greatly, O daughter of Zion: shout, O daughter of Jerusalem: behold, thy King cometh unto thee" (Isaiah 9:6; Zech. 9:9). It would otherwise be a cold commendation of love which Paul describes, when

he says, "God commendeth his love toward us, in that, while we were yet sinners, Christ died for us" (Rom. 5:8). Hence, again, we infer that Christ had no regard to himself; and this he distinctly affirms, when he says, "For their sakes I sanctify myself" (John 17:19). He who transfers the benefit of his holiness to others, testifies that he acquires nothing for himself. And surely it is most worthy of remark that Christ, in devoting himself entirely to our salvation, in a manner forgot himself. It is absurd to wrest the testimony of Paul to a different effect: "Wherefore God has highly exalted him, and given him a name which is above every name" (Phil. 2:9). By what services could a man merit to become the judge of the world, the head of angels, to obtain the supreme government of God, and become the residence of that majesty of which all the virtues of men and angels cannot attain one thousandth part? The solution is easy and complete. Paul is not speaking of the cause of Christ's exaltation, but only pointing out a consequence of it by way of example to us. The meaning is not much different from that of another passage: "Ought not Christ to have suffered these things, and to enter into his glory?" (Luke 24:26).

Study Guide Questions

Section 1

1. When discussing the merit of Christ, what must we remember lies behind it?

2. Did "the man," according to Augustine, deserve to be the only begotten Son of God?

Section 2

1. What was God's ineffable demeanor toward us?

Section 3

1. What did Christ accomplish by His obedience?

He truly acquired and merited grace for us with His Father.

Section 4

1. What power did Christ's sacrifice have?

The power of expiating, appeasing, and making satisfaction.

Section 5

1. What is the definition of redemption in Christ's blood?

It is forgiveness of sins (Col. 1:14).

Section 6

1. Did Christ merit anything for Himself?

ANSWERS TO STUDY
GUIDE QUESTIONS

Chapter One

Section 1

1. **What ancient proverb does Calvin commend?**

    Know thyself.

2. **What echo of an earlier point in Calvin does this make?**

    Calvin begins the *Institutes* by saying that man must know God and know himself.

3. **What are the two essential parts of self-knowledge?**

    We must know the loftiness of our original estate, and we must also know the magnitude of the Fall.

Section 2

1. **Instead of true self-knowledge, what do we tend to seek out instead?**

    We seek out flattery.

2. **What does this flattery appeal to?**

    It appeals to the "pride spontaneously springing up" in our "inmost heart."

Section 3

1. **Does reflection on our original nobility create pride in us?**

    No, just the opposite. It creates humility.

2. **How are we then to divide our knowledge of ourselves?**

    We should meditate on the greatness of man's condition before the Fall, and we should weigh our own subsequent lack of ability to do anything right given the Fall.

3. **What will this do?**

    It will cause us to cast ourselves upon God.

Section 4

1. **Does Calvin believe that Adam was allowed to eat from the tree of life?**

    Yes.

2. **Was Adam's sin simply gluttony?**

    No. What God so severely punished cannot have been "a trivial fault."

3. **What was the root of Adam's sin?**

    Unfaithfulness.

4. **What was the progress of Adam's rebellion?**

    Unfaithfulness led to pride and ambition, along with ingratitude, which resulted in disobedience.

Section 5

1. **How does Calvin define the "death of [Adam's] soul"?**

    He defines it as estrangement from God.

2. **How does Calvin define "original sin"?**

    He defines it as "the depravation of a nature formerly good and pure."

3. **What was Pelagius' "profane fiction"?**

    It was that Adam sinned to his own hurt, and that his sin did not harm his descendants.

Section 6

1. **When are children defiled by original sin?**

    At their begetting.

2. **What is Adam's position with regard to the human race?**

    He is the root of human nature.

3. **What is, for Calvin, "out of all controversy"?**

That if Christ's righteousness and life is ours by communication, then we receive sin and death from Adam the same way.

4. **How does Calvin define that communication of righteousness from Christ?**

As the power of righteousness being transfused into us.

Section 7

1. **What should we be content to know with regard to all this?**

That God gave to Adam what He intended the human race to have, and so when Adam lost those gifts, he lost them for us all.

2. **Does the contagion spread through the substance of flesh or soul?**

No. The contagion takes its origin because it has been so ordained by God.

Section 8

1. **How does Calvin define original sin?**

As a hereditary depravity and corruption of our nature, diffused into all parts of the soul.

2. **Do infants bear the curse of original sin?**

Yes. Their "whole nature is ... a seed-bed of sin."

3. **Is this original sin nothing more than the absence of righteousness?**

No, it includes the active presence of every evil.

Section 9

1. **How far does original sin extend in a man?**

To every part of his nature.

2. **Is it true that the flesh is fallen, but the soul is not?**

No. No part of a man remains "exempt from sin."

Section 10

1. **What is Calvin's response to those who would write God's name upon their faults?**

He calls them perverse and says, "Let us have done [with them]."

2. **What is wrong with asking the question "Why did God not prevent the Fall?"**

   It manifests inordinate curiosity.

Section 11

1. **In what way is sin unnatural?**

   It is contrary to the creational intent that God had in making man.

2. **In what way is sin natural?**

   We call it natural because all men are in the grip of it by "hereditary law."

Chapter Two

Section 1

1. **What are the twin perils that threaten man, given his bondage to sin?**

   On the one hand, he becomes complacent because it is said that he cannot be righteous. On the other, if he resolves to attain to some moral stature himself, he robs God of His glory.

2. **What does Augustine say that the defenders of free will do?**

   He says that they trample on free will more than they strengthen it.

Section 2

1. **What do the philosophers believe about reason?**

   That it is suffused with divine light, and that virtue depends upon following it.

2. **Where do they believe our corruptions reside?**

   In our sense perceptions, in our physical nature.

3. **Where do they locate the will?**

   Midway between reason and sense.

Section 3

1. **Do the philosophers believe that things can go wrong?**

   Yes, certainly, as when a charioteer loses control of his chariot.

2. **At the same time, do they believe that virtue is a real possibility?**

   Yes, they do. Both virtue and vice are within our power.

3. **According to Cicero, should we thank the gods for our own virtue?**

No, because virtue was our own contribution.

Section 4

1. **Does Calvin believe that the church fathers handled the idea of free will scripturally?**

No, he did not.

2. **What was the reason for this?**

They tried to harmonize what they taught too closely with the teaching of the philosophers.

3. **What two things were they concerned to avoid?**

They did not want to expose themselves to derision from the philosophers, and they did not want to seem to make room for moral slothfulness.

4. **Which of the fathers was an exception to this?**

Augustine.

Section 5

1. **What were the three kinds of freedom that were distinguished in the schools?**

Freedom from necessity, freedom from sin, and freedom from misery.

2. **Does Calvin accept this distinction?**

Yes, with the caveat that necessity not be muddled up with compulsion.

Section 6

1. **What is necessary before men can do good works truly?**

Only the elect receive this special grace through regeneration.

2. **What ambiguity does Calvin object to in the teaching of Lombard?**

Calvin objected to the door that was opened to the idea that God offers grace, and we can either "nullify the first grace" by rejecting it or confirm it by "obediently yielding to it."

Section 7

1. What does Calvin think about "mere verbal disputes"?

He abhors them because their result is that the Church is harassed "to no purpose."

2. So why then does he reject the words "free will" so strongly?

Because it is virtually impossible to use the phrase without encouraging a "fatal confidence."

Section 8

1. What does Augustine teach about the will?

He teaches that man's will isn't free unless the Spirit has brought that freedom.

2. Does Augustine use the phrase "free will"?

Yes, but in a way that mocks "the emptiness of the name."

3. What is Calvin's approach to the phrase?

He prefers not to use it and advises others not to use it either.

Section 9

1. What is the problem with the other fathers?

Sometimes they exalt free will. Other times they give all the glory to Christ. Calvin objects to their inconsistency.

2. What does Calvin say in their favor?

That however excessive they are in "extolling free will," their intent was to "the main object which they had in view was to teach man entirely to renounce all self-confidence, and place his strength in God alone."

Section 10

1. When a man is utterly cast down in himself, what has he gained?

True knowledge of himself.

2. What is the problem with a man retaining to himself some of the honor found in "free will"?

It usurps God of His honor and is monstrous sacrilege.

3. Who may receive God's blessings?

One who is consumed with an awareness of his own poverty.

Section 11

1. **What did Augustine say were the three chief rules for eloquence?**

   Delivery, delivery, delivery.

2. **In a similar vein, what does Calvin say are the three chief precepts of the Christian religion?**

   Humility, humility, humility.

3. **Instead of relying on human nature, which is "bruised, and broken, and burnt" and "having no help," what do we need?**

   We need true confession, not false defense.

4. **In order for our war with God to be over, what must happen?**

   We must be unarmed. Our weapons of impiety must be "bruised, and broken, and burnt."

Section 12

1. **In the Fall, what happened to our supernatural gifts like faith and righteousness?**

   We lost them completely.

2. **What happened to our natural gifts, like soundness of mind and uprightness of heart?**

   They were corrupted.

3. **Have we fallen to the level of the brute beasts?**

   No. The "shapeless ruin" of our natural gifts still appear.

Section 13

1. **What are the two kinds of understanding according to Calvin?**

   Understanding of earthly things and understanding of heavenly things.

2. **What is included in the former?**

   Matters involved with the present life, like government, household management, mechanical skill, and the liberal arts.

3. **The latter?**

   Pure knowledge of God, the nature of true righteousness, and the mysteries of the heavenly kingdom.

Section 14

1. **What does virtually every human being possess?**
    Talent in some art.

2. **What do we learn from imbeciles?**
    Gratitude, because we see how much God has left to us.

3. **What is a natural gift?**
    One bestowed on the pious and the impious alike.

Section 15

1. **If we regard the Spirit of God as the sole fountain of truth, what follows?**
    We will not reject truth, no matter where it first appears.

2. **What should our response be to the great accomplishments of unbelievers?**
    Great admiration.

Section 16

1. **What do we learn from Bezalel and Oholiab?**
    That the Spirit works to bestow understanding and knowledge in the arts and sciences.

2. **Is the Spirit's work limited to believers?**
    No. Apart from His work in sanctifying believers, He also fills, moves, and quickens all things, and He does so in accordance with the law of creation.

Section 17

1. **What is proper to our nature?**
    Reason.

2. **What must we avoid claiming as our own?**
    That which flows from the sheer bounty of God.

Section 18

1. **What are the three characteristics of spiritual insight?**
    Knowing God, knowing His fatherly favor toward us, and knowing how to frame our lives according to His law.

2. What illustration does Calvin use to describe unbelievers when they have a true insight concerning God?

They are like a traveler in the field at night who sees everything lit up by a flash of lightning, but who is then immediately in the dark again.

Section 19

1. Do unbelievers have some illumination concerning God?

Yes, but not enough to comprehend Him.

2. How do we know men do not have spiritual understanding?

Because John 1 describes men as "darkness."

Section 20

1. How do men regain what nature lacks?

We regain what we have lost through the Spirit of regeneration.

2. How far may a man become spiritually wise?

Only as far as God illumines a man's mind.

Section 21

1. Where the Spirit of God does not shine, what do we have?

Only darkness.

2. What is the worst form of blindness?

Not knowing yourself to be blind.

Section 22

1. Does Calvin take the Gentiles in Romans 2:14–15 to be Christians or not?

He takes them as unbelieving Gentiles.

2. Does Calvin believe in natural law?

Yes, he does.

3. How does he define it?

As the apprehension of the conscience which distinguishes just from unjust.

4. What is natural law for?

It removes the excuse of ignorance.

Section 23

1. **Can unregenerate men affirm the right ethical choice generally?**
    Yes, they can.

2. **Where then do they fail, according to Calvin?**
    They fail in the particulars concerning their own life. They know
    adultery is wrong, but have rationalizations for their own adultery.

Section 24

1. **Where does human ethical knowledge fail utterly?**
    With regard to the duties found in the First Table of the Law.

2. **Where does it fail in a critical sense?**
    In attempts to obey the Second Table of the Law, human efforts
    are plagued by lack of endurance, by inconsistency of application,
    and by failure to take our concupiscence into account.

3. **What do the philosophers recognize and what do they ignore?**
    They recognize gross sins, but they ignore "depraved desires, in
    which the mind can quietly indulge."

Section 25

1. **Does Calvin hold that men are evil in every respect?**
    No. Otherwise how could that which is pleasing to God even
    enter our minds?

2. **But what is absolutely necessary in order for us to understand
    spiritual things?**
    The grace of illumination, and to be reborn as David was.

Section 26

1. **Choice belongs to what sphere in our makeup?**
    It belongs to the sphere of the will, not the understanding.

2. **What is necessary before we can say that a true moral choice
    has been made?**
    That a man discern the good by right reason, that he choose it
    while knowing what it is, and that, having chosen it, he follows it.

Section 27

1. Does Calvin believe that the description in Romans 7 is of a Christian or not?

He holds that it is the self-description of a Christian.

2. What does he make of the excuse "It is no more I that do it, but sin that dwelleth in me"?

He holds that only a regenerate man could say that.

Chapter Three

Section 1

1. Is all of man's nature fleshly?

Yes, and this is why no good can be extracted from it.

2. What is the only way to obtain anything of spiritual value from the Spirit?

By regeneration.

3. Whatever we have from nature is what?

Flesh.

Section 2

1. What passage does Paul turn to in order to throw down the arrogance of mankind?

Romans 3:10–16.

2. Is this passage limited to some men?

No, it applies to the whole race of Adam's children.

3. What are the two reasons men are this way?

They are this way not only because of depraved custom, but also by depravity of nature.

Section 3

1. Does Calvin agree that some unbelievers have some nobility in their nature?

Yes. Depravity is total, but not absolute.

2. How does Calvin account for this?

By saying that God gives enough grace to restrain sin inwardly, but not so much as to cleanse it.

Section 4

1. **Does Calvin agree that we must "put Catiline on the same footing with Camillus"?**

   Yes, but only if we refuse to acknowledge that carefully cultivated nature can be capable of goodness.

2. **Which way does Calvin take it?**

   He says that cultivated nature is capable of some good.

3. **How?**

   By means of "special gifts" that God gives.

4. **Do these virtues put these men in a right standing with God?**

   No, because the chief part of uprightness is still absent.

Section 5

1. **We must attribute conversion entirely to what?**

   Entirely to God's grace.

2. **What drives evil will, and what drives good will?**

   A corrupt nature drives evil will, and grace drives a good will.

3. **Those who are offended by this do not know how to do what?**

   They do not know how to distinguish necessity from compulsion.

4. **If necessity is the same as compulsion, what must be said about God?**

   That He is good under compulsion.

5. **Calvin agrees with whom in these matters?**

   With Augustine, and the agreement of all the godly.

Section 6

1. **What must we not divide?**

   We must not divide between God and ourselves what He claims for Himself alone.

Section 7

1. **What does Calvin think of Lombard's idea of "preventing grace"?**

   Not much. He says that Lombard "preposterously wrests" a saying of Augustine to get there.

2. **What is prior to all merit?**

   Grace.

Section 8

1. **Why does Calvin cite Augustine?**

   To answer those who claim that Calvin is twisting Scripture.

2. **What is the basis for Calvin's assertions on this topic?**

   Calvin says that this teaching has been drawn from Scripture.

3. **How do we know that faith is a free gift of God?**

   The whole of Scripture proclaims it.

Section 9

1. **What antithesis must we always remember?**

   The antithesis between the perverse motions of disobedience and the correction of God.

2. **How does Calvin describe the license of our pride?**

   As strange and monstrous.

Section 10

1. **Does God's grace give us a chance to be good or not?**

   No. Grace disposes efficaciously.

2. **What must we not claim?**

   The slightest part of God's praise.

Section 11

1. **What is perseverance *not*?**

   It is not distributed as a reward for good use of earlier grace.

2. **Is grace a co-worker with us?**

   No. Those who think of grace as a "fellow-laborer" are deluding themselves.

Sections 12–13

1. **Can man take credit for even one good work apart from grace?**

   No, not at all.

2. **What, according to Augustine, brings about every good work in us?**

   Grace alone.

Section 14

1. Does grace eliminate the will?

No. The will is changed from evil to good and helped when it is good.

2. What is the right relationship of grace and freedom?

The human will does not obtain grace by freedom, but rather freedom by grace.

Chapter Four

Section 1

1. Does man sin willingly, even though of necessity?

Yes. He sins under necessity, not under compulsion.

2. What comparison of Augustine's does Calvin approve?

That of a horse and rider. Man is the horse, and the rider is God or Satan respectively.

Section 2

1. Who was involved in Job's loss?

God, Satan, and the Chaldeans.

2. What distinguishes these various agents?

First the end and then the manner of acting.

3. What aspect of God's sovereignty is Calvin not addressing here?

His universal activity whereby creatures are enabled to do anything at all.

Section 3

1. Why do the early fathers not want to attribute "hardening" to God?

They are concerned the impious will speak of it blasphemously.

2. What does Calvin think of this?

He sympathizes but says that Scripture does not speak this way.

3. What does Calvin call the idea that hardening is nothing but permission or a matter of foreknowledge?

He calls it a subtlety that Scripture does not admit.

4. **Considering the editor's footnote, how does Calvin chide Augustine unnecessarily?**

   He accepted as genuine a work attributed to Augustine that was not his.

Section 4

1. **Are there passages that describe God as acting on the godless by simply "deserting" them?**

   Yes, there are.

2. **Does this explanation cover all the scriptural data?**

   No, there are "other passages which go farther," describing God as actively hardening.

Section 5

1. **What error must be avoided when discussing the "evil spirit from the Lord"?**

   This spirit must not be confounded with the Holy Spirit.

2. **Can God and Satan work in the same man at the same time?**

   Yes, but to different ends.

Section 6

1. **When actions are neither good nor evil, is God still involved?**

   Yes. God is sovereign in all things.

Section 7

1. **How is God's control of kingly actions (Prov. 21:1) a "how much more" argument?**

   If any man might be expected to be free to do as he wishes, a king would be. And if God controls him, how much more everyone else?

Section 8

1. **For Calvin, is free will to be determined by whether or not a man chooses what he wants?**

   No. The question is internal to the man and is not a matter of outcomes.

Chapter Five
Section 1

1.　What is the first objection to Calvin's teaching on free will?

That in order to be sin at all, an action must be voluntary. Necessary sin is not sin.

2.　How do his opponents support this objection?

By means of "common sense" and certain scriptural arguments.

3.　How does Calvin answer?

By distinguishing (again) necessity and compulsion. The fact that it occurs necessarily does not mean it occurs involuntarily.

Section 2

1.　What is the second objection to Calvin's teaching on free will?

That the loss of free will means that reward and punishment lose their meaning.

2.　How does Calvin answer?

He answers with a solid dose from Augustine. Scripture teaches that God rewards the grace He gives, so that sins are our own, while our virtues are gifts from God.

Section 3

1.　What is the third objection to Calvin's teaching on free will?

That this obliterates all distinction between good and evil.

2.　How does Calvin answer?

He answers what he considers to be a closely related point, one concerning perseverance. He says that some persevere and some do not because God upholds those who do and does not uphold those who do not.

Section 4

1.　What is the fourth objection to Calvin's teaching on free will?

That all exhortation becomes meaningless.

2.　How does Calvin answer?

Again with an appeal to Augustine, followed by citations from the Bible. The basic answer is that this is a scriptural doctrine, and yet Scripture is full of exhortation. Therefore there is no inconsistency.

Section 5

1. If an impious man scoffs at exhortations from God, what can he not do?

He cannot condemn those exhortations.

2. What rests entirely upon God's grace?

All the righteousness of the pious.

3. In what two ways does God work upon His elect?

He works within by His Spirit, and He works from without by His word.

Section 6

1. What is the central objection to Calvin's views of free will?

That God's precepts must indicate the measure of our strength.

2. Do his opponents have no Scripture at all?

They have a host of passages, all of them misunderstood.

3. How does Calvin state this objection?

By saying that God is either mocking us when He enjoins personal holiness, or He is requiring only what is within our power to do.

Section 7

1. If the law does not show what we ought to do and are able to do, what does it show?

It reveals our condition of sinfulness. It reveals that we are unable to do what is right.

Section 8

1. How has Calvin broken up this particular objection?

Into three categories—the commands to be converted, the commands to honor God, and the commands to remain in God's grace.

2. What does he then do with these categories?

He shows various scriptural passages in each category that show God giving to His people what He has commanded them to do.

Section 9

1. **How is the work of conversion divided between God and man?**
    It is not divided.

2. **When God gives His law, what can we say about the grace of the Lawgiver?**
    That it is both necessary and promised to us.

Section 10

1. **To whom are the promises offered?**
    To the impious and believers alike.

2. **What effect do the promises have on the impious?**
    They prick the conscience, showing them how unworthy they are of His continued kindnesses.

3. **What effect do the promises have on the believers?**
    Since our sluggishness is not sufficiently aroused by His precepts, He gives us promises to sweetly entice us to love the precepts.

Section 11

1. **Why can unbelievers not find fault with God for His reproof of them?**
    Because they must find the source of the evil within themselves, and not from external causes.

Section 12

1. **How does Calvin interpret Deuteronomy 30:11–12, 14?**
    With reference to the interpretation Paul gives it in Romans 10.

2. **And what interpretation is that?**
    The words in Deuteronomy, according to Paul, apply to the gospel and not to the law.

Section 13

1. **What is the next objection that Calvin deals with?**
    The objection is that if God waits for men to respond, this must mean that they can respond, one way or the other.

2. How does Calvin answer this?

By saying that Scripture elsewhere teaches that men who are forsaken by God cannot do right. And if his opponents say that grace is necessary, then what is the problem?

Section 14

1. What objection is addressed in this section?

The objection is that the Bible calls righteous works of men "our works."

2. How does Calvin answer?

By pointing out that the bread God gives us in response to the Lord's Prayer is called "our daily bread." It is ours because God gave it to us.

Section 15

1. In what sense are our good works ours, and in what sense God's?

They are ours because they were a gift to us, and God's because He gave them.

Section 16

1. What is the next objection?

That God tells Cain that he must master sin. This must mean that he could.

2. What is Calvin's view of this passage?

He says the verse applies to Abel. But for the sake of argument he supposes that it speaks of sin and says it is either command or promise. If command, he has dealt with this earlier. If promise, why was the promise not fulfilled?

Section 17

1. What argument for free will is drawn from Romans 9:16?

That if it is not of him who wills and of him who runs, willing and running must have some kind of place.

2. What word does Calvin use in dismissing this argument?

"We must therefore abandon this absurd mode of arguing."

Section 18

1. Does Calvin reject the author of Ecclesiasticus?

Surprisingly, no. Although he says that he has the right to.

2. How does he handle this appeal?

By interpreting Ecclesiasticus in an orthodox way—although he doesn't have to. The book is not in the canon of Scripture, so it could be just wrong.

3. What does man need instead of an advocate?

A physician.

Section 19

1. How does Calvin handle the allegorical argument from the fact that the man beat up on the Jericho road was "half dead"?

He rejects the allegory.

2. What ought allegories not be allowed to do, according to Calvin?

They ought not go beyond the limits set by the rule of Scripture, and they should not be used as the foundation of any doctrine.

3. And how does Calvin handle the assertion that mankind has "half a life"?

By pointing to the Scriptures which describe sinners as dead.

Chapter Six

Section 1

1. What illustration does Calvin use to describe heaven and earth?

He calls it "this magnificent theater" and says that it is crammed with innumerable miracles.

2. What is our problem then?

Looking at these wonders, we ought to have known God. But because of sin, we do not.

3. What does God do for us in this situation?

He calls us to the faith of Christ—we need a Mediator, a Redeemer.

4. Has any worship apart from Christ ever pleased God?

No, not at all.

Section 2

1. **Is the need for a Mediator revealed to us for the first time in the New Testament?**

   No. The doctrine is found throughout the Old Testament as well.

2. **In order to be propitious toward the human race, what does God need?**

   God needs a Mediator in order to save us.

Section 3

1. **When is Christ prefigured in the Old Testament?**

   Whenever solace is promised in affliction, especially when the deliverance of the Church is in view.

2. **In the Old Testament, on what did our redemption and eternal salvation depend?**

   On the coming kingdom of David.

3. **The hope of all the godly has always reposed where?**

   In Christ alone.

Section 4

1. **What will happen to someone's faith in God without a Mediator?**

   It will gradually disappear.

2. **Why can we not attain to God's majesty?**

   It is too lofty, and we are like grubs crawling on the earth.

3. **What teaching of Paul's should have been more commonly known among the Jews?**

   That Christ was the end of the law.

4. **Are Muslims true theists because they worship one God?**

   No, because without a Mediator they are idolaters.

Chapter Seven

Section 1

1. **What does Calvin mean when he uses the word "law"?**

   The form of religion delivered to Moses.

2. What was the basic reason for giving the law?

To set the people's mind on Christ, to kindle a desire for Him.

Section 2

1. What should we remember with regard to the Ten Commandments?

That Christ is the end of the law for the one who believes.

2. The righteousness taught by the commandments is all in vain until what happens?

Until Christ confers that righteousness by free imputation and by the Spirit of regeneration.

Section 3

1. What else does the law do?

It renders us inexcusable and drives us into despair.

2. How many men are affected by the law in this way?

All of us, to a man.

Section 4

1. Are the promises attached to the law all in vain because of our disobedience?

Not at all. The promises make us realize they will not be fulfilled unless God does the fulfilling.

Section 5

1. What does Calvin mean by the impossibility of obedience?

He means something is impossible when it has never been, and what God's ordination and decree prevent from ever being.

2. What has plagued every human being?

Concupiscence.

3. What ought we not pit against one another?

God's power and God's truth.

Section 6

1. Without seeing ourselves in the mirror of God's law, what happens to us?

Drunk with self-love, we deceive ourselves.

2. **When we stand on our own judgment, what do we tend to do?**

Pass off hypocrisy as righteousness.

Section 7

1. **The law is compared to what?**

The law is like a mirror, showing us our sins the way a mirror shows us the spots on our face.

2. **As we grow tired under the burden of sin, what does God never tire of?**

He never tires of benefitting us and heaping new gifts upon us.

Section 8

1. **Does the first use of the law apply to unbelievers only?**

No, it works upon believers and unbelievers both.

Section 9

1. **When we are condemned by the law, what does this make us want to do?**

It makes us desire to call upon the grace of God's help.

Section 10

1. **What is the second use of the law?**

To restrain the public ungodliness of the wicked.

2. **Is their conformity to this law true righteousness?**

No, but this constrained and forced righteousness is necessary for any public community of men.

Section 11

1. **The law of God restrains us externally until what time?**

Until we are regenerated by the Spirit and begin wholeheartedly to love Him.

Section 12

1. **What is the third use of the law, according to Calvin?**

It provides admonition to believers and exhorts them in living a life of love.

2. **Is this a minor use of the law?**

No, it is the principal use.

3. How does the law help the believer?

It is a spur to doing right.

4. Is this use dependent upon precept alone?

No. Grace sweetens what is bitter.

Section 13

1. What do certain ignorant persons do?

They cast out the whole law of Moses.

Section 14

1. In what two ways has the law been abrogated?

With regard to the sting of conscience and through the discontinuance of the ceremonies.

Section 15

1. What part of the law is abrogated to liberate the conscience?

The part of the law that enforces its precepts—the thunderbolt of the curse.

2. How would that curse work on the conscience?

Through fear of death.

Section 16

1. Have the ceremonies been abrogated the same way?

No, not at all.

2. In what way have the ceremonies been abrogated?

They have been abrogated, not in effect, but only in their use.

Section 17

1. What does Calvin do with the "handwriting of ordinances" of Colossians 2:13–14?

He applies it to the ceremonies, provided those ceremonies are understood as a confession of sin.

Chapter Eight

Section 1

1. What is the written moral law?

It is a written statement of the natural law.

2. **What does God reprove us for through the law?**

   For our impotence and for our unrighteousness.

3. **Why is the written law necessary?**

   To make the force of natural law in our conscience more plain and to provide a clearer witness.

Section 2

1. **When do we render God the reverence due to Him?**

   When we prefer His will to our own.

2. **In what way is God always like Himself?**

   As the friend of righteousness, as the foe of iniquity.

Section 3

1. **What does the law teach us about ourselves?**

   Two things: first, our comparative unrighteousness, and secondly, our impotence to fulfill the law.

Section 4

1. **Why has God added promises and threats to the law?**

   In order to stir up in us a love of righteousness and a hatred of wickedness.

2. **What deserves no reward?**

   The payment of a debt.

Section 5

1. **Nothing is more acceptable to God than what?**

   Obedience.

2. **What religious affectation is rooted in man's nature?**

   To dream up religious rites in order to deserve well of God.

3. **What is an intolerable profanation of divine righteousness?**

   Any zeal for good works that wanders outside God's law.

Section 6

1. **If an earthly king forbids a particular action, what is not included?**

   The heart attitudes involved.

2. **How is this different from what God forbids?**

   God searches out the heart, and so He evaluates that as well.

Section 7

1. Who is the best interpreter of the law?

Christ Himself.

2. Did Christ add to the law?

No, He restored it to its original integrity.

Section 8

1. Does a refusal to go beyond the law require that we interpret the law woodenly?

No, the law must not be interpreted according to "the strict letter of the words" but must allow for figures of speech.

2. What is our central duty with regard to each law?

We must investigate what it is concerned with in the first place.

Section 9

1. What is conceded by all?

That if a virtue is commanded, then the corresponding vice is prohibited, and vice versa.

2. What mistake is commonly made in this?

That if, for example, murder is prohibited, I have fulfilled the law if I simply refrain from murder. But Calvin says this entails that we give our neighbor's life all the help we can.

Section 10

1. Why does God rebuke sin so strongly in the law and put the worst possible light on our behavior? For example, why call hatred "murder"?

Because we tend to gloss all of our sins. God intends to teach us to detest sin rightly.

Section 11

1. How does Calvin divide the law given in the Ten Commandments?

Into two sections—the first having to do with our duties to God, the second having to do with our duties to man.

2. What is vanity to attempt?

To cry up righteousness without religion—to praise righteousness toward men without a right relation to God.

Section 12

1. Why do some number the commandments differently?

In order to get the prohibition of image worship into the background somehow.

Section 13

1. How does Calvin take the preface to the Ten Commandments?

As the preface to the entire law.

2. Why is the preface important?

Because it highlights and underscores the nature of the God who gives the commandments.

Section 14

1. What is meant by "I am the Lord thy God"?

By this phrase God declares Himself to be God of the Church. He is emphasizing that He is our God, and we are His people.

Section 15

1. What does Calvin identify as one of the greatest crimes?

The crime of ingratitude.

2. Why does God reveal Himself through certain particular titles?

To restrain us from inventing absurdities about Him.

3. What did Israel's enslavement in Israel represent typologically?

Our slavery to sin, and so the motivation to godliness in the preface applies to us as well.

Section 16

1. What does the first commandment reveal about God's authority?

That His authority is complete and total.

2. What four things may we not transfer away from God to another?

Adoration, trust, invocation, and thanksgiving.

Section 17

1. **What is the grossest fault of a superstitious style of worship?**
    Outward idolatry.

2. **What happens whenever idols appear?**
    True religion is corrupted and adulterated.

Section 18

1. **Penalties for idolatry extend how far?**
    To children, grandchildren, and great-grandchildren.

2. **How far does His kindness extend to those who love Him and keep His word?**
    To thousands of generations or, as Calvin phrases it, to remote posterity.

3. **What is the act of bowing down to an image compared to?**
    To the act of adultery.

Section 19

1. **Does Calvin interpret the threat to "visit iniquity" to subsequent generations as a reference to temporal difficulties only?**
    No. He grants that it does happen, but he insists that it encompasses spiritual judgments as well.

Section 20

1. **Why did Ezekiel tell the people to stop using the proverb about the father eating grapes and the children's teeth being set on edge?**
    Because Israelites were using it to describe a wicked father and a son experiencing consequences, a son who was supposedly righteous.

2. **What therefore descends to subsequent generations?**
    Not only the judgment, but also the sin. It does not accord with God's justice for "a righteous son should suffer for the iniquity of a wicked father."

Section 21

1. How is this promise to be interpreted? As an absolute, or as a general rule?

As a general rule. The offspring of the wicked sometimes repent, and the children of the righteous sometimes fall away.

Section 22

1. What does the third commandment require?

That we hallow the majesty of God's name.

2. What three things constitute adherence to this command?

First, everything we think, say, or do should "bespeak his excellence"; second, we must not rashly abuse His word or His mysteries; and third, we must not defame or detract from His works.

Section 23

1. What is an oath?

It is calling God to witness the truth of our word.

2. What is one way of identifying a man's religion?

By the name he uses in taking an oath.

Section 24

1. What is it when a man swears falsely in the true name?

It is no small affront; it is what Scripture calls a "profanation."

Section 25

1. What renders God's name cheap and common?

When it is invoked for true but needless oaths.

2. When men swear unnecessarily, what are they doing?

They are departing from its lawful use.

Section 26

1. Who condemns all oaths whatever, and why?

The Anabaptists, on the basis of a mistake concerning Christ's words in the Sermon on the Mount.

2. Interpreting Christ's words as forbidding all oaths whatever does what to the relationship between Jesus and His Father?

It makes Christ His Father's enemy, because God permitted and sometimes required oaths.

3. What was Christ forbidding then?

He is forbidding the form of oaths that He uses as illustrations. He "refutes the sophistical subtlety of those who thought it nothing vainly to utter indirect oaths."

4. What is the relationship of God's name to all His benefits?

His name is actually engraven on all His benefits.

Section 27

1. Did Paul interpret Jesus as forbidding all oaths?

No, he swears without hesitation, sometimes even adding a curse.

Section 28

1. What did Calvin think about the early fathers who interpreted the Sabbath as a type of Christ?

He says that they spoke truly, but that they did not go far enough.

2. What are the three elements of obedience to this command?

First, it represents spiritual rest. Second, there is a need for a particular day to hear the law and perform the appointed rites. And third, a day is necessary to give rest to those under authority.

Section 29

1. What lesson occupied the chief place in the Sabbath?

The foreshadowing of spiritual rest.

2. When should we be at this place of spiritual rest?

All the time.

Section 30

1. What does the number seven represent in Scripture?

It is the number of perfection and denotes perpetuity.

Section 31

1. Can the Sabbath be kept merely by abstaining from physical labor?

No. The prophets repeatedly refer to this.

2. What must Christians shun completely?

Because the substance of the shadow belongs to Christ, Christians ought to completely shun superstitious observance of days.

Section 32

1. For Calvin, the Sabbath has been abrogated in Christ. But what two things do we still need to do?

We still need to gather on stated days to hear the word, break the mystical bread, and conduct public prayers. We also need to give relief to servants and workmen.

Section 33

1. Is there danger in Christian superstitious observance of the Lord's day?

Yes, but less than there is for the observance of Jewish holy days.

Section 34

1. For Calvin, is the Lord's day a continuation of the Sabbath or a replacement of it?

It is a replacement. Calvin is not a sabbatarian.

2. Why was the first day chosen as that replacement?

Because Jesus rose from the dead on that day.

3. Does Calvin condemn churches that have other solemn days?

No, he does not—provided there is no superstition.

Section 35

1. Who is encompassed under the fifth commandment?

Anyone that God has placed over us.

2. Is honor a word with a narrow definition?

No, in Scripture it has a very broad meaning.

3. What do fathers, princes, and lords all have?

A share in God's honor.

Section 36

1. Are we allowed to withhold honor based on the recipient's lack of merit?

No, it makes no difference whether they are worthy of it or not.

2. What are the three components of honor?

Reverence, obedience, and gratitude.

Section 37

1. **Does the promise attached to this commandment apply to us today?**

    Yes, this "promise has ... reference to us also."

2. **With the "exceptions," is God breaking His word?**

    No, no more than if He gave a man a hundred acres when He had promised him one.

Section 38

1. **Are there sanctions connected to this commandment?**

    Yes, an inevitable curse awaits all stubborn or disobedient children.

Section 39

1. **What is the purpose of this commandment?**

    Because God has bound all humanity together in a certain unity, each man must concern himself with the safety of all.

2. **What is hatred?**

    Nothing but sustained anger.

3. **Does this command address heart attitudes?**

    Yes, because the God who sees the heart does not issue commands solely to the body.

Section 40

1. **What are the two reasons we are to refrain from murder?**

    Because all men bear the image of God, and because we share a common flesh with all men.

Section 41

1. **Why should all uncleanness be far from us?**

    Because God loves modesty and purity.

2. **What effect does fornication have?**

    It brands our bodies with its mark.

Section 42

1. **What makes men doubly subject to women's society?**

    Our created nature and the effects of the Fall.

2. What two ways is the gift of celibacy given?

It is granted entirely to a few and to others just for a time.

3. Why can men not count on God's help for any attempt at celibacy?

Because God helps only those who walk in His ways.

Section 43

1. Can celibacy be achieved by great zeal and effort?

No, it has to be a special grace from God.

2. If a man is not able to be celibate, what does God require of him?

That he marry.

3. Is it adequate for a man to control external sexual behavior?

No, a true celibate knows how to be pure in body and spirit both.

Section 44

1. What can we say about sexual association within marriage?

That it is blessed by the Lord.

2. What follows from this?

That married couples ought not to give way to uncontrolled lust.

3. Is anything permitted, just so long as the couple is married?

No, there are a number of practices unworthy of the marriage bed that would exhibit extreme lewdness.

Section 45

1. What is the eighth commandment?

That we honor the possessions of others.

2. What is prohibited in this commandment?

The evil deprivation of another's possessions.

3. Does it matter if we figure out a way to do it legally?

No, a court action cannot cleanse the guilt of a theft.

Section 46

1. What sort of gain should we pursue?

Only that which is lawful and honest.

2. **What do greedy men look like?**

They madly scrape together from everywhere, by fair means or foul.

3. **What should we do if we have to contend with faithless and deceitful men?**

Give up something rather than contend with them.

Section 47

1. **What is the ninth commandment?**

That we refrain from false witness against our neighbor.

2. **What is the first form of this that Calvin mentions?**

Maligning him with false or slanderous charges.

3. **For Calvin, what are the two parts of this commandment?**

That we refrain from injuring a man's reputation, and that we refrain from depriving him of his goods by lying.

Section 48

1. **What peculiar temptation does everyone experience in this regard?**

We all tend to delight in a certain poisoned sweetness in ferreting out and disclosing the evils of others.

2. **What is not included under this prohibition?**

Private or public correction meant to remedy the evil.

3. **What else is excluded?**

Bitter taunts under the guise of joking.

Section 49

1. **What is the tenth commandment?**

That we not covet anything whatever that belongs to our neighbor.

2. **If the prohibitions of adultery and murder forbade heart intent, then how is this commandment not superfluous?**

Calvin distinguishes an intent to do something from a prickling or tickling with that desire. This commandment is therefore functioning at a much higher internal plane.

Section 50

1. What happens if we entertain any desirable object in our minds?

Our hearts leap with excitement.

2. What does God require of our heart?

He requires a marvelously tempered heart, not allowing the tiniest pinprick of anything that is not love.

Section 51

1. What is the purpose of the whole law?

To form human life to the archetype of divine purity.

2. What is a mistake to believe concerning the law?

That it is simply the rudiments or preliminaries of righteousness.

Section 52

1. Why is the keeping of the law sometimes summarized in the second table only?

Because it is speaking of that by which a man proves himself righteous.

2. What are the two indicators of keeping the first table?

Heart condition and keeping the ceremonies.

3. Why is this inadequate for identifying true godliness?

Because only God sees the heart, and hypocrites busy themselves with ceremonies. And so we tell who loves God by who loves his neighbor.

Section 53

1. What is the fulfillment of the law?

He who loves his neighbor fulfills the law.

Section 54

1. What life best conforms to God's will?

A life that is most fruitful for its brethren.

2. What stupid imagination did the Sophists advance?

That self-love was of first importance.

3. How does Calvin refute this?

By pointing out that God was simply using a given from the midst of our depravity and by citing 1 Corinthians 13:5. Love does not seek its own.

Section 55

1. Does Calvin resist the priorities we have for those closest to us?

No, this does not offend God. His own providence leads us to it.

2. Does love for a man depend on his character?

No, it depends on our love for God.

Section 56

1. What did the Schoolmen do with all these divine requirements?

They turned them into mere "counsels," obligatory for monks only.

2. How did Calvin respond?

With scorn and multiple citations of Scripture.

Section 57

1. How was the command to love our enemies diluted by some?

By making the instructions in how to love exhortations, not imperatives.

2. What early church fathers did Calvin appeal to in rejecting this?

Chrysostom and Augustine.

Section 58

1. What is the definition of venial sin that Calvin works with?

The definition from Aquinas—"Desire unaccompanied with deliberate assent, and not remaining long in the heart."

2. But how do these sins even get an opportunity within us?

Because of some empty place in the soul—we were already not loving God with all our heart, soul, mind, and strength.

3. So what does all sin deserve?

All sin deserves death.

Section 59

1. **Why is every sin deadly?**

   Because every sin sets God's authority aside.

2. **If those who distinguish mortal from venial sin "indulged this madness too long," what should we do?**

   Bid them farewell.

3. **What should the children of God hold?**

   That all sin is mortal.

Chapter Nine

Section 1

1. **What did God attest through the Old Testament promises?**

   That He was Father.

2. **What did the teaching and ceremonies of the Old Testament point to?**

   They all pointed to Christ.

3. **Did this make this teaching valueless to the prophets themselves?**

   Not at all—they enjoyed a slight taste of what we possess.

Section 2

1. **Taken in a broad sense, what does the word "gospel" include?**

   It includes the testimonies God gave to the patriarchs of old.

2. **Taken in the higher sense, what does it mean?**

   It refers to the proclamation of grace manifested in Christ.

Section 3

1. **Are the promises of the Old Testament abrogated with the law?**

   No, contrary to the teaching of Servetus.

Section 4

1. **For Calvin, is there a legitimate contrast between law and gospel?**

   Yes, provided the contrast is not made too sharply.

2. **Did the gospel bring a different way of salvation than the law, rightly understood?**

    No. The gospel confirmed and satisfied what the law had promised.

Section 5

1. **What kind of office did John the Baptist hold with regard to law and gospel?**

    An intermediate office.

2. **What was his role with regard to the disciples?**

    To prepare the disciples for Christ.

Chapter Ten

Section 1

1. **What point does Calvin believe is very important to make?**

    That all men adopted into the company of God's people through-out the history of the world have had the same law and the same doctrine.

2. **What was said concerning the Jews by Calvin's opponents?**

    In effect that they were nothing but a herd of swine, being fat-tened on this earth with worldly pleasures only.

Section 2

1. **How much alike are the various covenants that God has made with men?**

    So much alike in substance and reality that they are actually one and the same.

2. **Are these covenants similar?**

    In a way, but it would be better to say that they have unity.

3. **What are the three points Calvin makes here?**

    First, that the Jews aspired to more than earthly prosperity. Second, that the covenant they lived under was all of grace. And third, they knew Christ as Mediator.

Section 3

1. According to the Bible, what were the Old Testament saints looking forward to?

To Christ and to the gospel.

2. What was the Old Testament particularly concerned with?

The future life.

Section 4

1. What notable saying of the Lord does Calvin use in this discussion?

That Abraham rejoiced to see Christ's day (Jn. 8:56).

2. In passing, what does Calvin call the Lord's mother?

"The blessed Virgin."

Section 5

1. Does Calvin contrast the Jews in the wilderness with the Corinthians?

No, he compares them, showing their similarities.

2. If the Jews' baptism into Moses was carnal only, would Paul's argument have worked?

No, because Paul meant to disabuse Christians from thinking that they were superior to the Jews through the privilege of baptism.

Section 6

1. Does Calvin believe that manna was sacramental food?

Yes, he does.

2. How does he answer the objection from John 6:49, 54?

By explaining that Jesus was answering the Jews from the framework of their misunderstanding.

Section 7

1. In arguing for the spiritual benefits enjoyed by the Old Testament saints, what does Calvin point to in this section as their possession?

To their possession of the word, which has "such an inherent efficacy" in it that anyone who possesses it possesses life.

Section 8

1. **What else did they possess?**

   God was their God, as the Lord promises them throughout the Old Testament. And how could they have Him and not have spiritual life?

Section 9

1. **What is Calvin's next argument for the spiritual blessedness of the Old Testament saints?**

   God's promise to bless them in subsequent generations, which would come to fulfillment long after their deaths.

Section 10

1. **What is another reason for saying that they were not enjoying all the heaven they were going to get here on earth?**

   The fact that many of them went through extraordinary trials here on earth, just as we do.

Section 11

1. **Who was a preeminent example of this?**

   Abraham, who lived what Calvin describes as a "calamitous life." If all Abraham's blessings were to be enjoyed in this life, Calvin argues, something was seriously skewed.

Section 12

1. **Did Isaac live as troubled a life as Abraham?**

   No, but he still had a rough go. Calvin cites a number of examples.

2. **What about Jacob?**

   His earthly life was filled with various forms of grief, and he testified at the end of it that his life had been "few and evil."

3. **What are the implications of this?**

   Either that God's promises failed them, or that His promises were not directed at this life.

Section 13

1. **What Scripture settles the issue?**

   Hebrews 11:9–10, 13–16.

2. **What would the patriarchs have been if God had promised them earthly blessing which they did not receive?**

   They would have been more stupid than blocks of wood.

Section 14

1. **Did they ever express this hope openly?**

   Yes. For example, Genesis 49:18.

Sections 15–16

1. **What does David habitually call believers back to?**

   To the fact that their happiness reposes elsewhere.

2. **And what does he allude to throughout the Psalms?**

   That the prosperity of believers is not to be grasped without reference to a manifestation of heavenly glory.

Section 17

1. **How often did Calvin believe that promises of blessedness were fulfilled in this life for Old Testament saints?**

   Rarely or never.

2. **Did this cause these saints to despair of the fulfillment?**

   No. They looked for the fulfillment in the next life.

Section 18

1. **Did the wicked ever receive "blessings" in this life?**

   Yes, and it was a cause of temporary consternation. But the godly took refuge in considering their final end.

Section 19

1. **Did Job expect a future life?**

   Yes (Job 19:25–27).

2. **Was this an esoteric insight for just him?**

   No. Calvin denies that this was "hidden wisdom" for just a few.

Section 20

1. **If for Calvin the doctrine of the resurrection was clear in the earlier portions of the Old Testament, what happened later?**

   It became progressively clearer, as with a sunrise.

Section 21

1. How does Calvin interpret the valley of dry bones?

As a promise of restoration from exile which brought a promise of restoration in the afterlife.

Section 22

1. Which two prophets does Calvin cite here to reinforce this point?

Isaiah and Daniel.

Section 23

1. What was the first of Calvin's two remaining points?

That the Old Testament saints had Christ as pledge of their covenant.

2. The second?

That they put in Him all their future hopes.

3. So what doctrine falls to the ground?

The notion that God had promised the Jews nothing but a full belly.

Chapter Eleven

Section 1

1. How many differences are there between the Old and New Testaments?

Depending on how you count, Calvin says, four or five.

2. What is the first of these differences?

Calvin says that in the earthly possession which the Old Testament saints enjoyed, they had a teaching aid to help them see their future inheritance.

3. How did this differ from what Calvin's opponents said?

They said that the Old Testament saints had earthly benefits only, which provided us with figures of our future inheritance, not theirs.

Section 2

1. **Calvin reapplies an image that Paul used in Galatians. What is that image?**

   The figure of Israel, the people of God, in their childhood. Now, in Christ, we, the Church, have come to maturity.

Section 3

1. **What did Calvin believe about benefits and punishments in the Old Testament era?**

   He believed that they were displayed.

2. **What purpose did that serve?**

   They were functioning as types and symbols of the spiritual blessings and punishments to come.

Section 4

1. **What was the second difference between the two testaments?**

   The Old Testament represented the substance in a figure; the New in reality.

2. **What is the fulfillment of those figures?**

   The fulfillment, when all is "fixed and ratified," is Christ.

3. **When did the covenant become new and eternal?**

   Only after it was consecrated and established by the blood of Christ.

Section 5

1. **Was the truth understood clearly and distinctly in the time of the Old Testament?**

   No, Calvin says. It was understood, but there was no "light of revelation."

2. **What did the Law and the Prophets point to, then?**

   They gave a foretaste of the coming wisdom and "showed it afar off."

Section 6

1. **Is this view consistent with understanding that few Christians if any measure up to Abraham's faith?**

   No, it has nothing to do with how much grace was given to a few, but rather what the ordinary dispensation of grace was for His people.

Section 7

1. **According to Calvin, what is the third difference between the testaments?**

   The Old Testament is literal, while the New is spiritual.

2. **What does Calvin mean by those particular words?**

   For example, the difference between the Ten Commandments being carved into stone (Old Testament) and carved into human hearts (New Testament).

Section 8

1. **Why is the New Testament spiritual?**

   Because it is engraved spiritually on men's hearts.

2. **What is the final contrast between the testaments?**

   The final contrast is to be referred to the status of the ceremonial laws.

3. **What is the difference between the moral law and the ceremonial law in the Old Testament?**

   The moral law was weak through the weakness of the people. The ceremonies had the cause of weakness in themselves.

Section 9

1. **What is the fourth contrast between the testaments?**

   The Old Testament is one of "bondage," while the New is one of "freedom."

2. **How then were Old Testament saints saved?**

   They were saved as a fruit of the New Testament, working backward in time.

3.   Nevertheless, what did these true saints of the Old Testament still have to do?

They still had to offer sacrifices and observe the ceremonies.

Section 10

1.   How did the holy patriarchs live under the Old Covenant?

Not as to remain there, but rather to aspire to the New.

Section 11

1.   What is the fifth difference, which may be added?

According to Calvin, the Lord confined His covenant of grace to one nation (Old Testament), until the advent of Christ (New Testament).

Section 12

1.   What is therefore a "distinguishing feature" of the excellence of the New Testament?

The calling and inclusion of the Gentiles.

2.   Had the Old Testament foretold this?

Yes, but men were still surprised by it.

Section 13

1.   Why did God change His manner of administration?

Because the circumstances were different. A farmer does different things at different times of year. This does not make him inconsistent.

Section 14

1.   What is Calvin's basic assumption about all God's dealings with man?

That God does everything wisely and justly.

2.   Is God doing all this for His own sake?

No, He is taking our condition and situation into account.

Chapter Twelve

Section 1

1.   What was of the greatest importance?

That the Mediator be both true God and true man.

2. Where did this necessity come from?

From the heavenly decree.

3. Why did God have to descend to us?

Because it was not possible for us to ascend to Him.

Section 2

1. What were the children of men to become?

Children of God.

2. The heirs of Gehenna were to become what?

Heirs of the heavenly kingdom.

3. Christ took our nature upon Him ungrudgingly in order to do what?

Impart to us what was His.

Section 3

1. The Incarnation was necessary how?

As God alone He could not feel death, and as man alone He could not conquer it.

Section 4

1. What "speculation" does Calvin address next?

The view that Christ would have become a man even if Adam had not sinned.

2. What does Calvin think of those who "overleap these limits"?

He believes it is the indulging of foolish curiosity.

Section 5

1. Who is Calvin addressing in this section?

The Protestant theologian Osiander.

2. Does Calvin believe that Adam's fall precedes God's decree in time?

No. But it reveals what God determined before all ages.

Section 6

1. What is the basis of Osiander's teaching?

He holds that man is made in God's image because he was made after the pattern of the Messiah to come.

Section 7

1. **What is Calvin's reply concerning Christ's "precedence"?**

   He says that Scripture does not hesitate to describe Christ as a descendant of Adam. Not only so, but also as the second Adam.

2. **Does Calvin believe that Christ could have been "Head" of the human race without the Incarnation?**

   Yes. He is Head over the angels, and He never became one of them.

Chapter Thirteen

Section 1

1. **In this part of the *Institutes*, Calvin is answering three groups. Who are they?**

   There were two ancient groups, the Marcionites and the Manichees. The group contemporary with Calvin was the Mennonites, led by Menno Simons. Modern Mennonites have not followed their founder's heresy at this point.

2. **What were the two options suggested by these groups for the "body of Christ"?**

   One suggested a phastasm, while the other proposed Christ had a heavenly body.

Section 2

1. **What does Calvin say Paul is not doing in Philippians 2:5–7?**

   Paul is not teaching what Christ was, but rather how He conducted Himself.

2. **What is the basic approach to answering these heresies?**

   To simply quote the Bible in passage after passage, such as the one that simply says, "Christ shared in flesh and blood" (Heb. 2:14).

Section 3

1. **According to Calvin, the genealogy in Matthew was whose?**

   Joseph's.

2. **Although the male line is the basis for reckoning in the political order, does this exclude women?**

   No, Calvin says. Women must share in the act of generation.

3. **What does Calvin argue concerning Mary engendering Christ from her seed?**

   That Christ was begotten of Mary the same way that Isaac was begotten of Abraham.

Section 4

1. **When the Word in His immeasurable essence was united with the nature of man into one person, did He leave heaven?**

   No. He became one man; He was not confined to one man.

Chapter Fourteen

Section 1

1. **What two things must we not attribute to the two natures of Christ?**

   That the Word "was made" flesh or was "confusedly intermingled" with it.

2. **How then did the Son of God become the Son of Man?**

   Not by confusion of substance, but by unity of person.

3. **What illustration of this does Calvin use?**

   The illustration of a body and soul.

Section 2

1. **How do we know that this doctrine was not "of man's devising"?**

   Because of the many passages of Scripture that address it.

2. **Can we ever speak of the attributes of one nature in terms of the other?**

   Yes, but only "improperly" and not strictly. We do this because of the unity of the person—as when God laid down His life for us (1 Jn. 3:16).

Section 3

1. **When we speak of the office of Mediator, which way do we speak?**

   We do not speak solely of the divine nature or of the human.

Section 4

1. **Those who stumble over the question of Christ's two natures do not consider what?**

   They don't consider Christ's person, in which He was manifested as God and man, and they do not consider the office of Mediator.

2. **What does it mean when Christ calls His body a temple?**

   He did this because His divinity, as distinct from His body, dwelt there.

Section 5

1. **How does Calvin define the hypostatic union?**

   As one person out of two natures.

Sections 6–8

1. **What did Servetus teach about this?**

   That Christ was not Son of God before the Incarnation.

2. **Does Calvin struggle in answering the arguments of Servetus?**

   Not at all. It would be "superfluous" to refute it here, since he addresses it in another treatise.

3. **What is Calvin's summary of Servetus' position?**

   That "the Son of God was from the beginning an idea, and was even then a preordained man, who was to be the essential image of God."

Chapter Fifteen

Section 1

1. **According to Calvin, the office assigned to Christ consisted of what three parts?**

   Prophet, priest, and king.

2. **Is it enough to acknowledge the right names of these offices?**

No. The papists use them too, but "frigidly, and with no great benefit."

Section 2

1. **Which of the offices does the title Christ apply to?**

All of them, because under the law, prophets were anointed with oil, and not just kings and priests.

2. **Is the prophetic office extended to the Church?**

Yes, by virtue of the anointing being diffused from the Head to the members.

3. **What should be known outside Christ?**

Nothing is worth knowing outside Him.

4. **What is it not lawful to go beyond?**

The simplicity of the gospel.

Section 3

1. **What is the nature of Christ's kingship?**

It is spiritual in nature.

2. **What basic responsibility of a king does Calvin begin with?**

The responsibility of a king to protect his people.

Section 4

1. **How must we fight throughout our lives?**

Under the cross.

2. **Where does Calvin locate our happiness?**

In the heavenly life.

3. **In the midst of our trials here, what must we be content with?**

That our King will never leave us destitute.

Section 5

1. **What was the oil of gladness that anointed Christ?**

The spirit of wisdom and understanding.

2. **If Christ's kingdom does not lie in earthly pleasures or pomp, what does it lie in?**

The Holy Spirit.

3. **What can we not have one drop of apart from the Spirit?**

   Not one drop of vigor.

Section 6

1. **As priest, what does Christ do for us forever?**

   He is an everlasting intercessor.

2. **In this new and different order, what two roles did Christ play?**

   He was both priest and sacrifice, the one offering and the one offered.

Chapter Sixteen

Section 1

1. **Where did the name "Jesus" come from?**

   It was brought from heaven by an angel.

2. **What happens if we turn away from Christ, however slightly?**

   Our salvation, which is in Him alone, begins to vanish.

Section 2

1. **What must happen before we can accept God's gift of life with the gratitude we owe?**

   Our minds must be struck and overwhelmed by the fear of God's wrath.

Section 3

1. **Does God love us before our salvation?**

   Yes. Despite our corruptions He still finds something to love.

2. **Can He just receive us that way?**

   No. While we are still sinners, He cannot receive us completely. An atonement is necessary.

Section 4

1. **According to Calvin, did God love us before we were reconciled to Him?**

   Yes. His love motivated the provision of the atonement and did not follow after it.

2. **Which church father does he cite in agreement with this?**

   Augustine.

Section 5

1. **How did Christ accomplish salvation for us?**
   By the whole course of His obedience.

2. **We are freed from the curse of the law by what?**
   By the whole life of Christ.

3. **What passage in Galatians does Calvin claim as support for this?**
   Galatians 4:4–5.

4. **According to Calvin, was the means by which Christ died important?**
   Yes—He needed to be tried as a criminal and die as a convicted criminal.

Section 6

1. **What happened to the curse that was on us?**
   It was transferred to Christ on the cross.

2. **What exchange did the Son of God make, even though He was utterly clean of all fault?**
   He took on Himself the shame of our iniquities, and He clothed us with His purity.

3. **Christ cleansed our filth by what means?**
   By being covered with them by transferred imputation.

4. **Even though it was full of shame, what was the cross changed into?**
   A triumphal chariot.

Section 7

1. **What two things did the death of Jesus accomplish?**
   Our freedom from death (now conquered), and our freedom from the old man.

Section 8

1. **Does Calvin believe that the descent into hell belongs in the Creed?**
   Yes, he does, although he does grant that it was a late addition.

Section 9

1. **What traditional view does Calvin reject with regard to this article?**

   He rejects the idea that Christ descended into the nether world, into Hades.

Section 10

1. **If Calvin rejects the idea that Christ descended into the nether world, how does he take the phrase from the Creed?**

   He interprets it as referring to the soul agonies that Christ suffered while on the cross.

2. **Does the compiler of these study questions agree with this?**

   Nope.

Section 11

1. **How does Calvin undertake to prove this view?**

   By showing that the Bible teaches that Christ did in fact go through soul agonies on the cross, which He did.

Section 12

1. **How does Calvin answer his critics on this point?**

   By engaging with them on the question of whether or not Christ did suffer soul agonies, and he makes a strong case.

Section 13

1. **What must faith do in order to attain its full strength?**

   It must leap over the cross, death, and burial of Jesus and come to the resurrection.

2. **What is the summary of the effects of the death and resurrection respectively?**

   Sin was taken away by His death, and righteousness was brought by His resurrection.

3. **What should we understand in Scripture when the benefits of His death or resurrection are spoken of singly?**

   We should understand the presence of the other by synecdoche.

Section 14

1. What did Christ's ascension do for His relation to all things?

It enabled Him to fill all things, as Paul teaches in Ephesians.

2. The ascension of Christ's body did what to His power and energy?

The ascension of Christ's body diffused and spread His power and energy beyond all the bounds of heaven and earth.

Section 15

1. What is the central meaning of Christ's position at the right hand of God the Father?

The central meaning is rule and authority.

Section 16

1. What did Jesus do for us by means of His ascent into heaven?

He opened the way for us.

2. Do we look forward to heaven as with a "mere hope"?

No, but rather to our Head in whom we already possess it.

Section 17

1. Despite His present power, where is Christ's kingdom now?

It is hidden in the earth, under the lowness of the flesh.

2. Will any escape His judgment when He returns?

No one. He will judge the living and the dead.

Section 18

1. Who will share with Him in the work of judging?

Some of those who are to be judged.

2. What can a head not do?

A head cannot scatter its own members.

3. What does the Son do with the judgment He has been given?

He cares for our consciences.

Section 19

1. What do we find in every clause of the Creed?

We find Christ in every clause.

Chapter Seventeen

Section 1

1. **When discussing the merit of Christ, what must we remember lies behind it?**

   The grace of God.

2. **Did "the man," according to Augustine, deserve to be the only begotten Son of God?**

   No. It was entirely the grace of God.

Section 2

1. **What was God's ineffable demeanor toward us?**

   He loved us and was angry with us at the same time.

Section 3

1. **What did Christ accomplish by His obedience?**

   He truly acquired and merited grace for us with His Father.

Section 4

1. **What power did Christ's sacrifice have?**

   The power of expiating, appeasing, and making satisfaction.

Section 5

1. **What is the definition of redemption in Christ's blood?**

   It is forgiveness of sins (Col. 1:14).

Section 6

1. **Did Christ merit anything for Himself?**

   No. Calvin dismisses it as a stupid question.

www.ingramcontent.com/pod-product-compliance
Lightning Source LLC
Chambersburg PA
CBHW071312090426
42738CB00012B/2678